CORPOREAL READINGS OF CUBAN LITERATURE AND ART

Corporeal Readings of Cuban Literature and Art

The Body, the Inhuman, and Ecological Thinking

Christina M. García

UNIVERSITY OF FLORIDA PRESS

Gainesville

Publication of this work was made possible by a Sustaining the Humanities through the American Rescue Plan grant from the National Endowment for the Humanities.

Published in the United States of America

29 28 27 26 25 6 5 4 3 2

Library of Congress Cataloging-in-Publication Data
Names: García, Christina M., author.
Title: Corporeal readings of Cuban literature and art : the body, the inhuman, and ecological thinking / Christina M. García.
Description: Gainesville : University of Florida Press, 2024. | Includes bibliographical references and index.
Identifiers: LCCN 2023050471 (print) | LCCN 2023050472 (ebook) | ISBN 9781683404330 (hardback) | ISBN 9781683404415 (paperback) | ISBN 9781683404484 (pdf) | ISBN 9781683404569 (ebook)
Subjects: LCSH: Cuban literature—History and criticism. | Art, Cuban. | Gender identity in literature. | Gender identity in art. | Biology in literature. | Biology in art. | Race in literature. | Race in art. | BISAC: LITERARY CRITICISM / Modern / 20th Century | LITERARY CRITICISM / Caribbean & Latin American | LCGFT: Literary criticism. | Art criticism.
Classification: LCC PQ7371 .G28 2024 (print) | LCC PQ7371 (ebook) | DDC 860.9/97291—dc23/eng/20240201
LC record available at https://lccn.loc.gov/2023050471
LC ebook record available at https://lccn.loc.gov/2023050472

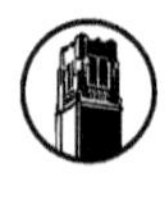
UF PRESS
UNIVERSITY OF FLORIDA

University of Florida Press
2046 NE Waldo Road
Suite 2100
Gainesville, FL 32609
http://upress.ufl.edu

CONTENTS

FIGURES

INSUFFICIENT ACKNOWLEDGMENTS

As a project that aspires to think ecologically, to imagine the imperceptible entanglements that constitute legible bodies, it is only fitting, if not imperative, to begin by acknowledging what is not visible in the final version of this book: the electronic drafts with track changes and lengthy inserted comments; the printed copies that bear underlines, circles, question marks, cursive elaborations, and suggestions in ink and pencil; the conversations over Zoom, in offices, and coffee shops; the expressions of faith and encouragement; recommendations to see an exhibit, to read that article, this novel; the friendships, the hospitalities, the voices, and hands that hold these pages together.

I have been the beneficiary of exceptionally generous mentorships. During my graduate study at the University of California, Irvine, I found a constellation of scholars where, in addition to deriving sustenance from their individual corpuses of knowledge, the exchange of ideas, of intuitions, of disagreements, of enthusiasms could flourish. Ivette Hernández-Torres has provided me with a model for academic rigor and creativity, a captivating set of pedagogical practices and philosophies, and a compassionate and challenging mode of advisement that I aspire to emulate. Viviane Mahieux, Gaby Schwab, Luis Avilés, and Raúl Fernandez have each played critical roles in shaping me as a scholar. I am deeply grateful for their kindness, humor, and brilliance.

Emily Maguire has impacted this project from its earliest iterations to its latest drafts. Her generous mentorship and attentive feedback have been essential in guiding me toward the larger implications of my readings. I am also indebted to the astute and inspired interventions made by dear friends and colleagues: Brennan Keegan, Tara Phillips, Lázaro González, José Chávarry, Fernando Hernández Jáuregui, and Jessica Gordon-Burroughs have each left their marks on sections of this book. *Corporeal Readings* also benefited enormously from its reviewers, who made absolutely critical suggestions. I am especially grateful to my editor Stephanye Hunter whose enthusiasm for my work and invitation to submit a manuscript were the catalyst for *Corporeal Readings*' materialization. And through this long process her faith and support have not waivered.

My home institutions at the College of Charleston, Languages Cultures and World Affairs, Hispanic Studies, Latin American and Caribbean Studies, African American Studies, and Women and Gender Studies, have each supported me to make this project possible.

I thank Martha and Ángeles Torres Méndez, Lauren Gaskill, James Hirsch, and Thania Muñuz for their friendship, wisdom, and academic adventures.

To my parents Martha and Charlie, my siblings Miriam, Charlie, Sebastian, and Michael, and the best *prima hermana* in the universe, Lauren, for tolerating me when I had to "write a paper" and the sky was going to fall; or rather, for teasing me at every opportunity and teaching me how to laugh at myself. For their unabashed pride, faith, and unwavering support.

To Dani, Luna, Santi, and the cats, Titus and Maeve, for being home, for being part of our dense ecology where affection and irreverence reign, and *calcetines* are also *medias, gambas* are also *camarones,* and *zumo* is also *jugo.*

Finally, there are sections of the book that were previously published as articles or book chapters. I want to acknowledge and thank the publishers for allowing me to reprint versions of those texts here. Fragments from "Of Souls, Skins and Leopard Prints: Queer and Animal Creations of *Cubanbeings,*" *Revista de Estudios Hispánicos* 55, 3 (October 2021), appear in chapter 2 and the Coda. "Baroque Revolutionaries, Communist Fags, and Risky Friendships: Reading the Politics of Friendship in Fresa y chocolate" from *Cuban Studies* 47 edited by Alejandro de la Fuente, © 2019, was reprinted by permission of the University of Pittsburgh Press. This modified article constitutes the section on the film of chapter 5. With permission of SNCSC, "Incorrect and Beautiful Anatomies: Becomings, Immanence, and Transspecies Bodies in the Art of Roberto Fabelo," in *Re-Encountering Animal Bodies,* edited by Matthew Calarco and Dominik Ohrem, Hampshire, UK: Palgrave Macmillan, August 2018, appears revised in the second half of chapter 2. The second half of chapter 3 is a modified version of "Among the Ruins of Ecological Thought: Parasites, Roaches, and Nuclear Imaginings in *La fiesta vigilada,*" in *An Island in the Stream: Ecocritical and Literary Responses to Cuban Environmental Culture,* edited by David

Taylor, Scott Slovic, and Armando Fernandez Soriano, Lanham, Maryland: Lexington Books, © 2019 by The Rowman & Littlefield Publishing Group, Inc., all rights reserved. Nicolás Guillén's poetry in chapter 1 was originally included in the volume "Motivos de son" (1930) © The Estate of Nicolás Guillén, 2023, courtesy of The Estate of Nicolás Guillén.

Introduction

At a distance from the exhibition wall, it would appear that one of Ad Reinhardt's all black, non-objectivist paintings had been slashed by a knife. The tear starts near the top left of the canvas and cuts straight toward the bottom, revealing flesh and fat. What might have been the pursuit of universal forms in the pure materiality of painting doubles as black skin that has been cut open. The painting is in fact by Afro-Cuban artist Roberto Diago, and part of a series titled *Wounds* from 2015. The illusion of the cut creates a depth at the surface of what would otherwise be an impenetrable plane offering no iconographic referents. Up close the illusion of the wound vanishes into a long strip of white and bright red paint on a canvas covered in a dense layer of charcoal black paint. The surface of the painting has a texture similar to that of bark. Underneath the paint, you can detect narrow rectangular pieces of canvas frayed at their ends and glued evenly alongside each other. Considered within the context of Diago's work and its references to *queloides*, "the raised scars of whipped slaves," we can read the rhythmic protuberances on the canvas as scarred skin. Indeed, art historian Elvis Fuentes describes this series as "The Art of Growing Skin."[1]

Diago's series *Wounds* presents us with an aesthetic that insists on its materiality, almost as pure form (black paint on a two-dimensional surface), with the exception of one referent: the wounded body (the illusion of the cut). In other words, we have so-called high art—traditionally associated with a universal language and human transcendence—intersected with, or made up of, that which we share with nonhuman animals, a corporeal vulnerability. Similarly, in this book I analyze how Cuban cultural actors undermine long held notions that art and discursivity are the exclusive domain of humanity and civilization. Instead, I explore how creative production is casted as a becoming-beast; that is, a becoming-undisciplined, unrecognizable, enfleshed, territorially interdependent, and even parasitic.[2] In so doing, I argue these Cuban writers and artists challenge the rhetoric that has justified imperialisms (its civilizing missions) and the sacrifice of

Figure 1. Exhibition view of Roberto Diago's paintings from the series *Wounds*, 2015, at the Halsey Institute of Contemporary Art, 2018. Each painting measures 118 7/8 × 78 3/4 in. Photography by Rick Rhodes. Courtesy of MagnanMetz Gallery and Roberto Diago.

some bodies for the benefit of others. More specifically, Diago's painting references Black embodiment and the wounds of slavery, and it does so not through narrative, identifiable tropes, or folklore. The shallow space of the composition forces one to reckon with layers of encrusted pasts through its texture and the visceral experience of a cutting. Rather than make Blackness visible, per se, Diago makes it palpable, felt in the nervous system.[3] While the painting refers to corporeal skin—the site of touch, contact, and separation, to other bodies—the surface of the canvas insists on its own painterly skin. As viewers we don't simply contemplate the painting from a safe distance but are compelled to trace its perturbances with our fingers.

Corporeal Readings of Cuban Literature and Art: The Body, the Inhuman, and Ecological Thinking is as much about a practice of reading and engagement as it is about the individual texts and images it explores. In sustaining our attention on the skin and the tactility of surface, Diago's thick layer of black paint denies the possibility of penetrating a deeper semiotic interiority. Instead, he makes Blackness an irreducible material fact that does not allow itself to be subsumed by a larger subjectivity. Following Diago's lead, this book carefully attends to the aesthetic as a site of relations and politics,

Figure 2. Close up of painting, oil on canvas, from Roberto Diago's *Wounds* series, 2015, exhibited at the Halsey Institute of Contemporary Art. Photography by Rick Rhodes. Courtesy of MagnanMetz Gallery and Roberto Diago.

reading closely without the pretense of identifying subjects or unearthing origin myths. As such, the book articulates an ethics of reading where consuming literature and art does not redeem the soul but transforms the body. If Diago's painting draws us in to touch its scars, we are necessarily implicated and impacted.

Geographies, Histories, and Materials

The devastation of human lives and the ruination of environments are often intimately intertwined. Where mining has been the main source of exploitation and extraction in South America, in the Caribbean it has been largely the production of sugar. For centuries its harvesting entailed the enslavement of Africans—an estimated 600,000 were brought from West Africa to Cuba,[4]—and, up until the present, ecological degradation in the form of deforestation, desertification, and contamination. In an essay titled, "Sugar and the Environment in Cuba," Antonio Benítez-Rojo provides a natural history of the Cuban archipelago starting from the tectonic "cataclysm[s]" that shaped its mountain ranges to a 2002 announcement that the state would dismantle seventy-one sugar mills no longer in use.[5] While this is a legacy of colonialism, it is under the "Socialist Machine" that sugar production in Cuba reaches its zenith. The famous sugar harvest of 1969–1970 was aimed at 10 million tons. It was considered a failed campaign since the goal was never met. Nevertheless the practice of monoculture continued, "producing an average of 7 million tons of sugar on the basis of an extensive agriculture that demanded deforestation, the use of enormous quantities of chemical pesticides and fertilizers, and the implacable pumping of underground and surface waters."[6] Benítez-Rojo explains, "Given that the ideology [. . .] had been announced as the only one capable of saving humanity from poverty and from other social inequalities, the conquest of nature was to be achieved at the quickest possible pace and at any cost [. . .] [I]t became a common practice to sacrifice the environment in favor of greater [. . .] production."[7] He provides a paragraph long inventory of the fruits, vegetables, herbs, and spices that became scarce, if not disappeared, during thirty years (1959–1990) of leveling the earth for the production of sugar. The list of botanical names conveys a diversity of cultures, languages, and histories erased in the efforts to provide the Soviet bloc with sugar. His essay closes with the various environmental initiatives the state has taken on, some in practice and others rhetorically, since the loss of Soviet subsidies and an inevitable deindustrialization.

Following the failure of the "Ten Million Ton Sugar Harvest," in the 1970s the country aligned itself more closely to its Soviet partners. While Cubans could consume very limited quantities of fresh produce through the system of rationing,[8] they would now have access to manufactured goods, such as clothing and appliances, from the Eastern bloc. In her study of material culture in 1970s Cuba, María Cabrera Arús identifies contradictions that existed between the revolutionary state's anti-materialist, egalitarian ideology, and its promise of material well-being. Security, modernism, and progress were signaled by the state through representations of mass-produced goods. Paradoxically a culture of consumerism was promoted and incentivized; workers might be rewarded with a television set if they went above quota. Interestingly, even during times of relative abundance, Cabrera Arús shows how Cubans would repurpose many of these prefabricated Soviet goods into unique or creolized Cuban products.[9]

This repurposing would become extraordinary in the 1990s, during The Special Period in Time of Peace, so called by Fidel Castro because of the economic crisis following the fall of the Soviet Union. The extreme scarcity of resources necessitated ingenuity in the manipulation of existing materials. Whether it's a pizza made with melted condoms, steak from a mop, or a fan from vinyl records,[10] the transformation of material goods into something totally different from what they were manufactured and intended for veers on the fantastic. The reinvention of fabricated commodities comes from urgent needs and serves instrumental ends. Contrary to the praise that Cuba receives from environmentalists abroad, many of the processes of recycling have created pollution and/or exposure to toxic fumes.[11] Nevertheless, these transformations, which Cuban designer Ernesto Oroza has described as a "Technological Disobedience," compels us to appreciate the irreducible, or inexhaustible potential, and even mystery and vibrancy in materiality that ecofeminists and new materialists profess. There is a "revaluing of discarded material"[12] that upends dominant structures of meaning and value. Similar to the contradiction that Cabrera Arús identifies between the anti-materialist rhetoric of the revolution and its promotion of a consumerist society in the 70s, the 90s were met by another disjunction between state representations of heroic sacrifice and the day-to-day experience of surviving. As we'll see in the creative works explored here, writers and artists appeal to a becoming-parasitic, to being corporeal beings with irreducible material needs, and as such exposing the hubris and violence of modernizing projects and their assumptions of conquering nature.

Since November of 2020 the Cuban public has mobilized itself and vocalized discontent with state policies and governance in an unprecedented manner; unauthorized protests and oppositional political parties have been and continue to be banned in Cuba.[13] At the forefront of these public demonstrations were artists, writers, and musicians, who were initially protesting President Miguel Díaz-Canel's 2018 Decree 349, making it illegal to exhibit or perform art without prior authorization from the government.[14] Notably, the San Isidro Movement, a group of "self-taught rappers, spoken word poets and visual artists, the majority of whom are Black," have staged a number of protests.[15] In November the group staged a hunger strike in Havana's San Isidro to protest the arrest and sentencing of rapper Denis Solís. "Security agents disguised as health workers," forcibly entered the house on the pretense of Covid restrictions, detained and later released the protestors.[16] This event sparked the protest on November 27th, 2020, where hundreds of well-known artists occupied the outside of the Cuban Culture Ministry and were successfully granted a meeting with the deputy culture minister. However, promises that were made to the artists were not kept, and the government has responded with more surveillance and arrests.[17]

The connection between medicalization and state repression would repeat itself when San Isidro member and performance artist, Luis Manuel Otero Alcántara, was locked up in a Cuban hospital for staging another hunger strike.[18] While Cuba's universal healthcare is undoubtably a model to strive for and emulate in many ways, the Cuban state has and continues to exercise repressive biopower. In the chapters of this book, I will often refer to the forced labor and rehabilitation camps that started in the 1960s, where religious believers, suspected dissidents, and people whose gender and sexuality were nonheteronormative were subjected to behavioral modification.[19] In her analysis of the Cuban state's strong public health policy and moral codes, Mirta Suquet Martínez describes the nation's archetype, *el hombre nuevo,* as an immune man, invulnerable to physical and moral contamination.[20] The violence of such an ethos is made evident in the involuntary quarantines of the 1980s for those with HIV and the 1960s camps where those that were perceived as a threat to the national body were segregated and essentially expulsed. It is not casual that the name of Cuba's coronavirus vaccine is *Soberana* (sovereign). Politically establishing an imagined immunity, protecting the nation's sovereignty against the threat of foreign incursions, has resulted in inhospitable practices and the sacrifice of its populace. While Cuba's health infrastructure facilitated an initially impressive containment of the virus, medical anthropologists have also noted the paternalistic and highly punitive actions taken to control the population.[21] By emphasizing corporeality and complicating the dynamics of incorporation, *Corporeal Readings* demonstrates how writers and artists contest presumptions of invulnerability, autonomy, and the moral righteousness of sacrifice. In Ena Lucía Portela's 1998 novel, *El pájaro: Pincel y tinta china,* for instance, I show how she represents a hospital as a necropolitical institution and challenges the authority of dominant medical discourse.

In addition to the new censorship, with Decree 349, public outrage grew as poor living conditions were exacerbated by the global pandemic, the return of a stricter US embargo and, most significantly, a return to Soviet-style repression in response to the protests. On July 11, 2021, there were spontaneous uprisings all throughout the island, ignited in towns that are small and rural, and largely by poor Cubans of color.[22] This resulted in 5,000 arrests, 500 of which are still detained today.[23] Not incidentally, those most vocal against the status quo have been Black Cubans. The Cuban state has been reluctant to recognize the persistence of racism it claimed to have vanquished; and its policies after losing Soviet subsidies in the 1990s—opening the country to tourism and making it the primary source of revenue—only increased lived material disparities. Tourist and retail jobs, which are the most lucrative, go disproportionately to white or lighter skinned Cubans. Meanwhile, remittances from abroad come mostly from white Cuban families who first exiled at the start of the revolution.[24] As the government has made economic policy changes toward privatization—in 2009 Raúl Castro decreased social services and subsidies—the lives of Black Cubans have become more precarious, revealing a structural racism that the revolution was unable to dismantle.

The aims of this book are not to analyze empirical policies or events, but rather structures of power and ways of seeing and organizing the world. Nevertheless, I reference the recent demonstrations and government responses not only because some of the cultural actors analyzed here participated directly and indirectly in the protests, but also because they reveal historical continuities. Moreover, the philosophies from which I draw imagine texts and images not as representations of an already existing reality but as embedded in and co-constitutive of lived materialities. Against the moralism, masculinist heroism, and presumed immunity of the Cuban state rhetoric, the writers and artists discussed here highlight ethics, vulnerability, and survival over sacrifice.

Ecological Thinking

In Rachel Price's assessment of contemporary cultural trends in Cuba, visual and literary works express not so much a disenchantment with the socialist project, characteristic of the 1990s, as a weariness with all things Cuban, with the discourse of national exceptionalism and identity, recently revived by the new tourist economy. Aptly titled, *Planet/Cuba,* Price's 2015 book looks at works that both refer to immediate localities (e.g., neighborhoods, factories, subcultures) and evoke planetary concerns: accelerating capitalism, rising sea levels, toxic waste, and deforestation among others.[25] Since the 1990s, Cuba has drawn the interest of environmentalists abroad. The loss of Soviet subsidies and resources, such as petroleum, necessarily led to deindustrialization, organic farming, and sustainable practices across all levels of society. Yet poverty and food scarcity continue to be prevalent and there is no assurance the country's environmental advances will be sustained. In addition to tourism, the Cuban economy relies on mining and oil exploration, while the state's newest development, through the assistance of foreign-owned companies, is the renovation of now the largest port in the Caribbean.[26] Price's project considers how cultural production might contribute "any new thought about, or solutions to, our contemporary crises."[27] To this end, she studies the emerging "ecological aesthetics" of the last decade, citing Cuban artists and writers engaged with environmental themes and issues.[28]

Corporeal Readings of Cuban Literature and Art: The Body, the Inhuman, and Ecological Thinking shares similar aims and observations. However, with the exception of Roberto Fabelo's drawings and sculptures, the texts and images explored here do not expressly address nor appear motivated by environmental concerns. Indeed, one could reasonably ask what does Nicolás Guillén's poetry collection, *Motivos de son,* whose poetic object is Afro-Cuban speech, have to do with material ecologies? The works selected for this book have each in different ways allowed me to consider how particular aesthetic practices might generate new and imaginative ways of relating. Irrespective of their iconographic representations, aesthetic forms—as organizing structures, compositions, patterns, systems, and networks—can tell us a lot about ecology, in terms of recognizing interconnections and non-anthropocentric relationships. And ecology, in turn, as a philosophical and analytical lens, can generate different practices of reading and engagement with cultural works. As such, an ecological paradigm also provides us with an alternative to identity and representational politics.

Accordingly, a guiding thread throughout this book is a form of ecological thinking; that is, an awareness of complex networks of interdependences and of the material as having its own transformative potential outside of human agency.[29] Such thinking is not exclusively concerned with vegetation, wildlife, or climate change, but entails attending to the ways we are always embedded and dependent upon particular territories and material configurations. If we consider how an ethos of production and a logic of compartmentalization have justified the exploitation of some bodies and landscapes for the benefit of others, emphasizing nodes of connection over models of autonomy becomes a critical ethico-political task. Ecofeminists encourage us to imagine the material as irreducible to instrumental ends, as agential and "vibrant."[30] Doing so not only highlights the imperceptible impacts of, say, non-biodegradable or nuclear waste, but also undermines a rhetoric and ordering of the world that has, at various historical moments, legitimated the commodification and disposability of people (e.g., Black, Indigenous, and colonized folks).

Fittingly, ecology as a science has always been multidisciplinary. The term, which first appears in 1885 as the combination of the Greek words *oikos* for house and *logos,* as the study of, was broadly understood as the study of the complex interrelations of organisms and their environment.[31] More recently, ecology has been defined as the study of "interdependent communities, integrated systems, and strong connections among constituent parts."[32] Where older forms of environmentalism sustain a dualistic perspective between humans and nature, ecology collapses that distinction in its attention to connections, be they biologic, economic, or sociologic.[33] Drawing upon its etymological root, *oikos, Corporeal Readings* extends its ecological analysis to that of hospitality and hosting. From a biological perspective of the body hosting various organisms to political and ethical notions of how subjectivities and communities are constituted by hosting foreign Others, *Corporeal Readings* closes with a reading of queer hospitalities that contest national subject models of autonomy and invulnerability. Since Queer Studies challenges the ethos of productivity and futurity in heteronormativity, and since it imagines subjectivity as constituted in relation to an Other, the discipline has generative overlaps with ecological thinking. Both ecofeminists and queer studies theorists are invested in rendering the ontology of the human indeterminate.

While *Corporeal Readings* adopts ecology as an analytical lens—and I will say more about this further ahead—it is important to distinguish the project from the field of ecocriticism. Much like Rachel Price's engagement with environmentally themed artworks from Cuba, Latin American ecocritics study stories that "raise global consciousness," and create "awareness of ecological realities."[34] As such, the discipline has been described as "an activist approach to the study of literature."[35] This type of awareness raising often entails making connections between the image or text and a recognizable environmental issue. With good reason there has been a significant shift in the Humanities disciplines from attending to "man-made" cultural products to the biologic, geologic, oceanic, and other such geographies in order to reorient ourselves from anthropocentric models and to engage with the world not merely as linguistic and cultural constructs—as old-school poststructuralists would have it—but as actors that exist outside of human subjectivity.

These ecocritical approaches are a necessary response to our planetary crisis and, more often than not, call for more imaginative and complex views of the world. However, in the relationship they establish between "art" and "world," they can also be reductive, reiterating ontological categories, such as reality, as tangible fact, and art (or culture) as an immaterial mirror that reflects reality either well or poorly. Even in some of the most provocative readings we find these essentialized distinctions. In his analysis of Fernando Ortiz's canonical text, *Cuban Counterpoint: Tobacco and Sugar* (1940), Héctor Hoyos suggests we read sugar and tobacco not as allegorical stand-ins for economic or cultural movements, but as literal protagonists, whose materiality and histories have an impersonal agency. Hoyos's re-reading of Ortiz's transcultural theory as a "transcultural materialism," to the benefit of my analysis here, underscores the non-anthropocentric orientation already present in this pre-revolutionary Cuban text. Moreover, his non-allegorical approach is a critical interpretive gesture away from using nonhuman beings as archetypes and toward respecting their singularity. Notwithstanding, Hoyos's defense for the relevance of literary analysis restates ontological distinctions and their attendant hierarchies of value: "unlike philosophy, literature can be part and parcel to the objective world."[36] Inadvertently, in his endeavor to privilege the material over the ideological, Hoyos reifies a Christian metaphysics of body and soul. For example, he explains that transcultural materialist literature "infuses the realm of externality with storytelling and literary language. It presents compelling, enduring stories about people and processes which, by virtue of being outside of narrative, are an easier target."[37] That literature might "infuse the realms of externality" suggests a form of divine incarnation, while the description of people and processes "being outside of narrative," coincides with a platonic divide between art and life and suggests that, ultimately, the political potential of art lies in its capacity to speak for or make visible the underrepresented.

Corporeal Readings of Cuban Literature and Art heeds the caution of ecofeminists that ontological categories—even when value is inverted—have served to pathologize and exploit different life practices and forms. Bringing poststructuralist thinkers in conversation with new materialists compels us to be vigilant of conceptual compartments, such as philosophy and literature, or artifice and nature, and to question their constructions, while also attending to the very materiality in those constructions. Ideas, thoughts, sounds, images, texts, the seemingly immaterial and intangible, Jane Bennett and Karen Barad suggest, as well as the poststructuralist Jean-Luc Nancy, are in fact material, and come into contact with other bodies. *Corporeal Readings* privileges literary texts and visual works as its primary objects of study. However, rather than engage with these objects as evidence of human transcendence or as artefacts of human sociality, I return to literature and art from the perspective of a posthumanist and new materialist, equipped with the tools of deconstruction. If as Bennett says, materiality is vibrant and irreducible to instrumental ends; it is mysterious and has an agency outside of human will, then can we not say the same of texts and images? Prompted by the works themselves, I engage with poems, narrative fiction, sculptures, drawings, and film from Cuba, not as existing outside of life reflecting back some truth or misrepresentation, but as occupying space and weight, intervening and constituting lived materiality. Moreover, if these works are embedded in our contexts, how might our perception and relation to them be transformative in ways that exceed making visible or creating awareness?

The Shit of Art

There is Cuban, and as we shall see further ahead Caribbean, philosophical precedence for thinking texts and images in ways that go beyond the logic of representation. The now celebrated playwright, poet, novelist, and essayist, Virgilio Piñera (1912–1979)—ostracized by the Cuban revolutionary government for being openly gay—famously described the production of literature as defecation. Not incidentally, Piñera is known for his absurdist theater and emphatically corporeal texts, such as *La carne de René*. When asked if a collection of his 1940 short stories could be considered "Cuban," rather than list nationalistic tropes or link narrative contexts back to recognizable social or historical events, the Cuban author provides a description of his physical body's consumptions and processes:

> [C]uando estos cuentos fueron escritos, mi cuerpo se movía en lo cubano . . . en una palabra respiraba lo cubano por todos sus poros. Un cuerpo que se alimenta con productos cubanos—tanto materiales como psíquicos—solo puede expulsar residuos cubanos. Y digo expulsar y digo residuos porque la literatura no es otra cosa que una defecación de la materia transformada.[38]

Piñera not only lowers literature from its lofty, civilized pedestal, but also exemplifies how art is made up of, and inextricable from, our embodied lives. Conceived as such, art cannot serve as a mirror or a model—be that of a subjectivity or a political project—to emulate, if it is the metabolized and metamorphosed material of corporeal and ecological entanglements. As remainder and waste, it will always be singular and non-instrumental.

What's more, thinking of art as the residuals of our cycles of territorial interdependence, means that art is always a process and never outside of politics or society. Its politics, moreover, are not prescriptive or propagandistic given its constant transformation.

Moving from a scatological to a more utopian, but no less irreverent thinker, I couple Piñera's ideas to those of the Martinican philosopher-poet Édouard Glissant. Much like Piñera who challenged the deployment of art in the service of a recognizable political project,[39] Glissant's later work was critiqued for its ambiguity and being "non-adversarial." However, as Michael Wiedorn points out, Glissant's later writings did not lack political commitment, they were simply too ambitious to be affiliated with a known party. Glissant conceived of imaginative work as having the potential to create "cognitive upheaval[s]," transforming the ways we relate to each other. Perhaps not unlike Piñera saying, "literatura no es otra cosa que una defecación de la materia transformada,"[40] Glissant looked to "reformulate categories of Western thought."[41] To this end, the Martinican used paradox and opacity, which in turn also act as strategies to sustain the irreducible singularity of the Other. Wiedorn writes, "[w]e readers of Glissant might do well to focus not on the *products* of our engagement with his texts, that is, on what we might grasp in them or get out of them, but rather on the *process* of reading them, of experiencing them [. . .] 'The imaginary of the world,' *Philosophie* [*de la Relation* (2009)] explains to its readers, refuses to deal in possession or even in knowing."[42] Glissant's insistence on a poetics of relation, as that which constitutes existence, and his embrace of unknowing indicates that the type of ethical close reading I find solicited by Cuban writers and artists, extends beyond the island nation to the Caribbean archipelago. There is, of course, a shared geography and colonial history.

In his theory of *tidalectics,* the Barbadian poet, Kamau Brathwaite takes the ebb and flow of the tides as a way to imagine a relationship with difference. Unlike the violence implicit in dialectics, where differences are resolved, synthesized into a new third, and in that gesture, an assumption of triumph and progress, *tidalectics* sustains difference in "a recursive movement-in-stasis that is anti-progressive."[43] Brathwaite's theorizing from the seashore, where two limits touch and overlap, recede and return, is much like Glissant's insistence on unbound horizontal relations. As opposed to arboreal motifs in which identity is rooted, based on vertical, or historical filiations, the surface of the ocean with its potential to move astray and obfuscate with reflective light becomes the philosophical locus for Caribbean thinkers.

Not surprisingly the geography of the archipelago in Caribbean studies has displaced the trope of the island. As an isolated body, the island not only served conceptually as a blank slate for the fantasies of colonizers, but also its imagined limits sustained fictions of autonomy and closure. Meanwhile, its physical limits have operated as a means to imprison and/or exile those bodies that do not correspond to national subject models.[44] An archipelago by contrast, presents irregular fragments connected by water ways; its composition is that of a net. And if you're positioned from the water, as Puerto Rican philosopher Juan Carlos Quintero Herencia suggests, then hegemonic binaries on land become indistinguishable; they are rendered dysfunctional by the dizziness and confusion caused by the waves.[45] This oceanic sensorium allows for more transformative ways of relating to the world.

Although *Corporeal Readings* focuses exclusively on work by Cuban writers and artists, the aesthetic tendencies it explores have implications for understanding cultural production from the Caribbean, not because Cuba is exemplary of a uniform island condition. Rather, in adopting an ecological lens, and tracing continuities as opposed to ruptures, notions of national sovereignty, exceptionalism, and the limits of the national body are necessarily contested, while territorial interdependences are foregrounded. Moreover, if the archipelagic geography of the Caribbean gives rise to an aesthetic of surface and opacity, we can also point to the impetus to counter a shared legacy of plantation monoculture. Focusing on texts and images from Cuba demonstrates that even in a communist state that had separated itself from US imperialism, that ethos of productivity and mono-cultivation persisted. The Cuban writers and artists discussed here transform materials and construct narratives that render the logic of productivity and sacrifice inoperable.

When Glissant writes in all capital letters, "RELATION CONNECTS, RELAYS, RELATES, IT DOES NOT RELATE ONE THING TO ANOTHER, BUT RATHER THE WHOLE TO THE WHOLE, THE POETICS OF RELATION THUS ACCOMPLISHES THE DIVERSE,"[46] I suggest another way we can understand this is ecologically. Not incidentally, the English anthropologist Gregory Bateson, who devoted much of his work to mapping "an Ecology of the Mind," was emphatic that what interested him in his study of aesthetic works was not "identifiable relata," "perceived objects or persons," but rather "relationships," "integration," "mutual dependency," and "circuity."[47] In order to approximate the systemic nature of the world, Bateson argues we need dreams, art, and poetry, to come to the aid of purposive rationality. For a sense of the whole does not allow itself to be compartmentalized and trying to do so results in pathogenetic practices. Relatedly, Glissant found that "rooted" or sedimented identity, as opposed to one that is relational, leads to fascist politics. We can see these exclusionary and pathologizing effects emerge in Cuba as the revolutionary state imposed a homogeneous identity.

This constellation between Piñera's notion of literature as corporeally transformed material, Glissant's poetics of relation, and Bateson's ecology of the mind sets in deeper relief my use of ecology as an analytical lens. In short, I explore how literary and artistic works insist on complex relationships that destabilize ontological hierarchies and conventional categories of thought.

Where Bodies Meet

Returning to Roberto Diago's cut, the exposed flesh and fat invites us to dwell on our environmental entanglements. In recognizing such dynamic relations, ecological thinking also acknowledges the impossibility of mastery or of knowing absolutely.[48] My interest in Diago's *Wounds* paintings are as sites of mediation; skin is where bodies meet. Diago's soliciting a touching as opposed to accessing knowable, reproducible content, expresses an epistemological humility as well as a relational existence. If, as Jean-Luc Nancy claims, "Being is 'outside itself,'" an "exteriority that is impossible to recapture [. . .] an outside that it cannot relate to *itself,* but with which it entertains an essential and incommensurable relation,"[49] then we can understand exteriors, exposures, epidermises, surfaces, artifices not as that which contain or cover an immaterial or more meaningful substance, but as the very sites of sense-making and transformation.

Locating existence at the point of touch, or where bodies meet, reorients attention from individual self-actualization, or national development, to that of co-constitutive relations, to collectivities and networks that exceed discursive boundaries. My emphasis on corporeality entails thinking of bodies not as incarnations of an immaterial ideal, or as discrete organisms. In drawing from thinkers, such as Nancy, Gilles Deleuze, and Roberto Esposito, I think of bodies as configurations in continuous exchange with other bodies. Guided by these philosophical expositions, *Corporeal Read-*

ings focuses on the work of writers and artists who draw our attention to the shared materiality of what we often think of as different kinds of bodies. Subsequently, these works challenge dominant models of subjectivity and belonging, soliciting more expansive forms of thought and practice.

While the first half of the book emphasizes exteriority and an impenetrable materiality—working against nationalistic projects that assume the incorporation of marginalized Others—the second half penetrates the body through a more biological notion of incorporation, or hosting and hospitality. Doing so allows me to further nuance an ethics and practice of reading, especially through the notion of cannibal reading or textopofagia. The word incorporation has a particular political resonance in the Cuban context, as it was ubiquitous in state rhetoric and referred to the involvement or obligation of citizens to participate in political organizations, the military, or even work in the sugar fields.[50] Antonio José Ponte underscores the subversive and baroque way José Lezama Lima used the word in opposition to the state's usage. Rather than forming part of a larger institution or subjectivity, the verb *incorporar* in Lezama Lima's texts signifies to eat or to have sex, in other words, to literally put inside the body. In eating, digesting, and metabolizing, or even in intercourse and eroticism, one is affected and changed but not fused with Other. There is also an expenditure or waste in consuming food and sex—and one that can result in literature if we recall Virgilio Piñera's scatological statement. Ponte's analysis of Lezama Lima's *incorporar* is especially apt for the way I read incorporation in the selected texts and images. Through Ahmel Echevarría's 2013 novel, *Búfalos camino al matadero,* with its references to letter writing and ingestion, the book argues that reading the Other might lead to a form of incorporation, but one that transforms the body and does not resolve the tensions posed by the Other. Put otherwise, if representations of the disenfranchised in art and literature have been understood in Cuban Studies as ways of allegorically incorporating them into the national body,[51] *Corporeal Readings* demonstrates that such incorporations do not harmoniously fuse or eliminate difference, but rather add parts to a dynamic composite.

This understanding of incorporation and emphasis on hospitality allows me to look at a mainstream work like *Fresa y chocolate* and underscore a radical politics. Although the film adopts the conventions of melodrama and works within the confines of the establishment—produced through the Instituto Cubano del Arte e Industria Cinematográficos (ICAIC, Cuban Institute of Cinematographic Art and Industry) and promoting the teleological narrative of the revolution—my analysis of the film points to irresolvable tensions. The film's makers, Tomás Gutiérrez Alea and Juan Carlos Tabío, may have intended to make the figure of the homosexual consumable to a general audience, but the imagined incorporation of this figure, I argue, necessarily transforms the body politic and does not diffuse the challenges it poses to the status quo.

Corporeal Contributions and Chapter Summaries

In her critical analysis of Enlightenment humanism, Denise Ferreira da Silva explains that the human subject was imagined as transparent, its agency and autonomy located in an immaterial interiority. Racial differences to white European man, as well as differences of gender and sexuality, were imagined as affectable exteriorities, in other words, objects to be manipulated and determined by subjects of authority.[52] I suggest Diago's doubling of black paint and Black skin collapses the universal and the particular. The painterly skin that refers to corporeal skin insists on a radical exteriority that resists co-optation and hermeneutics. Given that the logic of humanist thought has often resulted in totalizing and hierarchal structures[53]—and in the context of Cuba the imposition of a militarized and invulnerable national subject—I focus my attention on works that underscore a shared corporeality across human and nonhuman bodies. Bypassing the Cuban state's formulation of a binary opposition between the promise of *el hombre nuevo* (the new man) and the rejection of dissidents as *gusanos* (worms) and *escoria* (scum of humanity),[54] I examine how the figure of the human is unworked or rearticulated in literary and visual works. Put otherwise, I underscore an ecological attunement in these Cuban texts and images, as they diminish the superiority and differentiation of the human. As we shall see, certain literary and visual compositions operate as host-organisms in dynamic exchange with their environments, contesting models of the individual sovereign subject and gesturing toward the figure of the *gusano* (or the parasite).

Where Cuban and Caribbean Studies have been largely guided by a politics of representation, this book's original contribution lies in its setting Cuban aesthetic practices in conversation with Ecofeminist, Critical Race, and Poststructuralist theories. *Corporeal Readings* traces instances of impenetrable materiality and irreducible corporeality across diverse texts and images, unsettling systems of value and meaning. Drawing from texts, such as Fred Moten's *In the Break: The Aesthetics of the Black Radical Tradition* and Jane Bennett's *Vibrant Matter: A Political Ecology of Things*, I underscore an aesthetics in Cuban made texts and images that works against the logic of identity, the logic of substitution and, as such, the economy of sacrifice. The project of fulfilling a unified communist society, modeled on the self-sacrificing heroism of masculine figures, such as Che Guevara and Fidel Castro, meant the ostracization and expulsion of gays, religious believers, the sick, the lazy, the extravagant and anyone deemed in excess or unproductive to its ends. While Caribbean scholars, such as Thomas Anderson in his book *Carnival and National Identity in the Poetry of Afrocubanismo* and Rosamond King in *Transgressive Sexualities in the Caribbean,* have attended to the representation of Afro-Cuban identity and transgender subjects, respectively, this book reads racial, gendered, and species differences in art and literature not as (mis)representations of already existing subjects or cultural properties, but as surplus that refuses to be consumed. By sustaining a practice of reading that attends to the aesthetic materiality of works and adopting an epistemological humility—a form of reading that does not presume to penetrate coded essences—*Corporeal Readings* demonstrates how Cuban writers and artists have undermined regimes of seeing and organizing bodies.

The book breaks with conventional periodization as it moves across a wide expanse of time and a diversity of media, genres, and themes, discussing works such as Nicolás Guillén's 1930 collection of poetry, Roberto Fabelo's 2009 bronze sculptures, the 1993 film *Fresa y chocolate,* and novels by the neo-vanguard Severo Sarduy, as well as narrative fiction by contemporary writers Ena Lucía Portela, Antonio José Ponte, and Ahmel Echevarría. Through this unique and heterogeneous assemblage of works, *Corporeal Readings* engages with a variety of social differences and issues—race, gender, sexuality, class, species, and the environment—while resisting the tendency in area studies to mine for cultural symbols and ethnographic representations. Instead of reiterating monolithic historical periods (e.g., the Republican, Revolutionary, and Post-Revolutionary eras) or demarcating literary generations and artistic movements, *Corporeal Readings* explores how the limits of the national/human body are contested not just in Post-Soviet Cuban production, or in avant-garde work, but as early as the 1930s and in work as commercially successful as *Fresa y chocolate.*

I begin with two canonical Cuban works, Nicolás Guillén's 1930 avant-garde poetry collection, *Motivos de son,* and Severo Sarduy's 1963, neo-vanguard, novel *Gestos.* In so doing, my first chapter straddles the historical divide between the first decades of Cuba's independence (1902), known as the Republican period, and the start of the Cuban Revolution. Where previous scholarship considers the 1959 revolution as a "radical break with the past," defining history "by the dramatic extremes *before* and *after*,"[55] my pairing of these two authors foregrounds historical continuities: both periods share the hubris of modernizing projects and the articulations of a national subject. *Motivos de son* and *Gestos* have been understood as preoccupied with representing aspects of *cubanidad*. In contradistinction, I trace resistances to identity and subject formation in their texts. Within Cuban intellectual discourse these are tendencies ascribed to a postmodern zeitgeist that presumably arrives only after the disillusionment of the Soviet Union.[56] After 1959, Cuban historians mark 1991 as the next dramatic break; with the loss of Soviet subsidies came hunger, disenchantment, and a questioning of the Revolution's ideology. Many of the primary sources *Corporeal Readings* explores fall within this "Post-Soviet" period and self-consciously contest the narrative and authority of the Cuban State, such as Ena Lucía Portela's and Antonio José Ponte's narrative fiction. Nevertheless, by employing a particular strategy of reading, what the narrative arc of *Corporeal Readings* demonstrates is that even in works that do not historically correspond to this postmodernist moment or in works whose authors are not consciously, or explicitly, challenging national discourses, we can find traces of the inhuman, of non-identitarian community and ecological entanglements. In other words, despite spectacular political and ideological shifts, there are certain artistic practices that persist. This is not to suggest that these works are not co-constitutive of their historical contexts, but rather that despite changes at a state level, the lived material experiences of social differences, as well as corporeal and environmental interdependencies, have and continue to defy pretenses of sovereignty and co-optation.

In what follows, I provide a summary for each of my five chapters. Drawing from both literary and visual disciplinary practices, I provide a close reading of each work tracing the different ways in which corporeality and materiality are made manifest. My aim is to theorize from the works themselves allowing each to raise their own set of issues and questions.

Against the grain of reading Guillén and Sarduy as producing expressions of *cubanidad*, in chapter 1 I trace an impenetrable materiality in their texts that works against identity formation. A critical question that guides this book is the relationship between aesthetics and ethics; specifically, how literary and visual forms, conditioned by their particular historical contexts, are implicated in an ethics and politics of community. In this chapter, I argue that Guillén's and Sarduy's formal experimentations change the coordinates of dominant perception so that race, class, gender, sexuality, or species material differences are made palpable while sustaining their singularity to a politics of representation.

Importantly, through Guillén's and Sarduy's literary experimentations, this first chapter elaborates an ethics of reading as touching. Marking moments of impenetrability in their texts allows us to come into contact with sonic and visual material differences, without the pretense of expertise. This practice of reading, suspending the production of knowable content, has implications for the way we interact with social Others.

Chapter 2 expands the notion of impenetrable materiality to that transmateriality, or ontological indeterminacy, through Sarduy's 1972 novel *Cobra*, with a transgender protagonist, and Roberto Fabelo's artwork of transspecies figures. More specifically, by reading Sarduy's novel in tandem with Fabelo's drawings, paintings, and sculptures, my second chapter goes on to explore the reconfiguration of human-animal forms and the undoing of classificatory systems. I examine how Sarduy and Fabelo subvert representational techniques that presume unmediated access to the "natural" world, and in so doing unsettle the secure boundaries of the human and its attendant nationalisms. Drawing from both poststructuralism and new materialisms, this chapter intersects two theoretical camps often treated as mutually exclusive. I argue that Sarduy and Fabelo demonstrate how performative (un)doings of social constructs, be that gender or species identity, are embedded in lived material relations. Specifically with regard to Sarduy, I also consider the ethics of a baroque ecology, the indistinction it produces between life and death and its implications for biopolitics.

My third chapter focuses on the link between writing and becoming-nonhuman in Ena Lucía Portela's *El pájaro: Pincel y tinta china* (1999) and Antonio José Ponte's *La fiesta vigilada* (2007). In both novels we find characters deemed futureless and abandoned; their means of surviving abject conditions are at once the source of nonhuman becomings and a practice of writing. These novels recall the use of animalization as a figurative device in Latin American literature to address a series of social and political issues, most significantly the dehumanization of the dispossessed. However, in my treatment of these texts, I complicate the possibility of an allegorical interpretation—or, better, of simply reading animals as metaphoric stand-ins—and, thus, undermine attempts to establish an equivalence between the nonhuman and the abject.

Where writing in chapter 3 appears as a parasitic practice, in chapter 4 it's cannibalistic. Through Ahmel Echevarría's two novels, *Búfalos camino al matadero* (2013) and *Caballo con arzones* (2017), we continue to explore the notion of creative production as corporeal and animal, and how the distinction between the human and the nonhuman, or rather flesh to be nourished and flesh to be consumed, is culturally and politically determined. Importantly, this chapter expands upon and complicates the ethics of reading discussed in chapter 1, moving from the outside in, and shifting our focus from the material to the corporeal. Through the trope of cannibalism, which I tease from Echevarría's 2013 novel, I elaborate a practice of reading and writing as dependent upon and nourished by other bodies. "Trágame. Pero no me leas," a repeated request in *Búfalos camino al matadero,* is taken up as an ethical call in this chapter, as an ethics of the Other.[57]

My fifth chapter continues to complicate a politics of incorporation through an analysis of queer friendships in Gutiérrez Alea's seminal film, *Fresa y chocolate* (1993) and Portela's novel, *Cien botellas en una pared* (2002). Adopting the biological and political trope of immunity, this chapter considers friendship and hospitality in relation to the dynamic exchanges between host-organisms and their environments. Scholars have rightly critiqued cultural and governmental representations, such as the Centro Nacional de Educación Sexual (National Center for Sex Education), as attempts to neutralize the oppositional charge posed by marginalized figures to the Revolution's narrative of progress.[58] However, through inoculation's aporetic logic, I argue that consumable representations of queer figures inadvertently affirm what they aimed to deactivate. In the desire to incorporate the figure of the homosexual, to immunize itself against the poison of the Revolution's error—its persecution of gay citizens—these representations necessarily corrupt the integrity of the body politic.

Starting from Jean-Luc Nancy's assertion that it is "precisely the immanence of man to man, or it is *man,* taken absolutely, considered as the immanent being par excellence, that constitutes the stumbling block to a thinking of community,"[59] this book considers texts and images that insist on the limits of comprehension, on a writing that allows us to move away from human agents and teleological narratives, to reconsider collectivities, configurations, and assemblages. Against the backdrop of modern nation-building and its desire for a unified political body, the Revolution's messianic promise of *el hombre nuevo,* the State's rhetoric of progress, its violent enforcement of productivity (as in the UMAP camps)[60] and Castro's prescription to intellectuals manifested in "Palabras a los intelectuales,"[61] I explore how particular texts and images may insist on, or betray, a sense of excess and unproductivity. Ultimately, *Corporeal Readings* offers alternative ways of thinking community: Departing from the notion of human exceptionalism and its willingness to sacrifice for future ends, community here is imagined ecologically, as a shared vulnerability and difference.

In the coming pages we will discuss ecofeminists' deployment of Quantum Field Theory, prompting us to imagine the seemingly fixed and tangible world as enveloped in virtual particles, in relation to Sarduy's and Fabelo's metamorphoses. We will consider Guillén's untranslatable Afrophonemes as a Black radical aesthetics; that is, an "animateriality" that resists subjection and "embodies the critique of value, or private property, of the sign."[62] Returning to Diago's *Wounds*, and by way of closing this introduction, let me suggest that in the shallow space of the painting, the texture of bark, the illusion of the wound, and the impenetrable black paint, there is a virtual potentiality, a field of becoming that demands our relating to it with humility and imagination.

1

Reading as Touching

Tracing Impenetrable Materiality in Nicolás Guillén's *Motivos de son* and Severo Sarduy's *Gestos*

In the literary supplement of the Havana newspaper, *Diario de la Marina,* under *Ideales de una raza,* a subsection meant to attract Afro-Cuban readers, Nicolás Guillén's collection of eight poems titled *Motivos de son* was first published in 1930.

The collection features a cast of eight characters, stereotypes of Black Cubans drawn from vaudeville-like shows, such as the pimp, the *mulata,* and the dandy.[1] Perhaps more striking than the ironic adaptation of these codified figures was the graphic appearance of non-standard orthography, reproducing the vernacular speech spoken in Havana's poor Black neighborhoods. The collection's opening eight syllabic line, "¿Po qué te pone tan brabo,"[2] with its repetitive bilabial consonants, the missing *r* at the end of "Po" [por], and the use of *b* instead of *v* in "brabo" [bravo], make it almost irresistible to read silently. In fact, the poems' misspelled words would require most non-native speakers to phonetically sound out its letters in order to determine their meaning. With the stanza "sin acoddadte de mí"[3] one might repeat it several times, fumbling with its multiple *d*'s at the tip of the tongue and behind the teeth. Among *Motivos de son*'s playful banter and colloquial vocabulary, we also find sonorous refrains composed of Afro-phonemes, "sóngoro cosongo,"[4] that remain indecipherable, at least to the inexpert philologist. Adding to its auditory and performative quality, the structure of the poems follows that of the *son,* a popular Cuban dance form composed of both Hispanic and Bantu (African) musical elements. The poems' eight count rhythm and call and response chorus might induce in its readers steady forward propulsion with a subtle sway in the hips and the shoulders, as they pronounce the words out loud, imitating an accent like a stage actor, an impersonator, or a ventriloquist.

Motivos' departure from traditional rhyme schemes and syllabic counts, its irreverent break with the polished and erudite language of modernist Hispanophone poetry, and its textual reproduction of a popular musical form, not only challenged aesthetic sensibilities, winning Guillén immediate praise from the literary vanguard, but also the self-image of affluent Black Cubans.[5] Having placed so much stock in the cultivation of literature and the mastery of language, Cuba's Black bourgeoisie found the picaresque poems' lack of linguistic formality and allusions to the working classes damaging to their efforts of assimilation and racial equality.[6] Nicolás Guillén was not the first to articulate an Afro-Hispano speech in a literary context if we recall seventeenth-century writers such as Lope de Vega, Góngora, and Sor Juana Inés de la Cruz.[7] Critics have noted that these Spanish Golden Age approximations of slaves' creolized language were often placed adjacent to that of monolingual speakers, with the aim of producing humoristic and parodic effects.[8] Closer to Guillén's temporal and geographical context, starting in the 1920s, there is a surge of African inspired images and sounds in the cultural production of Cuba and other Caribbean islands. In the Puerto Rican author Luis Palés Matos's 1928 poem "Danza negra," and the Cuban José Zacarías Tallet's "La Rumba" from that same year, we find onomatopoetic phrases composed of Afrophones, Caribbean and African nations listed alongside each other, references to folklore and popular dance forms that "vibrate" with the "soul" of Africa, "El alma africana que vibrando está/ en el ritmo gordo del mariyandá" (Palés Matos).[9] Whereas Palés Matos's and Tallet's poems are narrated in the third person, situated in particular contexts, "Haití, Martinica, Congo, Camerún" (Palés Matos), and ripe with visual images, "Ella mueve una nalga, ella mueve la otra./ Él se estira, se encoge, dispara la grupa" (Tallet), the first-person speakers in Guillén's *Motivos* perform, as it were, on a bare stage, with no scenic descriptors or folkloric props, and little to no visual cues.[10] In effect, Guillén distills the sonorous, isolates an Afro-Cuban speech on the page, making its tonality and texture its sole poetic object, if not also the graphic materialization of an incorrect writing: "tu inglé era de etrai guan,/ de etrai guan y guan tu tri."

Rather than referring to Africa by name or symbols, rather than describing "vibrations" and "rhythms," rather than identifying the properties of the *son*, Guillén's 1930 collection, as I aim to explore further, produces the rhythm of the *son* and the sound of Afro-Cuban speech through its composition, grammar, and orthography, that is, the minima of language.

With respect to representation and its politics, one of my aims in this chapter is to consider the ethical implications of foregrounding the sonorous over a semiotics of words and images. If vibrations in *Motivos de son* are not *seen,* offering no narrative description of dancing bodies, I suggest vibrations have the potential to be *felt* in the process of reading the poems. This prompts a central question for this chapter: How might reading, solicited as an affective, visceral process, instead of one that mines for signification, complicate representation and generate a different relationship with the Other?

Notwithstanding Guillén's status as Cuba's national poet, I aim to explore how *Motivos* brings the reader into contact with a racial difference in such a way that resists its assimilation and co-optation by nationalist projects. In the second half of this chapter, I will turn to the work of another writer who might be considered Guillén's stylistic and political opposite. While Severo Sarduy's abstract and disorienting texts are anathema to the seeming simplicity and playfulness of *Motivos de son,* both Camagüey-born writers allow me to theorize an ethics of reading where the expert interpretive practices of the literary analyst must give way to a sensuous and "unknowing relation."[11] While Guillén's 1930 collection takes on a materiality through rhythm and the sonorous, Severo Sarduy's 1963 novel *Gestos* does so through the spatial composition of the canvas: visual artifice and two-dimensionality pervade throughout the text. As I hope to illustrate, both writers keep their readers on the surface and at the same time do the critical work of bringing to the fore a difference. In this chapter I try to imagine how it might be possible to accomplish this foregrounding while avoiding the pitfalls of converting difference into a property; that is, a positive substance that belongs to and is proper to a subject, a substance that can be reflected in institutions and heads of state, reproduced and commoditized. Through the work of Guillén and Sarduy, I consider how certain aesthetic or formal experimentations, in tangent with a particular practice of reading, can change the coordinates of dominant perceptions so that race, class, gender, sexuality, or species material differences are made palpable while sustaining their irreducibility to a politics of representation.

With Sarduy's *Gestos* we cross the historical divide marked by the 1959 Revolution, an event with providential weight. That said, Guillén's and Sarduy's periods share the hubris of modernizing projects and the articulation of a national subject. While Guillén's early poems coincide with the preoccupation of establishing an ethnic national identity, a mulatto fusion, or "color cubano," Sarduy's texts might be seen against the backdrop of establishing a revolutionary subject and an ideal communist society. In an article titled "Pintura y revolución" published on the 31st of January 1959, Sarduy warns against a post-revolutionary tendency to prescribe an art that is figurative with "cuadros que 'signifiquen' algo, que den opiniones . . ."[12]

> Sí, queremos arte nacional, pero puede hacerse pintura nacional sin llenar los cuadros de guajiros y palmas, puede hacerse teatro nacional donde no aparezcan gallegos y negritos, puede hacerse poesía nacional que no cante a los turistas y a los soldados.[13]

The instrumentalization of an art work, making it signify within and contribute to the progressive narrative of the Revolution would be implied in Castro's famous quote, "dentro de la Revolución, todo; contra la Revolución, nada" from his 1961 speech, "Palabras a los intelectuales."[14] As we shall see through close readings of *Gestos*—a novel that could be summarized as the detonation of bombs in 1959 Havana and, accordingly, a representation of the Revolution and *cubanidad*—Sarduy very consciously works against such purposive notions of art and identitarian politics.

Although his appeals against a didactic Social Realist art were already formulated in his 1959 article, another context should be noted when we consider Sarduy's aesthetics. In 1960 he leaves on a state scholarship to study Art Restoration in Paris.[15] There he would befriend Roland Barthes and immerse himself in the intellectual world of the poststructuralists, contributing alongside Derrida, Lacan, and Sollers to the *Tel Quel* journal.[16] Not surprisingly, Sarduy's novels are distinguished by their semiotic displacements and the prevalence of diegetic passages over the elaboration of plot and characters. When his student visa expired in 1961, Sarduy stayed in Paris, never returning to Cuba. Given his deep familial attachments and expressed desire to return home, Roberto González Echevarría speculates Sarduy's decision to remain in exile was in part out of fear of persecution as a homosexual and a dissident: "Ya para esa fecha [1961] el gobierno cubano daba claros indicios de que llegaría a convertirse en un régimen totalitario. . . . [E]empezó también por esas fechas la persecución sistemática de disidentes políticos, entre ellos muchos homosexuales, entre los que se encontraban no pocos artistas."[17]

In sharp contrast to Guillén, who was assigned the title of National Poet and served as the first president to the *Unión de escritores y artistas de Cuba* in 1961, Sarduy, as a writer in exile, would become persona non grata to the Cuban establishment; up until he died in 1993 none of his works had been published or reviewed in Cuba.[18] Considering their positions in relation to the state and the distinctiveness of their literary styles, my pairing of Guillén and Sarduy is at first glance incongruous. However, my interest in Guillén's vanguard *Motivos de son* and Sarduy's neo-vanguard *Gestos* is in a politics implicit in their formal experimentations and the type of reader engagements they solicit.

In developing an ethics and practice of reading from their literary texts, I have found the work of three theorists to be especially generative; in this chapter I devote space to the elaboration of their thought as they also inform organizing concepts for the book as a whole. The poet and critic Fred Moten helps me better formulate the relationship between racial difference and aesthetics. In his book, *In the Break: The Aesthetics of the Black Radical Tradition,* Moten considers how the conceptualization of the avant-garde and its production are antithetical to Black politics, since they rely on Eurocentric notions of historical progress and the appropriation of non-European forms (made rhetorically and materially possible through colonialism), as in Modernist Primitivism and, arguably, the *afrocubanismo* movement of which *Motivos de son* is considered exemplary. However, "oxymoronically," Moten asserts, "the avant-garde is a black thing [. . .] and blackness is an avant-garde thing."[19] In their rupture from dominant culture, their experimentalism, illegibility, and marginal status, blackness and the avant-garde, Moten argues, are the material surplus, the remainders reproduced in the very processes that attempt to subjugate and appropriate them. Black performance, as "the extremity that is often unnoticed as mere accompaniment to (reasoned) utterance,"[20] he writes, "embodies the critique of value, or private property, of the sign."[21] Ecofeminist Jane Bennett's concept of "vibrant matter," to which I will turn at the end of the chapter, similarly theorizes materiality in a way that challenges systems of exchange value, semiotics, or any other such sciences of equivalence. To think matter as vibrant, rather than inert and passive, demands a reexamination of the logics of utility and exploitation. Moten's and Bennett's combined theorization on animated materiality support my efforts to consider the merely aesthetic or technical aspects of Guillén's and Sarduy's work as having an ethico-political potential, in their resistance to instrumentality and their thwarting of the knowing subject. Finally, the poststructuralist Jean-Luc Nancy's notion of reading as touching, as opposed to a practice of decipherment or the culling of knowable content, prompts me to dwell on the tactility of language in Sarduy's *Gestos,* much like the triple *d*'s in Guillén's poetry. Through close readings of Nancy's philosophical texts on corporeality, intertwined with those of Sarduy's novel, in the second half of the chapter, I further elaborate a practice of reading that sustains an impenetrability. Reading Sarduy and Nancy alongside each other allows me to complicate the difference between literature and philosophy and its attendant binary distinctions between body and soul.

The Logic of Incorporation

The social significance of showcasing in poetry a music and a speech that had been disparaged by the cultural elite at that time cannot be overstated. In his famous prologue to *Sóngoro Cosongo,* the collection immediately following *Motivos de son,* Guillén himself acknowledges, "No ignoro, desde luego, que estos versos les repugnan a muchas personas, porque ellos tratan asuntos de los negros del pueblo." Matching the audacity of his poetry, Guillén's response to this "repugnance" is "No me importa. O mejor dicho: me alegra."[22] Indeed, following Jacques Rancière, we might say that Guillén's placing of Black working-class speech on the stage of high art demonstrates a redistribution of the sensible, in which the distinguishing (sonic and linguistic) features of a particular racial and class population, whose cultural imports had been unrecognized, are accorded poetic value.[23] Before considering artistic movements such as *afroantilleanismo* or *afrocubanismo,* it is important to remember the rhetoric and policies that followed four hundred years of slavery and natal alienation. Latin American and Caribbean nineteenth and early twentieth-century nationalist projects went to great lengths to pathologize, criminalize, and deny the persistence of African cultural practices. Discourses that circulated imagined Latin America as an organism sick with racial impurities, prescribing miscegenation as a form of diluting these pollutants and social progress through an education that located the birth of civilization in ancient Greece and Rome.[24] In the first decades of Cuba's independence (1902), the *comparsas,* carnival processions with musical roots in African religious rituals, were banned, as were the religious Afro-Cuban secret societies of *nañingos.*[25] Political organization along racial lines had also been made illegal, leading to protests by Black and mulatto Cubans; the military's brutal response to these demonstrations resulted in what historians now call the "Racist Massacre of 1912."[26] In addition to these laws, there was the continuation of Christian missionary work, a colonial Spanish education, and government propaganda that framed African derived traditions as primitive, at best.[27] Specifically, with regard to the genesis of Cuba's *son,* the composer and historian of Cuban folk music, Eduardo Sánchez de Fuentes (1874–1944) denied that African descendants had contributed anything to Cuban culture and instead identified the traditions of the Spanish and the indigenous *taínos* (a population made almost extinct in the colonial process) as the sole ancestral sources of musical forms on the island.[28] Buttressing such claims, US and Anglophone Caribbean sociologists as late as the 1960s posited that the memory of practices originating in Africa could not have survived the trauma of the Middle Passage.[29] In the face of such erasure, the effort to unearth and celebrate "the African presence"[30] in cultural production of the Americas becomes a critical political labor. And yet, such claims to "presence" as, for instance, Palés Matos's stanza in "Danza negra," "El alma africana que vibrando está," and its implication of definable properties are not unproblematic, as I will elaborate further ahead.

In contradistinction to the likes of Sánchez de Fuentes, there were other thinkers, such as Juan Marinello (1898–1977), who identified the descendants of African slaves as the very "marrow and root" of the people.[31] Although Cuba's Black population was in the minority, many artists and writers looked to Afro-Cuban culture as a "protest" and "authentic alternative" to the legacy of Spanish colonialism and an encroaching US imperialism.[32] In fact, for the Barbadian poet and cultural theorist Kamau Brathwaite, there is an imminent radical politics in the Black aesthetics deployed by Cuban and Caribbean artists, to which I will return. However, critics have also noted that the incorporation of presumably African images and sounds often reproduced stereotypes, such as the sensuous *mulata,* or romanticized African folklore as originary and immemorial, effectively evading ethnic tensions and lived material conditions.[33] These artistic productions, if not explicitly co-opted by nation-building projects, structurally coincided with the desire to assimilate whatever posed a threat to national unity. In the development of a Caribbean modernist poetics, Michael Dash identifies a "nostalgia for a prelapsarian mythic past" and a desire for the reconstitution of an organic whole.[34] Tracing the political manifestations of creative movements such as Negritude and Indigenism, Dash links this nostalgia to "totalitarian impulses." We see this in the fascist politics of the 1940s Haitian monarchist Charles Maure whose appropriation of "indigenist poetics" allowed him to exercise a politics of exclusion.[35]

Afroantilleanismo, afrocubanismo, poesía negra, negrismo, and *negritud,* among other artistic movement monikers, all signal a turn toward African-derived traditions in the early twentieth century, but each has also come to signal different political inclinations. Cultural theorists, then and now, have aimed to distinguish these various artistic manifestations, marking the difference between aesthetic and anthropological trends that participated (consciously or unconsciously) in forms of colonial appropriation and primitivist fantasies, inspired by a European "negrophilia," against those meant to celebrate and recover Black culture from racist practices of erasure.[36] If *negrismo* designates white creole writers that fetishized Black culture for their own artistic gain, *negritud* is said to name those of African descent who where committed to enacting political and social change.[37] While these distinctions are no doubt important, the question has often, reductively, become that of determining which representations of Blackness are authentic and positive and which are not. More nuanced readings of cultural and intellectual production of these years (20s, 30s, and 40s), recognize that individual works are not so easily catalogued.[38] Miguel Arnedo-Gómez's 2016 book, *Uniting Blacks in a Raceless Nation,* has made critical interventions in these debates. He not only underscores the essentialist logic underpinning questions of authenticity, but also shows how critiques of *afrocubanismo* have failed to consider the socio-cultural singularity of the historical Cuban context. In adopting the same critical frameworks drawn from European and North American cultural production, scholars have conflated *afrocubanismo* with French Negritude and Modernist Primitivism.[39] Accordingly, late twentieth-century Afro-Hispanists have come to understand *afrocubanismo* as a predominantly white elite movement that sought to assuage political tensions and mask material inequalities through a unified image of the nation.[40] Although these strategies were largely true, Arnedo-Gómez argues, these critiques foreclose the possibility of Afro-Cubans having been active agents in their own representation, appropriating some of the ideological elements of the movement to stage cultural and political resistance. By situating *afrocubanismo* literary works within the context of Cuban Black intellectual writings and considering the reception and interpretations of contemporaneous readers, Arnedo-Gómez makes a case for their counterhegemonic potential.[41]

The debates surrounding *afrocubanismo* have inevitably structured readings of Guillén's *Motivos de son.* For critics that consider the movement an emulation of a European fashion for Blackness, Guillén's 1930 collection has been described as "superficial," "pintoresco," and "folklorista."[42] Counter to these descriptions, in a 1973 essay Nancy Morejón calls the denomination of *Motivos de son* as "poesía negra" a bourgeois pigeonhole, from which she seeks to rescue the poems by underscoring how they contribute to the nation-building process. These critics, Morejón writes, "No entendieron jamás que se trataba de la aparición de una poesía que hablaba al negro y del negro para hallar su justo papel en la cultura nacional y para definir su aporte a ella. No es el negro como elemento aislante sino integrante."[43] She draws a direct correlation between the poems and Guillén's lived experience to show that *Motivos* was more than a formalistic experimentation. Similarly, Richard Jackson defends Guillén's poems, arguing for the legitimacy of their representations by pointing to the author's membership within the community as an Afro-Cuban.[44] Later scholars such as Vera Kutzinski and Luis Duno-Gottberg, for whom *afrocubanismo* is a discourse of *mestizaje* deployed by an intellectual elite, will consider the nationalist, integrationist work Morejón underscores as part of a project that sought to resolve racial tensions for the benefit of the dominant class. For them, Guillén's poems contribute to the fantasy of racial harmony.[45] In response to critics that have dismissed the emancipatory potential of *Motivos de son* as a superficial engagement with Black cultural forms,[46] others, such as Roberto González Echevarría, have mined the poems for originary African signs.[47] In Arnedo-Gómez's treatment of *Motivos de son,* read in light of contemporaneous socio-cultural events and Cuban Black intellectual debates, the poems combat the intraracist behavior of the Black middle classes.[48] Arnedo-Gómez, not unlike those engaged in a semiotic recovery, articulates his aims as a process of unearthing meaning and identifies an "antiracist didacticism" in the poems' contextual meaning, that is, in what its poetic speakers communicate.[49]

In my treatment of *Motivos de son,* I'm interested in locating the political not in what the poems intelligibly communicate or how they correlate to identifiable subjects or a historical period, but in what scholars have deemed aesthetic and superficial, the "mere accompaniment of (reasoned) utterance."[50] Returning to Morejón's statement, her use of the words "integrante" and "aporte" signal a logic of incorporation and a conception of artistic renderings as having the capacity to stand in for already existing subjects. If a concern with movements such as *afrocubanismo* has been the appropriation and assimilation of Black cultural forms, perhaps a way to circumvent co-optation is to think of these forms not as a representation of a positive substance or property, but as irreducible materiality. Where "poesía negra" might have been a delimiting designation, I find that thinking how the poems perform as opposed to represent Blackness, insisting upon its exteriority to dominant national models as a non-integrational surplus, allows that Blackness to remain an oppositional charge to the presumed unity of the nation.

To better understand the conflicts that arise in the effort of making visible that which has been negated or accorded an inferior status, and the effects of particular aesthetic strategies, I find it useful to turn to José Martí's notion of "Nuestra Mestiza America." When Martí published his seminal essay "Nuestra América" (1891), in which he defines the substance of Our America as precisely that which had been considered its contaminant—peoples of Indigenous and African descent—this was nothing short of revolutionary. Through a densely figurative language, Martí constructs various binary oppositions that invert those inherited from a colonial rhetoric and perpetuated in the profoundly Eurocentric intellectual climate of his time. Notwithstanding his appeals to inclusiveness of ethnic diversity, Martí's strategies produce inevitable exclusions. The title's possessive pronoun, "nuestra," converts America into a property, prompting the following assumptions: There is a subject, "nosotros," that possesses this America, and this America may be defined and represented. And by its very grammar, this *nosotros* constitutes an *ellos*. Throughout the essay, unity is invoked through a series of filial and arboreal metaphors; like the roots of a tree, the (American) autochthonous is assimilated to the virile and unwavering, and the (European) exotic, impermanent like leaves, to the feminine and weak. Martí's insistence on rootedness and brotherhood coupled with his rejection of the foreign establishes a paradigm that leaves little room for an ethics of hospitality. In the need to represent that which had been omitted from dominant discourses, Martí produces images, identifiable American properties, that result in reductive abstractions e.g., "masas mudas de indios" and "El negro, oteado [. . .] solo y desconocido."[51] Ultimately, through such formal mediations, as Julio Ramos has argued, the authority to represent comes to rest with the literary writer.[52]

At the close of "Nuestra América," Martí appeals to the universal identity of man and his soul, "El alma emana, igual y eterna, de los cuerpos diversos en forma y en color." Significantly, he claims there can be no racial hate in *Nuestra América* or, for that matter, the concept of races because "el mestizo autóctono" has vanquished the exotic Creole.[53] The concept of *mestizaje* (or *mulatez*), which would later become almost synonymous with Cuban national identity,[54] diffuses, blurs, blends, mixes, dilutes racial material differences. As a form of racial amalgamation, or miscegenation, *mestizaje* has been promoted in Latin American nation-building projects as both a form of whitening and a multicultural celebration, "disavowing divisive social realities."[55] Likewise, the concepts of syncretism and transculturation, which hold high currency in the cultural theorization of the Caribbean, invoke a hybrid new third composed of two distinct properties. In Fernando Ortiz's formulation, transculturation does not disavow the violent and complex context of which it emerges, "each of them torn from his native moorings, faced with the problem of disadjustment and readjustment, of deculturation and acculturation."[56] Nevertheless, the Cuban anthropologist elaborates the neologism through the tropes of grafting and sexual reproduction, not only relying on gendered roles, but also reinforcing a sense of community through filiation.[57] Although these tropes recognize diverse "parents" and their "offspring" as different from them, offspring are ultimately of the Same, related to each other like Martí's roots and brothers, "hermanos . . . han de encajar, de modo que sean una, las dos manos."[58] Ortiz's metaphor of the *ajiaco* stew for Cuba's diverse demographic similarly evokes a whole composed of different parts, parts which can be enumerated as individual ingredients.[59] What I would like to underscore is that in the conceptual mixing of properties the result is an imagined fusion or harmonic synthesis, like the ideal shade of a color or just the right taste. As long as *ajiaco* is composed of individual ingredients, other ingredients are inevitably left out, as its delicate flavor is consigned to a recipe.[60]

Through the concepts of *mestizaje,* syncretism, and transculturation community is imagined as the sharing of a property (or properties, however diverse).[61] Community imagined as a fullness, an interiority, the unity of individual subjects forming a larger subjectivity, will inevitably have immunitary impulses, protecting its body from the incursion of foreign others.[62] It is this traditional conceptualization of community that has fed nostalgic desires to recuperate an imagined past and resulted in the formation of totalitarian regimes.[63] Accordingly, philosophers, such as Roberto Esposito, have aimed to untie the concept of community from its historical association to the semantics of *proprium,* arguing that instead it is the absence of a property, the negative, or the concave from which community happens. It is an unfulfilled duty, a sense of debt, or an insufficiency, that create the conditions for a being-with. What we have in common, Esposito writes, "is an otherness that withdraws us from our subjectivity."[64] This negative, or non-subject-forming community, instantiated in exposure and exteriority, provides an alternative to the logic of incorporation and its inevitable exclusions. However, as I hope to elaborate in this chapter and those that follow, it is not so much the sharing of an absence I wish to underscore, as that of a materiality, a materiality irreducible to an identity and, therefore, unassimilable.

Like Martí and Ortiz, Nicolás Guillén will also formulate tropes, such as the "cóctel Cubano," that suggest a fusion of properties in the unification of a single body. Returning to his 1931 prologue to *Sóngoro Cosongo,* referenced above, Guillén's recourse to floral metaphors treat nation and race as organically constituted:

> Opino por tanto que una poesía criolla entre nosotros no lo será de un modo cabal con olvido del negro. El negro -a mi juicio- aporta esencias muy firmes a nuestro cóctel. Y las dos razas que en la Isla salen a flor de agua, distantes en lo que se ve, se tienden un garfio submarino, como esos puentes hondos que unen en secreto dos continentes. Por lo pronto, el espíritu de Cuba es mestizo. Y del espíritu hacia la piel nos vendrá el color definitivo. Algún día se dirá: «color cubano».[65]

The eventual correspondence between "espíritu" and "piel" in what will one day arrive as "color cubano," suggests a metaphysics of incarnation, the union between soul and body, as well as a teleological projection. Ultimately, "color cubano" is the blending of two whole races, the totality of "dos continentes" that lie submerged in the depths of the water. Notwithstanding Guillén's conception of race and nation, in my reading of *Motivos,* I aim to show that the sonorous, or that which is registered as aesthetic and artificial, works against such organicist assumptions and easy appropriation.

In his seminal work, *The Voice and Nothing More,* Mladen Dolar observes, "The voice is the instrument, the vehicle, the medium, and the meaning is the goal. This gives rise to a spontaneous opposition where voice appears as materiality opposed to the ideality of meaning."[66] Considering the extent to which *Motivos* preoccupies its readers in the production of a particular voice, in my treatment of this collection I sustain my attention on its sonic materiality, on the tension between meaning and nonmeaning. Put otherwise, I aim to read the poems as nonrepresentational, resisting the hermeneutic tendency of identifying subjects or reproducible knowledge. It is important to remember, as Vera Kutzinski has aptly argued, music is no less representational than images and phonic patterns "are no less stereotypical than more familiar physiognomic signifiers of blackness such as skin tone and hair texture."[67] That said, if we consider that the acoustic has the potential, as Julio Ramos states, "to remove the body from the plane of perception dominated by perspective, by the division of sensory work in the proliferating optical, geometric, dominant schemes of modernity,"[68] then perhaps holding our attention on the sonic, as *Motivos* invites us to do, might generate a form of relating that does not presume to render an Other legible and enhances the possibility of being affected and transformed by the poems.

Sonorous and Semiotic

Published in 1961, at the cusp of structuralist and poststructuralist intellectual production, Vladimir Jankélévitch's book, *Music and the Ineffable,* called for an engagement with music that would not only recognize the impossibility of arriving at stable meaning, but altogether resist the treatment of the sonorous as semiotic material. "Music acts upon human beings," he writes, "on their nervous systems and their vital processes. . . . [It] takes possession of the listener. This process, at once irrational and shameful, takes place at the margins of truth, and thus borders more on magic than empirical science."[69] Current musical theorists, such as Carolyn Abbate, have argued that the corporeal and emotional vulnerability that Jankélévitch underscores in both the production and the reception of music offers an ethical form of engagement with human others.[70] If music, as Jankélévitch insists, does not present us with a discourse from which we can tease out reproducible knowledge, but rather an impenetrable phenomenon experienced in time, then the musical presents us with an opportunity to relate to an unknown without the pretense of expertise.

On a similar note, drawing from Hans-Georg Gadamer's thoughts on music, Andrew Bowie writes in his introduction to *Music, Philosophy and Modernity:*

> It is when we don't understand and have to leave behind our certainties that we can gain the greatest insights. Given that this situation is in one sense almost constitutive for music, which we never understand in a definitive discursive manner, it is worth taking seriously the idea that such non-understanding might be philosophically very significant.[71]

Echoing Bowie's assertion that we gain insight from uncertainty, literary theorist Doris Sommer has argued for the benefits of submitting oneself to the untranslatable. The incomprehensible, she explains, opens the possibility for reflection; we come to see "the world is complicated beyond our understanding and worthy of our respect."[72] Indeed, music as indecipherable is not unlike the experience of encountering a foreign language. However, it is the verbal, or reasoning generated through a system of signs, that thinkers like Jankélévitch and Abbate insistently define music against. In opposition to the gnostic—a practice which presumes to make "the opaque transparent" through a "knowledge based on semiosis and disclosed secrets"—Jankélévitch privileges what he calls the drastic, an experience which "connotes physicality . . . desperation and peril."[73] Taking seriously the idea that non-understanding is philosophically significant, as Bowie suggests, it is the very opposition between the intelligible and the sonorous, or the gnostic and the drastic, that I am interested in bringing to bear on literary analysis.

Where dialectical synthesis is the sublation of difference and the production of signification is the making instrumental of a work, Jankélévitch's description of music as a synchronism of voices that says nothing offers an alternative model with which to engage literary texts that would potentially bypass the reductive economy of the former. Although he states that only music is capable of this *concordia discors,* or the superimposed voices of polyphony,[74] as I will demonstrate through the work of Guillén, poetry can also produce a non-dialectical *concordia,* imbued with a magical charge of its own.

Not incidentally, debates regarding the political or emancipatory potential of *Motivos de son* tend to focus on the question of nonsense or indecipherability. That is, those that seek to defend *Motivos* from aestheticist critiques insist on the presence of meaning where others find only linguistic or sonorous play. Roberto González Echevarría, for instance, claims, "It is a revealing fact that Guillén's poetry, no matter what the real color of the critic, has been the object of exclusively 'white' readings. . . . [I]t may be necessary to awaken all of us out of a massive process of repression." Such criticism is "repressed" because it has dealt with "what sounds to the lay ears like music (or noise) as if it had no meaning."[75] For González Echevarría, what critics have described as "purely sonorous facts" in *Motivos de son* is a Eurocentric simplification, the abnegation of meaning in the Bantu phonemes. Thomas Anderson's recent analysis of Guillén's poem "Sensemayá: canto para matar una culebra" (1934), echoes González Echevarría's complaints when he argues against the treatment of some lines as "apparent nonsense" and posits that the highly anthologized poem is "still misunderstood."[76]

González Echevarría's and Anderson's attentive readings produce compelling and novel interpretations of Guillén's work that underscore the poems' response to socio-political events and cultural practices. Anderson, for instance, reads "Sensamayá" as "a carefully constructed response to the many bans that were enacted against Afro-Cuban carnival processions during the early decades of the 20th century."[77] However, by implication, their arguments assign value and complexity to recoverable meaning and the process of decoding, a process that necessarily relies on a degree of expertise and logocentric thinking. Like González Echevarría's philological labor to unearth the repressed Bantu signification, Anderson sets off to "uncover . . . latent connection[s]" between images in the poem and religious iconography.[78] In the pretention of laying bare the encrypted, these readings also entertain the fantasy of recovering mythical origins: "Through this gesture the poem is reaching back to the original *Son,* the mythical 'Son de la Ma Teodora,' modeled on African and *taíno* rituals (*areítos*) whose function is to awaken a collective memory."[79] Such readings, providing icons and founding narratives that may be easily co-opted, structurally coincide with ideological movements that aim at formulating national and ethnic identities. In my engagement with Guillén's *Motivos de son,* I propose an alternative form of reading in which the apparently nonsensical or the exceedingly musical is not subjected to a hermeneutic practice that would mine for reproducible meaning. Rather, I consider and take seriously the ethical potential immanent to a reader's confrontation with obstinate phonic materiality.

In developing this reading, I have found the work of Fred Moten to be particularly helpful. In his book, *In the Break,* which gives sustained attention to the aesthetics of the Black radical tradition, Moten suggests that Black performance is precisely that which is registered as noise, a "*mate*-*r*ial" remainder that is irreducible to patrilineal logic, an impropriety that irrupts attempts at a nostalgic suturing. Moten reminds us here that the children of slaves were born outside of a familial structure; male slaves were not recognized as legal fathers, leaving mothers, as reproducers, to be the dominant figure of heritage. Motherhood, however, was "not perceived 'as a legitimate procedure of cultural inheritance.'"[80] Accordingly, Blackness is birthed in illegibility; it is improper and dispossessed, lacking the legitimacy of a filial lineage and its generational acquisition of property. For these same reasons, Moten argues that Black artistic production is always necessarily avant-garde. Where one might expect an analysis of the Black radical tradition to entail the political insistence on Black human subjectivity, Moten instead locates this tradition's radicality in the "resistant object," in "objection to subjection," in the impassioned shriek of a slave (as in Frederick Douglass's narration of Aunt Hester's beating) or what he also describes as a "speaking commodity."

In his analysis of the theory of exchange value immanent to the capitalist mode of production, Marx facetiously makes recourse to the impossible scenario in which commodities speak.[81] Moten argues that the limits of this impossibility are shattered with the phonic irruption of the slave. If a slave as a commodity can speak, shriek, and/or sing, then value or meaning may no longer be attributed solely to human sociality; "break[ing] down the distinction between what is intrinsic and what is given by or of the outside," the science of economy, as well as that of semiotics and its reliance on the difference between spirit and matter, is rendered inoperative.[82] Moten writes,

> My argument starts with the historical reality of commodities who spoke—of laborers who were commodities before, as it were, the abstraction of labor power from their bodies and who continue to pass on this material heritage across the divide that separates slavery and "freedom." But I am interested, finally, in the implications of the breaking of such speech, the elevating disruptions of the verbal that take the rich content of the object's/commodity's aurality outside the confines of meaning precisely by way of this material trace.[83]

Although Moten is mostly concerned with the work of North American Black artists, his analysis provides me with a model with which to treat *Motivos*. As Thom Donavan elaborates, "in Moten's book, the resistance of the object is related through certain ways of reading (and seeing, and hearing) it without reducing its materiality, or reducing this materiality through the object's representation."[84] Guided by Moten's claim that "such blackness is only in that it exceeds itself; it bears the groundedness of an uncontainable outside,"[85] let us hold our attention on the sonorous difference Guillén makes the poetic object of *Motivos de son*.

Black Is Beautiful

Caribbean scholars, such as Édouard Glissant and Kamau Brathwaite, have long noted the privileging of the voice and oral traditions in Caribbean poetic production as a response to institutions of writing and their links to

Eurocentric constructions of history.[86] Foregrounding of the voice is also a strategy of concealment or what Glissant has called a "forced poetics," "one in which the true meaning of words 'is hidden from the master's ear by the non-meaning of the noise and staccato, which is the true meaning. This non-meaning hides and reveals hidden meaning.'"[87] Accordingly, scholars have understood the noise and sound that challenge "master-codes of the plantation system" as "sustain[ing] a symbolic or semiotic system of cultural resistance."[88] Teasing out hidden, double meanings has been the aim of many critical readers of Caribbean texts, as noted above with González Echevarría's and Anderson's treatment of Guillén's work.[89] The recovery of such meaning is particularly significant, when we recall practices of erasure and the belief that African cultures could not have survived the trauma of the Middle Passage.[90] However, returning to Glissant's contradictory statements, where "true meaning" is located in the "non-meaning of the noise," it would seem that rather than treat these fragments as a secret language, what is significant (but does not signify)—reiterating Moten's argument about Black aesthetics—is the phonic matter.[91]

Viewed in relation to the various Negritude movements of the early twentieth century, critics of Guillén's work do well to remind us that the search for African origins often produces essentialist conceptualizations.[92] With regard to his poem "Negro bembón" from *Motivos,* which begins with "¿Po qué te pone tan brabo,/ cuando te disen/ negro bembón,/ si tiene la boca santa,/ negro bembón?,"[93] Guillén explains "va contra el prejuicio racista en Cuba, exaltando los valores auténticos de la raza negra en lucha obstinada contra una discriminación racial que duró más de cuatro siglos."[94] This claim to authenticity at once encapsulates the best intentions of Negritude and that which impede its project to combat racism. On the one hand, the recognition and valorization of African traits in the face of dominant European cultures and their strategies of erasure are critical to self-empowerment and emancipation. On the other hand, the generalization of "la raza negra" and the search for cultural origins results in reductive archetypes.

Whereas González Echevarría insists on *Motivos de son*'s meaningfulness, other critics have treated the collection as an aesthetic and artificial engagement with Afro-Cuban culture, from which Guillén would depart, gradually expanding his perspective from the local toward the universal conditions of the proletariat.[95] It was this small collection of poems published early in his career where he first wrote in an Afro-Cuban register.

Dismissing its distinct style as a product of Negritude essentialism, Jorge Ruffinelli explains that the focus on a Black aesthetic ignores social and economic realities. He characterizes *Motivos* as a stage in Guillén's oeuvre preoccupied exclusively with Blackness in contrast to his later poetry, which addresses neocolonial themes (e.g., his collection *West Indies Ltd.*). In Adriana Tous's study, *Motivos* is also presented as narrowly focused on Cuban popular culture, while its merit resides in its great rhythm and stylistic features. And according to its most reductive and critical reception, *Motivos* perpetuates racial stereotypes in its imitation of a vernacular speech and the use of pejorative racial terms.[96]

Ruffinelli valorizes Guillén's later work for transcending the scope of Negritude; however, in these more explicitly political poems, such as "Balada de los dos abuelos" (1934) where he represents the legacy of slavery and his European and African ancestry through the figuration of two grandfathers, Guillén develops binary metaphors and an exclusive identity. The effort to equate the value of African traditions to those of Europe resulted in the construction of complementary Black and white subjects; in other words, it reiterated a colonial rhetoric. This bipolarization is also exhibited in a poem titled "La canción del Bongo" (1931). Here we have the Afro-Cuban deity, Changó, alongside the Catholic saint, Santa Bárbara; together they operate as icons for Africa and Europe. Gathered under their respective signs, the diversity of cultures is reduced and sublated. Moreover, this symmetry of origins in the mulatto identity that Guillén proposes based on the syncretism of Spanish and African cultures excludes indigenous and Chinese Cuban minorities.[97] In response to those who would dismiss the political potential of *Motivos de son* for its emphasis on artifice and those who would dispute its artificiality by insisting on recoverable meaning (González Echevarría), I suggest that by bringing the reader's attention to the materiality of language—note the pattern of single syllable words and dental consonants in a line such as "te lo da to"[98]—and by not providing symbolic substitutes (e.g., Changó and Santa Bárbara), this first collection does not so easily lend itself to abstractions of race and resists the pitfalls of identity formation. Racial caricatures, such as "Negro bembón" and "Mulata," remain just that, superficial constructions that lie at the surface of the text.[99] That is, the already codified characters stand in for nothing other than their artificiality.

Concordia Discors

Where one might associate poetic language with the creation of metaphors, images, and lyricism, in *Motivos* the objective is almost exclusively the reproduction of audio, that is to say, voice, rhythm, and music:

> Con tanto sapato nuebo,
> ¡qué ba!
> Con tanto reló, compadre,
> ¡qué ba!
> Con tanto lujo, compadre,
> ¡qué ba![100]

Punctuation here acts like a musical notation. The repetition and alternating refrains produce rhythm and a call and response chorus. Like Jankélévitch's *concordia discors,* the verbal exchange forms a polyphony of voices, a harmony achieved through synchronism rather than a dialogic resolution. With every repetition "¡qué ba!" becomes less the exclamatory expression of "no way" and more the sounding of trumpets. This is not to say that the stanzas are illegible. In his reading of this sixth poem in the collection, which begins with "Búcate plata,/ búcate plata,/ poqque no doy un paso má: etoy a arró con galleta,/ na ma.,"[101] Antonio D. Tillis explains "[it] thematically speaks to the social, economic and political plight of Afro-Cubans in a communicative form understood by them. [. . .] The poetic voice expresses the level of poverty and struggle in this community."[102] While not dismissing the value or validity of such interpretations, in my effort to privilege the sonorous—or that which exceeds representation—I suggest that the content of these lines is not so much their semantic meaning as it is their exclamations and accents; it is the tone and texture of the phonemes that come to the fore. In the alternating refrains, the alliteration, and the omission of consonants and syllables, the reader's attention is sustained not by the formulation of a narrative or an image, but by an acoustic polyphony. So distinctive is its style and so overpowering its rhythm that critics like Ruffinelli overlooked the socioeconomic content of the poems.

In her study of the humorous word play, or *choteo,* in *Motivos,* Emily Maguire explains that these linguistic expressions, "poking fun at what is too serious," are a strategy that undermines established order (e.g., calling out the self-disparagement of African features in "¿Po qué te pone tan brabo,/ cuando te disen/ negro bembón,/ si tiene la boca santa,/ negro bembón?").[103] Indeed, the above stanzas from "Búcate Plata," like the rest of the collection, exhibit a picaresque and quotidian tone that is irreverent toward the elevated status of lyric poetry. Guillén inverts the romantic legacy of the poet as a heroic figure, who offers an interior monologue and a new vision. Throughout the eight poems in *Motivos*, it would be difficult to identify any reference to the subject of the author or an expression of introspection. To better appreciate this, recall Pablo Neruda's *Canto General*, a work of epic proportions where the author states, "Yo vengo a hablar por vuestra boca muerta [. . .] Hablad por mis palabras y mi sangre."[104] Whereas the poetic voice of *Canto* assumes the responsibility of speaking for the community, for those who are voiceless, *Motivos* is a community of voices: fragments of conversations, complaints, gossip, and songs. Each poem has an implied interlocutor: "Mira si tú me conose," "pero biejo," "compadre," "mi negro" are just some of the invocations. In this way, "Guillén's poetic voice rejects the literary descriptive conventions of a 'literate' speaker,"[105] and consequently, the reader, as a sophisticated literate figure, is never addressed.

In his discussion on the impenetrability of music, Jankélévitch explains that whereas the listener to a lecturer "is the second person—'you,' the object of invocation or allocution," the listener "for the pianist sitting at the piano," "is the third person, the outsider."[106] In a similar manner, I want to suggest that as "readers" of Guillén's ensemble of voices, we are the third person, the outsider. *Motivos* does not draw us inside the psyche of its speakers. As we recite the poems, we hear ourselves produce the voices of this Afro-Cuban community, but we are not given access to it. To further illustrate this point regarding the characters in *Motivos*, González Echevarría explains,

> Guillén's figures [. . .] had already been codified by Cuban literature, particularly by the theater. Hence, as they speak there is a double distancing, a layering that fixes the figures. The pimp, the mulatta, the dandy, the pretentious *catedrático* are stereotypes, which heightens their artificiality, their dependence on given codes in which black Cuban culture has been objectified. In so doing, the poems of *Motivos de son* are clearly denouncing the process by which black culture identifies itself.[107]

Significantly, in this collection, Guillén does not counter these flat personas with the representation of a more three-dimensional subjectivity. *Motivos* leaves us with an exteriority and, in so doing, does not position itself as inside this Black community. Although Guillén was often touted as a more "legitimate" representative of Afro-Cuban culture for being of mixed race in contrast to other white *negrista* poets, Miguel Arnedo-Gómez argues that *Motivos* remains a representation of the Other, given that Guillén came from the upper middle class and not the poor urban neighborhoods of his characters.[108] Arnedo-Gómez's critique is not meant to undermine the legitimacy of Guillén's representation, but rather to counter the evaluation of his work as more authentic than that of white *afrocubanistas.*[109] Such evaluations suggest that it is possible, and politically preferable, to write as a self-identifying member of a group, from the position of sameness and thus erasing what differences emerge in writing or the relation from one singularity to another. My concern, by contrast, is not whether Guillén did or did not *belong* to the community of voices he produces—especially since we're working against the paradigm of community as a cohesive body made up of members—for remembering Moten's argument, the Black radical aesthetic is dispossessed; "it bears the groundedness of an uncontainable outside."[110] In *Motivos,* if we are to speak of the author's voice, then it is one that does not assume a position of authority or of knowing, but that of a performer, reproducing an irreducible material sound, a resistant object.

Perhaps the most distinctive characteristic of this poetry collection is its orthography. In phrases like "búcate plata/ poqque no doy un paso má," Guillén reproduces an Afro-Cuban phonetics through non-standard spelling that forces the reader to very deliberately sound out the letters. The musicality of the poems demand that they be read out loud, or rather recited. Starting with exclamatory forms of calling out or drawing the attention of their interlocutor, "'Mira si tú me conose,' 'pero biejo,' 'compadre,' 'mi negro,'" are just some of the invocations.[111] Guillén imbues his poems with a performative quality. Notably, traditional poetic devices that ask to be unpacked, such as symbols and metaphors, are absent in this collection. In fact, visual descriptions are also sparse. If we consider that traditional European culture is ocularcentric, basing objective and empirical knowledge on what is visually observed,[112] then the lack of visuality here is another way the poems insist on their musicality and their unknowability. Put differently, if we note that the single instance of a simile reads, "la narise como nudo de cobbata,"[113] and descriptions such as "negro bembón" and "mulata," the poems demonstrate how visual language and assimilation have served racial discrimination. Instead of inviting us to penetrate a vision, or *read* its signification, the poems force us to reckon with its materiality while entertaining us with its rhythm and onomatopoeia. The reader/performer becomes a ventriloquist of Afro-Cuban speech, while the poems resist being interpreted. That is, beyond their literal meaning, or the sound of their indecipherable fragments, the poems do not elicit a deeper, or more expert, analysis.

The Cuban sociologist Fernando Ortiz describes the "untranslatable neologisms" in Guillén's poetry (e.g., "sóngoro cosongo") as "signifying nothing word by word, but as a whole expresses just this: an unintelligible black song." The value in these nonsensical constructions, explains Ortiz, is not simply in their artistic properties but in their imitation, their very precise onomatopoeia of "the emission of an African song" as heard by the uninitiated.[114] As Jean-François Lyotard discusses in his essay "A Few Words to Sing," onomatopoeic constructions "decompose linguistic behavior," making the materiality of language, its vocal sounds and their affects, the content of its expression.[115] Shifting our attention from the discursive to the sonorous allows us to treat *Motivos* not as an identitarian flag for Afro-Cubans, but instead, as presenting the voice of an unassimilable Other. In a similar vein, Maguire argues that while references to Afro-Cuban folklore had been in vogue with the aim of "co-opting Afro-Cuban culture to create an ahistorical national essence," in *Motivos,* Guillén sets himself apart from this trend "by locating his poetry within the [. . .] linguistic parameters of daily urban life."[116] This becomes all the more evident when we turn to the poem "Tú no sabe inglé," where there is an explicit preoccupation with the production of language. Here the poetic voice teases her interlocutor for his pretension of speaking English and, implicitly, for being an anglophile, as she advises him not to fall in love with American women. Again, we're left with the absence of a described scene, images, or metaphors. And aside from baseball, there are no references to cultural practices or African traditions. What does occupy the reader's visual frame are the misspelled words, a deformed writing printed on the page.

In "Tú no sabe inglé," Guillén not only reproduces the phonetics of an Afro-Cuban Spanish but also that of an English distorted in the mouth of an Afro-Hispanophone speaker.[117] The name of our interlocutor, Victor Manuel, is transformed to "Bito Manué." The letter *b* substitutes *v,* as the distinction between the two in Spanish is only etymological and orthographic; *ct* is simplified to *t;* the liquid consonants *r* and *l* are dropped; and the final vowel *e* is accentuated. We also find the characteristic *seseo* of Afro-Cuban speakers with the assimilation of *c* to *s,* "desí," and the dropping of the *s*'s at the end of words, both in Spanish, "inglé," and English, "yé." The lines "tu inglé era de etrai guan,/ de etrai guan y guan tu tri," which translate to "tu inglés era de strike one, de strike one, y one, two three" in standardized Spanish and English, would seem to be twice removed, a linguistic mise-en-scène. To understand the word "etrai," I repeated it over and over again trying to reach an approximation of an English word and ultimately had to rely on a secondary source reading. The three-strikes-and-you're-out reference to baseball, "de etrai guan,/ de etrai guan y guan tu tri" also operates as a rhythm count, "one two, one two, one two three." Indeed, the repetition of "tú no sabe inglé," like other lines in the poem, becomes a refrain. Its meaning recedes into the background; it is the syllabic count and the articulation of its phonemes that fill the mouth and preoccupy the reader. Instead of considering the linguistic variance exhibited in *Motivos* as representative of an ethnic or racial identity (notwithstanding my own identification of an "Afro-Cuban speech"), following Moten, we might say that the performance of Blackness is in the materiality of its incorrect writing, in the reader's repetition of "etrai," in the metamorphosis of the word "strike," in its becoming illegible, its rupture from a standard. The words themselves do not stand in for a subject. They are activated in their vocalization, in the production of difference that occurs at the minima of the writing.

Music and Magic

The third poem in *Motivos de son,* titled "Si tú supiera," whose chorus is made up of "purely sonorous facts," or indecipherable Bantu phonemes, becomes the focal point for questions regarding the collection's artificiality versus that of hidden meaning. "Si tú supiera" has also been the subject of numerous musical adaptations. Héctor Lavoe, Enrique Morente, and Fe Cortijo are just a few of the musicians to have performed the poem:

> ¡Ay, negra
> si tú supiera!
> Anoche te bi pasá
> y no quise que me biera.
> A é tú le hará como a mí,
> que cuando no tube plata
> te corrite de bachata,
> sin acoddadte de mí.
> Sóngoro cosongo,

sogo bé;
sóngoro cosongo
de mamey;
sóngoro, la negra
baila bien;
sóngoro de uno
sóngoro de tre.
¡Aé,
bengan a be;
aé,
bamo pa be;
bengan, sóngoro cosongo,
sóngoro cosongo de mamey![118]

In her analysis of *Motivos*, Maguire provides us with a succinct description of the *son* musical form, which "each of the eight poems in Guillén's collection faithfully reproduces": "the *son* is composed of an eight-line 'exposition,' consisting of one or two verses, followed by an *estribillo* (chorus, later called *montuno*), which features a call and response repetition of two different lines."[119] According to the musicologist Raúl Fernández, the format of the *son*'s instrumental ensemble produces "a deep melodic-rhythmic groove"; "its distinct eight tones [. . .] produce a feeling of steady forward propulsion [. . .] [with beats that] intensify dancing desires."[120] Such propulsion and desire recall Jankélévitch's statements on music as acting upon the nervous system and vital processes. In his chapter titled "Ontology of the Son," Fernández writes,

> [T]he son [. . .] is something that people listen to with their feet. It is a dance to which people give themselves body and soul, dancing sometimes for hours, tasting the music with their hips [. . .] approaching the spiritual levels of trance characteristic of Cuba's sacred ancestry of Arabic and African religious performances.[121]

Communication with divine beings through percussion, incantations, and especially through the process of possession is a key feature of African Atlantic religious practices.[122] With Ortiz's description of the neologisms as an African song heard by the uninitiated in mind, I would like to suggest that the musical structure reproduced in Guillén's *Motivos* might also be seen as an evocation of magico-religious oral practices.[123] In addition to the bodily affects (or trance) the poems' rhythmic composition would induce, the sonorous words with no available semantic meaning like "sóngoro cosongo" might operate as enchantments upon the reader/performer/listener. To clarify, I do not mean to suggest a recovery of an originary chant, but more that like these African oral traditions the poems have the potential to impact the body. We could also turn to the Greco-Roman myth of Orpheus who is both poet and musician; he enchants even inanimate objects with his lyre and voice, crosses from the world of the living to the dead, and is considered the founder of religious rituals.

Perhaps not surprisingly, Jankélévitch discusses music operating like a charm or an incantation, which he also associates to poetry. The Russian formalists were particularly interested in the trope of enchantment precisely because it brought language to its musical and material attributes, liberating it from the need to produce any signification. Velimir Khlebnikov writes, "poems may be understandable or they may not" but they do not lose their power, or perhaps we can say their affective potential. He affirms, "I mean only that we must not reject a piece of writing simply because it is incomprehensible to a particular group of readers."[124] "Sóngoro cosongo,/sogo bé;/sóngoro cosongo/de mamey" has been incomprehensible to most and yet the rhythmic phrasing has enchanted and delighted its readers.

Carolyn Abbate elaborates on the ethical implications of the experience of charm in music, saying, "the ways that one is transformed in response to it, is equivalent to the power of love, caritas and eros—the love of another or for an Other."[125] The corporeal vulnerability that Jankélévitch highlights in music—its ability to "possess," "intrude," and "irrupt"—is yet another aspect of this ethical engagement, as it puts the listener in a position of exposure and openness to an Other. The "tak[ing] up residence in our intimate self"[126] that he describes of music is no better illustrated than in the Afro-Atlantic religious practices where states of trance and spirit possessions are produced in devotees through percussion. Producing the Afro-phonemes dominated by unvoiced and fricative consonants, "Sóngoro cosongo,/sogo bé;/sóngoro cosongo," engages the body of the performer in the articulatory process—consider, for contrast, how vowels, produced solely through the vocal chords, sound more ethereal and less corporeal. The phonemes, which are unintelligible, can be said to possess the speaker as she pronounces them and her body is affected by the rhythmic quality of the verses, as the beats of the *son* intensify dancing desires. Like a "vibrating string" or "sound pipe," to use Jankélévitch's description of the reception of music or "man inhabited," the reader/listener/performer of

Guillén's poems momentarily loses herself and becomes a receptor for the voice of an unknown Other.

Reading Nonsense

In response to those who would say *Motivos* is merely aesthetic, González Echevarría, as mentioned above, has ventured into Bantu philology insisting that the seemingly purely sonorous aspects of *Motivos* are in fact "exceedingly meaningful," containing encrypted messages available only to the initiated, or in this case the trained philologist.[127] In my effort to privilege the sonorous over the intelligible, I do not mean to deny the various significations that can be teased from these phonetic fragments—after all, as González Echevarría himself concedes, "It is easy to make anything mean anything."[128] Rather, I propose a practice of reading that does not presume to know or aim at disclosing hidden secrets. In his analysis of the *son's* form, Fernández describes its open and closed structure as a unity of opposites.[129] Drawing from this structural antinomy, we can say that *Motivos* plays with both sense and nonsense. At the end of his essay, González Echevarría asks, "Why is it that no one has dared interpret the second half of the poem ["Si tú supiera"]? I believe that is partly because we are not meant to. The poem encrypts its meaning in an incomprehensible code [. . .] that leaves us babbling sounds not to be understood."[130] Following Doris Sommer's lead,[131] let us submit ourselves to the untranslatable, let us dwell on this babbling.

If Guillén's audible and rhythmic poems provoke in their readers the desire to dance, if his poems corporeally possess its performers, Severo Sarduy similarly affirms a relationship between writing and the body: "La escritura es como la danza. Es un ejercicio predominantemente corporal y el cuerpo lo siente."[132] The second part of this chapter will focus on this relationship between writing and the body through close readings of Sarduy's 1963 novel *Gestos.* Although music is also operative in his text, we will instead focus our attention on the predominance of a textual ekphrasis and its sensuous tableaux. In the place of psychic or emotional depth, exteriority and surface exposition collapse the scaffoldings of mimetic representation, denying his readers the pleasure of identifying with well-formed subjects or the voyeurism of a penetrating gaze. Not unlike the two-dimensional characters in *Motivos,* Sarduy's Black protagonist is drawn from popular culture; she speaks melodramatic lines lifted from *telenovelas, boleros,* and popular cinema.[133] Once again as readers we are left outside, and yet, as I will explore, Sarduy's text solicits a proximity between the reader and the writing, engendering an experience of reading that affects the body.

La deshumanización del arte

The title to José Ortega y Gasset's canonical 1925 essay on the growing movement of nonrepresentational and abstract forms in cultural production is "La deshumanización del arte." Whereas Beethoven and Wagner gave us cathartic works steeped in personal emotions, early twentieth-century artists had overturned an age-old hierarchy where people and the living took precedence over the inorganic. "[E]l veto del arte nuevo se ejerce con una energía proporcional a la altura jerárquica del objeto. Lo personal, por ser lo más humano de lo humano, es lo que más evita el arte nuevo."[134] In this new artistic zeitgeist, appeal to personal emotions and self-identification was thought to contaminate the artwork and impede its spiritual, intellectual, and universal aspirations.[135] Sarduy's novel corresponds to this hierarchal inversion, this *deshumanización,* but rather than approximate a pure, ideational state, what his text suggests is a corporeal contagion, as the decomposition of recognizable form brings the reader in contact with the limits of writing.

If the stylistic tendency of avant-garde painting is the lack of figuration, the flattening of space, and the exhibition of the techniques of painting, we could equally say that Sarduy's novel foregrounds the mechanics of writing. Producing images of Havana covered in posters, newspapers, flyers, and placards, Sarduy creates a two-dimensional space: "Bandas de chapapote enrejan las caras sonrientes [. . .] [y] líneas largas y espesas lo desaparecen todo." Through montage, shifting and occluded perspectives, the figure of the human is fragmented and dispersed: "aparece y desaparece, recortada, superpuesta sobre si misma."[136] In her study of early twentieth-century vanguards, Vicky Unruh explains that, in response to the critique of the dehumanizing tendency in modernist art, Latin American artists, in particular, looked for "an active engagement between art and existence," which she identifies as a "re-humanization."[137] However, considering, as Eva Hayward and Jami Weinstein do, that "[h]umanism delineates a normative standard of legibility by which all others are read, measured, controlled, disciplined, and assigned to fixed and hierarchical social statuses,"[138] I am interested in showing how the process of dehumanization in Sarduy's novel—giving precedence to technologies and the minimal mechanics of writing—might instead be that which allows for the encounter between art and existence. Put differently, the process of unworking the human, its logic of organization, its attendant nationalisms, and assumptions of sovereignty, allows for relations between singularities to flourish.

Set just before the triumph of the Revolution, the narrative in *Gestos* consists of the detonation of bombs, in particular one by a Black female cabaret performer at an electrical plant. However, her motives remain unclear, and the word "revolution" or explicit political references are absent in the novel. Instead, Sarduy sets off his own explosives at the level of the writing: "El letrero de las puertas [. . .] se desintegra: CASSO, PISSO, PICA. Ruido afuera. Todo asciende y desciende [. . .] casas llenas de bombas, jardines, raíces, ríos, manos que dicen adios, rifles, castillos que se viran y arden, granadas."[139] Having no discernible organization or internal logic, Sarduy here produces an inventory or assemblage where "raíces, ríos, manos que dicen adios, rifles" are on a parallel plane. The "letrero" that originally read Picasso, has been disintegrated into material fragments, highlighting the tactility of text and its entanglement in the ecology of the city. Moreover, in this cubistic, textual reshuffling, this taking apart of the sentence's anatomy, Sarduy also renders inoperative conventions of representation through which we order and understand the world, anthropocentrically.

Reading as Touching

In a 1976 interview on Spanish public television with the journalist Joaquín Soler Serrano, Sarduy describes his literary practice, stating, "poco importa si yo le comunico un relato o no [. . .] Se trata de ponerlo en una situación física [. . .] Lo que yo le invito no es que me lean [. . .] sino que hagan el amor conmigo."[140] While some critics have viewed Sarduy's disinterest in communicating an intelligible message as politically disengaged, reducing his work to "frivolous" textual games,[141] I'm interested in teasing out the ethico-political implications of such a "physical situation." His invitation, "que hagan el amor conmigo," as opposed to "que me lean," calls for a practice of reading not unlike the exhortations of the French poststructuralist Jean-Luc Nancy: "One has to understand reading as something other than decipherment. Rather, as touching, as being touched. Writing, reading: matters of tact."[142] In a 1990 essay titled "Corpus," Nancy makes an ethical and ontological call to undo the dichotomy between language and the body. Drawing from the Christian ritual phrase "this is my body" and its invocation of the transubstantiation, the spiritual incarnation of the blood and body of Christ into bread and wine, Nancy exposes how the demonstrative assumptions of language as in "*this* is my body," "the sign of itself and being-itself of the sign" depend on a magico-religious faith, or the metaphysics of body and soul.[143] Rather than producing a correlation, or perfectly containing its referent (as implied in a metaphysics of body and soul), words, categories, definition entries, he argues, generate new bodies. Words do not incarnate thoughts, as thoughts themselves are weighty bodies. Performing his own poesies though lists and catalogues, Nancy transgresses the disciplinary boundaries between philosophy and literature: "But a corpus, an ectopic topography, serial somatography, local geography. Stains, nails, veins, hairs, spurts, cheeks, sides, bones, wrinkles, creases, hips, throats."[144] Like the passage from *Gestos* cited above, Nancy here collapses structural frames; the anatomy of the sentence as well as that of the body is disorganized. Through his proliferating lists, Nancy deconstructs the well-formed or ideal body and, in so doing, disables its metaphysical and symbolic power.

With Nancy in mind, I want to suggest that Sarduy's invitation "que hagan el amor conmigo," does not imply a penetration, be that the interiority of a character or the disclosure of meaning, but rather the meeting at a limit. Limits—the boundaries, the outsides, the parts exposed, the skins that come into contact with other bodies—are the sites of pleasure and pain. That is, sensuousness (as opposed to an operative sense-making) is necessarily experienced at the place of exposure to another exterior. Alternatively, when Sarduy says, "lo que yo le invito no es que me lean," reading here, refers to the process of interpretation, of uncovering meaning. In other words, Sarduy prioritizes an aesthetic and visceral experience over one of knowledge production: "el placer que yo le comunico no es un placer intelectual."[145] Forcing the reader to reckon with the impenetrability of writing, with writing as a material body and not simply the hollow representation of a body, allows for a sensuous experience; it collapses the distance between the reader and the text bringing them into contact.

This lovemaking is not, of course, without corporeal vulnerability. Later in his televised interview Sarduy continues,

> Practicar la literatura es una especia de transgresión muy grande, es una especia de amenaza muy grande para la seguridad simbólica de nosotros y yo creo que hay una especia de represión en este acto apa-

> rentemente banal de escribir. [. . .] Se amenaza, se manejan conceptos simbólicos muy importantes para el cuerpo de uno y para el cuerpo de otros. Se ejerce una especie de violencia somática, de violencia corporal muy grande.[146]

From a poststructuralist's point of view, practicing literature threatens symbolic systems because of the excess and irreducible meaning that language produces. When we consider that hegemonic structures and their classificatory systems impose signs on bodies and seek to corral them through identitory markers, the link between the destabilization of symbolic systems and corporal and somatic violence becomes apparent. Sarduy's transgression, I hope to demonstrate, works against the union of the sign and the body.

The undoing of this union, moreover, helps us arrive at the material enmeshment between so-called art and existence. Thinking bodies not as the incarnation of something invisible (spirit, thought, idea), but as impenetrable materiality, keeps us from addressing bodies as anything but non-identical and singular beings. When Nancy writes, "bodies are impenetrable to language, and languages [are] impenetrable to bodies, bodies themselves, like this word 'body,' which already withholds itself and incorporates its own entry"[147] he is articulating an ontology where ideas, thoughts, or language (the seemingly abstract and immaterial) are corporeal: "Here is the hard point of this thing 'thought,' nodule or synapse, acid or enzyme, a gram of cortex." "Thought is itself a body," a physical mass that weighs and occupies space.[148] Signs, symbols, words, images, therefore, cannot be made to stand in for, or to take the place of, other bodies. Such an ontology bridges the distance between existence and art since art would no longer be a representation of an already existing, reproducible reality, but itself a singular and non-identical part of our relational existence.[149] This has important political implications. If the body cannot be reduced to its sign, or a sign equated to a body, then bodies remain unclassifiable. In this way we can approximate what Sarduy means when he says that writing challenges symbolic security. A symbolic structure, we should remember, be it a patriarchy, or monotheistic religion, transmits meaning from a center producing relations of power through fixed identities and social hierarchal organizations. Because writing inevitably "exscribes"—generates new bodies in its irreducible materiality—symbolic systems are always in danger of destabilization.[150]

Writing, Painting, Matter

In the following passage from *Gestos,* the fired missives of printed media become muddled in the city's ecology:

> A lo largo de los contenes el agua rueda arrastrando papeles y piedras, desaparece en remolinos los tragantes de las esquinas o se acumula detenida por grupos de piedras formando pequeñas represas, en las que los periódicos se mueven como barcos. La tinta de la tipografía deja sobre el pavimento manchas de titulares aún adivinables; la reproducción monstruosa de las figuras grabadas. Cuando los autos pasan, las ruedas proyectan grandes bloques de agua contra los muros y las páginas de los periódicos quedan fijas a la parte baja de las fachadas, donde el agua entintada chorrea formando sucios lamparones.[151]

The rain has rendered these newspapers inoperative. *Papeles* like *piedras* are physical objects, rubble and debris that are swallowed by the city's drains and at other times obstruct small rivers of dirty water. Paper, rocks, curbs, asphalt, water, cars, and ink form a vibrant assemblage where the uniform print of mechanical reproduction bleeds and births deformed, or "monstrous" copies.[152] Alongside the repeated question "ha leído usted los periódicos," the image of wet text that covers the city like wallpaper recurs as a leitmotif throughout the novel. Like the journalistic texts blurred by the rain, Sarduy's writing will smudge the sharp edges of meaning and deliberately fail to communicate knowable, reproducible messages.

While little is identified in the novel, Sarduy is precise with the context of *Gestos:* La Habana, its neighborhoods, its streets, and its clubs. In his deliberated visual, sonic, and gestural descriptions, it is as though he were exclusively concerned with conjuring the city, only that the images he produces by no means make use of perspectival illusionism or a single-point perspective, that is, modes of naturalistic representation:

> Las últimas vueltas descubren todo el panorama: el esquema, en círculos concéntrico, de la cuidad cuyas calles arrancan ondulando, interrumpidas unas por otras, mientras más lejanas más estrechas, hasta que en el horizonte no son más que líneas rayadas, mientras más lejanas más rectas, mas estrechas . . . , más grises . . . , mientras más lejanas.[153]

Here Sarduy converts the panorama of the city into a dynamic, geometric, two-dimensional image; not unlike an abstract expressionist painter, he flattens the space with large gestural brushstrokes. It is not surprising that Sarduy was fascinated with the work of Franz Kline during the time he was writing the novel and aspired to "pintar con palabras": "me preocupaba o me fascinaban las barras negras que un pintor bailando trazaba sobre inmensas telas blancas."[154] In the recurring passages of newspapers and other documents wet from the rain, "la tinta de los textos se va lavando, desdibujando."[155] As the printed text loses the definition of its contours we imagine its communications become illegible. Ink becomes paint and discourse becomes impressionistic images. Alternatively, the ubiquitous printed media textualizes the city and, like text on the flat surface of a page, the city becomes planimetric. In a similar vein to the New York School artists or the Cubists before them, Sarduy works against the pictorial conventions of receding space and makes his readers aware of the artifice, of its material components.

Is the "art of speech [. . .] only metaphorical?" Nancy asks, "What does a word touch, if not a body?" And yet, "A body is what cannot be read in writing." That is to say, the body in its "obstinate thereness"[156] is that which cannot be interpreted or subsumed by another sign. Of course, all speech is metaphorical, Nancy concedes, but in all speech there is also a limit, a border from which we separate and to which we come into contact. This point of touch is at the limits of comprehension, where writing stops operating as a sign. "In all writing, a body is traced, is the tracing and the trace—is the letter, yet never the letter, a literality or rather a lettericity that is no longer legible."[157] "[L]a reproducción monstruosa de las figuras grabadas" formed by the bleeding ink of Sarduy's wet newspapers, are an instance of such a trace. Following Nancy's ontology, *lettericity* is unavoidable, but there are practices of writing that pronounce these limits, that bring reading as touching to the foreground of the text. Nancy continues,

> To write the sign of oneself that does not offer a sign, that is not a sign. This is: *writing*, finally to stop discoursing. To cut into discourse. Corpus, anatomy. One must not consider anatomy of dissection, the dialectical dismembering of organs and functions, but rather the anatomy of configurations, of shapes—one should call them states of the body, ways of being in the world, demeanors, respirations, gaits, pelts, curlings, masses. Bodies are first to be touched. Bodies are first

> masses, masses offered without anything to articulate, without anything to discourse about, without anything to add to them.[158]

"Ways of being in the world, demeanors, respirations, gaits," is a fitting description of *Gestos,* as the novel opens with the narration of movement, the back and forth of the city: "Pasan de un lado a otro, de un lado a otro de la calle, El tránsito nunca cesa. No se detienen, no se vuelven sobre sí mismos."[159] Opening the novel in this manner, the reader has no point of reference for the subject of these actions. It is the actions themselves that take center stage. Returning to a passage partially quoted above, we see how the narration, describing the effects of an explosion at a Havana club called Picasso, "stop[s] discoursing":

> La puerta está próxima. La salida. La cabeza gira. El mural del fondo se precipita hacia la sala, se desune y rueda sobre la pista, contra los estantes, bajo el mostrador. El caballo rojo, dividido, veloz, salta sobre las líneas negras que lo enmarcan y galopa sobre el piano, se eleva, relincha, se diluye, estalla. El ángel sobre la contadora. El toro doble se agrieta y arde en el traganíquel. La lámpara azul se invierte y el aceite desciende sobre la pista. Los cascos de la bestia se escuchan. Las cabezas dilatadas, los cuerpos descompuestos, el brazo dorado que sostiene la pica la impulsa, la clava contra la pared. La puerta se abre de un tirón. . . . La pianista se desarma como un rompecabezas bajo los cascos negros y acerados del toro. El letrero de las puertas del refrigerador se desintegra: CASSO, PISSO, PICA. Ruido afuera. Todo asciende y desciende, huye y se acerca en ráfagas. Curva. Escaleras, casas llenas de bombas, jardines, raíces, ríos, manos que dicen adiós, rifles, castillos que se viran y arden, granadas.[160]

"Cuerpos descompuestos" is precisely (or literally) what this passage produces, riddled with fragmentary, single word sentences. Verbs, such as *desune, rueda, salta, agrieta,* and *arde,* enact a constant flux of images, forces, and intensities, on the vertical plane of the page. We can read, "El caballo rojo, dividido, veloz, salta sobre las líneas negras que lo enmarcan [. . .] diluye, estalla," as Picasso's *Guernica* painting trotting off the canvas and into the open space of the bar. The explosion of this canonical painting is coupled with the deconstruction of the artist's name along with its cultural authority, "CASSO, PISSO, PICA," becoming "lettericity." "Curva. Escaleras, casas llenas de bombas, jardines, raíces," produces what the philosopher calls for time and again in "Corpus": the compiling of a catalogue without a logos or hierarchal ordering. Vernacular words, such as "traganíquel" and "rompecabezas," standout in this anatomy of configurations, drawing the reader's attention to the mechanics of language in both its literal and metaphorical registers. In this difficult and dense passage, Sarduy brings the reader to the limits of comprehension, to point of touch.

Resisting Subjection

Insisting on a cartographic relation to the text, penetrating depth is denied on all fronts, perhaps most especially with regard to its protagonist. Referred to only in the feminine pronoun, "Ella," the text does not provide us with a name or a past history. We are given few physical descriptions and no inner dialogue, with the exception of what would appear to be the most inconsequential free indirect discourse: "(siempre haces la misma pegunta tonta: ¿este pull-over es blanco con rayas negras o negro con rayas blancas?)."[161] In fact, the novel does not provide emotional or psychological descriptions; its third person narrator does not presume to know or reflect upon characters' intentions. Instead, we are given gestures, movements, actions, and sensorial impressions seemingly without the guide of an authorial voice.[162] The novel lacks narrative frames and, as such, a fixed perspective. If narrative voice is considered the self-knowledge of a written work, then perhaps its absence here is an expression of what Nancy calls the "non-knowledge" of the body. "Massive substance is supported only by a spreading, not by interiority or by a foundation. So, as Freud remarks, 'Psyche is spread out'—adding 'she knows nothing about it.' This non-knowledge is the very body of Psyche, or rather, it is the body that Psyche herself *is*." Significantly, "knowledge wants an object" and "in the absence of an object there is no subject."[163] Following this logic, the apparent lack of a narrative voice and its object of knowledge is another way in which the text resists subject formation and reaffirms the corporeal.

Ella is always described carrying a small suitcase, the contents of which are repeatedly enumerated, as though they were fetishes or objects with symbolic potential. As readers we might attempt to decipher their meanings as does an investigator:

> Un policía toma la pequeña maleta [. . .] y va sacando los objetos, mostrándolos con la seriedad de un mago: un peine, un baniti, un espejo rojo, una pieza de música, un libreto de artista [. . .] una fal-

> da negra, una lata de sardinas, una novela, un candado, un abanico, un . . . , una . . .[164]

And yet, this catalogue of objects sustains an irreducible and enigmatic thingness, as suggested by the trail of articles and ellipses. Her script (and here I refer to the script that Sarduy has written her outside of her dramatic roles as a performer, which are often crossed and difficult to distinguish from those off stage) is sparse and can also be inventoried. Repeating the same melodramatic lines with little variations, her fragments of speech are simultaneously parodic and poetic:

> ¿Queda alguna aspirina? ¿O es que con este calor se han derritido hasta las aspirinas? Ah, qué calor; el calor ambiente y el de los focos. Dos calores en uno. Un calor doble. Uno frente a otro mirándose . . . ¡Ah, qué calor, qué asco de vida, qué mierda![165]

Recalling Nancy's "lettericity," speech here does not disclose an interiority, but remains on the surface of the text.

The Art of Assemblage

We might say that the character of *Ella* functions less like a protagonist and more like one of the Chinese Cabala icons with which the novel opens and serves as a unifying thread throughout the narrative. González Echevarría explains that the zoological symbols that reappear throughout the text—for example, "los caballos-sapo, los mariposas-piedra fina, los peces muerto grande, las culebras-niña bonita, los ratones-marinero, los caracoles-gato"[166]—refer to *la Charada China,* a system of interpreting dreams used to play the illegal lottery game, "la bolita," popular in Havana.[167] This system of metaphors and metonyms, explains González Echevarría, gives a certain coherence to the text. It not only prophesizes the Revolution and with it the explosion of all existing codes, but also corresponds to Sarduy's use of rhetorical devices.[168] Notwithstanding González Echevarría's hermeneutical unveiling (recall here my critique of his treatment of Guillén), that the narrative should be pieced together by a series of tropes reiterates Nancy's concession that all speech is metaphorical. Significantly for our purposes, these zoological symbols—"inexistente"[169] hybrid figures that come into being through the grammatical relation of the hyphen—makes apparent the mechanics in the production of texts and breaks the illusion of a realistic representation. At the start of the novel, in addition to the Chinese symbols, objects are listed, "una ferretería, una vidriera de números, un bar [. . .] un carro de ostiones, una casa de lámparas";[170] together these symbols and objects (like those in *Ella*'s suitcase) form a bank of signs of which the novel is composed. Repeated and reassembled, these icons produce different vignettes and, consequently, the impression that the novel is constructed on the reshuffling of a deck of cards. Conceived in these terms—as the reconfiguration of repeated icons—the development or penetration of subjects is made impossible while the composition of the icons, "caracoles-gato," made up of radical juxtapositions, demonstrates how meaning is not embodied in the sign, but rather produced through combinations and assemblages.

In the following passage that depicts a segment of a street parade, we see how Sarduy not only withholds markers of classification, but in the place of recognizable subjects he gives us a web of movements and forces:

> A ambos lados de la cadena el coro sigue los movimientos: las batas de encaje blanco, los espesos pañuelos amarillos amarrados en grandes lazos alrededor de la cabeza forman una marea ondulante que choca contra el público diseminado en las aceras. Un laberinto de metales dorados, de cornetas, trombas y flautas silbantes tiembla alrededor de los tambores. Las largas tumbas cilíndricas rayadas en blanco y negro parecen contraerse y estirarse con los golpes. La batería de bongoses, claves, triángulos, quijadas de vaca, simples botellas y cajones se desordena y cierra tras la cola de la comparsa.[171]

Significantly, this vignette of choreographed performers gives place to the movement and multitude of accessories and instruments. Without prior knowledge of Afro-Cuban cultural practices, the reader is left to trace the labyrinthine movement of yellow, gold, and brass in this visual and sonic configuration. With the exception of the word *cabeza,* no reference is made to the individual bodies that produce these gestures. Rather, what we see is "una marea ondulante" where flutes tremble and drums—or as Sarduy refers to them "long cylindrical tombs," invoking corporeality and finitude—appear to contract and shrink. Like the lists of objects in previous passages, here we have another assemblage made up of "claves, triángulos, quijadas de vaca, simples botellas y cajones" where no explicit reference is made to the figure of the human.

We might describe the above scene as displaying an "anatomy of configurations" and "states of the body," what Nancy calls for in opposition to an organized body.[172] The body as a seamless structure with functioning organs implies a complete and closed unit and, as such, an interiority without relation. Imagining the body as an individual whole or microcosm has led to regarding other bodies as aberrations, inferior or defective versions of an originary archetype. Against this model of the body, made up of working organs, or "members," where inside and outside are demarcated, Nancy insists on "parts outside parts." That is, an aerial, topographic view—an absolute exteriority, where existence is synonymous with exposure, where *techne*—as in technology, art, craft, and skill—rather than essence, creates bodies and where bodies are the very "separation and sharing" of sense.[173] Sarduy's "marea ondulante que *choca*" and "tambores [. . .] que parecen contraerse y estirarse con los *golpes*" (my emphasis) produces a context where corporeality comes to the fore in the impact, in the separation and the contact between bodies, between the skins of drums and hands.

Vibrant Corpse

In calling our attention to the limits, to the place of touch, Sarduy's writing brings us to the material enmeshment that connects singular bodies and allows us to move away from human agents and teleological narratives, to consider collectivities, configurations, and assemblages. While the notion of ecology is never made explicit in either Sarduy's or Nancy's text, treating the technology of writing as matter and thinking being, as being-outside, as the contact between bodies, necessarily foregrounds networks of relation, interdependencies, and vulnerabilities. I want to suggest that in their lists and catalogues Sarduy and Nancy express an ecological materialism, where the distinctions between artifice and organism become less apparent and where the seemingly immaterial—as in "demeanors, respirations, gaits, pelts" and gestures—becomes corporeal. In thinking the body not as the incarnation of something invisible, or an exceptional organism made in the image of God, but rather as impenetrable materiality, not only are the secure boundaries of the human destabilized but also the differences between life and matter. A definition entry of *corpus* reads "a person or animal, especially when dead"; as the title to Nancy's essay on the body, this meaning comes to the fore when he invokes the death of God, the death of the glorious sublime body that subsumes all others.[174] If life is no longer the embodiment of an immaterial force, then can we imagine a different notion of vitality?

Earlier I described a passage from *Gestos* as a vibrant assemblage in order to suggest a sense of aliveness in what would otherwise be understood as a conglomeration of inert and passive objects. Here, I am drawing from the work of Jane Bennett and her theory of "vibrant matter," an "impersonal affectivity" of things irreducible to their instrumentality. Her book, *Vibrant Matter: A Political Ecology of Things,* challenges anthropocentrism and calls for an attentiveness to "the capacity of things—edibles, commodities, storms, metals—not only to impede or block the will and designs of humans but also to act as quasi agents or forces with trajectories, propensities, or tendencies of their own."[175] Whereas historical materialism worked to demystify the fetishistic power of man-made things—recall Marx's speaking commodity—Bennett proposes cultivating "a bit of anthropomorphism—the idea that human agency has some echoes in nonhuman nature—[. . .] to counter the narcissistic reflex of human language and thought."[176] Interestingly, Bennett, as I see it, is theorizing along parallel lines to Fred Moten: Both thinkers depart from the demystifying strategies of historical materialism and, in so doing, challenge humanistic presumptions of spirit, matter, agency, and the social hierarchies that are generated from such presumptions. Where Moten is interested in drawing out a materiality that reproduces itself and resists subjection in the descendants of slaves and in Black artistic production, Bennett is interested in drawing out a vitality that *is* materiality and which she locates "alongside and inside humans to see how analysis of political events might change if we gave the force of things more due."[177]

Collapsing the divide between life and matter, Bennett's vital materiality also approximates and enriches Nancy's deconstruction of a Christian metaphysics:

> What I am calling an impersonal affect or material vibrancy is not a spiritual supplement of "life force" added to the matter said to house it. Mine is not a vitalism in the traditional sense; I equate affect with materiality, rather than posit a separate force that can enter and animate a physical body.
>
> My aim, again, is to theorize a vitality intrinsic to materiality as such, and to detach materiality from the figures of passive, mechanistic, or divinely infused substance. This vibrant matter is *not* the raw material for the creative activity of humans or God.[178]

The theoretical interventions of biopolitics have demonstrated how political techniques and culturally determined ways of seeing have ordered bodies in two camps: those as having a plenitude of life, as having futures and, therefore, bodies to protect, and those considered already dead, as abandoned, available for consumption and exploitation.[179] For bodies that do not correspond to a normative model, that are not politically recognizable as life to be valued, Bennett's vital materialism and ecological thinking upends the logic that would justify their sacrifice for instrumental ends. To quote her once more, "Such a newfound attentiveness to matter and its powers will not solve the problem of human exploitation or oppression, but it can inspire a greater sense of the extent to which all bodies are kin in the sense of inextricably enmeshed in a dense network of relations. And in a knotted world of vibrant matter, to harm one section of the web may very well be to harm oneself."[180]

Conclusion

In my reading of Sarduy's cabalistic icons "los caballos-sapo" and Guillén's sonorous phonetics, "sóngoro cosongo," what I have been particularly interested in underscoring is an impenetrable materiality. In his elaboration of Nancy's ontology, Ian James argues that matter can only be sensed from an outside; relating to it—whether that be through sight, hearing, smell, or taste—is ultimately a form of touching, that is, the coming into contact with a limit, or the mutual contact and separation of distinct bodies.[181] Accordingly, penetration would then be the dissolution of those distinctions, the fusion and assimilation of material differences. The presumption of penetrating interiority, as the expert analyst might do, implies accessing a closed system or knowable, reproducible content, demonstrating mastery over what would otherwise be irreducibly complex. The title of this book, *Corporeal Readings* expresses, therefore, an epistemological humility, as well as a co-constituting relationship. James offers a useful illustration; if we open an object up "dissect, X-ray, scan, or hugely magnify [it] we are simply creating another exterior surface or relation of contact-separation of sense."[182] In the chapter that follows, "Transmaterialities," turning to a 1972 novel by Sarduy and the contemporary drawings and sculptures of Roberto Fabelo, we will see how the work of the anatomist does not, indeed, reveal anything but another exterior surface; how dissection results in metamorphosis, in the reproduction of new bodies, rather than a seeing inside.

To insist on an impenetrable materiality is also to insist on an "unknowing relating." This phrase by Santiago Colas describes a practice of "writing the other." In the absence of a preposition—it's not "writing *about* the other"—the distinction between subject and object are collapsed; "to write" and "the other" share a plane of immanence.[183] Colas formulates an ethics of close reading through a short story by the Uruguayan writer Felisberto Hernández, in which the narrator describes a ritual of feeling objects in the dark with one's hands, a ritual capable of inducing discomfort and uncertainty, as much as pleasure. As a parable for the kind of close reading Colas is advocating, in the story "hands [. . .] compensate for the loss of vision, an unknowing relating in the place of the representational knowing associated with sight" and, thus, judgment is suspended and "thought [is disengaged] from narrow utilitarian ends."[184] Colas's ethical close reading is "a touching without knowledge," "an exploration, and in that way [an] unfolding of what we do not know in texts (and figuratively speaking in things)."[185] In this way, Colas echoes Sommer's and Abbate's arguments that encountering the unknown in literature and music (respectively) offers an ethical form of engagement with human Others.

In response to the aestheticist critiques waged against *Motivos* and *Gestos,* I have sustained my attention on the micro-compositions of their texts so as to locate an ethics and politics precisely where their work does not provide a prescriptive, empirical project or a knowable, reproducible subject. My engagement of *Motivos,* privileging the sonorous over sight and language, is an effort at unknowing relating, as well as a strategy of marking a difference while maintaining its irreducibility to representation. Following Moten, I suggested treating the phonetic materiality in *Motivos de son* as a resistant object, that is, resistant to the production of meaning, and its performative reproduction of racial caricatures as resistant to subjection, impenetrable to the analyst. Accordingly, *Motivos,* prompts us to consider its aesthetic form not as the empty container of a political content, but as the very material surplus—racial, gender, and sexual differences—that dominant culture aims but fails to subordinate.[186] While Sarduy's novel brings us back to semiotics and the visual, it does so in such a way that displaces an anthropocentric perspective. As we saw, human figures and so-called inanimate objects share a plane of immanence in the novel, while the reader's capacity to comfortably treat the book as an object of knowledge is also thwarted. Against the grain of reading these two canonical writers as expressions of a *cubanidad,* of mining their work for national properties, I have aimed to trace a tendency in their texts that works against identity formation.

Sarduy's statement on Spanish television, "poco importa si yo le comunico un relato o no [. . .] el placer que yo le comunico no es un placer intelectual," could not have been farther from the cultural climate of 1970s Cuba, particularly the state's edict that writers and artists have a civic obligation to contribute to the narrative of progress. In the continued administering of Castro's 1961 prescription to local intellectuals, "Palabras a los intelectuales," the 1970s, remembered as the "Quinquenio Gris," would be accompanied by an increasing Sovietization, most famously marked by the poet Herberto Padilla's 1971 forced *auto-da-fé*.[187] The state's polarizing rhetoric—"dentro de la Revolución, todo; contra la Revolución, nada"—justified its purging, its disposal of bodies deemed un-revolutionary as having no future in the ideal community to come. The 1960s labor camps designed to rehabilitate homosexuals, religious believers, and those considered anti-social were called *Unidades Militares de Ayuda a la Producción*—a means to make the Revolution's "lumpen" productive.[188] In this context, we can better appreciate the political implications of insisting on an inoperative aspect of writing.

2

Transmaterialities

Incorrect Anatomies in Severo Sarduy's *Cobra* and Roberto Fabelo's Art

> Before there was earth or sea or the sky that covers everything, Nature appeared the same throughout the whole world: what we call chaos: a raw confused mass, nothing but inert matter, badly combined discordant atoms of things, confused in the one place. [. . .] Nothing retained its shape, one thing obstructed another, because in the one body, cold fought with heat, moist with dry, soft with hard, and weight with weightless things.
>
> Ovid, *The Metamorphoses*

> Matter is not mere being, but its ongoing un/doing. Nature is agential trans*materiality/ trans-matter-reality in its ongoing re(con)figuring, where trans is not a matter of changing *in* time, from this to that, but an undoing of "this" and "that," an ongoing reconfiguring *of* spacetimemattering in an iterative reworking of past, present, future integral to the play of the indeterminacy of being-time.
>
> Karen Barad, "Transmaterialities"

Introduction—Creation Stories

In Book I of Ovid's *The Metamorphoses* the "primal chaos" and "raw confused mass" is given form by "a god and a greater order of nature."[1] It is the separation of the elements, the splitting, dividing, disentangling, and fixing that transforms obscure mass into distinct bodies, such as the earth, sea, winds, and sky. At the start of this creation narrative, in which Ovid calls upon the Gods to inspire his poetic endeavor, it would seem that creative vitality is infused into inert matter from an outside intelligent being. Order, hierarchy, and a linear development from the Silver, Bronze, and Iron Ages, are the modus operandi in this cosmology where Humankind is the "animal capable of higher thought that could be ruler of all the rest [. . .]

moulded into an image of the all-controlling gods."[2] And yet the composition of Ovid's *The Metamorphoses,* loosely referred to as an epic poem, defies all attempts at classification. Both mythical and historical, it lacks a single unifying hero or people, a characteristic of traditional epics.[3] Its themes and tones are varied and if moral reflection or insight were the purpose of myths, Ovid is said to make them "the object of play and artful manipulation."[4] Its fifteen books and two hundred and fifty myths might be better described as a proliferating catalogue of metamorphic accounts, restyled and, thus, *trans*formed through Ovid's poetic voice. Here we find ontological crossings as diverse as that of humans and gods into flowers, rocks, stars, mountains, birds; statues into young girls; spears into trees; two people into one, and so on.[5] It would seem that rather than reflect the "order of nature," Ovid's text comes closer to supporting a claim made by one of Severo Sarduy's narrators: "La escritura es el arte de descomponer un orden y componer un desorden."[6]

Drawing from the previous chapter's expositions on the body—imagined not as an organism made up of members but as an anatomy of configurations, coming to being through *techne* rather than essence—and its treatment of materiality as agential and vibrant,[7] in this second chapter, I consider the disarticulation and reconfiguration of human-animal forms through the various metamorphoses in Sarduy's 1972 novel, *Cobra,* and Roberto Fabelo's contemporary drawings, paintings, and installations. In the epigraphs above we find that, whereas in the fragment from Ovid's *The Metamorphoses* the chaos of indistinct inert matter is a primal stage before its organization by a supreme being, in the fragment from Karen Barad's "Transmaterialities: Trans*/Matter/Realities and Queer Political Imaginings," the indeterminateness of matter is not a quality of the past but the source of ongoing reconfigurations.[8] That is, if chaos is overcome by the act of creation in the former, creation is immanent to chaos in the latter. The passage from Ovid, we should remember, is just one among the many accounts of "bodies changed into new form"[9] of which he makes the object of play and artful manipulation. And it is this play and manipulation thought together with the notion of "transmateriality"—where the *trans,* as both prefix and preposition, does not signal this or that, but the process, the sharing of sense through which new bodies are infinitely engendered[10]—that will guide my readings of Sarduy's text and Fabelo's images. Treating matter as vibrant and not as "the raw material for the creative activity of humans or God,"[11] allows us to provincialize the anthropocentric narrative that Humankind is the "ruler of all the rest [. . .] moulded into an image of the all-controlling gods."[12] Following Barad's lead into the science of Quantum Field Theory (QFT), we can better conceive of materiality's vibrancy.

Whereas classical physics sustained the notion of the vacuum, a space of complete emptiness, through the science of QFT, Barad would have us reimagine this presumed nothingness as a field of virtual particles that "are and are not there as a result of the time-being indeterminacy relation."[13] That which we register as nothing or immaterial, is, instead, imperceptible matter that comes into contact *with* and separation *from* other bodies, a *trans*materiality. Accordingly, that which appears distinct or solid may be virtual. Virtual particles can also be understood as forces, energies and intensities, the invisible dynamics that constitute perceptible bodies, the memory of that which could have been or that which is yet to come.[14] Transformation is, thus, ongoing and recognizable form is always already incomplete or insufficient. QFT allows us to imagine a nonheteronormative creation story: "Nature is birthed out of chaos and void, *tohu v'vohu,* an echo, a diffracted/differentiating/différancing murmuring, an originary repetition without sameness, regeneration out of a fecund nothingness."[15] Such queer storytelling renders impossible a correspondence between so-called Humankind and an image, be that of the gods or otherwise. In light of this ontological indeterminacy, the categorical designation of Humankind is an artful manipulation. And images are a material part of our relational existence; they do not stand apart or as substitutes, but are themselves singular and non-identical.

Sarduy's and Fabelo's metamorphoses, as this chapter will explore, are the happenings at the intersection of technology, art, skill, and craft. It is the very artifice, the smooth texture of a painting on silk, or the glitter of eye makeup on which their transfigurations would seem to insist. Silk and glitter, however, do not mask or disavow the fleshiness of human-animal bodies, the rot of decay, or the tares of a corpse. Death and art, artifice and organic matter are intimately entangled in both their works. Considered together, Sarduy's novel and Fabelo's images break the illusion of the self-possessed subject at the other end of the Renaissance's linear single-point perspective. The use of geometric projection to produce the illusion of receding space on paintings and frescos not only assumed biological and inherent ways of seeing,[16] but also, following the tenets of a classical aesthetic, constituted the spectator as an individual subject or, more accurately, a five-foot-nine Italian man.[17] Remembering Aristotle's *Poetics,* his dictums for a sense of the whole and unity of space and time were predicated on the notion that a representation should be "easily embraced by memory" and "easily embraced in one view."[18] "Vast size," Aristotle writes, is not beautiful because "the eye cannot take it all in at once."[19] Later when the Latin Americanist Alejo Carpentier elaborated his theory of a destratifying baroque spirit, he opposed this spirit to the organizing structures of classicism, described as a geometrical harmony imposed through the partitioning of vacant spaces.[20] Accordingly, Sarduy's compositions would horrify the classist with their seemingly unrestrained textual *horror vacui:* the medieval tendency to leave no space unadorned in its proverbial fear of emptiness. As one of the theoretical engineers of a Latin American Neo-Baroque,[21] Sarduy constructs a novel that is dynamic, expansive, eccentric, and centrifugal. For instance, the text continuously draws its reader outside the purview of its pages with a minutia of technical and esoteric references that compel one to consult outside sources, be that medical, astrological, or art historical. And in its proliferation of vignettes, it becomes unclear for the reader what is transpiring within the frame of the main narrative versus that of a mise-en-scéne—the description of a painted canvas or a staged performance. The result is an indistinction between diegetic and exegetic passages that renders a single coherent interpretation impossible. In so doing, the text actively works against the classical tenets for a self-contained, conceivable, proportionate, and static representation intended to reflect the view of the individual sovereign subject.

In my reading of his novel *Gestos* in chapter 1, I suggest Sarduy textually reproduces the two-dimensional plane of the canvas. As an avid student of art history and a painter, it is not surprising that Sarduy invites his readers to imagine his literary work through the tropes of visual space.[22] This invitation is made all the more emphatic in *Cobra* with section titles, such as "PETIT ENSENMBLE CARAVAGGESQUE" and "PORTRAIT DE PUP EN ENFANT."[23] In his analysis of Sarduy's literary corpus, Pedro de Jesús underscores the preeminence of the plastic arts and suggests Sarduy inverts the ontological hierarchy between reality and artifice.[24] Following de Jesús's lead, I'm interested in tracing the implications of this inversion for other naturalized categories. In *Cobra* creativity and craft continuously manipulate and denature human forms. Through mutations, mutilations, drag performances, theatrics, cosmetics, and tattoos, Sarduy undoes the humanist figure of the ideal body. As though turning Leonardo da Vinci's *Vitruvian Man* upside down, the protagonist, "[s]e había suspendido [. . .] al techo, por los pies, ahorcado al revés: cadenas de cimarrón la colgaban por los tobillos al zócalo de una lámpara. Era un murciélago albino entre globos de vidrio opalescente y cálices de cuarzo."[25]

If Sarduy breaks with the classical universe, in which man is the measure of all things, through an aesthetic of excess and proliferation, Fabelo does so by employing the very techniques of the master Renaissance artists in such a way that he undermines their presumptions of an unmediated access to the "natural" world. In a series of ink drawings over the pages of a nineteenth-century medical encyclopedia containing illustrations of human anatomy, he produces a catalogue of figures displaying zoological physiognomies.[26] Overlapping the precise, uniform incisions of the text's original engravings with gestural cross-hatching and chiaroscuro modeling, Fabelo transforms anatomical parts into aesthetic material.

While Fabelo's illustrations of interspecies bodies transform naturalized taxonomies, in tampering with an encyclopedia, specifically Leo Testut's *Traité d'anatomie humaine* from 1887, still cited today by faculties of medicine around the world,[27] Fabelo is also transforming disciplinary boundaries and modes of knowledge production. In other words, Fabelo's drawings do more than intervene in the content of the encyclopedia. The integration of his drawings with those of the encyclopedia's engravers and the decontextualization of fragments of Testut's text—rendering instructional descriptions poetic—suggest the encyclopedia, as well as other sciences of compartmentalization, is a convention, a language, an art form, and not the repository of unmediated information. To better appreciate the implications of this intervention, let us recall that the encyclopedia is both a product of and emblematic of the eighteenth century. The Enlightenment ideology of progress through the acquisition of scientific knowledge nourished and laid the groundwork for twentieth-century modernizing and utopic projects, of which eugenics and the sacrifice of life for the imagined betterment of the human species was one manifestation. The rhetoric of progress and sacrifice, a predilection for taxonomizing, and models of an ideal man, as I will show below, are also operative in the discourse of the Cuban Revolution.

My interest in Sarduy's and Fabelo's work is not simply in the iconography of hybrid bodies, nor as reading these bodies as a direct response to a national subject model, but to consider how the destratifying work their texts and images do help us see the limits and processes of a dominant national discourse. To this end, I sustain my attention on their aesthetic practices, exploring the epistemological and, consequently, ethical implications of their artful manipulations. By aestheticizing presumably natural and scientific means of understanding and ordering the world and by foregrounding a shared biomorphic-materiality, Sarduy and Fabelo unsettle the secure boundaries of the human, its presumptions of sovereignty and its attendant nationalisms. The political significance of their non-anthropocentric strategies comes into high relief when considered against the backdrop of Che Guevara's seminal essay, "El socialismo y el hombre en Cuba" (1965). In Guevara's vision of the generation to come, "el hombre del futuro" is not only compelled by heroic duty, knowing that "libertad y su sostén cotidiano tienen color de sangre y están henchidos de sacrificio," but he is also free of "original sin," of the "infectious germs" and "perverse" tendencies of his bourgeois past.[28] The violent repercussions of this idealized, heroic subject and its sacrificial logic are made evident when we recall the 1965 forced labor camps where gay citizens and dissidents were interred and the involuntary quarantines for those infected with HIV in the 1980s.[29]

Interestingly, Guevara elaborates his own creation narrative with allusions to techniques and the malleability of clay:

> El esqueleto de nuestra libertad completa está formado, falta la sustancia proteica y el ropaje; los crearemos. [. . .] Nos forjaremos en la acción cotidiana, creando un hombre nuevo con una nueva técnica. . . . La personalidad juega el papel de movilización y dirección en cuanto que encarna las más altas virtudes [. . .] La arcilla fundamental de nuestra obra es la juventud, en ella depositamos nuestra esperanza y la preparamos para tomar de nuestras manos la bandera. [. . .] *Patria o Muerte* (author's emphasis).[30]

Here the future community is imagined corporeally, a skeleton in need of meat and clothes, but ultimately a cohesive organism that will be led by "un hombre nuevo." A Christian metaphysics is invoked not just in its messianic projection, but also in its allusion to body and soul, "La personalidad [. . .] *encarna* las más altas virtudes." In the previous chapter, following Jean-Luc Nancy, I suggested that conceiving of the body as an individual whole, a microcosm, or as the incarnation of an ideal, has led to regarding non-normative bodies as aberrations, inferior or defective versions of an originary archetype. Indeed, we see this in the context of Cuba, where those who did not match the Revolution's model of a hyper-masculine, morally and physically incorruptible New Man were categorized as *gusanos* and deemed disposable. In the Revolution's motto, *patria o muerte,* the grammar of one or the other leaves no possibility for deviations, for that which is unproductive to the coming community. Moreover, *patria o muerte* invokes the sublation, or the making operative, of death for the nation's providential fulfillment. Considered within this context—the imposition of a national subjectivity and its inevitable exclusions—it becomes critical to break the correlation between Humankind and an image, to decenter and fracture the single-point perspective, and to dwell on the creative potential of chaos.

Cataloguing *Cobra* from Frozen Orchids to Asthmatic Bishops

Sitting at her boudoir, the novel's protagonist "[s]e asilabla las enmarañada fibras de vidrio."[31] Taken literally, the reader is confounded. Glass hair? Is there such a thing? Tinsel comes to mind and David Bowiesque glam rock pink wigs. But can glass be untangled? Wouldn't the glass break? Read as poetic object, however, a wig of glass hair is emblematic of Sarduy's novel, a text that consistently conjures the paradoxical simultaneity, or the becoming-indistinct, between antithetical concepts—such as the organic and the synthetic—of a text that seeks to make the seemingly unbendable pliant, the solid porous, and the static unstable. Regarding a White Dwarf, a term for a celestial body that is small and dense, one passage reads, "ahora menos pétrea, menos densa de materia en su interior, ampollada."[32] The confluence of antinomies in the novel and their formal undoings recalls the chaos at the start of Ovid's *The Metamorphoses,* "Nothing retained its shape [. . .] because in the one body, cold fought with heat, moist with dry, soft with hard, and weight with weightless things."[33] Whereas in Ovid's myth the gods organize the elements into their proper places and create Humankind in their own image, in *Cobra* they seemed to have blundered. The novel's eponymous, transgender protagonist admonishes god, "Dios mío [. . .] ¿por qué me hiciste nacer si no era para ser absolutamente divina?"[34] Appeals to divine intervention notwithstanding, Cobra and company will go to any lengths to untangle glass hair.

Cobra is a performer/prostitute in the Lyrical Theater of the Dolls; its location is unspecified and historical context seemingly both fifteenth century and the 1970s. On its first page we find allusions to the Italian Renaissance, Chinese foot binding, and Calder's mobiles, all the while "en el tocadiscos, como es natural, Sonny Rollins."[35] As the star, "la reina," with the most admirers, she is almost perfect except for her feet. Cobra rarely appears outside the company of her diminutive double, Pup, also known as the White Dwarf [la enana blanca], and the Madame. Together they form an (un)holy trinity. In the first half of the text, sectioned "Cobra I," Cobra's obsessive experiments to decrease the size of her feet, in which science and magic intermingle, are complimented by those to enlarge her double, Pup. The denouement of these transformative experiments is Cobra's castration. The search for the elusive Dr. Ktazob who will perform "la conversión" takes the trio to Morocco and reproduces Orientalist fantasies of bazaars, hashish, and mosques. While the feminine gender is used during this first half, surprisingly, once Cobra emerges from the surgery—now possibly in a Parisian subway—on to the second half of the novel, "Cobra II," the adjectives switch to the masculine, as though grammatically insisting on the improper, on that which does *not* belong or correspond to its subject. Following her castration, phalluses and ejaculation abound as Cobra is now in the company of biker thugs who perform orgiastic initiatory rituals and go by the names Tundra, Escorpión, Totem, and Tigre. They also appear at times as Tibetan Lamas and drug traffickers in Amsterdam. The text ends with the section entitled "Diario Indio" in a Buddhist monastery in Nepal or perhaps the West Indies, given its allusions to Columbus's error.[36] Although Cuba is no doubt present in the text, whereas in *Gestos* it might be identified as its leading star, in *Cobra* its most explicit reference is in a footnote on the Mambo, which Cobra sings in Esperanto.[37]

The "novel," not unlike Ovid's "epic poem," is composed of a series of metamorphoses. In the place of a larger narrative arc, or a discernible plot, there is instead a catalogue of transformations. Even summaries of *Cobra* by other critics take on the form of lists. Emir Rodríguez Monegal, for instance, lists eleven transformations and observes that they occur "at the same time, or successively (there is no valid chronology although there is a succession of episodes in the conventionally bound solid called a book)."[38] Of course the quantification of eleven is arbitrary, for as Rodríguez Monegal notes the text itself performs its own metamorphoses.[39] A single sentence, such as the following, conjures for the reader continuously shifting images from one unexpected noun and modifier to the next: "A las sorpresas térmicas respondieron los invasores con grandes maniobras: de las uñas brotó un violeta vascular que tiraba a orquídea congelada, a manto de Obispo asmático, bajo un refectorio que se derrumba, comiéndose una piña."[40] In the comma that both separates and brings together "frozen orchid" and "asthmatic bishop," Sarduy's writing stops discoursing and instead enacts a transmateriality, a zone of indeterminacy in which the reader must sustain an imaginative doing and undoing from one word to the next. If "linguistic structure [has] shape[d] . . . our understanding of the world, believing that the subject and predicate structure of language reflects a prior ontological reality of substance and attribute,"[41] Sarduy upends this presumed correspondence and, in so doing, a prior ontological reality. Put otherwise, although grammatically, a vascular violet, a frozen orchid, and the robe of an asthmatic bishop correspond as attributes of the nails, as unique, idiosyncratic composites, they do not refer back or stand in for the nails, but occupy in the mind of the reader their own substantial space, like added objects to an expanding composition.

Before exploring this becoming at the level of the writing further, we can say that at the macro level of "the book," identifying a unified, well-organized body, or at least one led by a head, becomes an impossible task. Like an assemblage of found objects, the text contains, among other things, passages by Octavio Paz, surgical procedures, allusions to Caravaggio, a recreation of *Las Meninas,* the Chinese torture Leng T'che, linguistic terms [trigramas], Lotus Pose, Derrida, Coca Cola, cocaine, Italian glazed pottery [mayólica], Taíno statuettes, Astronomy [enanas blancas] and so on. And this is to say nothing of the various stylistic forms, tones, and shifts in narrative voice the text exhibits. The abundance of literary, visual, musical, scientific, religious, popular culture, and philosophical references over spill the boundaries of its narrative frame, so much so that it begins to resemble a disorganized encyclopedia, one that necessitates the use of another encyclopedia. It is as though Sarduy might have anticipated the spreading, virtual, web-like connections of the Internet. A twenty-first century reader, such as myself, will often refer to Wikipedia several times within the span of a single sentence. And with each search the text continues to expand; its virtual potentialities proliferate, for example: "Cobrita—que para ser breves, es una ventana de Tomar con dos patas."[42] For those unfamiliar with a "ventana de Tomar," a Google Image search will reveal a dizzyingly ornate window from a twelfth-century convent founded by Templar Knights in Portugal. "Para ser breves," this image of our diminutive, *Cobrita,* provides a visual counterpart to the text's accumulative composition and transmorphic figures: The Tomar window is framed by Gothic pinnacles, reliefs of vegetal, animal and choral motifs, a human head and set of hands, ropes in elaborate knots and sections of geometric shapes. All intricately carved, stylized and tightly spaced, the sculptures form repetitive, exuberant patterns.

As previous readers of *Cobra* have done, and in this way continuing a tradition, like a ritual invocation, I will list here some of the title's allusions: 1. An anagram for a group of experimental 1950s painters, (Appel, Alechinsky, Corneille, Jorn) from COpenhagen, BRussels and Amsterdam 2. Other anagrammatic possibilities are the Spanish verb "cobrar" 3. Barroco 4. Córdoba, Cuba 5. The name of an actress killed in a plane crash over Fujiyama 6. "The hypnotic snake that bites its own tail." 7. Octavio Paz's poem "La Boca Habla."[43] While each of these signals a particular aspect of the novel, my interest is in noting the multiplicity of meanings and directions that are conjured just at the title, before the novel has even "started." Like an elaborate knot of a Tomar window, or the dense consistency of a White Dwarf star, individual words and phrases in *Cobra* operate as concrescences of signification that dilate and expand the space of the novel.[44] Significantly, as González Echevarría has noted, the string C-O-B-R-A has infinite semantic potential:

> A computer study might reveal that the string C-O-B-R-A contains the phonic groups most often repeated in Western languages, perhaps in all languages: a sort of minus-zero degree where phonology turns in on itself, a point at which negations and oppositions which compose language cancel each other out: the non-origin of language.[45]

Perhaps not unlike the aesthetics of *horror vacui*—the meticulous and compulsive covering up of surfaces in fear of empty space—the polysemic nature of the title is meant to fill the vacuum of what González Echevarría calls the "non-origin of language" and later "an empty center" and "originary loss."[46] Other readers of *Cobra* have similarly reiterated this sense of absence. Considering that Sarduy himself describes his writing as a linguistic psychoanalysis,[47] *Cobra* has generated various Lacanian and poststructuralist readings. The text performs its own deconstruction and, as such, analysis of the novel, particularly by thinkers, such as Roland Barthes, Philippe Sollers, and Hélène Cixous,[48] result in poetic expositions, forming not so much interpretations of the text as continuations of its desires and metamorphoses. The title to Cixous's essay, "O C, o, b, r, a, b, a, r, o, c, o: A Text-Twister," is perhaps a literal example of this textual expansion. These material regenerations of the novel notwithstanding, the poststructuralist attention to the deferral, elision, and erasure in the production of meaning insists on an absence. Suzanne Levine, for example, writes, "[t]he text tells us that what is left after the recognition of the lack of a concrete center [. . .] are doublings and mirror images [. . .] rather than the objects themselves. [. . .] In Saussurean linguistics, they are signs minus sense or 'signifieds.'"[49] Following language's dialectics of negation—for example, to say that something is present is to also say it is not absent—and the correspondence between a sign and its signified, suggests that to destabilize this relationship, to make the sign nonsensical (or *minus* a signified) is to make it empty. This lacking is reiterated in the Lacanian formulation of the subject; its psychic structure is conceived as linguistic and, like the deferral of meaning, constituted in the desire for a lost object.[50] Accordingly, readers of *Cobra* have traced its heterogeneous and accumulative style back to an originary dispossession:[51] The protagonist's metamorphoses are driven by a desire for that which she is wanting, be that smaller feet, a divine body, or erotic ecstasy.

In my engagement with the novel I would like to slightly deviate from these readings, perhaps following another line of flight, another metamorphic desire of the text. Drawing from Barad's writing on Quantum Field Theory and its treatment of the void as virtual particles and a "fecund nothingness," I would like to reimagine what others have previously designated as a loss or an empty center as a plenitude of indeterminate materiality. Sarduy's own theoretical writings, in fact, support a rethinking of loss and emptiness. In an essay devoted to the metamorphic work of the transvestite, in which he cites Buddhism and Chinese theories of painting, Sarduy writes that instead of the full presence of god, man, or logos classical philosophy assumes, there is "*una vacuidad germinadora cuya metáfora y su simulación es la realidad visible* [. . .]. [El] estallido inicial no [es] de un átomo de hipermateria [. . .] sino de una pura no-presencia que se traviste en pura energía, engendrando lo visible con su simulacro" (his emphasis).[52] Although Sarduy posits a pure non-presence, the nothingness of which existence is birthed, "una vacuidad germinadora," is fecund and what we perceive as "realidad visible" is a transvestism of pure energy or, alternatively in the terms of QFT, virtual and infinitely transforming. Imagining a plenitude of indeterminate materiality where others have an empty center allows me to attend to other dynamics of the text, such as fields of becoming, constellations, assemblages and collectivities that do not reiterate subject formation—its constitution in opposition to an Other, self-knowledge, (mis)identification, or its splitting into many selves—and the negative dialectics of sign and signified. Returning to the string c-o-b-r-a, to its *lettericity*,[53] rather than point to its negations and oppositions, I suggest this graphic configuration appears like a string of malformed pearls one can touch, or at least trace the curvilinear lines of its graphemes on the page.[54]

Painting the Void as Full . . . of Drag, Dolls, and Toy Cats

At the opening lines of the novel we encounter our first act of transformation:

> Los encerraba en hormas desde que amanecía, les aplicaba compresas de alumbre, los castigaba con baños sucesivos de agua fría y caliente. Los forzó con mordazas; los sometió a mecánicas groseras. Fabricó, para meterlos, armaduras de alambre cuyos hilos acortaba, retorciéndolos con alicates; después de embadurnarlos de goma arábiga los rodeó con ligaduras: eran momias, niños de medallones florentinos.[55]

Corporeality comes to the fore in this passage in the verbs of enclosure, pressure, twisting, and binding, but the objects [Los] and subject of this punishment and submission remain unclear. Repeated every morning, like a ritual, these vulgar mechanics [mecánicas groseras] suggest perverse devices or even sadistic torture. At the end of the passage, *Los,* the object pronoun of these actions, a grammatical particle, are not *like* but *were* [eran] mummies and the children of Florentine medallions. Significantly, Sarduy does not give us an analogy. It would seem that the objects of these mechanics are at once an embalmed corpse and a lithograph, bandaged in strips of cloth and smeared in gum arabic: A viscous edible substance that was not only used by Egyptians to coat the bandages of mummies, but is also a key ingredient in traditional lithography, a mode of making medallions. We can consider "children" here as the multiple copies, the material and mechanical reproduction of lithographic printmaking. The materiality of the corpse and that of the lithograph is not inert matter, but alive, "eran . . . niños." In this opening passage, where subject and object remain indistinct, Sarduy entangles corporeality, mechanics, ritual, perversity, and art. Repeated later in the novel, the passage becomes a refrain, like the text's own ritual invocation. However, by the second encounter, the reader associates the "vulgar mechanics" to the protagonist's foot binding. "Cayó en el determinismo ortopédico."[56]

The Madame, a.k.a. la Madre, la Matrona, la Buscona, and la Señora—note the collectivity of names and roles—is the director of the show at the Lyrical Theater of the Dolls: "Aun allí seguía dirigiendo la mise-en-scène, el tráfico de tarimas y atuendos entre el espectáculo visible—donde ya cantaba la Cadillac—y el teatro generalizado en los sucesivos aposentos."[57] Between "el especáculo visible" and "el teatro generalizado," there is no unstaged or un-crafted scene. This sense of artifice is reiterated at the level of the writing. After the self-referential statement, "La escritura es el arte de la digresión," the narrator goes on to say, "Hablemos pues de un olor a hachís y a curry, de un basic english tropezante y de una musiquilla de baratijas. Esa ficha señalética es la del indio costumista."[58] Drawing on an orientalist stereotype, the reader is made aware that rather than referring to an outside knowable subject, this figuration is another sign within the tapestry of the text, a single plane that "el especáculo visible" and "el teatro generalizado" share.

Nevertheless, this artifice marks the skin. "El indio costumista" is also referred to as the Dermic Silversmith, "El orfebre dérmico":

> Iba pues decorando las divas con sus arabescos teta por teta, que éstas, por redondas y turgentes, más fáciles eran de ornar que los pródigos vientres y nalguitas boucherianas, rosa viejo con tendencia al desparramo. Desfilaban las divinidades roncas ante el inventor de alas de mariposa y allí permanecían estáticas, el tiempo de repasar sus canciones; aplicado, el miniaturista en vivo de las heladas reinas de grandes pies iba encubriendo la desnudez con orlas plateadas, jeroglíficos de ojos, arabescos y franjas de arcoíris, que según la inserción y el aguaje las adelgazaban o no; disimulaba de cada una las desventajas con volutas negras y subrayaba los encantos rodeándolos de círculos blancos. En las manos les escribía, con azafrán y bermellón, los textos de entrada a escena [. . .] La Señora las revisaba, les pegaba las pestañas y una etiqueta OK a cada una y les daba una nalgada y una pastilla de librium.[59]

The transformation of bodies occurs through artistic and illusionistic devices: "el aguaje las adelgazaban o no; disimulaba [. . .] y subrayaba." Arabesques reiterate the curvilinear lines of breasts, buttocks, and swollen bellies. And yet in this transformation, the nakedness of the bodies is at moments lost for the reader behind the description of "orlas plateadas, jeroglíficos de ojos, arabescos y franjas de arcoíris." Phrases, such as "el miniaturista en *vivo* de las *heladas* reinas" juxtapose and invert the lifelike and the inanimate; the suppleness of the bodies is contrasted to their static postures, "allí permanecían estáticas." The passage where "[l]a Señora las revisaba, les pegaba las pestañas y una etiqueta OK" evokes the image of dolls moving down a conveyor belt on an assembly line; whereas, the spank on the buttocks and the dose of Librium suggests these are bodies with corporeal and psychic vulnerabilities. The rusty pink, "con tendencia al desparramo," recalls the images from *Gestos* where ink runs outside its circumscribed boundaries. Using the same colors of henna tattoos, "azafrán y bermellón," "[e]n las manos les escribía [. . .] los textos de entrada a escena." Textuality here is produced not on an inert, flat, surface that passively receives the writing, but on one that is supple, porous, irregular, absorbent and curvilinear; textuality, moreover, is not only semiotic. At times tiny, consistent, and tightly spaced, its graphemes appear like a decorative nonrepresentational design. The trope of tattooing, of course, links art, skin, and pain, as suggested in the name Dermic Silversmith: "[T] anta nalguita rubensiana a su alrededor [. . .] intenta una pincelada y da un pellizco."[60]

Soon after the description of the paintings on the skins of the "dolls," the narrator brings us to another diegetic passage. What follows is a segment from the Dermic Silversmith's biographic background, which will later be dismissed as another fiction: "¡solo un tarado pudo tragarse la a todas luces apócrifa historieta [. . .]!"[61] Consequently, what constitutes the main narrative and that of other fictions or tableaux becomes indistinct.

> Un espejo abombado y otros doce más pequeños que lo rodeaban multiplicaron su imagen cuando entró con una sirvienta mofletuda en una casa de muros y puertas blancos que cerraban aldabones negros.
>
> Por las ventanas ojivales rondeles de vidrio opaco filtraban un día gris y húmedo. De un baúl sienés sobresalía un tapiz flamenco. Colgaban de las vigas arenques ahumados y racimos plateados de ajo. En una mesa había una balanza y una biblia abierta cuyas iniciales eran hipogrifos mordiéndose la cola, sirenas y harpías; entre las letras saltaban liebres. Junto al libro un reloj de arena. Reflejo de un vaso de vino, temblaba sobre el mantel una línea transparente y roja.

Like the curves of the "heladas reinas," our first surface here is a convex mirror whose image is multiplied in twelve smaller mirrors. What follows is a description of an interior whose contents recall those of a Dutch seventeenth-century painting with smoked herring and garlic hanging from the beams. Within this scenic arrangement there is another composition, the pages of a bible whose illuminated medieval script shows hippogriffs biting their tails, mermaids, and harpies. There is yet another still life embedded within the scene: a book, an hourglass, and a glass of wine whose reflection is "transparente y roja." In terms of narrative action, nothing happens. As readers we are presented with an image that fractures into other ones, producing an inventory of very disparate objects (e.g., mermaids, bibles, and garlic). Like the *horror vacui* composition of medieval European, Islamic, or Hindu art, Sarduy produces a multiplicity of images on a single plane. What action occurs is not at the level of the story but at the level of the writing, in the conjuring of images that transform from one to another in the imagination of the reader. Accordingly, the textual here—in the spatial work it demands of the reader to reconstruct the described scene—operates less like a narrative and more like a visual composition.

While Cobra might momentarily succumb to "el determinismo ortopédico," her cosmetic process before the drag show takes on a semi-religious discipline, something she endures for hours like a faithful devotee:

> Empezaba a transformarse a las seis para el espectáculo de las doce; en ese ritual llorante había que merecer cada ornamento: las pestañas postizas y la corona, los pigmentos, que no podían tocar los profanos, los lentes de contacto amarillos—ojos de tigre—; los polvos de las grandes motas blancas.[62]

False eyelashes, color contact lenses, pigments and powder—articles one might associate with fakeness, artifice, and illusion—are treated like the vestments and liturgical objects of a priest, "que no podían tocar los profanes." Except that unlike the theatrics of a Catholic mass, the ornamental here does not invoke a more substantive immateriality. The reflective surfaces of "mirror images," "what is left after the recognition of the lack of a concrete center,"[63] have depth; they are both sacred and profane. This paradox is reiterated in Sarduy's irreverent treatment of eastern religious and philosophical practices, references to which abound in the text: mosques, the Ganges River and Lotus Pose, to name a few. The iconography of the Buddha appears in one instance as a kitsch object: "No quedó Buda inflable, elefante de celuloide tamaño natural con dos arqueros en el lomo, seda, sari, raso, wash and wear indian silk ni electric sitar."[64] On the one hand, its mass-produced materials are a mark of its commercialization, of its iconography made trite and cliché. On the other hand, in its very syntheticness, the inflatable celluloid signals the Buddhist belief that the material world is but mere appearance, an illusion.

In the edited volume, *Materiality,* the anthropologist Daniel Miller begins by noting the relationship between the material and immaterial in many religious belief systems:

> For religions such as Buddhism and Hinduism, theology has been centered upon critique of materiality. At its simplest Hinduism, for example, rests upon the concept of *maya,* which proclaims the illusory nature of the material world. The aim of life is to transcend the apparently obvious: the stone we stub our toe against, or the body as the core of our sensuous existence. Truth comes from our apprehension that this is mere illusion. Nevertheless, paradoxically, material culture has been of considerable consequence as the means of this conviction.[65]

If all material and corporeal sensation is an illusion, then it stands to reason that art is no more illusory than everyday life. In this way we can better appreciate the novel's insistence on artifice and its interweaving of the organic and the synthetic, or the life-like and the seemingly inanimate. Thinking Buddhism with the science of QFT, we might consider the religion's insistence on the illusory as virtual particles, a state between being and non-being. Significantly, for Buddhism, as noted earlier via Sarduy's elaboration, the void is not an empty space of negativity as it is in traditional European thought, but instead a space that is generative with potential becomings,[66] and in this sense corresponds well with QFT's understanding of the void as indeterminate materiality. Surrounding the figure of Cobra, we find "gatos vivos y de peluche," "juguetes mecánicos" and the fleshy bodies that perform as "las muñecas."[67] I suggest these doublings do not cancel each other out, but rather signal to the non-essentializing *techne* and virtual becomings that make up a shared, vibrant materiality. Rather than transcend materiality, as most theologies would compel us to do, what we find in *Cobra* is a plane of immanence, one of paradox and indeterminism.

Returning to Cobra's cosmetic transformation, we also find a becoming-animal, invoked in the camouflaging of the color contacts, in the color of tiger-eyes. Rolando Pérez writes in his book *Severo Sarduy and the Neo-Baroque Image in the Visual Arts,*

> for Sarduy there is little or no difference between human transvestism and the kind of animal mimicry described by Roger Caillois, where certain insects mimic other insects, for no other reason than for their own non-teleological pleasure. In other words, the transvestite is not making some kind of statement about "X," but is instead, if one can put it this way, "communicating" through a logic of sensation.[68]

We might relate this unpurposive sensation to Barthes's notion of jouissance, in which our own subject positions are dissolved in the impossibility of self-identification with, or the extraction of knowable content from a text. Put differently, the bliss produced in *writerly* works takes us outside ourselves.[69] Whereas art has traditionally been conceived as the domain of the gods or Humankind, here the creative act of transformation, the ecstasy of writing, or the communication "through the logic of sensation," brings us closer to nonhuman animals.[70] Indeed, Sarduy's text does not elicit any kind of identification, but rather compels one to take an oblique or decentered (i.e., non-normative) perspective.[71] The perversity implied in the punishing and submissive "mecánicas groseras"[72] of Cobra's foot binding suggests that in creation, in the act of changing bodies into new form, there is a transgression of normative values, a disordering of an order as Sarduy's narrator states. And in this creative process, "en ese ritual llorante,"[73] there is also discomfort and pain. The novel's insistence on suffering in tandem with its subversion of the "natural" speaks to feminists' critiques of the super textualization in postmodernists' theory and "its utopian disregard for the lived relations of domination that ground the 'play' of arbitrary reading."[74] Let us recall Sarduy's statement about the somatic violence of language, "Practicar la literatura es una especie de transgresión muy grande, es una especie de amenaza muy grande para la seguridad simbólica de nosotros."[75] Language, after all, affects how bodies are distributed and spaced, made visible and invisible through identitory markers. When Sarduy's narrator describes Cobra as "desde los pies hasta el cuello es mujer; arriba su cuerpo se transforma en una especie de animal heráldico de hocico barroco,"[76] he is not only drawing upon the performativity of gender, but also that of species and its impact on the body; she is "maquillada con violencia."[77] Interestingly, when we move on to Roberto Fabelo's images we'll see that some of his hybrid figures wear wings tied to their torsos or beaks as helmets, as though performing species-drag.

Stages, Screens, Surfaces and Flipping the Channel

After a comical exchange of insults between the Madame and Pup (a.k.a. la Enana Blanca)—"frijol podrido," "desdentada trecemesina, alcahueta, bruja," "repugnantísima enana, aborto fétido," "gusarapo hediondo"—the former warns the latter, "prepárate una vez más para el cambio," and then using the imperative, "Vas a transformarte."[78] Since characters in the novel are not given a substantive form, be that in appearance or in psychic interiority, they transform for the reader in the very act of name-calling; that is, language acquires an incantatory effect. Having no stable image of Pup, the White Dwarf is transformed as we read "—Dios mío, ¡pero si es una lagartija!"[79] The change the Madame is threatening, however, is an agonizing process that will involve injecting Pup with snow (or possibly cocaine) to enlarge her. The passage leading up to her metamorphosis, and what I am particularly interested in, sets the stage:

> Rumor de aceitados aros metálicos deslizándose a lo largo de una varilla. Ábrense las cortinas de terciopelo púrpura: mi reducida pantallita cuca—rachienta se va agrandando . . . ya es una vasta superficie blanquísima, sutilmente curva. Sí, mi 16 mm blanco y negro—lo sé: en realidad carmelitoso y amarillento—, de bordes carcomidos, que interrumpían a cada rato números porosos, cabezas al revés y un tembleque de letras, se transforma en un Cinerama a todo Metro-color. Himnos estereofónicos. En la pantalla se va definiendo un paisaje.[80]

What follows are a series of disparate scenes that might correspond to those of classical and pop films, as though someone were flipping through channels on the television, whose screen and technology are described in the above passage. If we consider "una vasta superficie blanquísima" as a reference to a blank page (in addition to the surface of a White Dwarf star, a mound of snow, or a mound of cocaine), we might take this passage as an analogy of the text. Like a television screen, the virtual images that are conjured as we read appear on a single impenetrable plane. The surface of this plane—again like that of the convex mirror or bodies of the dolls—has a subtle curve [sutilmente curva], a distorting effect, and as such depth. While images transpire on its surface, this plane itself transforms from that of a stage with curtains to that of a 16 mm black and white TV and, finally, to that of a color Cinerama. Similarly, the plane of the text shifts; one notes, flipping from one page to the next, how its graphic body changes from paragraphs of prose to poetic arrangements, from a screenplay to disparate fragments, columns, or lists. Sarduy draws our attention not only to the page, the stage, the screen and its surface, but also to its very materiality, its deterioration, its becoming—"cuca—rachienta," "carmelitoso y amarillento," "de bordes carcomidos." Language is not simply an abstract, formal structure, but historically and geographically constituted; an organic/synthetic body that wears and tears, grows and transforms. As the sharing of sense, or of sense-making, language is in perpetual metamorphosis, infinitely engendering new bodies.[81]

As we saw with *Gestos,* Sarduy does not take his readers inside his characters but to a field of material encounters, from one sensuous exterior to another. With passages and scenarios that repeat themselves we are brought to do cartographic (as opposed to a penetrating) reading, marking its patterns, and interconnecting nodes. One such node is Cobra's sexual "conversion."[82] The character of Cadillac (a performer at the Lyrical Theater of the Dolls), who assists the Madame in the transformation of Pup, appears once again dressed as the elusive Dr. Ktazob, who will perform Cobra's "castration." This assemblage of figures—Madame, Pup, Cobra, with the assistance of Cadillac/Ktazob—form a network or algebraic formula in Cobra's transformation, "{Sra + Cobra (+/ =) Pup = (3/2)}."[83] The doctor/Cadillac, while smoking a Romeo y Julieta cigar (another nod to Cuba), insists that Cobra must be conscious during the operation otherwise she might not recognize herself in her new body.[84] One could consider this potential risk as the misidentification that occurs before the Lacanian Mirror, both a developmental stage [stade] as well as a performative one. To move forward with the operation without anesthesia, the doctor draws from math, the Sufi martyrs, whirling Dervishes, the logic of scapegoats, and devises a diagram in the shape of a diamond. This diamond-diagram, illustrated in the text, shows how the signs of pain will be transferred ["hay que disipar todo signo de dolor"][85] from Cobra to her diminutive double Pup, her residual excess: "No es más que tu desperdicio, tu residuo grosero [. . .] Tu excremento, tus senos falsos, ¡qué asco!: cuerpo de ti caído que ya no eres tú."[86] The projection of what one rejects in him or herself upon another is a process that psychoanalysts have identified in the constitution of one's subjectivity.[87] We might even say that in the deferral of one sign to another we are brought to the empty center of language and the subject's lost object. However, rather than treat "la conversión" as a developmental stage, as a self-determination, or even a misidentification—a process of individuation symbolized by the diamond—I suggest reading the diamond as a map, or a constellation, that expresses a cosubstantiallity, a shared enfleshment.[88] In Cobra's operation signs are not simply differed to other signs, but also have a physical impact on Pup's body; she writhes in pain. As readers of *Cobra* we are distributed along its networks, disoriented by its dense tapestry, brought into contact with other bodies in an *extimate* relationship: Sufi metaphysics, poststructuralism, algebra, psychoanalysis, and surgical procedures are made proximate within the space of the page but remain un-dialecticalizable. "La conversación" does not result in a fully actualized, autonomous, self-possessed Cobra, but in another complex configuration of figures—Tundra, Totem, Tigre, and Escorpión—changes in narrative voice and tone, and, as we shall see further ahead, an irreducible corporeality.

A Baroque Ecology

Decadence, lack of restraint, unremitting movement, excess and unmeasured expansiveness are some of the characteristics of a baroque aesthetic. These pejorative descriptors were reclaimed by Latin American thinkers, such as Alejo Carpentier, as expressing a counterhegemonic ethos against the self-contained, proportioned, and exclusive compositions of a classical aesthetic, associated with imperial and totalitarian systems.[89] In "The Baroque and the Marvelous Real," Carpentier illustrates the spatial mastery of these systems through three iconic buildings that stand in contradistinction to the baroque spirit:

> In the architecture of Versailles, the Escorial or the Parthenon, there is something very important, which is that empty spaces, naked spaces, spaces without ornamentation are in and of themselves as important as adorned spaces or the shafts of grooved columns. [. . .] Their boundaries [. . .] create a sort of geometrical harmony. [. . .] The construction [of all three buildings] is complemented by vacant space, by space without ornamentation whose beauty resides precisely in its circumscription [. . .] majestic beauty stripped of every superfluous element.[90]

Remembering that for the Roman architectural theorist Vitruvius (80–15 BC) a building stood for that most perfect creation, the human body, contemporary theorists of architecture argue that we perceive buildings in relationship to our own bodies, as stand-ins for our own psychic and corporeal structures.[91] After all, "experience in art and beauty strengthens the ego, if only because balance, pattern, harmony, welcome a composite whole."[92] Accordingly, the classical buildings Carpentier describes reflect an autonomous, independent ego-bound subject whose boundaries are clearly circumscribed against a vacant background. In juxtaposing these structures to the following passage describing the interior of Cobra's room, we might better appreciate what a baroque composition does to that most perfect creation:

> Un vaho verdoso, de alcanfor, emanaba del tugurio de Cobra, arabesco que se iba ensanchando hasta abrirse en una banda espiral, nebulosa, en un caracol que se expandía, de menta. Encerrados en frascos transparentes por todas partes retoñaban cepos, hojas anchas y granulosas, retorciéndose, pestilentes arbustos enanos, flores enfermas cuyos pétalos roían larvas diminutas y brillantes, helechos estrujados que en los pliegues albergaban huevecillos translúcidos, en multiplicación constante. De lo estilizado vegetal art nouveau el cubículo había pasado a la anarquía yerbera—buscaba sin tregua los zumos, el elixir de la reducción, el jugo que achica—. [. . .][93]
>
> Pronto comprendieron su presunción. El mal carcomía por dentro. Los invadió una erupción blanca, una escarcha que iba ascendiendo, sarna arborescente que formaba en los tobillos dibujos coptos. Flores palúdicas, naves perforadas: los pies de Cobra iban al caos.[94]

Cobra's "den" recalls a scientific lab or a medieval herbalist's workspace overrun by the specimens of biomorphic experimentations. Once again organic matter and artifice are intertwined. Vegetation morphs from the stylized designs of art nouveau to an undomesticated proliferation of greenery. The arabesques, spirals, and floral illustrations we saw painted on the bodies of the Dolls, are here the product of a superabundant organic life. "[L]a multiplicación constante," the sprouting, gnawing, and anarchy recall Barad's description of the ongoing reconfiguration of transmateriality, the undoing of this or that.[95] An indiscriminate regeneration of larvae, eggs, and foliage leaves no ground vacant. Not unlike the passage describing the interior of a room from the Dermic Silversmith's fictional backstory, or the paintings on the skins of the dolls, here we have another diegetic passage that leaves no space unadorned. Every clause produces another image, another composition. Meanwhile, the boundaries of the body are obfuscated, perforated, erupted, and invaded by foreign bodies: Cobra does not have sovereignty over her feet; they are taken over by a chaos that leaves its marks as Coptic drawings. Significantly, decay, sickness, and degeneration are part and parcel of creation. Against the empty center of poststructuralist thought, the vacuum of classical physics, the autonomous and independent structures of Renaissance compositions, what we have here is a plenitude of indeterminate materiality. Nothing appears isolated in the novel;

characters, ciphers, objects are always part of complex configurations. What Sarduy expresses through this aesthetic is a dense material ecology.

When Cobra eventually dies in the narrative, in "homenaje póstumo," we do not find the memorialization of a subject (nor the cause of death). While rituals are performed over the dead body, what is produced in the text is an engagement with its very corporeality. The decaying of the corpse is made viscerally palpable for the reader, "un tufillo grasiento y dulzón subía desde los depósitos inferiores:—la esponja de los intestinos abriéndose."[96] The same arboreal and floral designs that invaded her ankles reappear, "bajo la piel transparente se abrían minúsculas flores capilares, negras."[97] Recalling the opening of the novel where her bound feet "eran momias, niños de medallones florentinos,"[98] we now read that Cobra is both "embrión y momia."[99] Death and life cannot be disaggregated, especially in an ecology where "pestilentes arbustos" and "flores enfermas" are the place where "roían larvas diminutas y brillantes."[100] As such, death never belongs to anyone; finitude is communicated but death cannot be compartmentalized, sublated, and exchanged through the economy of sacrifice.

Exploring the textual and cartographic potentialities of the corpse, the section that follows is appropriately titled "Lección de anatomía":

> Estabas diagonal, amarillabas. Eras un puro peso, una madera unida, sin nudos, un objeto encontrado que los cuatro curiosos escrutaban.
>
> Te leían. Te señalaban. Confrontaban tu cuerpo con un cuerpo dibujado—un mapa del Hombre abierto—; enumeraban tus partes, nombraban tus visceras, te abrían los párpados—globos empañados—, tomaban notas, volvían la página.
>
> Junto a tus pies callosos, impregnados de azufre, como una partitura, se desplegaba un libro.
>
> Te hundían en la carne la punta de los dedos: quedaban las depresiones de las yemas, las ranuras de las uñas: eras de cera, de papel, de mármol blando, de arcilla.
>
> Con un bisturí te cortaron las muñecas; te apretaron el brazo con ligaduras, desde el hombro. Por la herida brotó una pasta negra que recogieron en un cofrecillo. En otros dos conservaron de tu orine y tu excremento.
>
> Esos tres residuos, disueltos en vino, rociaron el banquete funerario.[101]

In the second half of this chapter, we'll see what Roberto Fabelo does to that very "cuerpo dibujado" (anatomical illustration) with which Cobra's body is confronted, and its presumptions of being "un mapa del Hombre *abierto*" (my emphasis). If anatomy texts are objective, addressed to no one specifically except the medical student, this "Lección de anatomía" is notably different; narrated in second person, it is addressed to you. It is your body that is being read and taxonomized according to the representation of a so-called human physiognomy, "Te leían. Te señalaban." And yet, your yellowing diagonal corpse would resist such interpretations; it is "puro peso," or dead weight as the English idiom goes, an obstinate impenetrable materiality: "una madera unida." Against the map of "el Hombre abierto," your body presents another text, "se desplegaba un libro." Nevertheless, this text that is your body is meat, "Te hundían en la carne la punta de los dedos." And the act of pointing and identifying has effects on the body, "quedaban las depresiones de las yemas": the other's touch leaves its marks. The phrase "eras de cera, de papel, de mármol blando, de arcilla," again links art and the corporeal, creation and death. Your body might be read, but there is always an excess of body. From these residues, the blackened blood, excrement, and urine, they get drunk, "disueltos en vino, rociaron el banquete funerario." Were we to read Cobra's corpse as an analogy for the body of the novel, Sarduy here brings our attention to our imposing other representations and structures of thought onto it, and how the text will always be in excess and irreducible to these structures.

Considering that what Sarduy has presented us in *Cobra* is a series of visual tableaux whose transitions are metamorphic, rather than a chronological unfolding of plot, and considering his explicit allusions to art historical works, turning now to Roberto Fabelo's compositions of hybrid bodies is in many ways a continuation along the same plane. If Sarduy embedded Cuban icons within a web that is transhistorical and transcultural, Fabelo will similarly make references to Cuban art history—conch shells, roosters, full-bodied nudes, vibrant color palettes, and baroque compositions—entangled and impossible to disaggregate from a shared materiality that exceeds Cuban identity markers. Jumping from the publication of *Cobra* in 1972 to the 2010s of Fabelo's images, what becomes urgent is a planetary concern, environmental disaster, and the threat of a nuclear annihilation. Our material and territorial interdependence, expressed in Sarduy's dense stylized ecologies and complex configurations, are in Fabelo's work made explicit through human and animal compositions and its allusions to the environment.

Animals and Art

In *The Postmodern Animal* (2000), the British art historian Steve Baker observes a reemergence of animal bodies in contemporary art after a long absence in the early and mid-twentieth century. Whereas modernist artists might have abstained from representing animals in order to avoid referential images that draw the viewer's attention away from the formalistic aspects of their work, animals now populate the work of contemporary artists, many of whom aim at making their singular bodies present in a literal or "obstinate thereness."[102] Whether this aim stems from a political commitment to animal welfare or the desire to undermine anthropocentric constructs, Baker takes "obstinate thereness" as a starting point for mapping an ethics of engagement with animal bodies in visual art. Looking at various artists that recycle the bodies of taxidermied animals, producing morphologically incorrect forms or hybrid species—as in a piece from a series titled *Misfit* by Thomas Grünfeld where bat wings were fixed upon the body of a fawn—Baker formulates his notion of the postmodern animal as "botched taxidermy."[103] This practice results in "messy confrontations" and "new baffling whole[s]" through the deliberate use of "wrong" materials and clumsy suturing.[104] The smooth bodies of professional taxidermied animals acquire a "tattiness" that indicates "something went wrong." Their botched appearances not only disrupt species identities but also, as physical objects that spatially incorporate the body of the viewer, insist on a proximity to the animal body without the pretense of expertise.[105]

In a series of ink drawings over the yellowed pages of a nineteenth-century medical encyclopedia containing illustrations of human anatomy, Fabelo produces a catalogue of human figures displaying zoological physiognomies in a variety of ways: As an integral part of the body, like a reptile spine or a set of insect eyes; sometimes as a worn accessory like a bird beak helmet or feathered wings tied to a torso; and, in other instances, simply the stacking and overlapping of farm animals over a human head (see fig. 4). The assemblage of human and animal anatomies exhibited in these drawings recalls the hybrid morphologies that Baker identifies as botched taxidermy. Interestingly, the material source of a nineteenth-century anatomy text like that of a taxidermy piece is necessarily a corpse. Whereas the biologist dissects the body to display its interior, the taxidermist empties and seals the body in order to preserve its exterior. Both Roberto Fabelo and Thomas Grünfeld recycle and tamper with materials—encyclopedias and hunting trophies—that are emblematic of authority and power. We might also consider the instrumentalization of bodies their artwork alerts us to as indicative of a *necropolitics,* in which sovereignty (exercised by the hunter) and absolute knowledge (produced by the anatomist) are expressed through the work of death.[106] In his account of the material destruction of populations, Achille Mbembe argues that the calculus and compartmentalization of modernizing projects are not so much guided by reason as the need to constitute the limits between those who must live and those who must die.[107]

There are, however, significant differences between Fabelo's work and that of the various artists Steve Baker studies as exemplary visual engagements with animals. Significantly, Fabelo's images would seem to fail the criteria of "obstinate thereness." There are no messy confrontations or clumsy arrangements, but instead we are lured by the drawings' masterful skill and beautiful compositions. Monstrous as its iconography may be at times, we admire its statuesque nude torsos, its floral ornamental designs, the texture and quality of its lines, and the seamless integration of its mismatched parts. In *Sin título,* a giant sewing needle or skewer both pierces through the figure of a body and divides the space of the composition in equal halves. Fabelo's black ink drawing of a nude human body in a fetal position, anatomically well proportioned, volumetric and muscular, wears a conch shell on its head—its geometric spirals are visually seductive and reiterate the curvilinear lines of the body—extending from its spine we see a long dorsal fin, like that of a Marlin, and in the place of feet a caudal fin. The sharp points of the dorsal fin are both uniform and irregular; their rhythmic repetition running along the beautifully arched back produces another pleasurable pattern for the eyes. Drawn over a page from the medical text devoted to cerebral veins, Fabelo has not only superimposed his ink figure over the original illustration, but integrated it in such a way that the cerebral veins now run along the length of the figure's spine and its skin appears translucent, revealing subtle muscles and veins that lie beneath its surface. The image is attractive; Fabelo is well skilled in creating the illusion of a three-dimensional body and a composition that delights the eyes. But this alluring image is also violent. Struck through by a sharp needle, the figure might serve as a specimen of medical inquiry, a nineteenth-century cabinet curiosity, or meat prepared to be grilled.

Considering their expert execution, soliciting aesthetic contemplation, we might ask if their morphological transgressions remain at the safe distance of pure fantasy or if they have the potential to unsettle anthropocentric notions. Put differently, can his figures be easily reduced to psychic

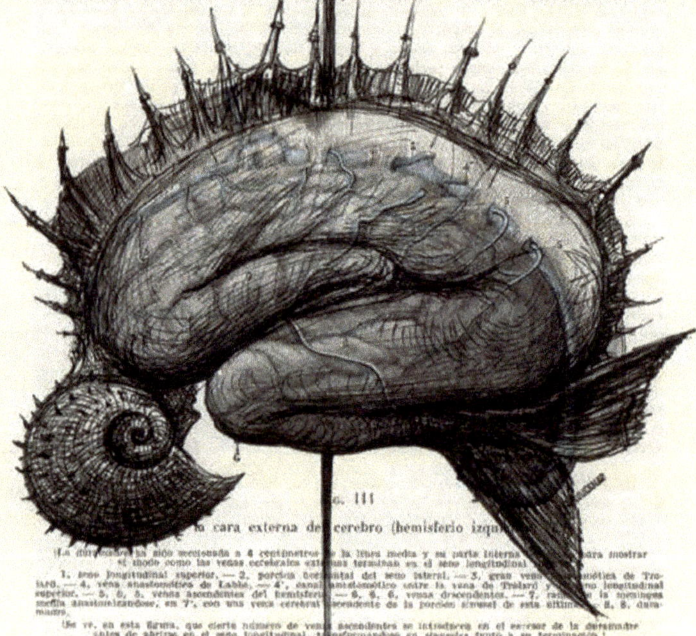

Figure 3. *Sin título,* 2014, by Roberto Fabelo, ink on print paper, 25 × 15 cm. Courtesy of the artist.

archetypes in a human-centered drama or do they evade a hermeneutic decoding and, in so doing, uproot our sense of the real and empirical in the daylight of consciousness? Given that for Baker so much of the undermining of "the secure sense of the human" at work in botched taxidermy is contingent on a display of inexpertise and an assault of the viewer's sensibilities,[108] I'm interested in how Fabelo's images may offer alternative ways of disrupting identitarian and hierarchal thinking. Throughout the trajectory of his work, he has demonstrated a sustained attention to environmental themes and human-animal compositions. Following Gregory Bateson's lead, let us pose the question: "What sort of correction in the direction of wisdom [or an ecology of the mind] would be achieved by creating or viewing this work of art?"[109]

Thinking Ecologically

In *Metamorphoses: Towards a Materialist Theory of Becoming,* Rosi Braidotti takes to task conservative psychoanalytic interpretations in which the figures of animals, be that in dreams or the literary imagination, are treated as iconographic substitutes within a patriarchal narrative. In theory, the unlocking of hidden meaning through the use of a master code will lead to the patient's psychic resolution and a well-formed subjectivity. Nonhuman creatures and uncivilized behavior remain just that, while the ontological border crossings in imaginative metamorphic processes—epitomized by figures such as the wolf-man or the vampire—are pathologized and treated as cautionary tales.[110] In referencing these interpretive strategies, Braidotti makes evident that much of a work's transgressive potential lies in the approach of the reader. Rather than assuming the expert knowledge of the analyst who can penetrate the meaning behind Fabelo's figures, and rather than treating his figures as figurative stand-ins,[111] following Braidotti's lead, I will adopt a cartographic approach, not unlike my readings of *Cobra.* In privileging "the organization of the multiple elements" over a semiological reading, we find a "web of interconnections" in Fabelo's two-dimensional planes.[112] This is an approach that does not focus its attention so much on content as it does on style, in an effort to bring an ecology in Fabelo's work to the foreground of our analysis. In a chapter titled "Style, Grace, and Information in Primitive Art," in his *Steps Towards an Ecology of Mind,* Bateson argues that form and pattern in art objects—the stuff of context and relationships—reflect a "larger patterned universe."[113] For him, data is never simply "raw," but always embedded in complex interactive systems.[114]

Since skill, as Bateson explains, necessarily involves large components of an unconscious or a Zen-like process, "art becomes in this sense an exercise in communicating about the species of unconscious."[115] Bateson's interest in art—or for that matter poetry over prose—is its relation to a different form of knowing that produces involuntary and irreducible meanings, dislocating the central authority of the individual subject. Because consciousness or "mere purposive rationality" tends to compartmentalize and address issues in an isolated manner, the result is "necessarily pathogenic and destructive of life."[116] In a powerful statement, Bateson writes, "unaided consciousness," that is, unaided by art, poetry, or dreams, "must always tend toward hate" and "[the] extermina[tion of] the other fellow."[117] Art, poetry, dreams, by contrast, bring to the fore connections and potentialities that are imperceptible to dominant modes of seeing and, in so doing, create the possibility for unconventionalized forms of relating. "The consummate skill of the draftsman validates the artist's message about his relationship to the animal—his empathy."[118] Grace, as that exhibited in artistic skill, or the unselfconscious movement we associate with animals, is the result of psychic integration, an overall wisdom that recognizes "interlocking circuits."[119]

Making a similar case about the limiting and violent aspects of how consciousness operates, Braidotti writes:

> [The] potency of Life is experienced as "other" by a mind that cannot do anything else but fold upon itself and go on patrolling its own constitutive elements as if it were in charge of them. This inner inversion by negative passions is a deeply-seated, uneasy form of mild schizophrenia, which we gloriously call "consciousness."[120]

Again not unlike Bateson, for her "Artists have crowded into this in-between area [of mind-body dualism], offering a number of interconnections," and she draws a parallel between artists and animals: "Like artists, animals mark their territory physically, by colour, sound or marking/framing."[121] We could consider these marks—the buzz of an insect, a cat's bodily fluids, or the howl of a wolf—as the intersection between *bios,* discursive or intelligent life, and *zoē,* all matter of life that exceeds discourse. Braidotti writes, "In the process of recognizing, coding and coping they transcend their sheer animality, joining up with the human in the effort of expressing, inhabiting and protecting their territory."[122] Imagining a posthuman "bio-centered egalitarianism," Braidotti not only seeks to unfix the categories of human-*bios* and animal-*zoē,* but also to recognize an intimately shared materiality that is lacking in negatives and therefore un-dialectical. We might also consider here Barad's notion of the void, as a field of indeterminate materiality that does not allow for a logic of antagonisms on which dialectics relies. Working from various Deleuzian concepts, Braidotti counters the ego-bound human with the notion of philosophical nomadism that considers animals' "attachment and interdependence on a territory" as "a model of radical immanence that needs to be revalued."[123] What Braidotti and Bateson both offer us is an analysis of art where becoming-animal, as opposed to a transcendental human spirit, is the source of creativity. Moreover, this becoming-animal, that is, the unself-conscious state of grace (Bateson) and an attachment and interdependence on a territory (Braidotti), provides an ethical alternative to the destructive forces of the ego-bound subject. It is useful to recall here Achille Mbembe's linking of subject formation to a necropolitics. Following Hegel, Mbembe writes,

> [T]he human being truly *becomes a subject*—that is, separated from the animal—in the struggle and the work through which he or she confronts death (understood as the violence of negativity). It is through this confrontation with death that he or she is cast into the incessant movement of history. Becoming subject therefore supposes upholding the work of death.[124]

Becoming-subject, Mbembe elaborates, entails a negation of nature, in which the human reduces nature to a material resource for his or her own needs. The negation of nature, or of the animal, achieves its fullest expression in the conscious decision to risk one's own life, so that "human death is essentially voluntary."[125] As such, death is attributed meaning and purpose; it operates within an economy (symbolically and/or materially) and can therefore be condoned.

Indeed, the work of thinking ecologically, that is, beyond categorical and exclusionary frames that have justified the extermination of different life forms, requires a move away from the privileged interiority of the Subject. It would require a move toward material surfaces, as Ron Broglio has argued, "deflat[ing] both cultural scaffolding of metaphor and truth by returning thought to the site where bodies meet."[126] In a quote that expresses a dislocation of meaning and agency from the subject to the material, Roberto Fabelo explains in response to one critic's reading of his drawings as poetic, "What you call poetry is an attraction that certain media have; they have their own memory, and all you do is intervene in that existence, in that memory."[127] Following Bateson, we might describe Fabelo's interventions in the pages of a medical encyclopedia as art coming to the aid of purposive rationality and, in so doing, an art that supplements and, significantly, challenges the hegemony of a necropolitics.[128] Fabelo further elaborates,

> The anatomy book pages are attractive in and of themselves. They contain solutions, tremendous creativity [. . .] I drew on top of those images, creating a new one, and also using some text as titles. Anatomical terms that, when decontextualized, when taken out of the sentence or of the book itself, the specific description, become poetry. It's a little game.[129]

This game, as we shall see, is one that exposes modes of knowledge production that presume unmediated, transparent access to the "natural word" as no less conventionalized than other cultural practices.

The Tricks of Illusionism

The title to one of Fabelo's drawings, taken from the medical text, *El antro está excavado* (The antrum is excavated), calls to mind the work of the anatomist who, after cutting a body open and revealing its interiority, dissects and identifies parts. It is a science of penetration and taxonomy. Turning our attention to the intervened page, perhaps what is most dynamic about this image is the integration of the minute, precise, uniform incisions of the text's original engravings and Fabelo's sketchy, gestural cross-hatching. Page sixty-seven, with section title "PARADES CRANEALES" (Cranial walls), appears to have been torn from the book's binding along the left edge of the paper. A fragment of a sentence, "el antro está excavado," is underlined, marking the place from where Fabelo lifted his title. The passage that remains un-obfuscated by his repetitive and irregular black ink lines begins with "Su *forma*" (its form) and goes on to describe an oval, vertical shape with numerous orifices and cavities. Removed from its medical context, we might read this passage as a formalistic analysis of an artistic rendering, rather than the scientific observation of an organ. Still visible is the engraver's name, S. Dupret, printed diagonally alongside each of four illustrations. However, recovering S. Dupret's original drawings from Fabelo's becomes a difficult, if not impossible, endeavor. While the quality of their marks is no doubt distinct, Fabelo has so effectively merged his lines with those of the engraver that the illustrations of the cranial walls have expanded and metamorphosed into something else altogether. Four busts, viewed in profile, emerge from the page like sculptures, modeled volumetrically in classical chiaroscuro. What anatomic parts the original illustration described are now illegible. Tissue, capillaries, cavities, muscles, bone, and cartilage have been transformed into headpieces with birds' eyes and beaks over two of the busts. On a third bust, the biological material has been outlined as a bird and the backside of a pig overlapping the face. And on a fourth, the original illustration that appears to sit over the bust's head remains unaltered and, as such, an unidentifiable organic fragment. Following Gilles Deleuze and Félix Guattari, I suggest Fabelo has changed the coordinates on this plane, moving from a molar to a molecular perspective. These engraved illustrations that had an instructional function are now aesthetic material; juxtaposed to Fabelo's dramatically gradated bodies they appear as two-dimensional designs. The body parts that had been cut open and laid flat to provide us with a maximal vantage point from which to view "nature,"[130] to penetrate its exterior and see inside, are now another material surface on the page. Deterritorialized, like the fragment of text that serves as its title, these medical illustrations, "un mapa del Hombre abierto,"[131] are made poetic.

The light and dark gradations produced through Fabelo's cross-hatching and to a lesser degree the small incisions of the text's engraver are techniques that were refined during the Renaissance to produce the illusion of three-dimensionality. Founded on the notion of Euclidean geometric perceptual fields in which the eye, through a single-point perspective, can penetrate, discover, and measure space, rendering what lies within that field knowable, these techniques assumed inherent and universal biological ways of seeing.[132] Whether illusionism was used to produce a landscape on a painted canvas or a botanical illustration in an encyclopedia, both artist and scientist presumed a transparent representation of the natural world. In poeticizing this encyclopedic text, and in juxtaposing similar and yet different forms of representation, Fabelo demonstrates how these are in fact conventionalized modes that produce knowledge rather than display raw data. Given that these are the tools that have been used to produce taxonomies and species identities, we can say that Fabelo unsettles the foundations of these categories. This unsettling is all the more significant when we consider the historical privileging of sight as an exclusively human faculty, whereas nonhuman animals have been relegated to the dominion of other senses. Fabelo, in effect, provincializes vision and situates its perspective alongside other senses in order to counter its presumed transcendental view.[133]

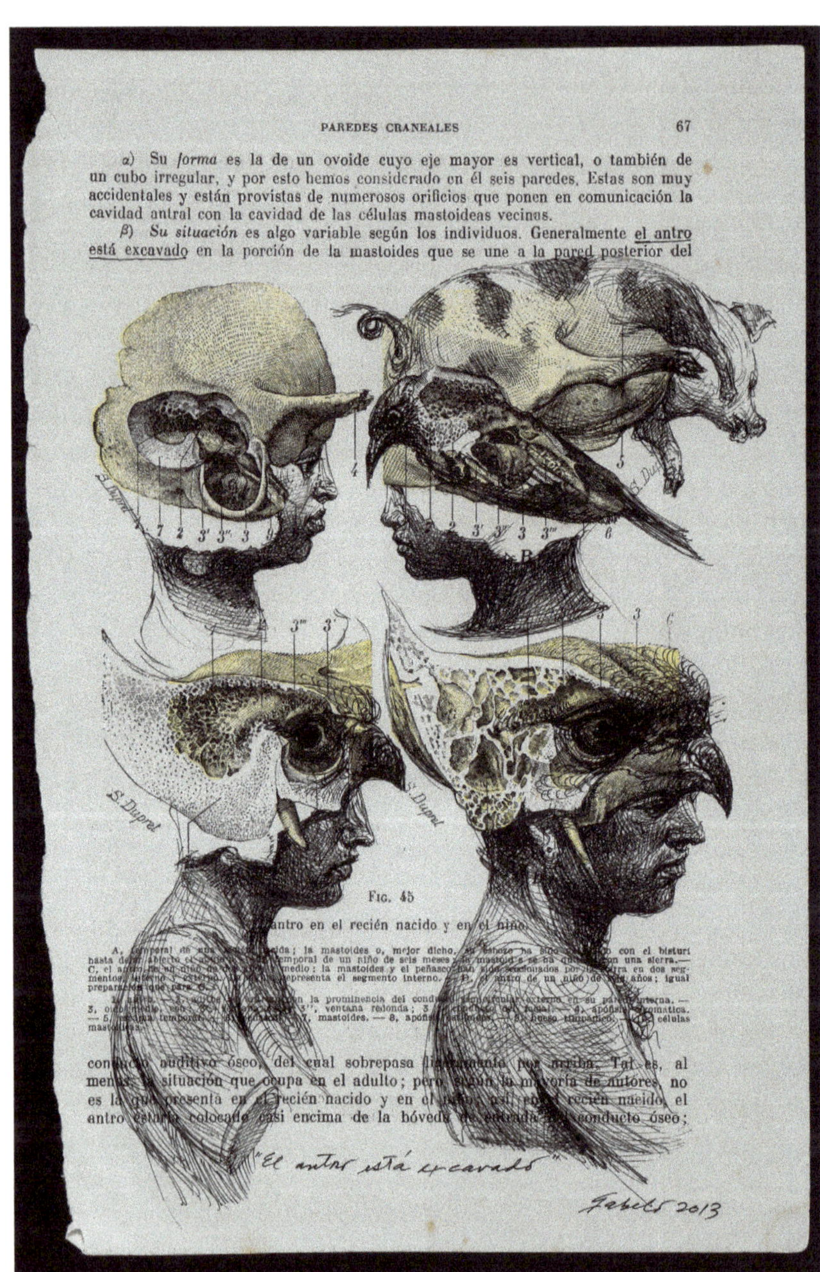

Figure 4. *El antro está excavado,* 2013, by Roberto Fabelo, ink on print paper, 25 × 15 cm. Courtesy of the artist.

Returning to the drawing's title, *El antro está excavado,* as a cavity, whose contents have been exposed to the light of day, calls to mind Plato's cave. In his essay "Corpus," Nancy writes,

> The body was born in Plato's cave, or rather it was conceived and shaped in the form of the cave: as a prison or a tomb of the soul, and the body was thought *from the inside,* as buried darkness into which light only penetrates in the form of reflections [. . .] This body is first an interiority dedicated to images, and to the knowledge of those images; it is the inside of representation [. . .] (author's emphasis).[134]

Nancy follows this line of thought further stating: "[T]he philosophical-theological *corpus* of the body is still supported by the spine of *mimesis,* of representation, and of the sign" (author's emphasis).[135] While the philosophical and biological caves may be at odds with each other, certainly technologies of representation and the relationship between seeing inside and the acquisition of knowledge are operative in both. As I have shown, Fabelo undermines the demonstrative pretensions of signs and mimesis; collapsing inside and outside, the body is rendered as surface. In fact, one could say Fabelo draws us toward his images through the illusion of receding space, seducing us with volumetric and sculptural bodies, only to effectively bring us to an impenetrable materiality.

Silk and Immanence

In a drawing that departs from the series' characteristic sculptural figures, *Sobre la cara* (On the face) shows a frontal view of a disembodied face. With disproportionately large eyes, a spiked collar, and the figure of a female nude emerging from the center of the forehead, the overlapping drawing transforms the text's scientific engraving into a surrealist composition with inexhaustible symbolic potential. While the bottom portion of the face is depicted through black ink cross-hatching, modeling a soft cherubic face that recalls those of Renaissance paintings, the top portion is painted over an anatomical illustration that depicts the intersection of various veins and capillaries that lie beneath the surface of the face. In this radical juxtaposition between the top and bottom half of the image, we can see the overlapping of *bios,* as in facial identity, and *zoē,* the indistinguishable stuff of life. In fact, if we look across this series of drawings in which both animal and human figures seem to share the same biological material,

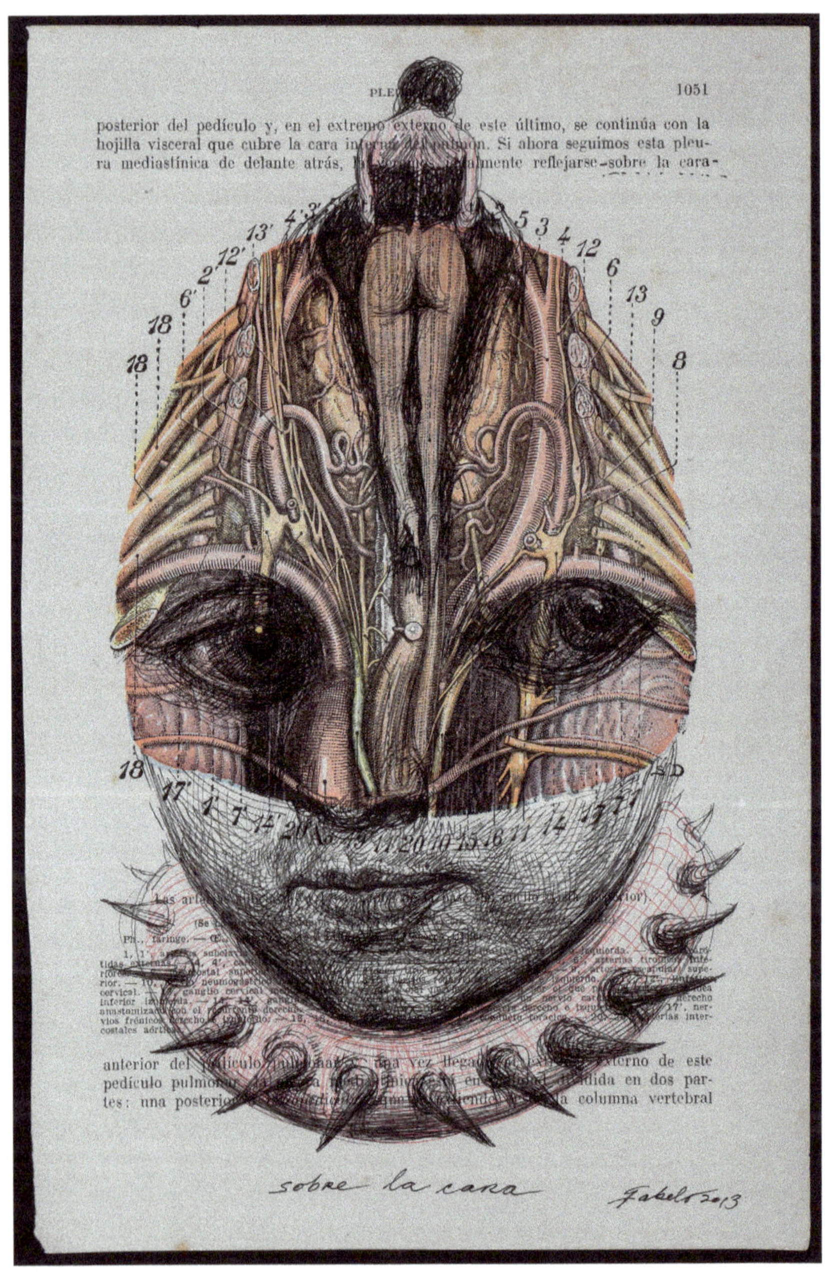

Figure 5. *Sobre la cara,* 2013, by Roberto Fabelo, ink on print paper, 25 × 15 cm. Courtesy of the artist.

it is as though Fabelo were exposing the pulsating *zoē* that runs through all species, as a web of interconnections.

This shared biological material is made even more explicit in a series of paintings where we find bodies brimming the tops of cauldrons and stacked on barbecue skewers. Human flesh as edible meat becomes a trope throughout Fabelo's work.[136] In *Perla*, an oil painting on canvas displaying a color palette of warm pinks and cool purples, blues, and grays, the viewer's perspective looks down upon a heap of nude female torsos and marine anatomies, over-spilling a deep metal cooking pot. Conch shells, squid tentacles, long dorsal and caudal fins, sharp spikes and claws extend from these voluptuous human-sea creatures. In this hearty stew of cold and warm-blooded animals, Fabelo's impasto and impressionistic application of paint heightens the fleshiness/meatiness of human bodies. Turning back to his ink drawings, we can similarly observe a becoming-animal not just on an iconographic level, as is suggested by the assemblage of trans-species figures but, especially, on the level of its organizational makeup, in the "restless, agitated, [and] repetitive"[137] quality of his lines. After all, for Deleuze and Guattari it is "through style that one becomes an animal."[138] They write:

> To become animal is to participate in movement, to stake out the path of escape in all its positivity, to cross a threshold, to reach a continuum of intensities that are valuable only in themselves, to find a world of pure intensities where all forms come undone, as do all the significations, signifiers, and signifieds, to the benefit of an unformed matter of deterritorialized flux, of nonsignifying signs.[139]

An essentially creative process, becoming "refers to the discontinuous regularity which marks the continuous present of energetic flows."[140] Indeed, this energy is not only expressed in the repetitive and dynamic quality of Fabelo's lines, but also in their interweaving with and contagion of the encyclopedia's text and engravings. Making the encyclopedia dysfunctional, Fabelo brings biology, chiaroscuro, medical terminology, cross-hatching, humans, birds, and pigs to the surface of the page; they are in effect collapsed from their cultural scaffolding to a plane of immanence. Overall, what we observe is overflowing and irreducible visual information that does not lend itself to an indexical reading.

This plane of immanence, or impenetrable materiality, becomes all the more evident when we turn to a series of large acrylic paintings that Fabelo made over embroidered silk. In his characteristic chiaroscuro,

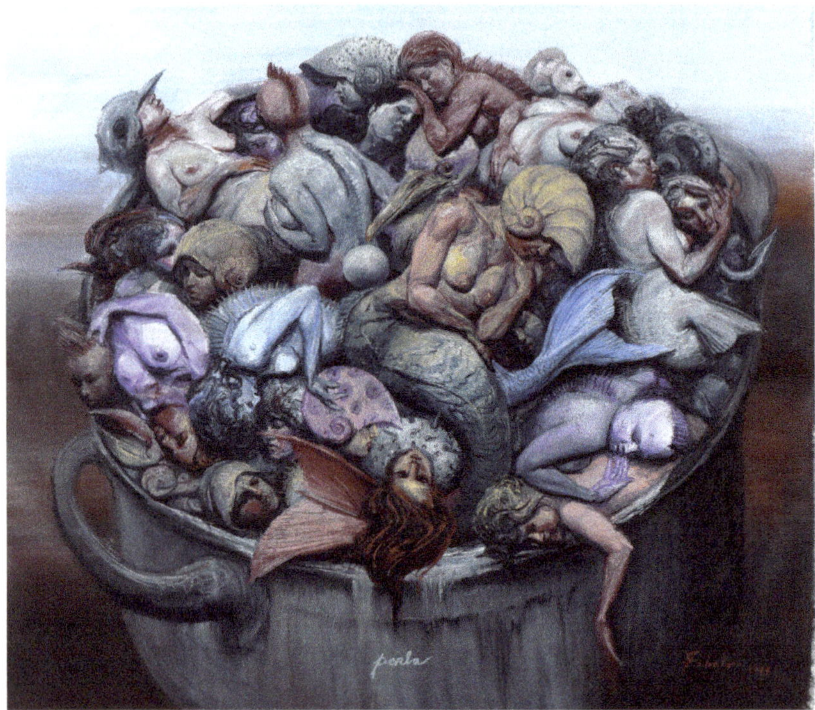

Figure 6. *Perla,* 2014, by Roberto Fabelo, oil on canvas, 210 × 230 cm. Courtesy of the artist.

convincingly three-dimensional female nudes emerge from a solid color background. Yet despite its very skillful volumetric modeling, the viewer is forced to reckon with its two-dimensionality. We are drawn to the silk fabric and the texture of its embroidery. The stitched ornamental floral patterns (like the "minúsculas flores capilares" we saw on the body of Cobra), both an aesthetic and a craft that has historically been associated with women, populate the surface of the painting, and break its perspectival illusion, that masculine gendered technology linked to mathematics and the so-called natural sciences. Instead, Fabelo's repurposing of the aged silk, not unlike the encyclopedia, brings us to a depth at the surface. (Let us recall here the skin of the "dolls," the curvilinear screen of the television, or the convex mirrors in Sarduy's *Cobra.*) The texture of the embroidered silk and the virtual memory it holds produce a depth that can only be sensed through touch or, as Deleuze might say, transmitted through sensation and the nervous system.[141]

Insects and Art

While most of these paintings depict full-bodied statuesque figures, in keeping with *Sobre la cara,* I'd like to turn to another disembodied face. *Meditación de Remedios* shows a lovely feminine face with full, heart-shaped lips and a delicate cleft chin. Her perfectly oval head is a model of symmetry and proportion, accentuated by dramatic lighting that casts a dark shadow, partitioning the face in equal halves. With her eyes turned to the left in a quiet, pensive stare, the figure seems unaware of, or unconcerned by, the swarm of flies that frame her head in the place of hair. The image is unquestionably beautiful, luring, and attractive and yet the idea of a swarm of flies covering one's face is repulsive. The flies are distributed in a way that works with the casting of lights and darks, helping model the three-dimensionality of the face so that the flies also operate as marks or brush strokes that when seen from very close—as one might, drawn to the gold sheen of the silk and its raised embroidery—become imperceptible, even ugly dark smudges. In other words, the artistic process and the figure of the fly are intertwined. As Braidotti argues,

> [Insect life] dwells between different states of in-between-ness, arousing the same spasmodic reactions in humans as the monstrous, the sacred, the alien. This is a reaction of simultaneous attraction and repulsion, disgust and desire. They pose the question of radical otherness not in metaphorical but in bio-morphic terms, that is to say as a metamorphosis of the sensory and cognitive apparatus.[142]

Looking through the trajectory of Fabelo's work, insects take on a predominant role. The simultaneity of attraction and repulsion is one that he seems to draw from very purposefully as noted above. And while part of the appeal is undoubtedly its unassimilable difference and metamorphic potential, Fabelo's insects also seem to express an anxiety that emerges from the nuclear imaginary. In an earlier installation titled *Mundos,* one of five suspended spheres was made of 17,000 cockroaches. One critic, reminding us that cockroaches are believed to be the only species to survive an atomic holocaust, describes the installation "as a reflection about the crisis that threatens the planet."[143]

In 2009 for the Havana Biennial, Fabelo produced another large-scale sculptural project involving the body of insects. Over the exterior walls of the Museo Nacional de Bellas Artes, he installed massive bronze sculptures of roaches displaying human heads. Each sculpture, rendered in detail, was executed with maximum fidelity to the roach's body (as well as its human face) and, I suspect, employing all of Fabelo's skills and resources. I point this out because large-scale sculptures using a material such as bronze have historically been reserved for the depiction of national heroes. I don't mean to suggest that the roaches are necessarily being revered (although that is possible to an extent), but rather to indicate an inversion of values, as well as scale. Titled *Sobrevivientes,* the piece has been described as "giant mutant roaches" that result from "the aftermath of a nuclear war or prolonged environmental pollution."[144] Interestingly, in an interview regarding the installation, Fabelo explains that the piece is a "reference to today's world where man in some form or another is surviving."[145] Provoking us to consider the ways in which we live in the shadow of nuclear objects' future effects, or what Gaby Schwab has recently called a "haunting from the future,"[146] Fabelo further elaborates that the installation is also an allusion to the threat of disappearance and "that here, in this piece, we do not know if it is the roach that turns into man or the other way around."[147]

It is not surprising to find allusions to the effects of a nuclear disaster and more generally to the theme of survival when we consider that so much of the Cuban state's *período especial* (Special Period in Time of Peace) rhetoric relied on evoking the threats of the Cold War era and the Missile Crisis to justify its inability to provide citizens with basic needs after the loss of Soviet subsidies in the 1990s.[148] To appreciate the political implications of Fabelo's roaches within a specifically Cuban context, it helps to take a look at Havana's topography. In the Plaza de la Revolución, on the facade of the Ministerio del Interior, another national building about five kilometers away from the Museo Nacional, we find a sculptural mural of Che Guevara. Made out of iron, the massive silhouette of the national hero's face, fitted to cover the entire sidewall of the concrete building, replicates Alberto Korda's now well-recognized 1960 photograph. Underneath the silhouette, we read the words "Hasta la Victoria Siempre" (Always toward Victory). While Che's mural was installed in 1995, a second similarly styled mural on an adjacent telecommunications building was added of Camilo Cienfuegos (another youthful martyr of the Revolution) in 2009, incidentally, the same year Fabelo's roaches were installed on the facade of the Museo. The images of Che and Camilo are ubiquitous throughout the country and have come to represent an aspired national subjectivity. They are the models of *el hombre nuevo,* the Revolution's messianic promise of a new generation of men whose sense of civic obligation would surpass the pursuit of pleasure.[149]

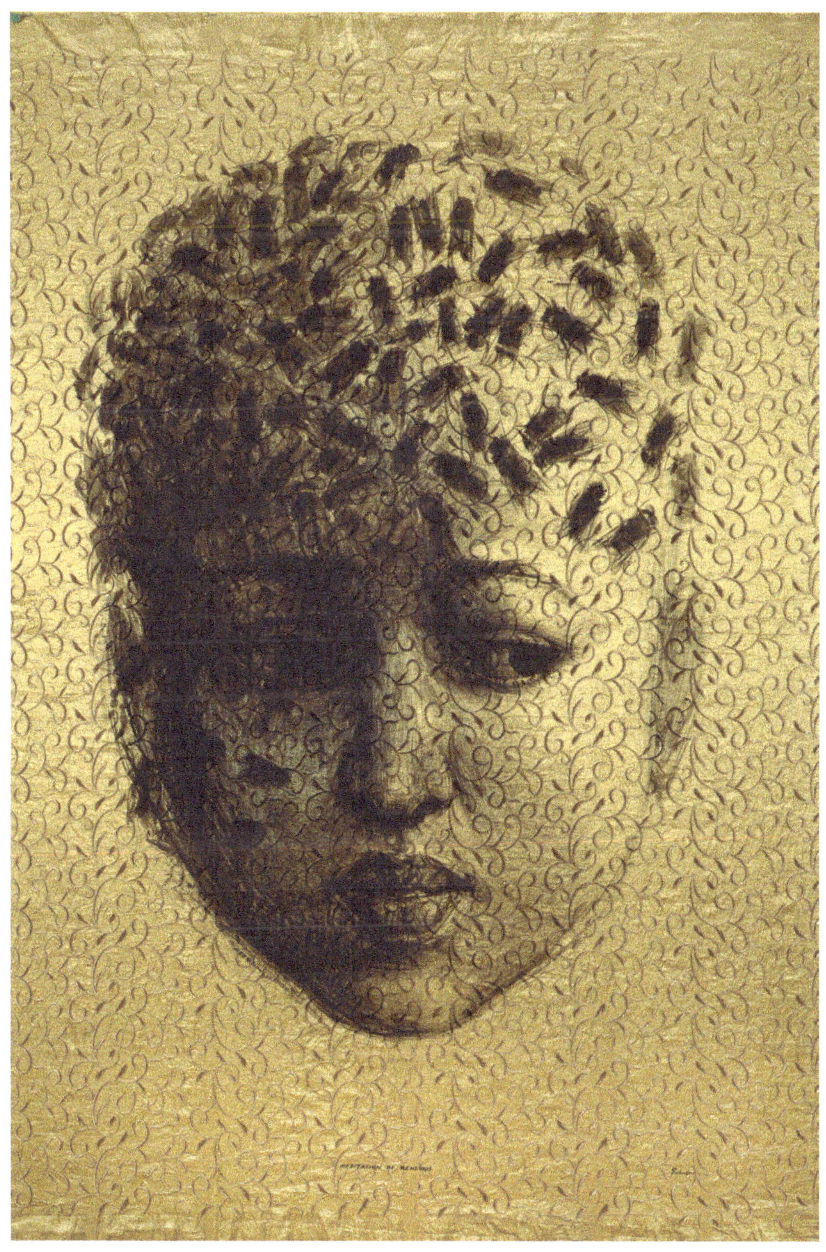

Figure 7. *Meditación de Remedios,* 2012, by Roberto Fabelo, acrylic on embroidered silk, 136 × 100 cm. Courtesy of the artist.

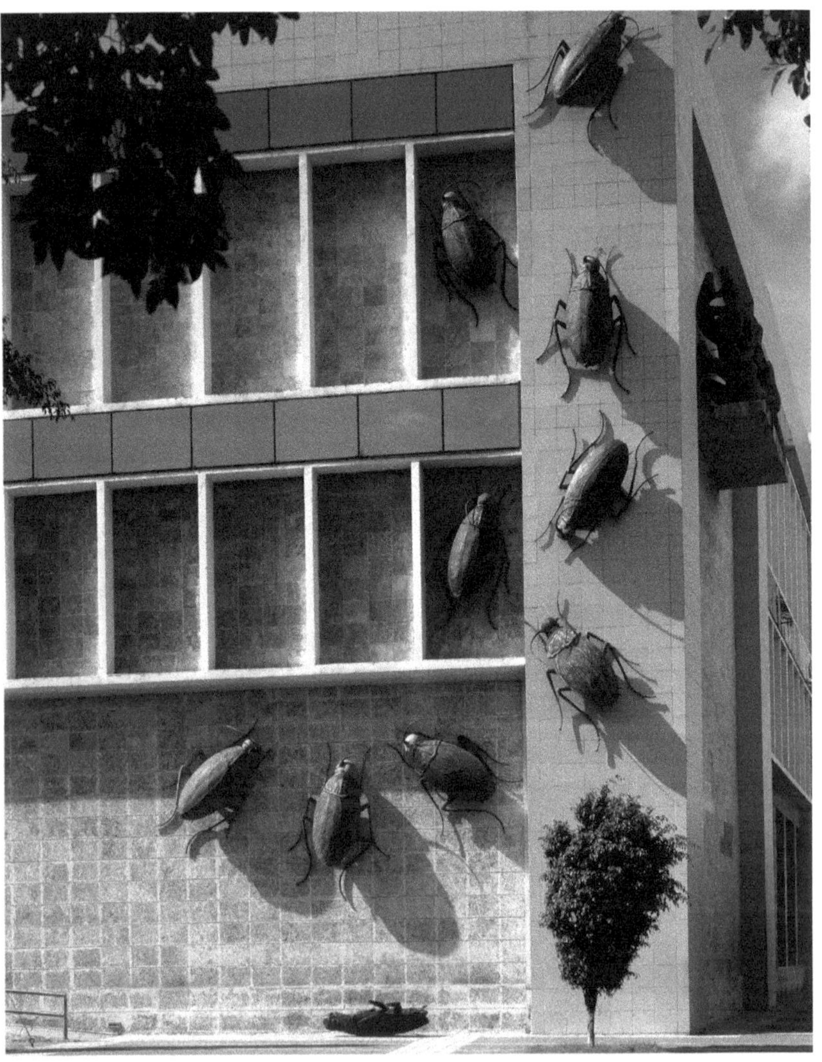

Figure 8. Installation view of *Sobrevivientes,* by Roberto Fabelo, 2009. Courtesy of the artist.

The narrative of the New Man like the slogan “Hasta la Victoria Siempre” represents a future community, a telos realized through the logic of sacrifice.[150] However utopic, this sacrificial logic is tied to a necropolitics; its violent repercussions discussed in the introduction of this chapter.[151]

Fabelo’s roaches and the indeterminacy of the installation—is it a de- or re- humanization?—allows us to pose the provocative question whether the New Man, the generation to come, is better represented by a human-roach hybrid than the handsome figures of Che and Camilo. These giant mutant roaches counter the futurity of the state’s rhetoric of sacrifice with a haunting from the future (Schwab). Moreover, Fabelo’s statement that the piece is a “reference to today’s world where man in some form or another is surviving” insists on thinking in the present, a task that impedes the efforts of teleological projects.

Conclusion

In Sarduy’s and Faeblo’s artful manipulations we see bodies as part of complex configurations. In *Cobra* the protagonist is always read as part of a constellation of other characters, at times indistinguishable from those of tapestries, stages, or proliferating vegetation. Meanwhile, in Fabelo’s drawings, his volumetric, voluptuous figures form part of and are formed from the two-dimensional engravings of the encyclopedic page. Language, printed media, ink, charcoal, paint, glitter, flesh and bones form vibrant material assemblages, interdependent and indeterminate. Exceeding an anthropocentric sense of scale through expansive, outward-bound texts (Sarduy) or giant mutant roach sculptures (Fabelo), their work incites us to imagine the imperceptible, the virtual particles that fill those seemingly empty spaces. The shared substance they bring to the fore suggests that to instrumentalize, or dispose of, one part of a collectivity will necessarily impact the rest. Returning to Gregory Bateson’s question, “What sort of correction in the direction of wisdom would be achieved by creating or viewing this work of art?”: Fabelo’s images and Sarduy’s text prompt us to consider community through an ecological lens, one that concerns itself not just for the green in the environment, but also recognizes the negative consequences of compartmentalization, or the corralling of bodies through fixed identities. This poses a significant challenge to the hubris of totalizing nationalist projects and particularly to the Cuban Revolution’s narrative of progress through sacrifice. In Sarduy’s baroque ecology, in its treatment of Cobra’s corpse, death is not presented as the finitude of a subject, as something which exclusively belongs to any one individual. Put differently, life does not exist independently (the "minúsculas flores capilares" on her corpse express the life that is embedded in death) and is therefore not available for the transaction sacrifice presupposes. Accordingly, in the passages describing Cobra's "conversion," the "cuerpo caido que no eres tú" cannot be neatly severed because of our shared enfleshment. Fabelo's images equally work against the logic of necropolitics, as he exposes the pulsating *zoē* that runs through all as a web of interconnections.

In making bodies impenetrable and in scrambling identities, Fabelo and Sarduy also challenge a metaphysics that treats bodies as the incarnation of an idea or that assumes a unity between the body and its sign.[152] The undoing of such a metaphysics, as discussed in chapter 1, has significant political implications when we consider that hegemonic structures and their classificatory systems impose signs on bodies and seek to corral them through identitary markers. Unlike Che and Camilo, Fabelo's roaches do not easily serve any state, psychological or mythical narrative. Instead, in their imposing size visible to the city, their detailed bodies that demand closer scrutiny, their feeling antennas, and scattered movements, acquire an obstinate thereness.

3

Inhuman Writings

Roaches, Parasites, and Radiation in Ena Lucía Portela's *El pájaro: Pincel y tinta china* and Antonio José Ponte's *La fiesta vigilada*

In Ena Lucía Portela's 1998 novel, *El pájaro: Pincel y tinta china,* an unnamed lecturer at the University of Havana is quoted by the narrator, "—Un escritor moderno es un ser retórico, exuberante, verboso, palabrero, sin conciencia alguna de la economía [. . .] Como diría un amigo, <<el escritor moderno escribe, no inscribe>>."[1] Although the distinction between "escribe" and "inscribe" is never elaborated, a character speculates it regards the writer's materials: paper versus stone. We might then deduce that a writing conscious of economy has substance, political import, and lasting permanence, whereas an exuberant wordy writing is superficial and ephemeral. An exuberant wordy writing with no consciousness of economy, moreover, is implicitly wasteful and unproductive. The difference between "escribe" and "inscribe" calls to mind Jean-Luc Nancy's neologism, *exscription,* in lieu of inscription. Through the prefix *ex* Nancy signals the exposure, the coming-into-contact of writing with an outside, another limit, be that the reader or another writing. As such, writing always traces a body, irreducible and in excess of its operative signification.[2]

Portela's novel is certainly culpable of trafficking in a writing that is rhetorical, exuberant, and needlessly verbose, consciously aware of its uneconomic *exscribing.* As in previous chapters, one of my interests here is to cull the ethico-political from the seemingly apolitical, of what might be dismissed as mere textual, visual, or sonic jouissance. More specifically, I'm interested in how her novel produces an aesthetic excess as a means to challenge the pretense of knowing and expertise, such as a literary analyst's grasp on the narrative or a medical doctor's diagnosis and pathologizing of a character. As I explored through the work of Roberto Fabelo and Severo Sarduy, in my reading of *El pájaro,* I pay special attention to the ways in which Portela transforms means of seeing inside, of penetrating surfaces—like those of a third person omniscient narrator reproducing a character's inner dialogue, or an obstetrician's determination of a fetus's sex through an ultrasound—into inoperative aesthetic material. In much of the same way that Fabelo tampers with the nineteenth-century medical encyclopedia—making an instructional object of authority dysfunctional—Portela tampers with technologies of representation, be they literary or scientific, and modes of knowledge acquisition. In so doing, her novel undermines dominant ways of seeing and organizing bodies.

In chapter 2 we ended with Fabelo's 2009 installation *Sobrevivientes,* which he explains is a "reference to today's world where man in some form or another is surviving."[3] I suggested that one way to approximate his designation of "today's world" and the installation's allusion to a disaster yet-to-come is through Gaby Schwab's notion of a "haunting from the future," as we live in the shadow of nuclear objects' future effects.[4] I also suggested that the indeterminacy of the piece—Is it a de- or re- humanization?—solicits a simultaneous attraction to the biomorphic potential of the insect and its ability to survive, as well as an anxiety regarding ecological concerns. Not incidentally, the indeterminism of Fabelo's installation, its potential for both attraction and anxiety toward nonhuman becomings, and its reference to survival are recurring themes in contemporary cultural production from the island. In her book *Cuban Currency,* Esther Whitfield observes that much of the Cuban state's rhetoric, following the loss of Soviet subsidies during the Special Period in Time of Peace (early to mid 1990s), relied on evoking threats of the Cold War era and the Missile Crisis to garner legitimacy as it failed to provide its citizens with basic needs.[5] It is not surprising, then, to find allusions to the effects of an atomic holocaust and more generally to the theme of survival in literary and artistic production. The effects of radiation on human biology, as well as paradoxical responses toward the body's metamorphosis, will figure in my reading of Portela's novel. *El pájaro*'s uneconomical, rhetorical, and exuberant writing moreover, thwarts the reader's desire to make determinations and distinctions within the narrative.

Antonio José Ponte's 2007 novel, *La fiesta vigilada,* in which he attends to the rubble and ruins of Havana's urban landscape, provides another rich example of a literary work that foregrounds survival and states of ontological indeterminism. Linked to the city's architectural ruins, we also find the ruination of subjectivities deemed unproductive to the Revolution's teleological project. Against the Cuban state's narrative of progress and victory, Ponte's novel traces the waste left behind by the incessant drive toward a future and the desire to cultivate "a scientific education necessary for the domination of available resources" [*la educación científica necesaria para dominar los recursos disponibles*].[6] This call for a "scientific education" by a bureaucrat in the novel is posed against what he conceives as an "erotic" and, therefore, inoperative aesthetic. Ponte's novel, as readers have noted, is explicitly concerned with assigning culpability to the Cuban state for allowing the perpetuation of inhospitable living conditions; a city in ruins, after all, supports the rhetoric of a country under siege.[7] That said, in its attention to Havana's inhabited ruins, the novel also illustrates networks of material and territorial interdependencies that exceed the limits of state politics. In my reading of the text, I will underscore these networks with the aim of bringing to the foreground an ecological thinking in Ponte's novel, as it challenges the instrumental logic of modernizing projects and displaces the centrality of the human as the agent of history. In *La fiesta vigilada* buildings and trash are anthropomorphized and the inhabitants of Havana's seemingly war-torn buildings appear at moments as parasites, insects, and even algae; they are survivors of an incoming implosion.

Portela's and Ponte's novels attest to dehumanizing conditions. In *El pájaro* and *La fiesta* we find state institutions, a hospital/psychiatric ward and a nursing home, respectively, in which individuals are treated as disposable bodies, left to die or experimented on like laboratory rats. While the international community with regard to the Cuban state often invokes the discourse of human rights, Ponte's and Portela's novels, as I aim to explore here, do not appeal to a shared humanism nor do they seem to advocate for a politics of representation. In their novels the survivors of these necropolitical institutions do so precisely in their capacity to scurry away or behave parasitically. Moreover, in Ponte's and Portela's texts the practice of writing and of creative production—that which is often cited as evidence of a human spirit or intelligence, and charged with the duty to humanize and represent legible political subjects—appears to emerge from an irreducible corporeality and territorial interdependence. In other words, cultural production in their texts is not imagined as transcendence from mere "animal" subsistence but the result of creatively surviving.

In a chapter titled, "Can Thought Go on Without the Body," from his book *The Inhuman,* Jean-François Lyotard considers early on, "Technology was not invented by us humans. Rather the other way around."[8] Even the simplest life forms operate as technological devices, absorbing and processing information from their environment in order to survive. Although humans demonstrate a higher capacity for storing information, differentiating, and reflection, they are, ultimately, material, technological systems. The question, then, more specifically for Lyotard is whether human thinking can be technologically reproduced outside of its corporeal and terrestrial environment. Restated philosophically, can "the life of the mind," like that of the soul, be segregated from that of the body? The answer is no. Unlike artificial intelligence, human thought does not operate in a binary mode; it works intuitively, hypothetically, accepting imprecise, ambiguous data, or what Kant called reflective judgment. Lyotard goes on to demonstrate how reflective judgment is conditioned by and generated from our perceptive, phenomenological experience. Just as our vision is marked by blurry, peripheral limits, anticipating always a horizon beyond reach, infinitely unfurling, so too does thought make inferences and imaginative leaps of what it has not yet determinately encountered. In order to make these leaps, to think the *unthought,* Lyotard continues, one must be irresolute in their thinking, resist arriving at a conclusion, and patiently wait in the discomfort of the unknown, "letting a givable come towards you." Much like an actor, a painter, or a calligrapher, one needs "a kind of suspension of ordinary intentions of mind associated with habitus, or arrangements of the body" for the grace of the right brushstroke, gesture, or thought to be evoked. And this "doesn't happen without suffering. An enjoyment of what we possessed is now lost. [. . .] [T]here's a necessity for physical experience and a recourse to exemplary cases of bodily ascesis [. . .] if the mind is to think."[9]

Interestingly, while Lyotard makes a case for the singularity of human thought, he does so by arguing that it is both technological and corporeal. Put otherwise, corporeality is technological and intelligent in its very survival and attachment to a particular environment. If "the life of the mind," in its transcendence over mere material need, is what conventionally distinguishes human from nonhuman life, following Lyotard's elaboration, what constitutes human thought is its inhumanness, its technicity and corporeal dependence on an environment, that which it shares with the simplest of life forms. Drawing from Lyotard's theorization on thought and the inhuman, an important consideration in my treatment of Portela's and Ponte's novels, as indicated by the chapter title, is how these writers prompt us to reconsider our conceptualization of "culture" as that which marks humans from non-humans. If artistic creations can be considered part of the zoological, ecological, "natural" domain, then what distinguishes a political being, whose life is worthy of protection, from raw, material, instrumental resources?

Chinese Brush Painting

The title to Ena Lucía Portela's novel, *El pájaro: Pincel y tinta china,* presents us with a grammatical convention more akin to that of academic essays or non-fiction works. Though audibly it reads as a list—such that the bird, paintbrush, and Chinese ink are ontologically parallel—graphically, the three nouns are organized by a colon. Following the logic of this punctuation, the paintbrush and Chinese ink elaborate or explain the bird; put otherwise, the bird *is* brush and ink, an artificial figure. Setting its grammatical arrangement aside, the three nouns recall the tradition of Chinese brush painting, in which artists, drawing from the disciplined craftsmanship of calligraphy, meticulously apply ink over silk or paper using a very fine tip brush.[10] The cover to the novel's first edition displays one of these paintings, a black silhouette of a bird surrounded by an Asian script; both title and cover image provide a particularly evocative paratext for my reading of the novel. Composed historically by so-called scholar painters, Chinese brush paintings of birds, flowers, rocks, and bamboo also integrate poetry. Notably, it was (and continues to be) the custom for the recipient of the work, or a later appreciator, to inscribe his or her own response to the original poem—painting in the empty spaces of the blank background. To accommodate the proliferation of responses, additional panels of silk or paper are attached along the length of a scroll.[11] In its display of various authorial voices and artistic hands, one is reminded of the notations found at the margins of ancient Greek scrolls by later translators or the supplemental and decorative illustrations of medieval illuminated manuscripts. And not unlike the stylized renderings of these manuscripts, a formalistic feature of Chinese brush painting is its reliance on line. That is, rather than modeling through lights and shadows, with economical precision, the "scholar painter" aimed to distill an ideational form, "capturing" both the outer silhouette and inner essence of the represented figure.[12] For contrast, recall how European naturalistic conventions adhere to a particular angle of view and a source of light in order to produce the illusion of receding space and volumetric bodies. Whereas a fifteenth-century Italian painting was conceived as a window through which the spectator can see a landscape or the interior of a room, the linear calligraphic compositions of these Chinese paintings reiterate the flatness of the picture plane, drawing the viewer's eyes from top to bottom, vertically, as though scanning a text. It is then not surprising to learn that a traditional way of appreciating a painting in Chinese is often expressed as "*du hua,* 'to read a painting.'"[13]

To be clear, Portela's novel, *El pájaro: Pincel y tinta china,* is not "about" Chinese brush painting, nor much less a bird, a paintbrush, and Chinese ink. In fact, references to the translation of ancient Greek texts, classical Roman sculpture, and portraits of the Florentine Renaissance play a far more visible role within the novel. And yet, el pájaro, pincel, and tinta china will reappear in the text, in grammatical arrangements that read more like a litany, becoming a refrain, couched between clauses and sentences, with no explicit meaning for the reader: "Entonces todo era recorrer la casa [. . .] a la ida y a la vuelta el pájaro enjaulado, no pincel, no tinta china"; "De nuevo sufrir el tiempo . . . el pájaro desbordado, no pincel, no tinta china"; "Lo hace con sus pájaros, ya sean grises o lluviosos (pincel y tinta china, grabados)."[14] And later in a metatextual reference, "Así era *El pájaro: Pincel y tinta china,* una historia como la seda. Envolvente, translúcida, sensual."[15] I want to return to the narrator's self-referential description of the story as enveloping, *trans*-lucent, sensuous silk. But first let us consider the following: While the colon in the title announces something explanatory like an essay, within the body of the novel the three objects operate as enigmatic tropes. As readers we are misled, if we expect to learn about el pájaro, or the tradition of Chinese brush painting. What follows the colon does not explain or substitute the bird, but adds objects to a list or an assemblage, like "parts outside parts,"[16] or additional panels of silk along the length of a scroll.

By way of introduction, the tradition of Chinese brush painting provides a rich analogy for how Portela's text does and does not operate. With the aim of "capturing" the inner essence of the object represented, brush painting's linearity and symbolic figuration present images as text and not naturalistic representations. In no way does Portela's novel presume to capture an inner essence and will in fact play with the impossibility of doing so. However, like the ink brush paintings, the novel suggests that its representation is based on conventions within a long and expansive literary tradition, to which recipients and future readers will supplement, (miss) interpret, and (miss)translate, adding their own responses at the margins of the text. *El pájaro* continuously brings the reader's attention to the artifice of its narrative with a hyper-self-awareness, making the process of writing and storytelling ever-present themes. Discussion of literary styles, such as Nuevo Realismo and Neobarroquismo; critical theory by Barthes and Derrida; as well as intertextual references to literary works by J.D. Salinger, Djuna Barnes, and Lewis Carroll, to name only a very few, abound in the novel, populating its pages with citations, stories, voices that do not belong to, or are not proper to, its author.[17] That is, Portela deliberately undermines the authorial and proprietary boundaries of her own text.

In Chinese brush painting not only is visual representation textualized, but the textual, in turn, is made visually palpable. The calligraphic scripts, while conveying linguistic meaning, are also meant to please the eye through the disciplined marks of the artist's hand, which sought both regularity of form and originality. As readers of a brush painting, we can take our fingers and trace the lines of ink script dried on the silk fabric. Put otherwise, the art of calligraphy allows us to better imagine what Nancy and Sarduy have theorized with regard to language and corporeality: writing always *exscribes* another body, irreducible to its conventionalized signification. Language is always both metaphorical—displacing its referent, attempting to stand in for something absent—and absolutely singular in its *lettericity,* its tangible materiality.[18] What's more, as a specialized craft, Chinese brush painting prompts us to consider how the textual and visual bodies of *El pájaro* are the result of honed skills, a *techne,* and not the incarnation of an already existing bird. While the concept of technology is often thought in opposition to the organic, recalling Lyotard, consider that in order to achieve the controlled and precise application of ink, the calligrapher-artist is said to suspend "ordinary intentions of mind associated with *habitus* [and] arrangements of the body."[19] In order that grace may be received—that the iteration of a character may also display an unexpected gestural mark, something unimagined before—an emptiness and evacuation is solicited, which "doesn't take place without some suffering [and] discomfort."[20] In other words, artistic creation, here, is not imagined as a disembodiment, a purely intellectual process, but happens from and with corporeality. I find it significant that the title of the novel should refer to an artistic practice which calls for the disciplining or un-conditioning of the body, to sit with the discomfort of the unknown, when Portela's text, as I will explore in the pages that follow, links creative production with states of paralysis, loss of bodily control, disease, contagion, and possession. It is also telling that Portela's title should reference an artistic practice that rejects the use of a direct light source and a fixed point of view, for the novel might be summarized as the manipulation of light and the destabilization of perspective: the very sources postmedieval European art and science relied on to see "nature" and "discover" knowledge.

Staging the Abject

Camila, a.k.a. "la sacerdotisa" and "la Mirada," Fabián, a.k.a. "ese loco de rostro renacentista," and Bibiana, a.k.a. "Beatriz," "la Modelo," and "la niña ilustre," provide the main casting for the narrative, with minor roles given to Zarathustra, as aborted fetus, Dr. K. Schilling, as what his name conjures—a fascist medical doctor that performs human experiments—and Emilio U, as contemporary Cuban writer and sometimes double for Ena Lucía Portela. In addition to writing, Emilio U will also play the role of Fabián's lover and murderer. Main set locations are a home, a hospital, and a university in early 1990s Havana, such that, hospitality, medical treatment, and the production of knowledge within a context of power outages play thematic roles in the novel. The three main characters, as "la Mirada," "la Modelo," and "ese loco de rostro renacentista," also stage the spectator, the object of the gaze, and an enigmatic work of art. Accordingly, the question of perspective, where the spectator is situated, seeing and not seeing, and interpreting or diagnosing will be guiding concepts for my reading of the text.

Camila is an eighteen-year-old aspiring actress from the provinces that has come to study theater in Havana on a scholarship. She is described as having "una personalidad y un cuerpo pequeños y grises," who through a series of errors discovers the advantages of being a spectator, "de ser espectador, actuar de espectador."[21] We are introduced to Camila's character in a subsection titled "Posiciones humillantes" and a passage that runs about two pages in length with no periods. In an informal conversational style that implicates the reader with phrases such as "mira tú," the narrator often switches from using the third person feminine singular, referring explicitly to Camila, to the impersonal and passive "uno," "lo," and "se," as though the actions narrated are not exclusive to her, but commonplace and possibly applicable to the speaker as well: Getting drunk by day, cultivating and selling marijuana in order to buy and snort cocaine, getting kicked out of school, and landing on the street, homeless, sifting through trash and talking to oneself, with no one to notice or care. As "pequeña" and "gris," Camila does not stand out, but is overlooked, invisible. "Ni siquiera la miran. Solo tú y yo sabemos que ella está allí," our narrator confides in us.[22]

At other times, Camila "está por completo fuera de foco, *old fashioned,* en plena disonancia, haciendo la payasada del siglo [. . .]."[23] Dissonance and out-of-focus are adjectives that not only signal discursive strategies Portela deploys—continuously destabilizing the reader's perspective—but also the construction of her characters; they do not conform to conventional subject models, or certainly not "respectable" ones we should emulate.

Camila's "payasada" is the result of a series of missteps, one inevitably leading to the next:

> como quien dice, personaje del aire bajo la corona de pámpanos, de ser posible con ron, llegado el caso con pediculicida de plátano—producto de la conjunción entre la química, el vicio y la miseria, horrendo como su nombre indicia: pedi, culi, y SIDA, preparado a base de alcohol, que también sirve, mira tú, para matar bichos—y fumar marihuana con alegría, como no, cultivarla, matica linda de mi corazón, en algún sitio donde nadie la reconozca—venir a La Habana a cultivar, qué mal chiste—[. . .].[24]

The narrator's phonetic breakdown of "pedi, culi, y SIDA," is not insignificant. That Camila should be associated with something that exterminates insects, "para matar bichos," and semantically evokes feet, ass, and a virus, points to the abjectness with which her persona is continuously imagined. If that weren't enough, our narrator makes clear that Camila does not fit-in anywhere, she has no home, no friends, and no belongings: "se carezca de amigos, de sentimiento de pertenencia a un grupo cualquiera, de dinero, de ropa, de comida [. . .] se pone a dormir en las aceras y a husmear en los latones de basura, hablando solo sin que nadie lo mire ni se asombre."[25] The image of Camila sniffing [*husmear*] through trash like an animal, is reiterated with a description of her as a "liebre marceña"—a reference to Alice in Wonderland—, "con las orejas paradas," and in the following page, "se siente cucaracha," and has the face of a mouse [*cara de ratón*].[26] But as to why Camila should find herself marginalized and dehumanized is unclear; or at least from a legible social justice issue, Camila is not stigmatized by a disability, racial, class, or sexual difference.[27] It would seem, instead, that Camila's fall into "posiciones humillantes" is the result of her own hubris, a tragic flaw in Greek theater:

> entonces se advierte que uno se ha malogrado—al menos es lo que dice la peruana del cuarto, inca de mierda—, uno se ha pasado de los límites con mucho *hybris* sin saber por qué (mentira, uno sí sabe), si

> no había una Causa por la cual luchar ni nada de qué quejarse, si uno tuvo en sus manos las mejores oportunidades y las dejó pasar porque eso es precisamente lo que le gusta hacer a uno con las malditas oportunidades.[28]

There's much to be said about ruination and hubris in Post-Soviet Cuba during the economic crisis of the early 1990s. The narrator's mention of a lack of a Cause, with a capital C, there being nothing to complain about, and the best opportunities, implicitly, made available to its citizens, might be read as an ironic reference to the Revolution's assumed accomplishments. However, our narrator does not appear to be making a critique of the status quo, and the absence of a Cause, with a capital C, may also be a reference to the tenets of a logical cause and effect in Greek tragedy.[29] Without a justifiable Cause, Camila's actions are seemingly the result of a morally degenerate character. She has squandered her scholarship, which would necessarily be a gift from the Cuban state. Recalling the ethics of Che's *hombre nuevo,*[30] Camila has failed to fulfill her debt to the revolutionary forefathers and her obligation to her fellow compatriots. Like a bacchanal figure, "personaje del aire bajo la corona de pámpanos," Camila is an unproductive citizen. It is only reasonable then that she has been expelled and left to survive on trash, or so the tone of our narrator would lead us to believe.

The narrator's citing Camila's roommate, "al menos es lo que dice la peruana del cuarto, inca de mierda," situates him or her within the world of the novel. It also demonstrates that this speaker, who confides in the reader "(mentira, uno sí sabe)," makes racists statements. But identifying who the narrator is becomes a difficult, if not impossible, game. At one point the reader is outright challenged to do so: "si adivinas quién soy yo, te doy un premio."[31] And before you judge, the narrator asks "antes de pensar que soy un <<sexista abominable>> que <<reincide en estereotipos represivos>>, considera, te lo ruego, que esto del *kalós* y el *agathós* no es tan simple."[32] The ancient Greek terms that translate to "beautiful and good" or "fine and noble," were used in reference to an ideal of life and behavior. The usage of these terms also corresponds to the philosophical position that "[t]he more elements of the ideal were realized in an individual, the more fully human that person was. If he had few or none of the elements, his life was essentially subhuman and not worth living."[33] I find the narrator's questioning of "*kalós* y el *agathós*" especially relevant. Camila will be hospitalized in a so-called rehabilitation ward, where she and the other patients are described as "anormal," treated as though,

> carecían de espíritu o cosa parecida, eran puro cuerpo, muñecos a los que no había necesidad alguna de tratar como a personas, nada de hablar con ellos, por ejemplo. ¿O es que uno, humano ciento por ciento, *zoón politikón,* conversa con los ratones blancos o con los monitos de los modelos experimentales?[34]

The assimilation of the hospital's patients to animals in a lab is indicative of the "dehumanizing" treatment they receive there, of the indignities they must endure. However, Portela's novel does more than expose exploitative conditions. As I will explore in more detail ahead, her novel undermines the authority and the metrics used to determine "[un] humano ciento por ciento," or what gives *zoón*—undifferentiated animal life—*politikón*—a political identity—distinguishing a life as worthy of living from that of an instrumental material resource. If artistic creation has served as both evidence of Humanity and as a means to humanize, *El pájaro* will also complicate the notion that art—as discursive and intelligent life that transcends mere material need—and animal life—as immanent, attached and interdependent on a territory—are mutually exclusive.[35] Were we to judge from the Humanist tradition and its notion of "*kalós* y el *agathós,*" *El pájaro* is neither an edifying nor civilizing work; there are no morally good characters with which to self-identify and pity, a necessary requisite for a hearty cathartic purging. Within the discourse of the Cuban Revolution and its call for artists to contribute to the nation's progress, the novel also seems to renege on its civic duty to produce a socially committed, purposeful art.[36] Certainly, statements such as the following mock any endeavor to make art purposeful, "[E]n última instancia todas las ocupaciones humanas resultan por igual inútiles."[37] In case the reader had any expectation about the novel's redemptive potential, in one of the text's many self-referential passages, Fabián tells the writer Emilio U (sometimes double for Ena Lucía Portela), "Eres un puñetero mosquito [. . .] vas a terminar creyéndote tus propias ficciones y confundiéndote con los personajes de tu novela, los cuales, me disculpas, no son nada dignos de imitación." Followed sarcastically by, "¡es tan edificante lo que estamos hablando!"[38] And yet, it is creative production, a literary work, which will *inexplicably* instill in our abject character, deemed unworthy by the powers that be, the desire to survive.

Perspectives, Possessions, Parasites

With phrases such as, "desentona, según muestran las superficies pulidas que la repiten," "[a]sí la veía él en los cristales de un hombre," "[c]olocada desde siempre en el mismo centro de la luz," "de pie junto a la lámpara," "la iluminación en la azotea es de pocos watts, amarilla casi ocre," "mirarlos [. . .] a través del ojo de una cerradura," "mirando desde el suelo," "desde el fondo de la penumbra," "desde su precaria posición," "desde ese punto de vista," "[d]esde la sombra," "[d]esde el sofa más alejado de la lámpara," *El pájaro* constructs visual scenes by marking a spectator's perspective, situating the object of the gaze, and determining the source or quality of light.[39] These perspectives and light sources, moreover, are usually oblique, unstable, and opaque. In the following exchange between two characters, Portela ironically underscores the artifice of what is seen, mediated by lighting and staging, "<<[N]o vamos a poder vernos ni las caras [. . .] Quedaremos murciélagos. [. . .] Hoy toca el apagón, ¿no te acuerdas? ¡El apagón! ¡Je je! Te lo digo para que no vayas a pensarte que esta oscuridad de mierda es pura escenografía o algo así.>>"[40] Similarly, when we are first introduced to Fabián, a series of consecutive paragraphs each begins with, "El espejo del baño," "El espejo era un cuadro," "Inmóvil y enmarcado," "Aunque era el hombre de la medalla"; so that, the elaboration of this character emerges from a two-dimensional plane or a framed composition. Whether the image is a reflection on a polished surface, displaced, multiplied, or miniaturized on a pair of spectacles, it is always from a situated, singular angle, "desde su ángulo singular," and not an unmediated "transcendental view from nowhere."[41] Writing also happens from a particular standpoint, "Quizá lo que deberías hacer, desde tu escondrijo, desde debajo de tu piedra, es escribir una novela."[42] In this case, our narrator writes not from an upright, sovereign, human perspective, but from that of a vulnerable quadruped close to the ground.

Portela not only plays with perspective at the level of representation, but also at the level of the writing. If narrative voice provides a focal point, that which situates the reader, Portela constantly destabilizes our position and, in so doing, our ability to fully grasp the novel's characters and actions. From one clause to the next, narrative voice might switch from a situated, unnamed character expressing their love for marijuana, to a third person omniscient, to that of Emilio U, Fabián, a female narrator, possibly Camila, or a self-identified neighbor and friend.[43] Fabián's warning to Emilio U, that he will end up confusing himself with the characters of his novel—

incidentally, titled *El pájaro: Pincel y tinta china*—is both a metatextual nod to the reader and a way in which Portela undermines authority: The error of "creyéndote tus propias ficciones y confundiéndote con los personajes" falls on the writer, "un puñetero mosquito," and not, necessarily or exclusively, the reader.

In his study of perspectival illusionism, the art historian W.J.T. Mitchell notes that the metaphors "taken in" and "capture" have historically been used to describe the deceived spectator, or "beholder," of a naturalistic representation. These metaphors are an indication of how "the problem of illusionism is deeply interwoven with structures of power" and implicated in a process of social othering. In his *Treatise of Painting*, Leonardo da Vinci describes various instances of animals being deceived by perspectival illusionism in order to prove, Mitchell explains, "that painting is superior to poetry because it is a 'natural' and scientific medium that produces true representations of the visible world." Quoting da Vinci's claim, "I have seen a picture that deceived a dog because of the likeness to its master . . . likewise I have seen a monkey that did an infinite number of foolish things with another painted monkey," Mitchell points out that in these stories "the 'error' [. . .] is not the painter's, but the beholder's: the dog, not the master, is taken in by the illusion of the master." The binaries it relies on—"human/animal; painter/beholder"—base illusionism "in [a] structure of alterity [. . .] characterized by inequality in power, self-consciousness, or self-control."[44] Moreover, perspectival illusionism has been deployed as a method of domination through "the perfection of the panopticon, 'lures,' and 'decoys,'" while its presumed objectivity has buttressed notions of expertise, social hierarchies, and fixed identities.[45] The pretense of producing a "true representation" or the endeavor to create verisimilitude is not exclusive to painting; I want to suggest that in narrative fiction similar devices of illusionism are also operative, in its elaboration of so-called three-dimensional characters and a believable progression of events. In bringing our attention to the question of perspective—"desde ese punto de vista"—, in destabilizing the reader's viewpoint through shifts in narrative voice, and in constructing visual scenes that are fragmentary, cubistic, where lighting dramatizes, but rather than illuminate, obfuscates and veils (we will see this in more detail in the following section), Portela breaks the illusion of her fictional world and insists on a writing that is immanent, interdependent on a particular territory.[46] As such, the novel upends authorial modes of knowledge production and their attendant structures of power. Efforts to fix and hold the object of the gaze are consistently thwarted: "De nuevo guiña el ojo y se me desdibuja entre las manos cuando ya creía haberla atrapado."[47]

When Camila's and Fabián's paths cross, the narrator in third person omniscient will provide us with Camila's thoughts through indirect discourse. However, later in a scene that describes the two having sex, the narrative voice switches to first person: "Las manos de ella, muy poco lo que se espera sean las manos de una muchacha, se apoyaban en mi cabeza [. . .] Ella gemía de placer aunque a mí no me gustara su voz y me empujaba todavía más [. . .] me empujaba hasta el vacío que yo temía [. . .]."[48] The phrases correspond to Fabián's subject position and for a moment, one might, as I initially did, assume that Fabián has been the narrator the whole time. In the following paragraph, this assumption is immediately countered: "Fabián no podía evitar en esos momentos la acometida de una tristeza oscura."[49] This confusion, both the reader's and ostensibly the narrator's, generates a becoming-other, moments where subject and object are intersected, or where the spectator becomes the model and vice versa. Put otherwise, if, as readers, our position within the world of the novel comes from the narrative voice, then in one passage we are "watching" Camila and Fabián have sex, and in another we are Fabián having sex with Camila.

I find the literary critic Chiara Bolognese's explanation of these narrative transitions especially evocative: "el narrador habla por la boca de los diferentes personajes; les roba la voz."[50] The act of stealing and of speaking through another's body conjures the act of possession, or an unwelcomed, parasitic, hosting. In the novel's first pages, we read that Fabián, "personaje misterioso [. . .] del cual, a pesar de su elegancia y rara belleza, sabes que es el malo, el rufián, el sinvergüenza," "lamentaba perder el tiempo. Como si antes hubiese sido suyo, como si pudiera ser suyo."[51] The expressed lamentation of losing something which could never have been his, of imagining something like time as a property, is soon followed by his desire to possess, "poseer algo, si no el continuo, quizás un algo más modesto, en cuya posesión pudiera creer sin la sospecha de una nueva estafa, de un nuevo descalabro en este mundo tenebroso signado [. . .] Hubiera deseado poseer limpiamente."[52] A world darkly signified is an apt description for the novel itself. Let's also not forget Fabián's fear of the void [*el vacío que yo temía*] and dark sadness [*tristeza oscura*]. The impossible fulfillment of this desire to possess "limpiamente" without deceit or injury, that is, to possess with total certainty, is further elaborated as a failed attempt to recall a lost paradise or "alguna otra ucronía a contrapelo."[53] Given that Fabián, not unlike Camila, does not belong to any particular group, he has been abandoned by his family and lives alone, it is perhaps not surprising to read, "Desde la sombra Fabián extendía la mano, cada vez más ansioso. Quería, por decirlo de algún modo, acceder a alguien, estar de acuerdo. Poseer. La misma angustia de siempre."[54] This anxiety to have access to someone and to be in accord might be understood as an anxiety for communion, to commune with someone, to be of one mind. In fact, Fabián will later describe his sexual rendezvouses as "comunión con otra persona."[55] But to possess "limpiamente," without remainder, within the context of recovering "la *belle époque*," or a univocal community without the ambiguity of a darkly signified world, would necessarily entail violence, the elimination of difference, of disagreement. Unlike Camila who does not try to understand *el vacío*, "lo aceptaba como había aceptado la calle," "[a] Fabián siempre le preocupaba el fondo de todo," otherwise described by our narrator as "una vulgar angustia metafísica."[56] Fabián's fear of the void, of the unknown, of that which is impenetrable and impossible to decipher—interestingly, he spends his time translating (poorly, our narrator says, for he is not a trained philologist) ancient Greek texts, "una lengua muerta,"—and his anxiety to access and to be in accord, to possess, is perhaps manifested in the torture and rape of Camila. As Freudians, we might diagnose Fabián's inability to recall a lost paradise as melancholia and the self-abasement and self-destruction that follows is projected onto an Other; in this case Camila, as small and gray, becomes the void upon which his violence is inscribed.

I see possession as operative in at least two ways in the novel: 1) to possess *limpiamente*, without ambiguity, a structural impossibility that necessarily entails violence, and 2) to possess and be possessed through confusion, a confusion generated through writing. In those shifts of voice, following Bolognese's lead, the narrator possesses the body of its protagonists and, I would add, the protagonists, in turn, possess the body of the narrator. These are messy transfusions difficult to trace and disaggregate. In the following statement we can observe what begins as the narrator's self-critique, "Esto no es ya narración, sino retazos de ideas, aburrimiento, analogías discordantes que, tras la tormenta tropical, iban apareciendo sin más ni más en la mente de él,"[57] become inscribed in the mind of Fabián; the discordant fragments of ideas the reader attributes to the narrator become, in the last clause, Fabián's thoughts. Significantly, this statement follows almost immediately the passages where the narrator speaks through Fabián, "se apoyaban en mi cabeza." And consequently, in the act of "stealing" his voice, in becoming-other, the narration becomes scrambled, discourse comes to a halt, "Esto no es ya narración." I want to suggest that here writing operates as a parasitic form of inhabiting, or a form of contamination, and the reader is not immune. When the narrator asks, "considera, te lo ruego" or simply "mira tú," this call to the reader, this plea, not only implicates the reader, but also instantiates an invitation, a possible hospitality, and hosting is not always welcomed. The question of hospitality and the risks it entails arise at the level of the plot. Fabián invites Camila who is homeless to his apartment for tea and a bath. The bath becomes a gruesome scene of cruelty; Camila becomes hostage to the sadistic whims, or anxious and anguished need to possess of a Renaissance man—Fabián, after all, looks like a Quattrocento Florentine model and translates classical texts. Camila never leaves and becomes a sort of live-in girlfriend to this "loco." To our surprise and feminist indignation, she tolerates his constant barrage of verbal and physical abuse. However, remembering our narrator's plea, "considera, te lo ruego, que esto del *kalós* y el *agathós* no es tan simple," for the sake of hospitality, let us not judge Camila, or too quickly pathologize her.

Making Bodies Trans-Lucid

Chapter 2 of *El pájaro* begins with a visual description of what might be the moving water, oil, and wax of a lava lamp, but that ultimately remains enigmatic:

> En el interior de la ampolla de vidrio, ambiente gelatinoso, se agitaba una multitud de figuritas brillantes, unas con forma de clave de sol y otras no. Triángulos, sombreros de copa, burbujas, explosiones calladas. El jardín de las delicias. Era uno de esos cuerpos que cuelgan multicolores de los llaveros o de cualquier otro cuerpo (siempre cuelgan) como calidoscopios asimétricos sobre los cuales gravitara el malentendido con sus vísceras doradas al descubierto.[58]

Portela's sentence fragment, "Triángulos, sombreros de copa, burbujas, explosiones calladas," recalls Severo Sarduy's lists with no hierarchal ordering, his anatomies of configuration.[59] Indeed, we might read the entire passage as a vibrant assemblage. The notion of asymmetric kaleidoscopes, much like Sarduy's glass hair [*fibras de vidrio*] in *Cobra*,[60] provides the reader with a seemingly ontological impossibility and, as such, a charged poetic object. Incidentally, lava lamps and kaleidoscopes delight the eyes with images that transform through light and mirrors, respectively. Also notable, the etymology of the word kaleidoscope comes from the Greek *kalos,* which we've already seen signifies beauty and goodness, *eidos* "form, shape," and *skopeo,* "to look or examine," so that the term literally translates to "observer of beautiful forms."[61] There is a third object, "cuerpos que cuelgan multicolores de los llaveros." And wedged between descriptions, a reference to Hieronymus Bosch's *The Garden of Earthly Delights,* a work that depicts carnal joys and temptations through a composition so dense and so imaginative it puts the juxtapositions of twentieth-century Dadaists and Surrealists to shame. The phrase, "Era uno de esos cuerpos que cuelgan multicolores de los llaveros o de cualquier otro cuerpo (siempre cuelgan)," brings us from the whimsical "figuritas brillantes" of a lava lamp, or an ornamental key chain, to the terrestrial gravity and weight of a body. The syntax of the sentence is difficult to follow; is it a multicolored body that hangs from a keychain, or a body that hangs multiple colors from a keychain, or from any other body, (siempre cuelgan)? What does come through is the notion that bodies are not sovereign, but attached, hooked, lifted, pulled, dragged, by other bodies, "como calidoscopios asimétricos sobre los cuales gravitara el malentendido con sus vísceras doradas al descubierto." This last clause combines the impossible asymmetry of a mosaic pattern multiplied through double mirrors and the exposed entrails of the so-called misunderstood. Gold entrails, that is. Unpacking Portela's paragraph, untangling literal from figurative bodies, determining the object of the narrators' gaze, becomes a chimerical task. What I would like to underscore is the figure of the body possibly seen as/through gelatinous, golden, liquid, light and its interior exposed, as a beautiful form to observe.

Following this paragraph we read that Camila, Fabián, and Bibiana have all been observing the enigmatic image with fascination, though Camila for a much longer time. We are also given Camila's location within the apartment and what would seem to be a further elaboration of what she sees in the lava lamp-kaleidoscope-keychain object, "[d]esde el sofá más alejado de la lámpara (y de su ignorancia), la sacerdotisa presentía que los delirantes paisajes de figuritas evolucionaban en un silencio total [. . .]."[62] However, the scene transforms into another composition. So that, the *figuritas* Camila now watches are those of Bibiana and Fabián:

> Camila los hacía contraparte de su propia experiencia. Pues ella tenía por costumbre observar todos (o la mayoría de) los cuerpos sigilosamente, en puntillas de pies. Como a través del ojo de una cerradura, una grieta, un claro de luna o el espíritu curioso de Monte palomar.

> Desde la franja oscura hasta la franja iluminada era *voyeur,* espectadora, espía de los pies increíbles de Bibiana, muchacha descalzada y sentada sobre la alfombra—unos pies demasiados bien formado para ser ella tan alta—, sus rodillas, el pañuelo con talento para el desorden, el bolso tejido, un ojo azul y el otro verde, las figuritas de un útero transparente. La alfombra misma, anacrónica a más no poder.[63]

As la Mirada, la espectadora, Camila, "[j]amás se le ocurría la idea de habitar esos espacios. Al menos no en el sentido de asimilarse a ellos, de pertenecer."[64] Again, we are reminded of Camila's un-belonging and the question of perspective is brought to the foreground. A view from a keyhole, a crack, or a fringe is an occluded and framed one. In keeping with the themes of light, reflections, and deceptive illusions, "Un claro de luna," is an astrological term for the nocturnal illumination of the earth by the light of the sun reflected upon the moon. What we see is always displaced, distorted, and mediated. Bibiana, la Modelo, seated on the rug, is evidently now the object of Camila's gaze. However, the ensuing composition is fragmented, an anatomy of configuration: We get her feet, knees, scarf, a knitted handbag, a blue eye, a green eye, and an anachronistic rug. But what on earth are "las figuritas de un útero transparente" doing in this frame? Eventually, we learn that Camila is six months pregnant. And when Fabián critiques the clumsiness of the *figuritas*' movements, Camila responds that one cannot expect a small child to have too much agility. I want to suggest that the lava lamp-kaleidoscope-keychain the three characters observe with fascination, in which bodies hang and where entrails are exposed, might also be read as a sonogram or the screen of an ultrasound monitor.

Let us recall that a sonogram is a two-dimensional image produced through the transmission of sound waves and their reflection; emitted through a probe, sound waves reach the boundaries of tissues and bone and produce an echo. In other words, the image that would seemingly make the womb transparent, allowing one to *see* inside, is, in fact, constructed by recording the distance of sound waves from their emission to the point of contact and separation, to the point of touch. Earlier I cited a passage from the novel that referred to itself as sensuous, enveloping, translucent silk [*como la seda. Envolvente, translúcida, sensual*]. A fabric that is translucent allows one to see through it, but what we see is mediated and obfuscated by the tangible material. Portela's text, as I aim to further illustrate, much like Sarduy's invitation to his readers, solicits a form of reading as touching, where decipherment or a penetrating decoding is stymied by enveloping—wrapping, covering, as a membrane or a sheath—sensuousness. Indeed, as one of its narrator's considers, "¿Y si en vez de la pluma, me pregunto, eligiéramos un pincel para acariciar?"[65] From the sonogram, a medical, scientific device used not only to examine a fetus, but to also diagnose symptoms, to identify the cause of an illness, Portela generates delirious landscapes [*delirantes paisajes*], images as imaginative as Hieronymus Bosch's *The Garden of Earthly Delights*. The sonogram, or ultrasound screen, becomes a gelatinous space of brilliant figures with the potential for an infinite number of compositional arrangements. Turning back to the object of the kaleidoscope, note that its exterior body is a long cylindrical tube, much like a telescope and a microscope, instruments which also rely on mirrors and whose etymology share the suffix *skopeo* "to look or examine." Portela, not unlike Fabelo and his treatment of the medical encyclopedia, transforms scientific devices, which would presume to see or discover nature, into kaleidoscopes, objects of play, illusion, and aesthetic pleasure. And kaleidoscopes, in turn, are not simply inert instruments for the production of artifice, but vibrant matter with a biology that operates like bricolage: As indicative of Camila's creativity, we read that she has a "funesta iniciativa de reordenar células en el hueco de un calidoscopio vivo, de un inasible calidoscopio, *ars combinatoria*."[66]

Before taking another look at scientific technologies made art and vibrant matter, I would like to sustain some attention on how the body, in particular the female body and its reproductive capacities, are imagined by some characters or narrators in the novel:

> Compasión y asco fue todo lo que expresó el rostro de Fabián. Sobre todo asco. Tan fatigada y lenta, con los senos hinchados y aquella barriguita de seis meses debajo de algo harapiento (en ella todo lucía harapiento), Camila se le antojaba, ahora sí, la peor de las cucarachas. Y él, por supuesto, un cucarachón. [. . .] *una mujer en casa?* Pues, bien, ahí la tienes. En toda su expresión multiplicadora y reproductiva [. . .] Tu Fabiancito, gran horror, o tu Camilita, horror de horrores. La sagrada familia, el Tondo Doni de La Habana. [. . .] [A]quello de reproducirse le parecía algo diabólico, más bien propio de las lombrices y las amebas, de negros, indios y chinos, del subdesarrollo más basto. Sus ideas al respecto [. . .]consistían más bien en el producto rígido y desaforado de la perplejidad, del asombro de que su cuerpo tuviese,

> en cierta forma, vida independiente. Aunque parezca mentira, nunca se había percatado. Contra la actuación del cuerpo se estrellaban los sentimientos y las filosofías; el cuerpo merecía su tributo, su vigilancia, su culto aparte. Era un demonio peligroso.[67]

Camila, pitiful, appearing homeless and incapacitated—she is fatigued and slow moving—inspires disgust in our handsome Florentine-Renaissance-look-a-like. Embedded in Fabián's animalization of Camila, we have the narrator's interjection in second person, "Tu Fabiancito, gran horror, o tu Camilita, horror de horrores. La sagrada familia, el Tondo Doni de La Habana." As a representation of Mary, Joseph, and baby Jesus, Michelangelo's painting of the Holy-three-member-Family is an iconic image of a patriarchal structure; it is also a work that reflects the High Renaissance and its classical values: Its composition is a perfect circle. Drawing the spectator's eyes right to its center, one can delineate the invisible intersection of equilateral and longitudinal lines of a mathematically harmonious space, and its figures display well-proportioned, idealized, volumetric bodies. Somehow imagining "el Tondo Doni de La Habana" incites horror and disdain in the narrator (or is it Fabián, our lover of all things Greco-Roman?) as though this classical image in the tropics is absurd. Moreover, this image of both a dominant organizing structure (the patriarchal family) and "high art" is juxtaposed to that of roaches and their ability for indiscriminant proliferation. That worms and bees are grammatically parallel to Blacks, Indians, and Chinese, is indicative of how racism and other discriminatory forms of organizing of bodies rest on the fictive distinction between *zoón*—undifferentiated life—and *zoón politikón,* "humano ciento por ciento."[68] And what exactly constitutes "el subdesarrollo más basto"; is it the absence of Michelangelo, of having not mastered the art of perspectival illusionism?

It appears that what really terrifies Fabián is the body's "vida independiente," the body's biological activities undomesticated by our intellectual domain. The perplexity and astonishment the body evokes is tellingly described as rigid and boundless [*rígido y desaforado*]. At the limits of the body, against its rigid, or impenetrable, perplexing mysteries, emotions and philosophies crash [*estrellar*]. For this, the body merits not only its own cult, but also vigilance against its dangerous monstrosity [*demonio peligroso*]. I want to suggest that here Humanism and the inhumanity of roaches are mutually co-constitutive. At the limits of what is known, measurable and compartmentalized by Reason's equilateral and longitudinal lines, is the body's becoming-roach.

From Fabián's living room, the reader suddenly finds him or herself in a hospital waiting room. Camila's contemplation of "el mismo espacio gelatinoso de las figuritas brillantes," transitions to a diatribe by Fabián on education without dogma, and from there to the images reflected on the surface of a man's glasses, a man wearing a long blue robe, whose face also happens to be blue. Indirect discourse weaves in and out from one character to the next, and narrative voice switches back and forth from third, to first, to second person. In effect, as one of our narrators aptly describes, "[l]as historias se cruzaban, se interrumpían, formaban una red, una malla doble, triple y pegajosa, difícil de leer."[69] Portela's narrative produces a dense, tangled ecology from which subjects, objects, viewpoints, actions, thoughts, opinions, and compositions are difficult to disaggregate, difficult to dissect and identify.

What exactly brought Camila along with Fabián and Bibiana to the hospital remains unclear, Camila simply states "<<Tuve un accidente.>>" Across the span of a number of pages and intersecting narrative strands, we come to speculate that, while at the hospital, Camila has crossed the threshold of a room, willingly or unwillingly, clearly labeled "NO PASE," where radiation for producing X-Rays is emitted. As a consequence of this transgression, her now eight-month-old fetus, "Zaratustra," also referred to as "la Cosa," would necessarily be affected, as the exposure to such radiation results in "anomalías embrionarias, malformaciones múltiples, el tipo de cosas que paladean los médicos." Notwithstanding the ionization of cells such exposure would cause, Camila's unborn child survives: "El feto estaba vivo, pero más le valdría no estarlo."[70] Note the use of "valdría" and its implication of a life "worth" living. In Portela's "malla doble," scientific explanations of the biologically hazardous material are entangled with, and reimagined through, literary references, "En ese horno de azufre tan lleno de íncubos y súcubos con las fantasías de Paracelso, las bodas químicas y los ingredientes de las brujas *Macbeth,* se cocina la nueva criatura óptima, el ciudadano modelo."[71] The denomination of the model citizen, "la nueva criatura óptima," an ironic jab at Che's *hombre nuevo,*[72] might be thought alongside Fabelo's human-roach sculptures crawling over the walls of the Museo Nacional, as the biomorphic creatures imagined to survive the effects of a nuclear explosion. Indeed, from the description cited below, in which modern X-Ray machines have the capacity to produce radiations comparable to those emitted by Gamma Rays, the power of this medical device is linked to that of a nuclear weapon. The figure of the doctor and the hospital, moreover, are described as authoritative and totalitarian, "todopoderso," so that the evocation of nuclear weapons further underscores a necropolitical institution.

> Los aparatos modernos de rayos X de alto voltaje, los cuales se emplean para el diagnóstico y la terapéutica, son capaces, dijo, de producir radiaciones de longitudes de onda comparables a los rayos *gamma* que emanan, por ejemplo del *radium*. [. . .] ¡Atención¡ Otro sistemas, decía, también productores de radiación, emplean cobalto-60, un emisor monocromático de rayos *gamma*. ¿Monocromático? ¿De un solo color? ¡Que aburrido![73]

Dr. K. Schilling is also monochromatic; with his blue robe and blue face, the stereotactic neurosurgeon is at once assimilated to radiation and rendered as a fanciful figure. Having possession of "<<una de las más sólidas y reconocidas experiencias internacionales en las novedosas técnicas quirúrgicas aplicadas en las neurociencias>>,"[74] Dr. Schilling has the institutional backing and power to perform secret experiments on "negras, sacerdotisas, veteranos de África, etc."[75] That is, anyone who does not conform to the dominant subject model (or the state's ciudadano modelo), whose life is not deemed worthy of living, is treated as a "muñeco."[76]

If the doctor's authority is grounded in a particular expertise, Portela's text undermines this authority by challenging certain modes of knowledge production, scientific and medical practices that presume an unmediated access to the body. Literary analysts are also denied entry; readers that attempt to dissect and compartmentalize the body of the text will find themselves continuously thwarted by Portela's "malla doble, triple y pegajosa," or sensuous enveloping silk. While some Gamma Rays are only emitted in cobalt blue, Camila's body is injected with a variety of colors "destinados a volver más nítidas y hermosas ciertas radiografías como retratos fantasmales."[77] The X-Ray, which is produced with the express purpose to see inside the body, is transformed into a portrait, made beautiful and phantasmal; the positivistic is now eerie, paranormal. In other words, the diagnostic power of the X-Ray is rendered inoperative, made into aesthetic material, while its hazardous effects are imagined to produce biomorphic anomalies—again another creative process. That said, the fetus is eventually aborted, "firmaron los papeles que contenían la sentencia de anulación," and Fabián is suspected of having pushed Camila into the radiation room. Accordingly, the "sentencia de anulación" is indicative of both the violence Camila suffers at the hands of her domestic abuser—who at one point says, "me tratan como si fuera la bomba atómica"[78]—and the necropolitical power the hospital exercises. We learn that Camila wanted to keep the child despite its prognosticated malformation and is not granted the opportunity to see "nada de los restos del Zaratustra, un varoncito o algo así, en la cubeta llena de algo sanguinolento?"[79] The aborted fetus is at once corporeal waste and all that its mythical and literary name conjures: "¡Qué gran personaje habría sido el (la) Zaratustra de las células rebeldes!"[80]

During the hospital scenes, noting the incongruousness of the simultaneous narrative strands, the narrator/Fabián makes the following assimilation, "[e]ran casi como el paraguas y la máquina de coser encima de la mesa de disección."[81] The phrase, which originally appeared in a nineteenth-century literary text, was adopted by the Surrealists to express their ethos of chance and radical juxtapositions, unsettling preconditioned notions of reality.[82] Portela's text certainly participates in this unsettling, juxtaposing kaleidoscopes and sonograms, for instance. However, the reference to the dissection table, reiterated again, "No le había gustado pensar en la mesa de disección," also draws our attention to a particular treatment of the body.[83] In the following passage we are led to consider the diverse implications of touching, dissecting, and possessing:

> Uno es tan ingenuo que a pesar de todo le encanta ver radiografías del propio cerebro. [. . .] porque esa porción grisácea, arcilla palpitante, no se puede tocar por muy cerca que se encuentre, qué fastidio. A mí, por ejemplo, me gustaría tocar mi cerebro, debe tener pelusitas. Mis ideas tienen pelusitas, ¿no se nota?. Los intestinos, en cambio, o el estómago, sí se pueden tocar en el supuesto caso de que a uno lo destripen y no se muera enseguida. Claro, da náuseas. Uno también se puede autodestripar con alegría, romper para conocer, para poseer como posee el niño que desarma un juguete. Para eso sirve la mesa de disección, ¿no es así?[84]

The impossibility of touching one's brain while still conscious, imagining its texture as greasy and clay-like, imagining also that this particular brain and its ideas would have small hairs or fuzz, prompts us to consider the materiality of the seemingly immaterial. Let us recall here Nancy's concept of thoughts as weighty bodies, "[h]ere is the hard point of this thing 'thought,' nodule or synapse, acid or enzyme, a gram of cortex."[85] That thoughts or ideas might have "pelusitas," that they can be touched, suggests not that thoughts can be incarnated, but rather that each and every thought is absolutely singular and therefore unpossessable, at least not *limpiamente.* How would one reproduce or understand a "pelusita"? Alternatively, "romper para conocer, para poseer," signals the violence that knowing and possessing entail, or more accurately that a particular form of knowing entails, in its assumption of being in full possession. The assimilation of taking apart a doll, as a child might do, to the dissection table alerts us to the instrumentalization of bodies as mere material resources, as well as to the whims of sovereign power, cutting and taxonomizing under the guise of reason and modernizing projects.

Inhuman Writings

Following the abortion of Zaratustra, Camila suffers from a sudden paralysis and is relocated to a famous research center that boasts integral rehabilitation and whose name the narrator prefers not to remember.[86] The cause of her paralysis evades Dr. Schilling and his cruel experiments.

> Vino una extrañeza que no había conocido antes, la levedad y al fin la parálisis acompañada a veces de espasmos [. . .] Una inmovilidad móvil, inquietante oxímoron [. . .] que durante varios meses impidió a diversos especialistas, unos con caras azules y otros no, establecer un diagnóstico.[87]

Camila's body, "conformada por lo indefenso de volverse gusano retorcido por no decir otra vez feto," is subjected to electroshock therapy and a diversity of injections and pills.[88] At one point she is denied sedatives, "<<a ver qué pasa>>," and her body goes into convulsions, palpitations, and spasms. Described by the narrator as a sack full of cats thrown into the water, Camila's body is no longer hers, nor an individual entity, but a force, a pack of animals desperate to survive.[89] "Siempre con el sádico propósito de hacerla caer [. . .] en un agujero [. . .] ¿Para qué sirve el poder si no se ejerce."[90] Between stimulants and depressants, Camila imagines Dr. Schilling telling her with a baroque flair for the infinitesimal, "no eres persona en el sentido recto de la palabra. Eres una cucaracha. ¿No lo sientes de vez en cuando? ¿Nunca te lo habían dicho? Un grano de arena entre todas las playas del mundo, un gorgojo entre quinientos quintales de arroz. Eso eres."[91] If Dr. Schilling's physical torture and imagined verbal abuse weren't enough, the hospital attendants speak in front of her assuming she cannot understand them: "<<Dicen que tuvo un hijo anormal, un

monstruo.>> <<Lógico: los hijos salen a sus padres.>> <<Quién sería el valiente, eh?>>[. . .]<<No hay una perversión sexual que es así, que hace que a la gente le gusten los anormales? [. . .] debe ser la mongofilia [. . .] estas retrasadas mentales que andan por ahí sueltas y sin vacunar casi siempre son tremendas putas.>>"[92] The attendants' gossiping, as though Camila were not in the room, is symptomatic of her invisibility and un-belonging. Although she may be reduced to a grain of sand or an insect, Camila clearly poses a societal threat: Her association with perversion, her suspected sexual proclivity and un-vaccinated body present her as a behavioral and corporeal contaminant. And no wonder she poses such a threat. When Camila attempts to speak in her semi-paralysis, her tongue trembles and her speech is illegible: "No entiendo nada de lo que estás diciendo. Sácate lo que tengas dentro de la boca."[93] Her inability to control her body and to articulate renders her defenseless. However, it also renders her incomprehensible and, as such, I want to suggest, instantiates, to quote the narrator again, "el producto rígido y desaforado de la perplejidad, del asombro de que su cuerpo tuviese, en cierta forma, vida independiente."[94] The incomprehension and perplexity Camila inspires is yet another mode in which she becomes-animal.

Earlier I proposed that Portela's novel does more than expose institutional abuse of power and inhumane treatment. As I hope to illustrate further, the text prompts us to reconsider the ways in which bodies are organized and made legible, to reconsider the distinction between undifferentiated animal bodies, as material resource, and political bodies, as lives worth living. When Camila finally regains control of her body and her speech, rather than confront Dr. Schilling and defend herself as "una persona en el sentido recto de la palabra," la sacerdotisa "prefirió escabullirse, suelta y sin vacunar."[95] In other words, Camila and the text's narrative voice do not disavow her being a vulnerable, un-immunized "bichito" or "animalejo"[96] that scurries away. It is survival, the desire to stay alive, and not heroics that conditions Camila's actions. For her, "no existe ningún sentido, ninguna trascendencia [. . .] Se trataba de vivir, circunstancia ajena a toda comprensión."[97] In her reading of *El pájaro,* Odette Casamayor-Cisneros echoes this sentiment when she writes, "Portela [. . .] parece decirnos solamente que lo importante es vivir."[98] Camila manages to escape the hospital and possibly stages a mutiny with other patients on her way out, but the events remain unclear. Portela's politics in this novel might be dismissed as indifferent or as having no import given that her characters do not insist on recognition or protest for the rights and representation of a particular disenfranchised group. Once out of the hospital, Camila will continue to be medicated and never demonstrates an autonomous agency that is legible or in accordance with a broader political agenda. In fact, Casamayor-Cisneros claims that in *El pájaro,* "no hay críticas ni elogios, la burla es ingrávida, y todo es más bien un deslizarse por entre estructuras, ideologías, y políticas y culturas [. . .] Esta literatura no pertenece a nada ni a nadie. Se pierde en ella toda noción de grupo."[99] While the observation is meant as a negative critique, considering this book's investment in exploring non-identitarian forms of community, I would argue that *El pájaro*'s belonging to nothing or no one, and its espousal of surviving over the fulfillment of a teleological project, is precisely where its political impact lies. In this last section, I will explore how Portela, in addition to deploying an aesthetic practice of impenetrability and impropriety, links creative production to a becoming-animal, as a means to challenge authority, dominant subject models, notions of autonomy, agency, and what it means to be *humano ciento por ciento.*

After having been read a short story—one written by Emilio U (sometimes double for Ena Lucía Portela)—Camila experiences a sense of well-being and the following day, to the "estupefacción" of Dr. Schilling, she regains control of her body.[100] Aesthetic pleasure, it would seem, provides the cure to Camila's un-diagnosable medical ailment. However, even before she recovers from her paralysis, the narrator illustrates Camila's capacity to creatively mediate the happenings at the hospital. From her outsider's perspective, or "desde la puerta, su ángulo favorito,"[101] and her "a-normality," Camila's spectatorship transforms the cruel and banal events at the hospital into fantastical pieces. As noted above, her X-Rays become beautiful phantasmal portraits. Through Camila's thoughts, her dramatic illusions, her visions, what happens in the hospital does so on a stage, "Y así por el estilo cada vez que aparecían en el escenario," "teatro total," "la tragedia," "majestuosos espectros," "proyectos."[102] When she watches a 1993 telenovela, *Corazón salvaje,* with other patients, Camila does not distinguish between commercials or the plot of the soap opera, but considers what transpires on the television screen as one continuous dramatic narrative. The doctor may be "todopoderoso," but what Camila conjures imaginatively remains outside of his jurisdiction.[103] Her inability to perceive distinctions—be that between fiction and reality, or commercial and soap opera—or rather, her capacity to un-restrict her vision by conventional limits, has political implications. After the death of one of the patients,

> Camila sintió curiosidad por el destino del cadáver, imagen ausente, y su fantasía voló en dirección a una siniestra cámara refrigerada, donde también habría jamones colgando del techo [. . .] <<Sería interesante si a la hora del almuerzo se confunden (o no, ¿quién sabe?) y nos sirven a los sobrevivientes un plato raro con forma de mano o de pie o de algo peor.>>[104]

In Camila's fantasy, where once again bodies hang, Portela prompts us to consider the indistinction between human flesh and animal meat and, consequently, between that which is protected, fed, and nourished and that which is consumable, disposable, and sentenced to death.[105] Through curiosity, fantasy, and confusion, not only does the ordering of bodies into human and animal come into question, but also, necessarily, other forms of societal discrimination. Drawing from the discourse of biopolitics, Gabriel Giorgi reminds us that hierarchal binaries of race, sex, class, and gender, while commonly understood as cultural constructs, are projected upon the limit that marks *zoón politikón* from indistinguishable animal life, a limit assumed to be natural, but that in fact is constituted by aesthetics, by a way of seeing and organizing.[106] When Camila wonders if Blacks or whites taste the same and speculates that Blacks must be more nutritious since Black slaves were more expensive than white ones,[107] Portela implicitly, if not ironically, demonstrates how structures of value and exclusion, disguised as rational and apolitical, are violently arbitrary—like a child taking apart a doll. Accordingly, the distinction between the living and the dead is also rendered cultural and political; Camila considers the contradictions of "una cultura que entierra a sus muertos y a veces, ¿por qué no?, también a sus vivos."[108]

In her search for the elusive Emilio U, author of the short story read to her at the hospital, Camila attends a lecture at the university. Discussions on Lacan, Foucault, Neobarroquismo, and a series of other ideas and assumptions about modernist and postmodernist literary writers are mentioned; each dismissed in one way or another with irreverence by the narrator. It becomes impossible for the reader to identify a particular thought or tradition with which Portela might align herself. Meanwhile through Camila's eyes the respected university professor is seen in the following way, "No usa pañuelo y el sudor le pega la camisa al cuerpo todo cubierto de pelos. Es un mamífero."[109] And the content of his lecture becomes material for more interesting compositions:

> Los garabatos y fórmulas que el orador <<inscribe>> en la pizarra semejan una composición informalista, cada vez más complicada, donde Camila de nuevo se propone descubrir cuerpos, latencias, enanos y sirenas de trapo que se escudan ahora tras la más citada de las frases, tanto así, que hasta yo la cito (ver en alguno de los capítulos anteriores), obra de un pe-pensador, un fi-filósofo, esc-cuela de Viviena. Ninguno de nosotros estuvo allí, ¿cómo creer en eso?, piensa ella y alguien susurra que Viena está de moda.[110]

The narrator may mock the orator's stuttering, "un tartamúdo rodeado de imbéciles,"[111] and dismiss those in attendance with their preoccupation for what is academically fashionable, but the narrator does not exclude him/herself from participating within this particular intellectual world, "hasta yo la cito." Camila, as always, goes unnoticed in the lecture hall even when she faints and falls to the floor. She observes her surroundings, from the ground, littered with cigarette butts and even an albino roach; "desde su angulo singular, aunque no desconocido para ella," the narrator notes.[112] But from her humiliating positions [*posiciones humillantes*], her obstructed perspectives, "[q]uizá la perspectiva no sea del todo buena, pues la sacerdotisa es bajita,"[113] she takes the formulas on the chalk board, abstractions and generalizations with an instructional function and (like Fabelo and Deleuze) changes the coordinates on this plane; she moves from a molar to a molecular perspective. Bodies, latencies, dwarfs, and mermaids made of rags are idiosyncratic, differentiating agencies that contaminate the authority of those so often deferred to citations.

Unlike people she speculates to be "incapaz de percibir la corriente de poesía que fluye de todas las cosas,"[114] Camila states, or so the narrator speculates,

> <<Soy una diáspora, la visión final del estallido>>, diría Camila si en verdad tuviese algún interés en explicarse. <<Estoy disgregada, puedo representar diversos personajes cuando yo quiera [. . .] Cualquier apariencia de unidad, de sujeto coherente deducible de lo que digo, es falsa, es una ironía. [. . .] Me gusta escuchar, aprender, puedo devorarlo todo, mi estómago es infinito. No hay escape. Soy una diáspora, soy mis fragmentos.>>[115]

Although Camila is never identified as a writer per se, her imagined ontology as a dispersed, fragmented, diasporic explosion, is certainly poetic, if not philosophical. Her perceptiveness of situations is later assimilated to that of the narrator's, "(como la sacerdotisa o el mismo narrador)."[116] Fabián and Bibiana, by contrast, are clearly not writers: "Fabián no era escritor, sino personaje."[117] Bibiana is imperceptive, unobservant, and incapable of expression, "[l]a modelo, daltónica para gentes, lugares y cosas, vagaba por el espectro sin distinguir entre sí los tonos complementarios," "[l]os signos [son] ignorados por sus ojos de colores distintos," "jamás hubiera conseguido expresarlo."[118] "Ante los ojos de la sacerdotisa," on the other hand, we get the most spectacular visions; "Camila [. . .] percibe ahora todos los detalles con nitidez anormal."[119] On each of Bibiana's fingernails painted with iridescent polish, Camila envisions mermaids, volcanoes, and figures from Bosch's paintings.[120] She is also a captivating storyteller, and one that does so all the while "acariciando ella a la modelo y haciéndola estremecer por caminos que sabe de memoria."[121] Camila's audience demands "Dime, ¿qué pasó después?" and she considers "qué es realmente lo que ellos desean escuchar."[122] Camila, as we've seen, does not look for meaning, she does not believe in the transcendental, she does not try to understand the void, she is not motivated by dignity or heroics, she will not jeopardize her survival. She is by no means a model citizen, nor much less a political activist challenging the status quo. Camila scurries away. And yet through her creativity she continuously transforms her surroundings; she subverts and undermines authorial ways of seeing and understanding the world around her. Creative production here seems to always be linked with "un bicho raro" or "un puñetero mosquito." The narrator states, "soy tímido, desmesurado (si lo prefieres, denso) y padezco de ansiedad. Me fascina figurar en mis inventos como las moscas en la comida vieja y los guajacones en el fanguito."[123] In other words, creative production is not that which redeems and transcends mere material subsistence, but is imminent and interdependent, even parasitic, on a particular territory. Accordingly, the text itself or, rather, texts in general are a territory, a mud, from which meaning cannot be disaggregated. With regard to a Greek-Spanish dictionary, one passage reads "con palabras en forma de bichitos que significaban otras y otras palabras y así hasta el infinito, calzaba los papeles."[124] So that the deferral that poststructuralism posits takes on here a materiality; alphabetic scripts are tiny bugs, proliferating pages upon pages from which meaning can never transcend, but only generates more insect-letters.

At the start of this chapter, in reference to the Chinese brush painting, I discussed how the calligrapher-artist was thought to suspend ordinary habits of mind and body in order that grace may be received, in order that an iteration of a character may reflect something unimagined before.

Interestingly, Portela's narrator denies having grace: "Para lograrlo, sin embargo, es necesaria la gracia de un talento especial, una suerte de sanción divina que no me ha tocado, pues aquí estoy, cada día más aburrido de mí mismo."[125] And with regards to the writer Emilio U, the narrator states,

> del cachorro no desprovisto de talento que todavía no ha llegado a creerse [. . .] tocado por la gracia divina; escribía con el descaro del aprendiz que aún piensa el lector sin hacer de ello un manifiesto, que busca erizar y divertir al lector, colársele por debajo de la puerta como una tarjeta de Navidad, en lugar de mortificarlo con inhóspitas densidades u otras malevolencias por el estilo.[126]

Recalling here Gregory Bateson's elaboration of artistic grace as a wisdom that recognizes interlocking circuits, a capacity for empathy—imagination unrestricted by identitarian limits—and the unselfconscious movements of an animal, I want to suggest that while Portela does not claim a divine grace, something immaterial and transcendent, what she does exhibit is an ecological grace. Her narrative style as a network, "una malla doble, triple y pegajosa, difícil de leer," is certainly laborious and arguably inhospitable to her readers. Her constant shifts of narrative voice disabuse us of any notion of a coherent subjectivity, of our ability to penetrate the text. Instead, we must submit ourselves to the dispersed, fragmented, diasporic explosions, to the enveloping, sensuous and translucent silk of her textual embroidery. She looks to "erizar y divertir" in place of a manifesto, in place of a political project. The image of the writer slipping through the bottom of a door, [*colársele por debajo de la puerta*], brings us again to that horizontal animal, that insect small enough to crawl through a crack like an uninvited guest. The absence of a legible project does not foreclose, but only enhances the political potential and impact of Portela's text. In its impropriety, in its uneconomic verbosity, in its refusal to provide self-identifying subjects, and in its predilection for non-anthropocentric perspectives, *El pájaro* destabilizes dominant modes of seeing, knowing, and relating; it challenges the limits of what constitutes the political and prompts its readers to consider alternative forms of community.

Unproductive and De/composing Bodies

Although Portela's novel takes place early in the 1990s, at the height of the Special Period, and makes references to power outages and characters stealing goods from stores exclusively available to tourists—Bibiana steals baby socks and clothing for Camila—its main characters do not suffer from inadequate housing or material shortages. Camila is initially unhoused due to her own reckless behavior (or so the narrator suggests) and later lives with Fabián who has inherited an apartment and receives funds from his family living abroad. Bibiana, through her modeling, has access to luxury apparel and opportunities to travel to cities like New York. In effect, their living conditions are not representative of the island at large, and in this way Portela's novel participates in the same un-belonging of her characters. Ponte's novel, *La fiesta vigilada,* to which we now turn, by contrast is very much focused on the housing crisis and dire need for basic material goods everyday citizens endure. However, both writers share a particular attention to the vulnerability of the body, its entanglements with its surroundings, and a strong critique of dominant subject models, institutional power, and a narrative of forward progress.

"Mea!', llegué a gritarle viendo que se dormía en el inodoro. (Una tarde la arrinconé con una escoba del mismo modo que se trata a las ratas.) Las noches se iban en ese tango y al final era dulce escucharla orinar"; this Ponte's narrator tells us about his maternal grandmother early in *La fiesta vigilada.*[127] Wedged between stories of literary enemies, the fall of the Soviet empire, the Eiffel Tower, and a statue of John Lennon sitting on one of Havana's park benches, we have the deteriorated body of an old senile woman, a body with the "consistency of a rag doll" [*consistencia de muñeca de trapo*].[128] In what turns out to be very infrequent in this novel, Ponte takes some eight uninterrupted pages to narrate an intimate and biographical story, a story, moreover, about incontinence and fragility.

As the first-person narrator, the unnamed author recounts his suspension from the Cuban writer's union, UNEAC. With the loss of his civic identity, expulsed from the "lettered city," he wanders through Havana's ruins like a "phantom."[129] And yet, the narrator rarely appears as a character in what would seem to be an autobiographical account.[130] With the exception of his voice and parenthetical digressions, he disappears for parts of the narration, as though exiled from his own text, or perhaps transformed into a ghost. The very idea of one's own proper text is called into question when we note the "novel" is composed of a series of retold movie plots, spy fiction, historical events, journalistic information, scholarly essays, topographies, and personal reflections. In short, *La fiesta* reads like a catalogue or a work of assemblage. Its pages are marked by an excessive use of parenthesis, as the narrator appears to slip in wherever he can, producing fissures and ruptures, parasitically. Novelistic conventions such as plot and character development—climactic and voyeuristic devices to lure its readers inside—are largely disused and, instead, Ponte draws his readers outside the text, situating *La fiesta* within a web of other archives, artifacts, and contexts. This is a text without a well-formed body, without a recognizable structure, and among the rubble of other stories, as I aim to demonstrate, we find a pulsating subterranean life, an insistence on corporeality, exposure, and survival.

Before taking a closer look at this life underneath, let's consider the following: The Cuban Revolution "domesticates time" [*doma el tiempo*], states Ponte's narrator; it institutionalizes "what was open adventure" [*lo que fuera aventura abierta*].[131] Shortly after the Revolution's triumph in 1959, leisure, laziness, festivity for the sake of festivity—otherwise considered "killing time while the fields of sugar cane needed cutting" [*mata(r) el tiempo en tanto los campos de caña de azúcar necesitaban macheteros*]—became a criminal offense.[132] Unproductive expenditure, to use Georges Bataille's phrase, was closely surveilled and each year was inaugurated with a mission: "Year of Agrarian Reform," "Year of Education," "Year of Planning." After exhausting specific missions, the years were simply commemorated as "Year Thirty of the Revolution."[133] Cabarets and beaches were closed so time and energy could be spent not just on the fields but, especially, missiles and radars.[134] With the advent of the 1962 Missile Crisis, "La Habana fue declarada campo de guerra que duraría décadas," eventually becoming "parque temático de la Guerra Fría."[135] According to our narrator, the revolutionary project was totalizing and, consequently, exclusionary. Invoking Fidel's famous 1961 speech to intellectuals, he writes, "Dentro de la Revolución, todo. Pero ¿quién conseguía estar adentro?"[136] The all-inclusiveness of Castro's original phrase, "Dentro de la Revolución, todo; contra la Revolución, nada," produces a grammar where what is not recognized as contributing to the aims of the Revolution is deemed valueless, "nada," and therefore disposable. Put otherwise, its all-or-nothing logic demanded absolute devotion.

Citing the protagonist from Graham Greene's novel *Our Man in Havana,* the narrator states, "a Wormold tocaba cierta epifanía frente al apocalipsis: <<los crueles vienen y van como las ciudades y los tronos y los poderes, dejando detrás de sí sus ruinas. >>"[137] While the threat of the Missile Crisis in the form of spectacular nuclear bombs was never realized, its promise of ruins did in a politics of perpetual antagonisms and slow violence.[138] Wormold's epiphany, regarding the powerful and what they leave behind, might be likened to what Brad Evans and Henry A. Giroux theorize in their book, *Disposable Futures.* Following Zygmunt Bauman, they write:

> Rather than seeing waste as politically useless, Bauman affirms that the production of wasted lives shores up the productivity of the whole system, as the very idea of progress requires the setting aside of those who don't or are unable to perform in a way that would appear meaningful. Criminalization [. . .] performs a vital task by providing scapegoats [. . .] such scapegoats offer an "easy target for unloading anxieties prompted by the widespread fears of social redundancy." [. . .] [T]he incessant drive to progress justifies a form of societal assay that allows for the casting aside of people [for] their own failure to have resources worth extracting.[139]

Although Evans and Giroux's analysis is largely based in contemporary capitalist economies, Cuba's 1971 law against vagrancy and its 1960s labor camps, Unidades Militares de Ayuda a la Producción, designed to rehabilitate homosexuals, religious believers, and those deemed anti-social are examples of this criminalization and casting aside.[140] Adding to Evans and Giroux's insights on the production of wasted lives, it is useful to recall Georges Bataille's ecological theorization of excess energy in his work *The Accursed Share.* Observing that living organisms ordinarily receive "more energy than is necessary for maintaining life," he argues that this excess should be spent luxuriously and unproductively; otherwise, the outcome will be catastrophic.[141] Material resources, in turn, exceed whatever instrumental work we might assign to them. Bataille writes, "Humanity exploits given material resources, but by restricting them as it does to a resolution of the immediate difficulties it encounters (a resolution which it has hastily had to define as an ideal), it assigns to the forces it employs an end which they cannot have."[142] To prevent a destructive and ruinous outpouring of energy, Bataille calls for a "general economy"—where transactions are considered within a larger framework that allows for expenditure without gain—against the instrumentality and productiveness of a "restricted economy." In other words, the "erotic" aesthetic the bureaucrat in *La fiesta* complains against (cited in the introduction)[143] and the unpurposive festivities the state aimed to prohibit are not only "inescapable" according to Bataille, but serve an ethical function, allowing for a dissipation of energy before its manifests itself violently.[144] As though expressing this inevitable dissipation, in one of the novel's parenthetical, sardonic, asides, we read that in 1971, assigned "The Year of Productivity," "En el país había más parásitos y gente ociosa que en toda la novelística rusa del siglo XIX."[145]

The casting aside of people that Evans and Giroux observe is operative in *La fiesta* in various ways. Following the verbal news of his suspension from the writers' union, the narrator is unable to recover any documents that would evidence his expulsion and censorship: "Mi etapa de fantasma comenzaba sin prueba alguna. [. . .] La orden, el documento oficial, el papel, no existía."[146] Juxtaposed to passages on the erasure of political identity and "civil death,"[147] Ponte narrates intimate, banal, and pathetic scenes in an imperturbable manner. In a less obvious instance of casting away, we learn about the decision to place his grandmother in a state asylum. "Encerrada cuando ya no cabía educación para ella, cuando no podía adaptarse a nada nuevo."[148] At the asylum:

> Las deposiciones eran limpiadas al amanecer, el día comenzaba con el baño de los cuerpos y la hervidura de la ropa de cama. (Imagino los racimos de cuerpos en la desesperación del insomnio, el orine desparramándose por la explanada de aquellas camas unidas, el hedor de las viejas.) Y en una de sus visitas mi mamá encontró marcas de golpes en la piel de su mamá.[149]

In depicting the indignity these incapacitated figures endure, in choosing the word "bodies" instead of "individuals," and in occupying the foreground of the narrative with biological needs, Ponte underscores a bare life. Whereas the discursive boundaries of civic and national identities are considered stable markers of differentiation, immune to changing environments, bodies, as illustrated here, are exposed, contagious, and vulnerable, always in relation to and, at times, indistinguishable from other bodies. The narrator and his mother eventually bring the grandmother back home. Under institutional care she had ultimately been abandoned, exposed to violence and theft.[150] Through her bruised skin and defenseless body, unable to even shout, [*no alcanza a la defensa ni al grito*],[151] Ponte conveys an image of absolute dependence.

This foregrounding of corporeality is consistent throughout the text. We are reminded that like the leather produced from a cow's skin, the skin of a man also serves to line material goods: "La historia podría ser tan cíclica y terrible como lo aseguraban la cigarrera forrada de piel humana."[152] And yet the narrator notes that in particular historical accounts "algo más de fondo parecía existir [. . .] Notas de color [. . .] frases al parecer inesenciales."[153] The city itself is described as a mortal body: "tantos cortes como cicatrices puedan contener los antebrazos de un suicida obsesionado con la idea de acercarse cada vez más al final."[154] "La capital cubana se anima a implosión, late en sístole y sístole."[155] "[L]as ruinas son arquitectura torturada."[156] And with respect to the pages of a text whose errors were marked in red, the narrator tells us it appeared to have "blood ink" [*tinta en sangre*].[157] With this sample of citations, I mean to underscore an insistence on a shared and irreducible corporeality, be that between humans, animals, buildings, and the pages of a text. Ponte, furthermore, animates through this enfleshment what would otherwise be considered inert material resources, or simply a repository of history with no vitality of its own. We might consider the "notes of color" and "inessential phrases" the narrator points to, as that which cannot be subsumed, made a work of, or used as a means to an end. Against the Revolution's taming of time and its narrative of futurity, "something more underneath appeared to exist." I want to note, a shared corporeality, in contrast to an identity, is necessarily improper, it belongs to no one; the phrases "my body," "my text," "my city" could never fully encompass their referents. Accordingly, to treat a shared corporeality, or a cosubstantiality, in an instrumental and compartmentalized manner, as though it was distinct and reducible to a property, will have destructive consequences.[158]

In the novel's depiction of the Revolution's handling of prostitution and gambling we see the negative impacts of treating something in an isolated manner. Ponte illustrates how the state's mission to exterminate what it perceived as immoral and decadent failed to recognize a larger system, an ecology of which slot machines and pimps are only some of its perceptible effects. Instead of addressing poverty and unemployment, cabarets and casinos were closed, leaving sex workers and gamblers to find more illicit and precarious venues.[159] During the Special Period, prostitution as a mode of survival returned with a vengeance. Curiously, Ponte describes it as an almost inoperative economy, or one whose transactions cannot be measured by monetary gain. Being willing to work in exchange for the pleasure of a cold beer, the comfort of a couch, or the simulation of personal affect confused the distinctions between necessity and desire.[160] Alternatively, the inefficiency of this prostitution according to a restricted economy, the unproductive expenditure in the fulfillment of a desire for a cold beer, might be considered an inescapable, and necessary, outpouring of excess energy. Resources, as Bataille argues, cannot be reduced to the ends we assign them.

Inhabited Ruins

The distinctions between what is proper and improper, or private and public, are further obscured when we consider the inhabited ruins.[161] The collapse between interiority and exteriority, as facades crumble, makes it difficult to determine the boundaries of these buildings. Their porosity and precariousness intensify their relationship with their surroundings. And just as a body harbors other organisms like bacteria and microbes, the ruins are described as inhabited by parasitic dwellers. Ponte observes that while Havana does not expand its vertical or horizontal limits, the city grows from the inside.[162] With the migration of easterners to the capital, expanding families, a housing shortage, and the collapse of other buildings, Havana's inhabitants or dwellers [*moradores*] build walls, divisions, and lofts within existing structures. Notably, Ponte hardly, if ever, uses the word residents or individuals, heightening the image of the city as a habitat and ecosystem. The proliferating smaller spaces are often described as corners, hideouts, or closets [*rincón, covacha*].[163] Even rooftops are converted into tiny rooms for which "one didn't know if it was humans or pigeons that should be accredited" [*no se sabría si adjudicar a humanos o palomas*].[164] While these inhabitants carve out spaces for themselves within these structures, chipping away at the buildings' foundations, they are also the ones to consistently repair its damaged roofs, patch surfaces, and drain rainwater.[165] In this continuous process of damaging and repairing, the inhabitants appear as integral parts of the buildings; they both animate the buildings and are a source of their destruction.[166]

Citing a Spanish essayist on the stages of ruination the narrator writes, "Durante el último acto aparecían los vegetales carroñeros. 'No hay ruina sin vida vegetal; sin yedra, musgo o jaramago que brote en la rendija de la piedra, confundida con el lagarto, como un delirio de la vida que nace de la muerte,' determinó María Zambrano."[167] The cyclical link between "life" and "death," the emergence of vegetation from within a crack, and the assimilation of its greenery to that of a reptile is, perhaps, a classic image of the persistence and indistinction of "nature." What is not however classic is the assimilation of human reproduction, or filial expansion, to that of proliferating plant life: "Lo vegetal [. . .] comienza por un árbol dentro de la casa, el genealógico."[168] In the poetics of this novel, human figures often cross into a zone of biological organisms, exhibiting qualities of rodents, insects, and even algae. The inhabitants of ruins are described as "scurrying" [*escabullían*].[169] At another point, they emerge from a power outage drawn to the bright windows of a hotel, like moths to a light. And these illuminated panes of glass appear as "fish tanks" in the dark of night [*la gente (. . .) emergía del apagón para acercarse a esas peceras*].[170] In a passage referring to the state's response to an epidemic we read, "En vista de que las fumigaciones volvían irrespirable el interior de los domicilios, también nosotros, moradores, salíamos a la calle."[171] With that "también nosotros," Ponte's narrator implicitly situates himself and his neighbors alongside that which needed to be disinfected and purged; as part of the same environment they are also vulnerable to the fumes. In a phrase that expresses the height of abjection, we read: "los albergues estatales guardan una capa humana tan legamosa como lo que cubre las aguas estancadas."[172]

People are not the only ones to adopt other ontologies. In the rapid deterioration of buildings in Cuba, we can observe processes of change in materials conventionally perceived as solid and stable. As suggested in the section on corporeality, materials in *La fiesta* are charged with a vitality of their own. In Ponte's grammar, objects, such as a potted plant, a fan, or the Eiffel Tower, occupy the position of subject; they are agents of action.[173] The presumably inanimate are also depicted as the recipients of emotional injuries: "he insulted her" [*la insultó*], the pronoun her standing in for the Eiffel Tower.[174] In the following passage we see how an architectural structure fought with its last breath to stay alive, so to speak:

> [E]l antiguo hotel Pasaje resistió el desequilibrio que le causaran. La vida pareció continuar igual que siempre por una noche y la mitad de una mañana. Hasta que la estructura no pudo más, lanzó un silbido, un chorro de polvo al cielo, y se vino abajo.[175]

That particles of dust should produce a stream [*un chorro de polvo*], transforming solid into liquid matter, is another example of how Ponte's poetics unsettle ontological categories. Illustrating the complex and delicate networks of which this structure is a part, heightened in its precarious state, the narrator surmises, in his characteristic parenthetical asides, "(El colmo pudo ser el cierre de una puerta, alguien que cerraba un refrigerador luego de servirse agua)."[176] The seemingly inconsequential and unselfconscious act of closing the refrigerator door has monumental effects, like the proverbial straw that broke the camel's back.

Recalling Georg Simmel's writings on ruins, the narrator explains that the German philosopher found inhabited ruins disquieting and blamed their inhabitants for abetting nature, a force they should have banded against.[177] For Simmel, ruins—that is, those not too demolished that their original form is imperceptible, and certainly not ones with people living in them—afforded the contemplation of nature's vengeance over culture's transcendental spirit. But to appreciate this dialectical relationship, these two antagonizing forces must remain distinct. The inhabitants of ruins, complicit with nature, collapse this distinction; "traicionaban a los hombres y demostraban cuán poca alma tenían."[178] What, then, might be gained or revealed from a sustained attention to Havana's ruins, a zone of indistinction, and abject living conditions?

As a self-identified ruinologist, Ponte's narrator expresses ambivalence toward his trade. He acknowledges that in representing Havana's ruins, in perpetuating this particular trope, he, inadvertently, not only contributes to an ongoing process of the city's museumification and its image as a Cold War theme park, but also supports the state's narrative of a permanent state of emergency.[179] However, as Esther Whitfield demonstrates in her reading of *La fiesta* and other works by Ponte, these ruins in their very persistence are also for him a source of hope. She explains,

> For Simmel, the people whom he saw living in Roman ruins were unambiguously agents of those ruins' destruction, parasites who could only weaken their host's structure and power to charm. Their very presence broke the spell of silence that surrounds a ruin proving them to be complicit with, as Ponte puts it, "one of the two adversaries," the one charged with destruction. [. . .] [T]he squatters had to be nature's accomplices. And yet, to what Simmel laments as the dilapidation of an aesthetic affect, Ponte opposes a hope that the buildings, and hence the life within them, will remain standing against the odds. [. . .] Rather than mere accomplices in the destruction of their dwellings, Ponte suggests, might not these survivors be double agents, in the service of both decay and hope?[180]

The imagined dichotomy that Simmel wants to guard between nature and culture buttresses the notion of human exceptionalism and its teleological projects. These modernizing and utopic projects, let us remember, have roots in Enlightenment rubrics and have relied on an instrumental and compartmentalizing logic to justify processes of exploitation and casting aside.[181] I want to suggest that in breaking the spell, in obstructing the distanced contemplation of "culture" and "nature," the inhabited ruins do *not* allow us to disavow a shared materiality with our environment; the inhabited ruins make evident that we are always in a relationship of interdependence.

While Ponte is certainly invested in exposing a system of censorship and social death—a mode of disposing those considered unproductive to the Revolution's ends—we have seen that intertwined with texts, buildings, and the city (all of which are associated with intelligent, discursive life), is the corporeal, the material, and the indistinguishable. In illustrating the simultaneity of being a political phantom, or politically "dead," and being corporeally "alive," the text draws our attention to the persistence of life underneath (or zoē), that which modernizing projects have strived to domesticate through "scientific education," "culture," and "progress." Following Whitfield, it is the very parasitic ability of the dwellers to survive that gives Ponte hope and not, I would add, a reclaiming of national identity or the exhibition of heroic sacrifices.

As I noted earlier, *La fiesta vigilada* does not provide us with a cohesive structure that would constitute a recognizable literary work. In appropriating other novels, essays, films, and historical events, assembled with seemingly insignificant accounts of invisible lives, Ponte, not unlike the inhabitants of ruins, expresses a symbiotic relationship; he destroys as he constructs, eating away at the integrity of other structures. The novel's lack of biographical information and the space allotted to summaries of other narratives, reiterates a sense of impropriety. Inserting digressions and personal reflections between parentheses, the narrator appears to burrow spaces in a structure of which he does not belong. In effect, he produces and inhabits a ruin at the level of the writing. Where one might expect for Ponte to insist on an enduring humanism or the recovery of his civic identity through an edifying work of literature, he, instead, adopts the very techniques of the parasitic dwellers. On the last page of the novel, referring to a museum's guest book, the narrator claims, "I managed to *scurry* away without writing anything in it" [*logré escabullirme sin escribir nada en él*].[182] Such scurrying and slipping away recall Fabelo's roaches on the exterior walls of the Museo Nacional. In place of leaving a legacy, his name for posterity, Ponte's narrator, like the parasitic dwellers, opts for survival. And in the same way his narrative strategies emulate their parasitic practices, we might consider the dwellers, in turn, as anonymous writers, who leave their traces and recreate the city from within.[183] Ponte's text is no doubt aimed at exposing "dehumanizing" living conditions, but rather than appeal to a transcendental spirit he elevates the less-than-human, the discarded and the useless.

Talking Trash

In her reading of Pedro Juan Gutiérrez's novels, Whitfield explains how Havana's residential quarters appear as "habitats" animated by the "human beings" who live in them.[184] Returning again to Jane Bennett, I would like to suggest that in *La fiesta vigilada,* Ponte allows us to imagine an ecology where buildings are not simply animated by humans but by their very own "vibrant matter." Indeed, as we have seen, objects in the text are often depicted as having agency and a capacity to feel. In her book *Vibrant Matter,* Bennett aims "to detach materiality from the figures of passive, mechanistic, or divinely infused substance," and argues, "vibrant matter is *not* the raw material for the creative activity of humans or God."[185] Echoing Bataille's theory of excess energy and material resources, she observes an "impersonal affectivity" of things that is irreducible to their instrumentality. Her book challenges anthropocentrism and calls for an attentiveness to "the capacity of things—edibles, commodities, storms, metals—not only to impede or block the will and designs of humans but also to act as quasi agents or forces with trajectories, propensities, or tendencies of their own."[186] Early in her text, Bennett describes an encounter with some debris—a dead rat, a white bottle cap, a black plastic glove, and a piece of wood—in the following way:

> [T]hese items shimmered back and forth between debris and [. . .] stuff that commanded attention in its own right, as existents in excess of their association with human meanings, habits, or projects. [. . .] [The] stuff exhibited its thing-power: it issued a call, even if I did not quite understand what it was saying. At the very least, it provoked affects in me.[187]

Ponte offers us a similar scene in *La fiesta vigilada.* Following an epidemic that broke out in a neighborhood due to standing water, there was an official campaign to "throw out all that was useless from homes"; consequently, "accumulated junk started to float outside" [*echar fuera de casa todo lo inservible y comenzaban a salir a flote los tarecos acumulados*].[188] Expressing an affective attachment toward this junk, as well as a parallel between the inhabitants and the discarded, we read "Costaba dar adiós [. . .] nos amarraba a desechos."[189] The passage continues:

> Un cascarón de huevo, una linterna rota, la suela despegada de un zapato: si en vida útil nos habían servido, deberían acompañarnos como

restos. [. . .] Los almacenes de la calle Murralla vomitaban bienes. [. . .] Bernaza amanecía alfombrada de fichas de un juego de mesa que nunca llegó a imponerse, suerte de *trivial* materialismo dialecto. (El viento barajaba ahora las fichas.) [. . .]

"Entonces todas las cosas desechadas que callan durante el día hallaron voces," escribió Lord Dunsay. Cada uno a su turno, en una de sus historias hablaban los artículos de un basurero:

a) un corcho crecido en los bosques de Andalucía,
b) un fosforo incólume,
c) una tetera vieja y rota que se decía amiga de las ciudades,
d) un pedazo de cuerda maldita desde el origen (<<Fui hecha en un lugar de condena, y condenados tejieron mis fibras en un trabajo sin esperanza. De entonces me quedó la mugre del ocio en el corazón>>)[190]

In Ponte's characteristic anthropomorphization, the stores "vomited" the material goods and fibers of a rope have a heart; these fibers, moreover, carry the sentiments of those who made them, "the filth of leisure." Arguably, Ponte is using a literary, allegorical device; however, we should note another theme of the novel: "miraculous static" [*estática milagrosa*]. As a term deployed by "experts" to account for buildings that remained upright against all knowledge of physics,[191] "miraculous static" is perhaps, in its mystery to human understanding, akin to "vibrant matter." With this inventory of random objects occupying space in the text and their becoming "remains," or auratic relics, in their very uselessness, Ponte illustrates, like Bataille and Bennett, how material resources exceed the utilitarian ends and even cultural meanings we ascribe to them. Ponte also shows how the "useless" does not go away. It floats on to the street. That which has been deemed trash has a power and affectivity of its own and continues to be a part of our environment. Tellingly, the narrator refers to the shuffled game cards as a "trivial material dialectic." Let us recall, historical materialism aims to demystify the fetishistic power of man-made things. Bennett, by contrast, proposes cultivating "a bit of anthropomorphism—the idea that human agency has some echoes in nonhuman nature—[. . .] to counter the narcissistic reflex of human language and thought."[192] Bennett's vital materialism and ecological thinking upends the logic that would justify the sacrifice of the "useless" for instrumental ends.

Stone versus Paper

At the end of chapter 2 with regard to Fabelo's installation of roaches, I made recourse to the sculptural murals of Che Guevara and Camilo Cienfuegos in the Plaza de la Revolución. Returning now to the steel outlines of Camilo's and Che's handsome faces, monumentalized for all the city to see, we find the archetypes of a national identity. Interestingly, in her analysis of different aesthetic strategies, Natalia Brizuela notes "nation-building narratives that are themselves based on structures of exclusion, differentiation, and value of particular kinds of ideological identification are enacted through the language and the pathos of the face."[193] The ideological identification, as elaborated in Che's writing, is one of heroism and sacrifice for a providential future.[194] Such calls to sacrifice have at times manifested in the criminalization and disposability of those who did not correspond to the model of a morally and physically incorruptible New Man.[195] Moreover, the historical narrative that is invoked in the memorialization of the Revolution's martyrs is one of sovereignty and human exceptionalism; it is a history grounded on a dialectical logic of clear antagonists, perhaps best epitomized by Cold War politics.

Roberto Fabelo's installation, on the other hand, presents us not with recognizable, historic figures, but with a swarm of roach-men. The hybridity of these creatures evokes a planetary threat, exceeding the discursive limits of the nation state and a politics of adversaries. Fabelo's statement that the piece is a "reference to today's world" alludes not only to the psychic effects this future catastrophe has on the present moment, but also the material deprivation that such a threat generated. The Special Period in Time of Peace, as Ponte has argued in *La fiesta,* inaugurated a state of exception that demanded from its citizens extraordinary measures in order to survive. While the threat of nuclear war posed by the Missile Crisis did not come to fruition, Havana still bears its wounds and is, at present, surviving. Fabelo and Ponte thus complicate a linear temporality and counter the futurity of the state's rhetoric of sacrifice.

Like Fabelo's roaches, in Ponte's depiction of Havana's inhabited ruins—buildings whose facades (or faces) have crumbled away, exposing delicate networks—we do not find individual heroic figures, but a swarm of survivors. The anonymity of the ruins' dwellers, who leave their traces and recreate the city from within, who work for the pleasure of a cold beer with no consciousness of economy, might be said to *escribir* rather than *inscribir.*

Conclusion

Portela's and Ponte's narrators are not "authors" or "historical agents" of their own accounts; they borrow, steal, and appropriate other texts, they inhabit bodies and spaces like unwelcome guests, they slip in and scurry away. Their *exscribing* leaves traces, but never a name or a legacy inscribed in stone. What I find most generative about both their texts is that art, literature, philosophical thought are imagined as forms of becoming-animal, as interdependent on a particular territory. These two writers elaborate tangled ecologies both on the level of their writing and representation. Against the national subject model of the Revolution as morally righteous, incorruptible, heroic and self-sacrificing, Ponte's and Portela's protagonists are vulnerable and motivated by survival. And it is in surviving, in becoming-parasitic, that creative resourcefulness, creative transformation and minor, if invisible, forms of rebellion occur.

Ponte's and Portela's ambivalence toward nonhuman becomings, or "células rebeldes," lead us to consider the critical question of how a literary or visual piece might do the work of protesting "inhuman" or "dehumanizing" conditions while not appealing to a transcendental humanism or resorting to the discourse of human rights. Through the language of their poetics, we are brought to imagine forms of relations that bypass and exceed conventional ontological markers; we are brought to imagine the material as having its own transformative potential outside of human agency. Given these dynamic relations, such thinking necessarily acknowledges the impossibility of mastery or of knowing absolutely. The corporeal vulnerability foregrounded in *La fiesta vigilada* and *El pájaro: Pincel y tinta china* undermines the presumptions of human sovereignty and calls attention to our communal interdependence, while the impropriety of their texts and the un-belonging of their characters insists on the impossibility of possessing *limpiamente.*

In the following chapter, through two of Ahmel Echevarría's novels, composed in the 2010s, we will continue to explore creative production not as that which humanizes, but as a becoming-beast. Specifically, we will imagine reading and writing as a form of cannibalism. In this textopofagia, there is an ingestion of the Other and a metamorphosis.

4

Eat Me

Cannibal Readings and Failed Incorporations in Ahmel Echevarría's *Búfalos camino al matadero* and *Caballo con arzones*

To the question, "¿Cómo hacer un poema, uno de amor, penetrante y bello?," Ahmel Echevarría's narrator responds with the following stanzas: "Ten paciencia / debo quedar carbonizado. / Muele la carne quemada, / la piel, los huesos. [. . .] Tritúralo todo, / polvo oscuro y fino. / Vierte un poco: tres rayas. / Enrolla un billete, luego aspirar."[1] If Antonio José Ponte's *La fiesta vigilada* prompts us to imagine the writer as a parasite (chapter 3), *Búfalos camino al matadero* by Ahmel Echevarría suggests the writer and the reader are cannibals. Burn me to a crisp, grind me to a fine dust, and snort me through a bill—these are Echevarría's writer-protagonist's instructions. Most empathically he pleads, "Nunca me leas."[2] "Trágame. Pero no me leas,"[3] a repeated request in *Búfalos camino al matadero,* constitutes the ethical and theoretical matrix of this chapter.

Búfalos camino al matadero's 181 pages presents itself largely as a novel, but one that is spliced with poetic fragments and sometimes the off-narration of a nature documentary. The text does not lend itself to plot summaries. Attempting to do so leads me to an enumeration, one of intimate encounters, bar fights, drunken pontifications, ketamine trips, sex, hangovers and vomiting, a lot of vomiting. As an Iraq war veteran, the first-person narrator possibly suffers from PTSD; he has a penchant for Heineken, whiskey, ESPN, and paying for sex. In addition to his monthly allowance as a veteran, he makes additional money in illegal trafficking; he has suicidal thoughts; he is an alcoholic, and very likely has cancer. Also, he is a writer.

In the previous chapter, through Ena Lucía Portela and Antonio José Ponte we saw writing as emerging from an irreducible corporeality and creatively surviving; in other words, art and literature are not that which transcend mere animal subsistence but emerge from a material interdependence. Through Nicolás Guillén's *Motivos de son* and Severo Sarduy's *Gestos,* we elaborated a practice of reading as touching (chapter 1). Marking those moments where their texts insist on an impenetrable materiality—be it in the form of indecipherable sonic matter or the ekphrasis of a two-dimensional plane—we explored reading as coming into con*tact* without the pretense of accessing a deeper semiotic interiority. In this chapter, through two of Ahmel Echevarría's novels, *Búfalos camino al matadero* (2013) and *Caballo con arzones* (2017), we will continue to expand upon an ethics of reading in which the Other is made perceptible, while resisting a politics of representation. We will also continue to explore creative production as corporeal and animal rather than a transcendent humanism.

However, where Guillén, Sarduy, and Portela sustained our attention on outsides, highlighting the tangibility of writing, or the body which writing *exscribes* (Jean-Luc Nancy) as that which cannot be subsumed/consumed by a larger subjectivity, in this chapter through Echevarría's novels, we will explore reading as incorporation. And here I am referring both to its literal meaning—to put inside the body—and its figurative, political meaning—to include and make part of the community. As such, Echevarría allows me to nuance and complicate our reading of surface and impenetrability, by bringing us *inside.* However, never in such a way that affirms the limits of discrete organisms. Through the trope of cannibalism, reading and writing are imagined as dependent upon, and nourished by, Other bodies. Furthermore, these incorporations do not result in a fused mestizo spirit (recall Guillén's "cóctel cubano" or Martí's "alma [. . .] igual y eterna") nor much less resolve the tensions posed by the Other.[4] Indeed, for the cannibal, consuming literature does not edify the soul but transforms the body. As I discussed in the introduction of the book, José Lezama Lima's use of the verb *incorporar* in lieu of *comer* and *templar* provides a useful model for the way in which we want to complicate nationalistic building projects that assume the integration of citizens. Whereas the Cuban state often used the term to refer to the obligatory participation of individuals in political organizations, the army, or the harvesting of sugar, Lezama Lima's use of the verb as eating or having sex implicitly refers to a metabolic process of change and corporeal expenditure, as opposed to the seamless incorporation of individuals within a greater subjectivity.[5]

Alongside Guillén, Ahmel Echevarría is one of the two Afro-Cuban writers discussed in this book and in many ways one of the two poets. His texts very loosely conform to the novel genre; in addition to interspersed italicized stanzas, the prose body is itself composed of refrains, oneiric vignettes, and a sparsity of narrative description. However, unlike Guillén, Echevarría does not explicitly engage Blackness nor lived disparities that result from inhabiting a recognizable social identity. That said, his attention to the body, its ailments, dysfunctions, desires, and needs, the body's dependence on and call to the Other, make Echevarría's texts an ideal space to think through marginalization and imagine community based on difference. Similar to Portela's flawed and unheroic characters, Echevarría's first-person narrators are unproductive citizens, preoccupied with sex, drinking, and the inoperativity of writing. As such, they not only challenge the Revolution's dominant subject models, but also work against the logic of identity; his narrators insist on an unknowability and shared incompleteness rather than a positive substance. *Búfalos* is set in an unspecified city in the United States and its protagonist is an Iraq War veteran whose race and ethnicity are impossible to determine. Cuba is only mentioned in an off-hand manner, as the nationality of a tertiary character and the music played in a cab. *Caballo con arzones,* by contrast, is situated in the specificity of Havana's neighborhoods and we can say that its narrator is a young Black man . . . but also a mature white woman. In other words, even though readers are given descriptive details, such as dreadlocks, black rimmed glasses, long straight black hair, and faint scars of acne, *Caballo con arzones* frustrates the hermeneutic desire to identify subjects or distill reproducible knowledge.

Búfalos camino al matadero and *Caballo con arzones* have received little critical attention. Other novels of Echevarría, such as *Días de entrenemiento* (2012) *or La noria* (2013), which are contextualized in Cuba and contain explicit references to Cuban political and literary figures, have been analyzed, as well as published in foreign editorials.[6] I suspect that because *Búfalos camino al matadero* makes it difficult for the critic of Cuban or even Latin American literature to identify empirical references to these contexts, the novel has not been studied critically. It was the recipient of the Premio Oriente of 2012 and, accordingly, published by Editorial Oriente in Santiago, Cuba, in 2013. Given Cuba's lack of material resources, the edition is a poor quality with some copies having been printed with pages upside down. Copies of the novel are scarce and finding one outside of Cuba is difficult.

Caballo con arzones was awarded the prestigious Premio Alejo Carpentier in 2017 and published by Instituto Cubano del Libro in Havana, Cuba, that same year. Aside from a few book reviews, critics have not studied the novel exclusively. Rafael Rojas, for instance, includes *Caballo con arzones* in his analysis of recent Cuban literary production, as it refers to monumental moments in Cuban history, such as the Mariel Boatlift.[7] Nevertheless, it is a novel that foregoes traditional plot and character development and exhibits a minimalism that does not lend itself to sociological or identitarian readings. Perhaps for these reasons it has not received the attention it merits.

Both novels are invested in writing and the illusions of representation and, as their titles suggest, both rely on animal figuration. However, as we will explore through the particular practice of reading solicited by these texts, animals in *Búfalos* and *Caballo* are not simply allegorical devices. Recalling here Rosi Braidotti's cartographic approach to dreams and the literary imagination (chapter 2)[8]—and dreams will figure prominently in *Búfalos* and *Caballo*—Echevarría's animals, I argue, cannot be reduced to a symbolic code, unlocking a deeper meaning, or leading to a resolution. Instead, we will see how these literary animals unsettle the secure boundaries of the human and stampede through civilizing culture. By reimagining reading and writing as practices that do not differentiate "man" from "beast," but rather collapse these categories, these novels challenge the assumptions of human exceptionalism and its symbolic economy. In so doing, Echevarría compels us to reexamine how society determines which bodies have futures and which are disposable.

The Latin American Cannibal and the Civilized Cuban

In the Latin American imaginary, we can trace the figure of the cannibal back to the earliest Spanish American text. Columbus writes, "Entendió también que lejos de allí había hombres de un ojo y otros con hocicos de perros que comían los hombres y que tomando uno lo degollaban y le bebían su sangre y le cortaban su natura."[9] Whereas the majority of what Columbus describes is chronicled as an eye-witness account, the cyclops and the cannibals are only something of which he has heard, a rumor in the background of an otherwise paradisaic landscape populated by an innocent, childlike people. Evangelization, after all, is only possible if we are dealing with human beings. Nevertheless, should there be any doubt this is a barbarous place, in the far distance is the cannibal, an inhuman figure with a dog's snout who savagely slits throats and cuts off genitals. Columbus's chronicles provide the blueprint for a dichotomy that would not only rhetorically justify the colonial project but has lasted well into the present, determining what constitutes development and progress.[10] In these accounts you have, on the one hand, your armored conquistadors that arrive with navigational tools, several surnames, ceremonies to claim the land, and banners with phonetic letters; these letters not only refer to the queen and king of Spain but evidence a kind of writing. On the other hand, you have a homogenously young, naked people, generous to a fault, godless, unaware of sharp objects and, implicitly, have no writing. In colonial representations that followed, where the figure of the cannibal represented the extreme of barbarism and the limit of the human, the figure of *el letrado*, or the evidence of writing, came to be the signal par excellence of civilization.[11]

To appreciate the prestige of phonetic writing and its equivalence to civility in the European imaginary we can turn to two colonial accounts. The sixteenth-century missionary, Pedro de Gante, wrote of the Aztecs, "they were people without writing, without letter, without written characters and without any kind of enlightenment."[12] Juan Bautista Pomar, a descendant of pre-Columbian nobility and a Spanish father, reports on the refinement of sculpting, painting, metallurgy, carpentry, and astronomy among other arts and sciences in the education of the Amerindian nobility, and later concludes with the following:

> [I]t is clear that if they had possessed letters, they would have come to grasp many natural secrets, but as paintings are little capable of retaining in them the memory of the things painted, they did not advance, because almost as soon as the one who had made the most progress died, his knowledge died with him.[13]

Letters, then, as opposed to painting or sculpture, is the only medium capable of operating as an archive. What these statements reflect was the growing idea in Europe that the only way to transmit knowledge from one generation to another was through alphabetic writing, books, and printing technology.[14] In the face of pre-Columbian sophistication, demonstrated through architecture, engineering, agriculture and other forms of cultural production, colonists and evangelists cited the seeming lack of writing as evidence of barbarism and the need for European civilization.[15] This evangelizing discourse was not necessarily deployed in Cuba, since colonizers did not need to reckon with a highly stratified society and the Taíno population was almost entirely decimated.[16] These accounts, nevertheless, express a European ethos that prevailed throughout the Americas.

Nation-building narratives that followed independence redeployed the dichotomy in such notorious texts as Domingo Sarmiento's 1845 *Facundo, o civilización y barbarie*. Classified together in Sarmiento's critique of a barbarous caudillo is the gaucho and the Indian, considered obstacles to progress and democracy. The 1838 landmark story *El matadero* by the Argentinian Esteban Echeverría also participates within this discourse. The matadero operates as a metaphor to the tyrannical rule of the de Rosas government and the killing of a bull is meant to be assimilated to the unjust killing of a young man from the opposition party. Echeverría equates poor Black women and their transactions within the slaughterhouse to the barbarism of the tyrant government. While Echeverría decries de Rosas's gross injustices and advocates for a modern and progressive government, he does so by evoking the opposition between civilization and barbarism and relegating non-European bodies to the category of barbarism. These nineteenth-century texts make evident the persistence of these categories and their colonial and racist legacies.

Despite its critique of imperialism and bourgeoise pretensions of refinement, the notion of being civilized would figure prominently in the rhetoric of the Cuban Revolution.[17] If the upper classes of the Republican period distinguished themselves through a particular kind of education, or their appreciation and access to high art, the Revolution would aim to collapse those class distinctions by making that education and art widely available. However, the distinction between civilized and uncivilized remained. When Fidel Castro stated in a 1972 speech, "creo que una de las metas que debemos proponernos es la civilización," Jacqueline Loss explains that civilization for him "entails technical advancement and equality. Yet the choice of words makes it difficult to unleash the association between 'civilization' and that bourgeoisie for whom certain modes of comportment are understood as innate."[18] I would also suggest that the paralleling of technological advancement with equity and progress is not unrelated to the pretense that navigational instruments and alphabetic writing made the colonialists agents of history.

I have sketched the trajectory of this Latin American dichotomy in order to contextualize and underscore the implications of Ahmel Echevarría's novels when they suggest the writer is a cannibal or a pig named Robespierre that philosophizes. As I will discuss later in the chapter, other twentieth-century writers, most famously Oswald de Andrade, have recast the figure of the cannibal to contest the legacy of colonialism and Eurocentric views. We will consider how Echevarría implicitly contributes and expands upon this growing cannibal corpus.

It is important to note, however, that the word cannibalism or its synonyms never appear in either novel, nor does a literal act of cannibalism occur, aside from the narrator's poetic instructions to snort his carbonized and grinded body in *Búfalos camino al matadero.* Before arriving at a more direct engagement with the practice of cannibal readings in *Búfalos*, prompted by the narrator's repeated request, "Trágame. Pero no me leas," I will first analyze aspects of the narrative that support the teasing of cannibalism as a subtext. In the sections that follow, we will see how Echevarría transforms human flesh and literary texts into meaty bodies. Because animals have historically been taken for granted as bodies that can be sacrificed and eaten, cannibalism necessarily complicates what is edible meat (animal) and what is flesh to be nourished (human). We will therefore also examine how the novel subverts the symbolic economy of humanism and the use of animals as literary tropes. If texts are meaty bodies consumed by readers, then bodies themselves are also texts; a section will be devoted to examining how Echevarría presents the wounded body as writing and, as such, destabilizes classical notions of cohesive and autonomous bodies that can be represented.[19]

In her book, *From Communion to Cannibalism,* Maggie Kilgour explains, following Mikhail Bakhtin, that the act of eating complicates the boundaries of the subject, where I end, and you start. Ingesting the Other,

> creates a total identity between eater and eaten while insisting on the total control—the literal consumption—of the latter by the former. Like all acts of incorporation, it assumes an absolute distinction between inside and outside, eater and eaten, which however, break down, as the law "you are what you eat" obscures identity and makes it impossible to say for certain who's who. Paradoxically, the roles are completely unreciprocal and yet ultimately indistinguishable.[20]

This indistinction and obscuring of identity will be explored in *Caballo con arzones,* discussed in the second half of the chapter. *Caballo* expands upon our practice of cannibal reading by underscoring forms of incorporation and hosting and presenting writing and reading as animalistic and beastly. Since the broader implications of cannibal reading are a destabilization of what constitutes civilization and the rhetorics that have justified the exploitation of some bodies for the sake of others, I will also look at the ways that Echevarría collapses the distinctions between art/culture and mere animal existence. Ultimately, both novels suggest that reading and writing are corporeal and dependent upon Other bodies.

Meaty Bodies

Charles Bukowski's Blue Bird, Charles Baudelaire's Albatross, William Blake's Tiger, and Herman Melville's Whale, a menagerie of literary avatars, or simply bait for the expert critic, populate *Búfalos camino al matadero* as intertextual references. Alongside literature's animals we also find sex workers, traumatized veterans, domestic violence survivors, cut limbs, cancered bodies, Catholic pimps, bruises, wounds, prosthetic eyes, and false teeth. In titling his novel *Búfalos camino al matadero,* the Cuban Echevarría evokes the Argentinian Echeverría's *El matadero,* and in so doing, a long Spanish American literary tradition, in which animals operate as allegorical devices to address the dehumanization of the disenfranchised. Foregrounding lives at the limits of society, one might expect Ahmel Echevarría to traffic in the substitutive logic where buffalos are a metaphor of abjectness in a human-centric drama, a linguistic instrument to be decoded by the literary analyst.

However, phrases, such as "Las mismas estrellas y el mismo cielo visto por Alejandro Magno, y por jerbos y chacales, buitres, perros y búhos,"[21] collapse a hierarchal scaffolding that would distinguish conquerors from desert rats. Echevarría's scavenger animals cannot stand in for abjectness any more than Alexander the Great when they share the same sky and stars and are made parallel to him through coordinating conjunctions. Other parallel constructions such as, "Mirábamos las obras y le tocaba el culo" or "llevaría mi culo y mi ojo de cristal a mi apartamento,"[22] equate seeing, "noblest of the senses,"[23] and its elevated pursuits, as in contemplating art, with carnal desire or even defecating. These sentences destabilize a regime of value and signification. In the pairing of "mi culo y mi ojo," the roundness of an anus is assimilated to the roundness of a glass eye, from which the proverbial soul cannot be seen.[24] If we recall Freud's *Civilization and Its Discontents,* it is the eventual privileging of vision over smell and organic repression that break humans away from animality.[25] As we shall see further ahead, *Búfalos* continually undermines that imagined break as it intersects high art with organic needs and foregrounds corporeality. Not only will the narrator repeat that modern or contemporary art is "Una estampida, una verdadera estampida," but also dripping with sweat or semen, "dibujaba pájaros y torpes muñecos en el vientre de Janela," or with blood, "pinté sus labios," "[e]n la herida metí el índice, para humedecerlo."[26]

In his recent study on the proliferation of animals in Latin American cultural production, Gabriel Giorgi explains that where animals had historically represented the opposite of humans and civilization, in more contemporary works, depictions of animals, rather than mark a limit, destabilize what had been taken as an ontological distinction. We begin to see literary animals shift from landscapes imagined as outside of culture and society to political spaces and, in so doing, put into question what constitutes politically recognizable bodies. Differences of gender, race, and class are recognized today as cultural and political constructions. However, these constructions and their attendant hierarchies have been drawn along an axis, assumed to be natural, that which divides human from nonhuman, or more accurately as Giorgi explains, *bios*—politically recognizable individuals—and *zoe*—undifferentiated life.[27] In his reading of animals in Latin American texts, Giorgi demonstrates that the distinction that had been taken as a fact of nature is aesthetically determined, contingent on how we see and organize bodies. Our reading of *El pájaro: Pincel y tinta china* exemplifies this trend (chapter 3); we saw how Ena Lucía Portela undermines ways of seeing and representing the world and, consequently, contests how society distinguishes between bodies to protect (*bios*) and bodies to exploit (*zoe*). Accordingly, the lines of an entire social map are unsettled. Moreover, if animals had operated as a way to signal the abuse of humans—the mistreatment of humans *as though* they were animals, or the abuse of power by a sovereign *as though* that sovereign were a beast—that assimilation no longer functions since humans and animals are now part of a contiguous continuity.[28]

In his book, *Animal Rites: American Culture, the Discourse of Species, and Posthumanist Theory,* Cary Wolfe makes clear the stakes of questing the limits between humans and animals when he explains:

> [A]s long as this humanist and speciesist *structure* of subjectivation remains intact, and as long as it is institutionally taken for granted that it is all right to systematically exploit and kill nonhuman animals simply because of their species, then the humanist discourse of species will always be available for use by some humans against other

humans as well, to countenance violence against the social other or whatever species—or gender, or race, or class, or sexual difference.[29]

Wolfe illustrates how the assumptions of humanism provide a "ready-made symbolic economy" that justifies the sacrifice, colonization, or expulsion of some bodies for the sake of those imagined to have transcended their bare material needs. More specifically, within the context of Latin America, the structure of the *matadero,* as a space designed to keep bodies sentenced to death isolated and hidden, is echoed in state camps and biopolitical practices.[30] Although these were not extermination camps, Cuba's notorious UMAPs and involuntary quarantines for those infected with HIV, as well as the government's recourse to the term *gusanos,* are instances where institutional topography and rhetoric enact the speciesist structures that Wolfe describes.[31] In other words, the forced labor camps, as they corral bodies deemed unproductive, together with "dehumanizing" labels, provide the state with the mechanisms and justification for the segregation and the eventual expulsion of bodies whose futures it no longer recognizes or values.[32]

Returning to Ahmel Echevarría's title, literary mataderos have historically been zones of indistinction between flesh and meat, life and death.[33] Even in such canonical works as the story by the nineteenth-century Echeverría, the literary matadero—in contradiction to what institutional mataderos attempt to do, keeping animal death hidden and isolated—is a space where human and animal body parts get confused, "los cuerpos se volvieron contornos imprecisos que los vuelven contiguos unos con otros." Giorgi goes on to explain that in the Argentine literary context these spaces of animal death were staged time and again, creating territories where classificatory systems that distinguish and distribute bodies are rendered inoperative. In the confusion and failure to make sense of which body is which, there is a transformation from "cuerpo" to "carne."[34] The Cuban Echevarría does not put the animal body, nor the slaughterhouse, front and center as Giorgi observes in the works he examines. However, as we shall explore ahead, much like these works, *Búfalos camino al matadero* does displace the topography of the matadero and produces zones of indistinction. Such an indistinction insists that we rethink what constitutes the limits of culture and politics.

The transformation from body to meat that Giorgi identifies as characteristic of literary mataderos is expressed in the first pages of *Búfalos.*

Refusing to be interpolated by the brotherhood of his fellow veterans, the first-person narrator states, "No quiero que ninguno de esos zombis intente estrechar mi mano para hacerme creer que somos parte de una hermandad."[35] If zombies are understood as the living dead, those "who no longer possess a will of their own and only obey orders,"[36] in assimilating the veterans to zombies, Echevarría subverts notions of heroic self-sacrifice for the nation. The narrator, instead, describes himself as part of a herd that emerged from the "bellies" of military aircrafts "cooked at a simmering temperature": "De la barriga de varios Hércules C-130 salió una manada que había sido cocida a fuego lento."[37] "Una manada" becomes a recurring trope through which fraternal belonging and human exceptionalism are consistently undermined.[38] Meanwhile, the metaphors, "la barriga" and "cocida a fuego lento," imagine the bodies of these soldiers as ingestible and even edible.

That human flesh might be slaughtered like animal meat is suggested in the following images, "una bala les taladraba el pellejo [. . .] mirábamos un estomago en erupción de tripas, mierda y sangre tras un rafagazo, un cráneo abierto o una pierna destrozada."[39] In the carnage of war, we no longer see coherent individuals but corporeal parts outside of parts,[40] "pellejo" instead of "piel," senseless and undignified death. The narrator's description of smells, tastes, and references to cooking, "Conozco el agrio sudor cuando el sol cae vertical y nos va cocinando desde las tripas. Es bien salado el sudor. Olemos como si ya estuviéramos muertos,"[41] reiterate the transformation from body to meat, as well as the social death one experiences when made disposable by war. Returning from Iraq with a glass eye, the narrator like other soldiers has "un solo plan: inventarme un plan."[42] The need to make a plan, a phrase that will be repeated like a mantra, is an indication of a life rendered futureless. Alcoholism and suicidal thoughts are always in the background, if not the foreground, of the narrative: "En El Albatros me he apuntado a la sien decenas de veces [. . .] Todavía sigo muerto."[43]

Literature and Animals

Echevarría's first-person narrator begins with a request to his readers, "Llámame Ismael." Repeated throughout the text, the interpolation becomes a choral refrain. The adoption by the US Iraq War veteran of the biblical and literary name underscores his preoccupation with writing and his position as a social outcast; it also impedes the reader's capacity to identify him with a recognizable community. His ethnicity and city of residence remain purposely indistinct. We assume the novel takes place somewhere in the United States. There's a bar called El Albatros, cheap motels, and a description of an art exhibit titled "Revolving Hotel Room," which after a quick Google search turns out to be a 2008 Guggenheim show. Otherwise, the setting of the novel is seemingly nowhere; the text displays a remarkable sparsity of contextual description. A tertiary character, the husband who beats his wife is Cuban and Buena Vista Social Club is played in a taxi, which occasions a list of Cuban stereotypes by the narrator, such as "todos los Cubanos están muertos de hambre. Todos los cubanos bailan salsa."[44] The character El Mexicano, the pimp and black-market trafficker, we learn is not actually Mexican. There are the veterans, T-Rex and Bob Esponga, and the bartender, Irish Coffee. We finally learn the full name of the sex worker, whose country of birth is continuously speculated by Ismael to be somewhere in Eastern Europe, only after her body is found abandoned in an alley. All of this to say that identity or recognizable markers of how we distribute and organize bodies are continuously displaced, circumvented, or subverted. The community of the novel, or more specifically, of El Albatros, that portside bar that smells of dried semen, alcohol, halitosis, cinnamon or mint flavored gum, false expensive perfumes, and the sour stench of sweat, as our narrator likes to enumerate, is a community of the marginalized: "la manada de búfalos, con sus números marcados en el lomo, atraviesa el portón de El Albatros. El paso es lento, avanzan como si fueran camino al matadero."[45]

We might say that the only shared identity and allegorical signification that coheres in the novel is that of being marginalized, deemed citizens not worth protecting, sentenced to a social death like buffalos on their way to the slaughterhouse. However, the narrator is also consumed with questions of writing and the novel itself is riddled with references to other well-known literary works. While the name Ismael is a reference to Melville's *Moby-Dick,* the novel is prefaced with stanzas from Bukowski's *Bluebird,* and that bird, which resides in the chest of the writer—"there's a bluebird in my heart that/ wants to get out/ but I'm too tough for him" (Bukowski)—is later replaced in the novel with a Bengali tiger that resides in Ismael, by which Echevarría implicitly references Blake's "The Tyger," "What immortal hand or eye/ Could frame thy fearful symmetry." Finally, the title of the bar is a reference to Baudelaire's poem "L'Albatros," which uses the maritime bird as a figure for the poet, "Le Poète est semblable au prince des nuées/ Qui hante la tempête [. . .] Exilé sur le sol au milieu des huées, / Ses ailes de géant l'empêchent de marcher."[46] After a cursory reading of these intertexts, what they all share is the figure of the animal and references to writing or artistic creation. As such, Echevarría aligns his narrator and/or himself to a community of writers through the figures of animals.

Traditionally, the animal has been reduced to an aesthetic object, a material resource, or vehicle to transmit meaning deployed by the artist/writer. But the link between artistic creation and the animal in this assemblage of intertexts points to a shared vulnerability (the bluebird as the author's emotional vulnerability and the tiger as the threat of being devoured by an Other) and a lack of mastery ("He cannot walk for his unmanageable wings") where the distinction between creator and animal-as-object (or stand-in) is no longer sustained. When we consider how poetry brings us to the limits of language in tandem with the perceived incommunicability of animals, the entanglement of the animal with the aesthetic that Echevarría brings to fore not only destabilizes the historical opposition between animals and culture, but also the operative transmission of meaning.[47] Moreover, if art and culture have been imagined as that which transcend bare material needs and wield nature, as that which mark humanity, here art and culture emerge from vulnerability or a failing.

Animal figures are so pervasive in the novel—"Eres muy tierno, mi osezno tuerto," "Era celoso como un perro," "nos revolcábamos como perros," "Así es el inconsciente: un caballo indomable," "es un animal perfecto"—they no longer operate as simple metaphors.[48] The novel is not only populated by literary birds and tigers. There is also the interspersed off-narration from an Animal Planet documentary on birds from the Galapagos Islands. Metaphorical and documentary representations intersect and are made contiguous. Meanwhile, Ismael's descriptions of individual characters and interactions might at first appear simplistic, lacking depth and complexity: "ella sí parecía un gorrión," "era altísima esa mujer. Una enorme gata," "la pelirroja Paola tiene piernas largas y un corazón pequeño," "Cabello negro y lacio sobre los hombros, delgada y tetas pequeñas."[49] And yet through frequent repetition (the narrator will repeat these same phrases with slight variations when referring to these characters), these descriptions become poetic; with each iteration they lose their literal meanings; they become refrains and lend the narrative a rhythm and circularity that break a linear progression of events. As we read the reiterated phrases, each time formulated somewhat differently, Echevarría is also taking his readers through the writer's process. In repeating the lines, it's as though we were rehearsing them, returning to the top of the page to evaluate their texture and phonetic value. As such, we are encouraged to reflect upon the novel's language, to suspect its lack of mastery.

In the following dialogue, we are especially prompted to question the text's efficaciousness:

> ¿Qué carajo sabes tú de poesía? Dijo mientras se limpiaba.
> Me encogí dc hombros.
> —¿Acaso eres escritor?
> Vi un gesto de dolor en su rostro. [. . .]
> Ella tenía razón: creer en los tipos atormentados no es saber de poesía. Tener fe en esos tipos que saben nombrar el dolor no es saber de poesía.[50]

This sentiment, in almost the exact phrasing, is repeated later in the text, "Nombrar el dolor o el amor no es saber de poesía. Tener cierta fe en esos tipos que saben nombrar el dolor no es saber de poesía."[51] The figure of the deeply feeling writer is not only presented as a cliché, but also the possibility of identifying, or accurately communicating feeling is a false pretension. Were we to associate "atormentado" with melancholic, psychoanalysts tell us that the failure of mourning is a failure at introjection—a process of finding a substitute for the missing object or something to represent an absence, in other words a metaphor—which results in the internalization of the loss. Put otherwise, the melancholic subject fails at the metaphoric process of substituting the absence and, instead, incorporates the lost object, subconsciously encrypting that loss within oneself.[52] I suggest we read the repetitions of descriptions that fall short of representing the Other as an indication of this psychic ingestion—the internalization of the absent Other—and, thus, another way in which cannibalism is expressed in the text.[53] We will turn to a passage of (failed) mourning further ahead where Ismael, alternatively, suggests smelling and touching the bones of the dead. While smelling and touching are not an eating per se, they are certainly a consumption of the Other as a corporeal body.

Importantly, I want to underscore an insufficiency or a failure of language to which the novel gestures in connection with incorporation or an irreducible corporeality. In the section that follows we will continue to examine how the structure of the novel works against the logic of representation, while also framing creative production as emerging from a wound or affective desire. With italicized poetic stanzas interspersed in the body of the text, the intersection of scientific and literary language, a sparsity of information, heavy use of tropes, and repetition, the narrative consciously undermines the transmission of reproducible knowledge and its novelistic representation. It offers us a configuration of parts rather than a unified coherent body and, all the while, addressing itself to an Other: "Te miraré a los ojos con mi único ojo, dejaré que vomites lo que tienes dentro. [. . .] No huyas. No huyas si sonrío. Extenderé mi mano [. . .]."[54]

"En el moretón está el poema"

In addition to intertextual references to well-known literary works where the figure of the writer is connected to that of the animal, the narrative is dense with references to writing in the context of a wounded body. The dialogue cited above, in which the figure of the writer is put into question, occurs between Ismael and a woman he finds outside the bar, Amanda Carter, who has escaped with her life from what appears to be a beating. Ismael, who has just left the bar inebriated with the stench of vomit on his coat, first spots the woman as "un bulto blancuzco junto al muro del litoral" and suspects the indistinct mass is a Labrador for which he might earn some money, "podría ganar dinero si lograba venderlo o hacerlo mi mascota." Instead, "aquel bulto" is the naked body of a woman with a broken lip and bruises, "uno de los hematomas le adornaba el ojo derecho."[55] That a bruise would be decorative is indicative of how art and corporeal vulnerability are intertwined in the novel. Realizing that this is not a dog, Ismael notes that for a bruised woman you can't earn a penny. The speculation over money and the initial indistinction of the woman's body are symptomatic of how society values certain bodies over others based on how they are seen and classified; in other words, the value distinction is aesthetic and not ontological. According to Ismael's calculations, the woman is worthless: "Lo triste es que por una mujer desnuda y con moretones en el pellejo no te ganas ni siquiera un centavo," and yet he states, "Tu cara es un maldito poema."[56] Phrased as a fact and not a simile, "tu cara es" instead of "tu cara es *como*," the body and its bruises are a form of writing. The statement invites us to imagine the marks of this face, its visible injuries and suffering, as irreducible expressions, interconnections, and histories. In what society has deemed disposable (he finds her among trash bags), of little or no value, Echevarría's narrator finds poetry and thereby overturns a system of meaning and value. Moreover, with the phrases "en el moretón está el poema," or "En la herida metí el índice, para humerdecerlo. Y pinté sus labios,"[57] the novel insists it is a corporeal vulnerability, or a material interdependency, and not its transcendence, from which art is produced.[58]

Immediately following a chapter titled, "Animal Planet," Ismael gifts one of his girlfriends the very rare and unique opportunity to spend a night at the Guggenheim Museum, as part of the "Revolving Hotel Room" exhibit. "La obra era una habitación con estructuras y cama giratoria. [. . .] Quien la alquila podría dormir en su interior además de visitar el museo. Una habitación con minibar, baño, ducha."[59] The exhibit allows Ismael and his girlfriend to spend "una noche dentro de una obra de arte"; they are hosted, and thus incorporated, or cannibalized, by the work.[60] Ismael describes the exhibit as a kinetic art piece, and it would appear that what is on exhibit—he speculates the museum guards must also be having a stimulating evening—is the simultaneity or the tension between their sexual arousal and the consumption of artwork: "En los corredores del museo nos estuvimos besando y tocándonos mientras intentábamos observar con detenimiento las obras. Creo que justo eso es el arte moderno."[61] Echevarría narrates their intercourse in such a way that emphasizes the penetration, or incorporation, of a body, "Mi cuerpo dentro de Janela." Note the use of the verb "taladrar," to drill: "Gemidos. La cama girando. Mi carne, dura, embistió la carne abierta entre sus piernas. Y comencé a taladrarla. Despacio."[62] Here the body, again, becomes meat, as well as beast, and the distinction between the museum and Animal Planet is less defined. Another passage reads, "Mirábamos las obras y le tocaba el culo. Comentábamos lo que nos parecía alguna pieza y Janela ponía su mano en mi entrepierna. Mi hueso durísimo, estaba amordazado por la tela de mi pantalón. Creo que justo eso es el arte moderno. Una estampida, una verdadera estampida."[63] Thus, art and becoming-beast, or art and corporeal touching, affective responses, and sexual desire are expressly linked. While artistic creation has served as both evidence of Humanity and as a means to humanize, in *Búfalos camino al matadero,* the production and consumption of literature and art is neither edifying nor civilizing. Incidentally, Janela will end up projectile vomiting in the Revolving Hotel Room, after consuming copious amounts of alcohol and a couple rounds of intercourse. "Me cubrí la nariz, la boca. Alguien debía limpiar aquella lava ácida que había brotado de sus tripas."[64] Vomiting, which happens frequently in the novel, might be read as a failed incorporation, while also bringing one's insides out, however repellent to those around them.

The connection between corporeality and creative production is also expressed in the novel through the suffering of writing; the phrase "padecer la escritura" is repeated variously in the text. In one instance, with regard to responding to someone's letter, Ismael says, "Cartas . . . padecer la escritura. [. . .] Pliegos de papel como cuchillos encajándose en la sien."[65] We can associate this physical pain with Jean-François Lyotard's notion of suffering the unthought. In chapter 3, we discussed Lyotard's theory that so-called human thought cannot be disaggregated from the body and the body's territorial interdependence. Thought is not binary like artificial intelligence but relies on our phenological experience and, like our vision, which is marked by blurry limits, a horizon without reach, our thought also makes inferences and leaps of what it has yet to perceive. To think the unthought, or arrive at the right brushstroke, one must be irresolute and patiently wait in the discomfort of the unknown, "letting a givable come towards you." The grace we associate with creative talent is one that demands "suspension of ordinary intentions of mind associated with habitus, or arrangements of the body." "[T]here's a necessity for physical experience and a recourse to exemplary cases of bodily ascesis [. . .] if the mind is to think."[66]

Although Ismael does not demonstrate exemplary ascesis, certainly loss, impairment (mi único ojo), and physical experience, as I have underscored, are at the foreground of the novel. The constant repetition of lines and subtle revisions, as well as Ismael's expressions of doubt "en esos tipos que saben nombrar el dolor," might also illustrate the irresolution and suspension of ordinary intentions that Lyotard describes.[67] The constant questioning of the text's language puts the writer, and potentially the reader, in a state of uncertainty and insecurity. Considering the unthought, or creativity, as something for which one must wait in discomfort also communicates a notion of art that relies less on authorial autonomy and mastery and more on humility and interdependence. Yet, another way in which the novel demonstrates a suffering or vulnerability in writing is through its use of the second-person voice and its various addresses to an Other, as in a letter addressee; we will explore this further ahead.

The material corporeality of writing is made most evident in the very composition of the novel. While Ismael asks himself, or more accurately the reader, "¿Dónde debería cortar para tener una nueva estrofa? Tomar la navaja, hacer un corte, luego poner una frase debajo de la otra sobre un papel en blanco,"[68] we experience this cutting and dismemberment as the first-person narration is often interrupted and interweaved with italicized poetic fragments. In addition to these fragments, the main narrative that seemed straightforward and unblemished—almost to a fault in its lack of description—progressively takes on a poetic register, as we've noted, in the continuous repetition of lines which become refrains. Like poems, mantras, prayers, invocations, Echevarría's writing stops discoursing and brings the reader's attention to its sonorous material surface and to its metaphoric, virtual potentialities. The refrains, in other words, interrupt an aesthetic of mimetic representation.

In his book *Corpus,* which we first discussed in chapter 1, Jean-Luc Nancy explains that mimetic representation partakes of a Christian metaphysics of soul and body. In the liturgical invocation of the transubstantiation, where bread and wine become the body and blood of Christ, the demonstrative phrase, "This is my body," presumes a union between the sign and the body, or a representation and its referent. The communal consumption of the wafer, moreover, is imagined resulting in a hypostatic union, that is, the incorporation of the individual bodies within a larger subjectivity. Significantly, Ismael will ask "¿O quién soy, sino un homúnculo, para negar que estamos hechos a su imagen y semejanza, que Él antepuso su muerte para darnos la vida a nosotros?"[69] But later he states as he suffers the agony of a toothache, "Supuestamente ni el cordal, ni las amígdalas ni el apéndice tienen ninguna utilidad. Sin embargo, están ahí, en el cuerpo, para nada o para jodernos. Y todavía dicen que el cuerpo es una máquina perfecta."[70] In listing parts of the body that are unproductive or in excess, Echevarría not only challenges the theology that man is made in the image of God, but more significantly a metaphysics in which the human body is the incarnation of an ideal, the outward representation of an immaterial interior. Doing so has ethical implications when we consider that conceiving the body as an indivisible whole or corresponding to an archetype allows for the evaluation of non-normative bodies as aberrations, inferior or defective versions.[71]

We might also read the composition of the novel, its narrative and iconographic references, as a challenge to classical notions of the well-organized body. Although Aristotle's biological perspective did not imagine the soul as an immaterial agent that animates physical bodies as in a Christian metaphysics, his conception of the soul and body does resonate with the Cartesian model of a unitary and indivisible subject. For the Greek philosopher, the soul of a vegetal or anthropic organism is that which gives matter its form; it is the intrinsic principles of a substance, which cannot be separated or partitioned. If the organic body is a body that has organs, parts that have specific functions, the well-organized body (or complex organism) is the means to develop the potentiality of the soul and from there an ontological hierarchy is generated. Aristotle writes:

> Suppose that the eye were an animal, sight would have been its soul, for sight is the substance or essence of the eye [. . .] when seeing is removed the eye is no longer an eye, except in name, it is no more a real eye than the eye of a statue or of a painted figure. We must now extend our consideration from the "parts" to the whole living body; for what the departmental sense is to the bodily part which is its organ, that the whole faculty of sense is to the whole sensitive body as such.[72]

Aristotle's reference to the eye "that is no longer an eye" once seeing is removed allows us to underscore an intentional inoperativity and impropriety of the novel. Ismael's glass eye, Amanda Carter's "dientes postizos," the numerous "prótesis, muletas, bastones" alongside the novel's fragmented and collage-like composition, counter the well-organized, or indivisible model of the body.[73] When Ismael makes "ojo" contiguous with "culo," or Alexander the Great with desert rats, he is collapsing an order, a hierarchy of being meant to be expressed in the differentiation and unity of organs. Moreover, the narrator's expressed lack of faith in the ability to name an emotion, his repeating a word just used with question marks, "¿desbasta?," to signal his doubt over its usage, and the destabilization of metaphors through the numerous and repetitious animal figurations, all gesture toward a failure of language or an organ malfunction. Writing, rather than represent a subject, becomes another part, another appendage, in excess to a subject.[74]

In addition to the malfunctioning or inorganic and prosthetic parts of which the characters are configured, there is a chapter where Ismael narrates a dream he had of cadavers, starfish, and hundreds of octopuses. Starfish and octopuses present a very different model to the well-organized body; starfish can be segmented, broken into smaller pieces, regenerate new limbs, and even entire bodies from the segmentation. Octopuses can think at any point of their bodies; their tentacles, the parts that we associate with touch, are also the place of intelligently processing information. Taken as the subconscious icons of the text (given that the chapter is a dream sequence), rather than read these icons as symbolic stand-ins for Ismael's unresolved trauma, we can instead read them cartographically. They can be diagrams of the text and, at the same time, points of touch. As parts-outside-parts, tentacles and star limbs can break off here and regenerate there, always reconfiguring new and un-organized bodies. While there is a general sequence of events in the novel, some chapters can be read as individual occurrences that do not necessarily lead up or connect to each other; they might be read out of order or skipped entirely. In other words, the text can be separated and partitioned, like tentacles and star limbs, and very much unlike Aristotle's well-organized body, in which every part serves a specific function.

Returning to the novel's repeated references to Christ, the text underscores and draws upon the corporeality in the passion of Christ, "no vi los clavos que atravesaron las manos y pies de Jesús. Tampoco pude ver el dichoso Santo Sudario," and, implicitly, the cannibalism of communion, that imagines a hypostatic union through the ingestion of the host.[75] The novel challenges messianic narratives where death is sublated, worked into a sacrificial logic—of which nation-building and political projects have availed themselves to justify war and the disposability of some lives for the sake of others. In the second half of this chapter, where we discuss *Caballo con arzones,* we will see explicit references to these calls to self-sacrifice in the rhetoric of the Cuban Revolution. In the following passage (partially cited above) we see how the novel invokes forms of social death and reveals the false promise of a meaningful or glorious death:

> Conozco el agrio sudor cuando el sol cae vertical y nos va cocinando desde las tripas. Es bien salado el sudor. Olemos como si ya estuviéramos muertos. Cuerpos que se agarran a sus fusiles incluso después de la muerte. Cuerpos a la espera de la última emboscada, esa que quizá nos impida ganar el cielo o lo que creemos vamos a ganar.[76]

Ahmel Echevarría's text invites us to dwell on the "dehumanizing" conditions and "inhumanity" of war, as bodies are cooked by the sun like meat. That said, the novel never disavows the relationship between human flesh and buffalos on their way to the slaughterhouse, but instead makes that shared corporeality the source of empathy and writing.

Cannibal Readers

A chapter from the novel, titled "Cementerio de elefantes," recounts the news of the manslaughter of one of Ismael's lovers, a sex worker who asked to be called Gunila. Ismael describes what he and the other veterans were doing at the Albatross bar when they heard the news and later his kneeling beside her dead body. In a spiral composition, the events of the night are retold over and over, each time articulated somewhat differently and each time approximating the reader closer to Gunila's body. Reiterating an earlier passage in the novel where Ismael finds Amanda Carter's injured body among trash bags, Gunila's dead body is also found near trash in the alley behind the bar, indicating her being perceived and treated as disposable life. Such disposability is challenged, as both Amanda and Gunila are deeply cherished and respected by the narrator: Amanda gifts Ismael poetry and Gunila the wisdom contained in nature channel documentaries. Once again, here, we have the pairing of the literary and the animal.

At the start of the chapter, Ismael asks "¿Cómo recordar entonces a Mónica, Mónica Sanders Samsonov o Gunila? ¿Cómo evocarla?"[77] The question might be rephrased as how does one mourn her or, more broadly, how does one mourn? The image of Ismael kneeling beside Gunila's body is interweaved with descriptions of elephants mourning their dead:

> Arrodillarse aunque estés muy fatigado. Alzar esos huesos. Olerlos. Mirarlos muy de cerca. Parparlos en silencio tal como hacen los elefantes cuando llegan a ese sitio donde reposan los restos de otros elefantes—la otro manada, o la verdadera sombra de la manada—aunque estén fatigados, hambrientos. Gracias, Mónica Sanders Samsonov, o simplemente Gunila, gracias por revelarme que hay todo un saber acumulado en esos documentales del Animal Planet y National Geographic.[78]
>
> Tocar en silencio los huesos sin saber por qué lo hacemos. Como los elefantes. En el documental Animal Planet [. . .] la voz en *off* dijo que los científicos no saben por qué los elefantes tienen esta rara costumbre para con sus muertos.[79]

If mourning, according to psychoanalysts, is a metaphoric process, one of finding a substitute for the absent object, then Ismael's repeated tries at narrating the night's events and his questioning of certain words expresses a lack of mastery and a failure at substituting the loss. And if, as Ismael speculates, what is called a metaphor is nonsense, "Supongo que a este desatino lo llaman metáfora," with regard to his rumination, "La personalidad se esculpe con el paso del tiempo y según lo que en vida nos haya tocado tragar y cagar," then maybe ingesting and defecating are simply, and not metaphorically, what constitute a life.[80] Where language fails, Echevarría's novel suggests, the alternative is to kneel like elephants, "Arrodillarse aunque estés muy fatigado." In this way, one is not only in a posture of humility, but closer to the ground from which humans had presumably left their animality. Remember that for Freud, "the origin of humans is located in an act of 'organic repression' whereby they begin to walk upright and rise above life on the ground among blood and feces."[81] Like elephants Ismael says, "aunque estén fatigados y hambrientos,"—signaling our embodied vulnerabilities—we should look at the remains of our dead up close, touch, and smell them. In recounting how elephants mourn their dead, the passage chips away at hierarchal distinctions between humans and animals. On the one hand, elephants demonstrate a cultural practice, "esta rara costumbre para con sus muertos," and, on the other hand, Ismael's appeal for us to do the same underscores a shared corporeality and finitude between humans and animals, a shared biology and psychology. Moreover, as I suggested previously, the smelling and touching of the bones in lieu of substituting the loss with the right metaphor, is a form of ingesting, or cannibalizing, the Other.

"Tocar en silencio los huesos sin saber por qué lo hacemos," I suggest, presents us with a practice of reading and writing that does not presume to know, or represent an absent Other, much like Santiago Colas's "unknowing relating" discussed in chapter 1.[82] Colas retells a Felisberto Hernández short story of a ritual of feeling objects in the dark with one's hands. In the story "hands [. . .] compensate for the loss of vision, an unknowing relating in the place of the representational knowing associated with sight."[83] Colas's ethical close reading is "a touching without knowledge," "an exploration, and in that way [an] unfolding of what we do not know in texts (and figuratively speaking in things)."[84] Echevarría's *Búfalos,* as it will become more evident, appeals for this kind of unknowing relating, or *tocar sin saber* from its readers, but more than being touched, it will ask to be ingested. Whereas writing had once been the sign par excellence of civilization, in *Búfalos camino al matadero,* writing (and art) we've seen is more often associated with interdependence and becoming-beast—"Óleos. Gemidos. El cuerpo de Janela bajo el mío. Esculturas. Gemidos. [. . .] Embestidas."[85]

Before taking a closer look at cannibalism in *Búfalos,* let us examine its philosophical implications in earlier texts. The cannibal, who has historically signaled the opposite of the lettered man, has been redeployed by twentieth-century writers to combat colonial thinking, as well as to convey a different relational ethics. In his 1928 "Manifesto Antropófago," Oswald de Andrade was responding to internalized Eurocentrism and xenophobic, essentialist national movements. Where Latin American cultures had been considered, domestically and abroad, as lesser copies of Europe, Andrade argues that the adaptation of European cultural and social practices is a cannibalizing and not a mere imitation.[86] Rather than stand for the opposite of culture, cannibalism, Andrade proposes, is how culture and politics happen. In so doing, he not only collapses the binary of civilization and barbarism, but also underscores the agency, power, and autonomy of Latin American cultural actors. The manifesto's statement, "Cannibalism alone unites us. Socially. Economically. Philosophically," counters the notion that what unites is a shared identity and introduces a different conception of how cultural production and appropriation work.[87] Instead of imagining art and literature as static representations of an already existing reality, or as copies of other art, imagining them as cannibalistic, as the predatory digestion and metabolizing of matter for sustenance, implies that art and literature are the transformation of material, forms of becoming and metamorphosis. In cannibalizing there is no original or copy.

Andrade's linguistic and irreverent play on Shakespeare, "Tupi or not to Tupi," references the Tupinambá indigenous people of Brazil and the colonials' debate as to whether they had souls. In war, the Tupi practiced an elaborately ritualized cannibalism where their captured enemies would be consumed as vengeance. Such consumption was also a form of reverence as it was imagined that in incorporating the enemy one was also incorporating the enemy's perspective. In his *Cannibal Metaphysics* the anthropologist Eduardo Viveiros de Castro explores the ethical potential in these indigenous cosmologies, which considers all things, even the seemingly inanimate, such as mineral and rocks, as having their own point of view and agency. Significantly, in what Viveiros de Castro calls perspectivism, one's being is constituted in relationship to other beings. In the Tupinambas' cannibalism there is "a transmutation of perspectives whereby the 'I' is determined as other through the act of incorporating this other, who in turn becomes an 'I' . . . but ever *in* the other—literally, that is, *through* the other."[88] The Tupian cannibalistic sacrificial rituals, thus, dramatize the belief that "[s]elf-consciousness is reached not through confrontation with the other and subsequent self-return but through temporarily occupying [. . .] the enemy's point of view, and seeing 'oneself' from there."[89]

This conception of subjectivity, as dependent upon and constituted by the other, is similarly expressed in Juan José Saer's seminal novel *El entenado* (1983), based on the sixteenth-century chronicle of a Spanish explorer who was taken hostage by an indigenous cannibal tribe. Saer's fictional tribe, the *colastiné,* practice cannibalism as a means to determine the limits of the community and of the self and Other. The narrator who is kept as a guest-hostage is meant to bear witness to these rituals. The tribe's cosmology resembles a twentieth-century existentialism wrought with uncertainty; their existence depends on their being seen from an outside. As such, *El entenado* advocates for an ethics of hospitality and, more precisely, for an ontological order in which the Other comes first, for psychic differentiation, or subjectivation, requires the perspective of the Other.[90] Where Andrade's cannibalism was a means to affirm autonomy and agency against colonial hierarchies, Saer's later twentieth-century cannibalism is a response to the Argentine state genocide of the Dirty War. Rather than assert autonomy, cannibalism here recognizes one's need and nourishment from the Other. Cannibalism also serves as a metaphor for a melancholic incorporation of a loss, as Saer implicitly addresses the Argentine state's disavowal of its crimes and lost lives.[91]

Turning back to *Búfalos,* we can begin to understand its cannibalism as an ethics of the Other. Much like the interpolation of the reader, "llámame Ismael," writing in the novel is always addressed to an Other, as a gift or as the response to a request. For example, "Soñar que con un solo ojo, torpe caligrafía y una promesa puedes complacer a una portuguesa que te pidió un intercambio de cartas."[92] Anticipating an insufficient fulfillment of such a debt generates a particular kind of writing: "Escribir una carta. Comenzar a desgarrarse las ropas y el pellejo en cada oración escrita."[93] In this undressing, I suggest, there is not so much a revelation as an exposure, a coming into contact with another body. When Ismael asks, "Trágame. Pero no me leas, aunque lo hayas pedido, aunque mis cartas lleguen a tu buzón,"[94] we might interpret this as an appeal to be incorporated, to be metabolized, transformed and, in turn, to transform his host. And all of this without the pretense of knowing or resolving the difference the Other presents. The plea is repeated numerous times. On one occasion Ismael states, "Nunca me leas, por favor. Nunca te he leído," by which he expresses a reciprocity and implicitly collapses the unilateral role between author and reader.[95] Instead of reading the letters, Ismael takes them "para olerlas y mirar las estampillas—y arrancarlas para quizá algún día hacer una colección—."[96] Recalling the passage with the elephants and the remains of their dead, in smelling, looking, and tearing there is corporeality and also violence. In reading/writing there is exposure, "desgarrarse las ropas y el pellejo," and risk of injury. By not deciphering the letter's written text, Ismael sustains that "sin saber" and instead explores its texture and materiality. Accordingly, writing is presented as the preparation of meat: "Cortar, deshuesar, botar el pellejo, las tripas, los tendones, la mierda. Moler, condimentar, mezclar. ¿De eso trata la poesía?"[97] Producing and consuming literature always involves meaty bodies.

Drawing from the Tupinambas, perhaps "trágame" is a plea to see oneself from another's perspective, but only ever through the other. In other words, this being seen or seeing oneself from another perspective is never a mirroring or a return to the Self. The novel ends with Ismael making a pilgrimage to see four albino alligators; local lore claims that achieving sustained eye contact with one of the fantastic beasts promises good luck. Having done so, Ismael, who has "un solo plan: inventarme un plan," because otherwise, "avanz[a] como si fuer[a] camino al matadero," concludes the narrative with hope for the future.[98] Rather than look at the face of God, as El Mexicano recommends, "Debes mirar al Señor. Míralo a los ojos y trata de sostener la mirada,"[99] Ismael opts for the inhuman face of a colorless reptile: "Me miró con sus frías y profundas canicas azules."[100] In reading/eating the Other, the Other does not become me, nor I them; we are each transformed. The text becomes something else as we incorporate it into our bodies and we, in turn, are different.

Talking Pigs

Published in 2017, four years after *Búfalos camino al matadero,* Echevarría's *Caballo con arzones* also destabilizes a human-animal divide and corporealizes reading and writing. However, whereas in *Búfalos* animals mostly figured as poetic tropes or nature documentary references, in *Caballo con arzones* they appear as philosophizing protagonists. The novel is highly conceptual and much of its theoretical discourse comes from the mouth of Robespierre, the penultimate pig to have been raised by the narrator's neighbor in the patio of his Havana apartment. The neighbor, who committed suicide, occasionally visits the narrator postmortem with a leaky brain, a bloody visage, and a loose eyeball. Robespierre now also spends a lot of time in the narrator's living room sniffing for truffles, "*Tuber melanosporum,*" under the black and white tiled floor.[101] This pig is not only wise and Socratic, but he also appears to have already been cooked.

In the following passage we see the suicide-neighbor's wife clean the grease stains left by Robespierre:

> Su mujer, lozano cadáver, hincada de rodillas iba detrás de Robespierre con un trapo. Apenada secaba las gotas de manteca, manaban a través de las grietas del pellejo tostado. Robespierre olía a zumo de naranja agria, ajo, comino, además tenía el toque ahumado del palo de guayaba. Entre caladas al cigarro liado con picadura de tabaco negro mi vecino observaba a la mujer, al cerdo, también a mí.[102]

> <<No hay más que un problema filosófico verdaderamente serio—dijo Robespierre y caminó hasta mi butacón, se alzó hincando los cuartos delanteros en el mueble—. Ese problema verdaderamente serio es el suicidio>>.[103]

Where the culinary in Cuban literary tradition has operated as a trope for Latin American singularity and baroque plenitude,[104] in Echevarría the well-seasoned pig alerts the reader to intense scarcity and precariousness, as he reflects, no less, on the question of suicide. The peculiar Cuban practice of raising pigs in urban contexts had its beginnings in the Special Period, when the government was unable to provide basic needs to its citizens. Raising pigs, which are considered property of the state, in your Havana apartment for your own consumption or profit is illegal, and thus a tactic developed out of mere survival. The narrator's description, "[m]i vecino observaba a la mujer, al cerdo, también a mí," places the narrator within the same frame as the dead woman and the cooked pig. All three, living or dead, man, woman, and pig are here animate bodies, and yet socially determined to be ontologically Other to one another. Couched within this absurdist narrative—where cadavers are healthy, "lozano cadáver," and the distinctions between the living and the dead, and humans and animals, appear to be arbitrary—"[e]se problema verdaderamente serio," *el suicidio,* calls into question the social conditions that render a life futureless, or determine, in Robespierre's words, "<<que la vida vale o no la pena . . . >>"[105]

Having been marinated deliciously, Robespierre's seasoned flesh alludes to the novel's own incorporation and digestion. Recall that in *Búfalos* Ismael asks, "Moler, condimentar, mezclar. ¿De eso trata la poesía?"[106] Although consuming a pig would not constitute cannibalism per se, Echevarría makes thought, dialogue, and representation taste good, or at least communicated through a meaty body. Jacques Derrida's interview with Jean-Luc Nancy, "'Eating Well,' or the calculation of the subject,'" provides us with insightful ways of reading Robespierre, as well as the larger structure of the novel. The French axiom "one must eat well" becomes a way for the philosopher to think through an ethics of the Other, that at once complicates subjectivity and resists prescriptive morals: "The moral question is thus not, nor has it ever been: should one eat or not eat, eat this and not that, the living or the nonliving, man or animal, but since *one must eat* in any case and since it tastes good to eat, and since there's no other definition of the good, *how* for goodness sake should one *eat well?*" (Italics in the original.)[107]

Derrida uses eating as a metonym for other forms of incorporation, in addition to the physical act of ingesting food; one interiorizes symbols, language, and social conventions. "All forms of identification and assimilation in relation to the Other (language, meaning, and so forth) and others (including animals, plants, rocks and so forth) are literal and/or metaphorical forms of eating."[108] Since one must eat in order to survive and since producing one's own subsistence is impossible without the help and sacrifice of others—be they vegetative or animal—eating is an act that reminds us of our interdependence and inestimable debt to one another. "One never eats entirely on one's own: this constitutes the rule underlying the statement, 'One must eat well.' It is a rule offering infinite hospitality."[109] Consequently, being perfectly moral is impossible since one's own survival depends upon the consumption and reliance of others.

This impossibility, however, provides a horizon to which we should always strive, and it means that the work of ethical reflection is never complete. As Derrida explains,

> For everything that happens at the edge of the orifices (of orality, but also the ear, the eye—and all the "senses" in general) the metonymy of "eating well" (bien manger) would always be the rule. The question is no longer one of knowing if it is "good" to eat the other [. . .] One eats him regardless and lets oneself be eaten by him.[110]

If "everything that happens at the edge of orifices" entails an eating, a transference of nourishment/depletion with/from others, then the limits between the Subject and the Other are porous and fluid. The question of the ethical cannot, then, be institutionalized or morally coded, but constantly reposed. Following this citation, Derrida goes on to talk about symbolic anthropophagy, particularly in the consumption of the eucharist. In Catholic communion the incorporation of the body of Christ transforms the devotee into a host of the sacrificial host. In French, the word host means both host and guest. Through this double meaning, Derrida elaborates his notion of infinite hospitality. In recognizing one's inassimilable (or indigestible) debt to the Other, one becomes hostage to their guest, and thus the roles between Master of the house and guest are collapsed. This becoming host to the host, or reverse incorporation, also destabilizes the roles between active subject and passive object. Put otherwise, who eats and who gets eaten is no longer clear; for in eating or assimilating the

Other, one becomes Other and is, therefore, eaten by the Other. Hence Derrida's statement, "[o]ne eats him regardless and lets oneself be eaten by him." This is not unlike Viveiros de Castro's reading of the Tupinambá's cannibalism, "whereby the 'I' is determined as other through the act of incorporating this other, who in turn becomes an 'I.'"[111]

The structure of *Caballo con arzones* similarly complicates the distinction between the I and the Other, as well as active subject and passive object, through a series of narrative frames and voices that produce double or reverse incorporations. To begin with, the narrator, who is a young Black man with dreadlocks and black rimmed glasses for myopic correction, is suggested to be the invention of an older white woman with straight black hair and the faint scars of acne; she needs glasses to see up close. However, as readers, we first encounter this woman through the eyes and voice of the young Black man. *Matrioska,* the name for the Russian dolls that contain a series of other dolls inside them, is tellingly the title of one of the novel's chapters and an apt trope for the novel's composition.

Like the black and white tiled floor of the Havana apartment, the descriptions of the characters, such as nearsighted/farsighted, male/female, young/old and Black/white, create complementary opposites. These details, which would constitute social and lived material differences, operate as accessories or iconographic accoutrements to subjects who remain unnamed, rather than essential markers. In other words, details, such as glasses or dreadlocks, become a way for the reader to distinguish between characters but not something that necessarily reveals an inherent quality about them. Alternatively, we might say that each nameless character is the configuration of their attributes. Although cadavers appear to be alive and well, what these characters all share, or what *is* essential, is their mortality, as the mourning of the dead will figure prominently in the novel.

The book is organized into fifty-two very short chapters, interspersed with unnumbered "Dudas" where philosophical questions are posed in an already philosophical text. The chapters read like vignettes, sometimes explicitly dreams, other times dreamlike, or individual occurrences typically between two people. The connection between the chapters is thematic rather than historical, although a family history involving an affair, the loss of a child, and the death of a father, a grandmother and, later, that of a mother are traced. These biographies also become details—like that of acne or hair texture—the reader uses to determine who is the speaking subject or with whom they are dialoguing, or whom they are observing and describing.

Ahmel Echevarría offers us the most succinct summary of the text when he explains in an interview,

> Solo sé que mi terquedad se traduce en observar al otro y verme en el otro, luego asociar. También sé que deseo escribir desde "otra biografía," desde una "biografía extraña."
>
> Solo sé, por ejemplo, que quiero ser una mujer blanca para entender su propia noción del mundo y para ello se inventa la voz de un hombre negro, el hogar de este hombre, y su familia.[112]

This "observar al otro y verme en el otro [. . .] desde una biografía extraña"—again another parallel to the Tupinambá's cannibalism—manifests itself in the novel through a textual transvestism: "no soy ese joven de los dreadlocks y las gafas [. . .] sino una mujer muy blanca de poco más de cuarenta años [. . .] Por lo tanto, soy una mujer. Una mujer real."[113] Although the descriptive sparsity of *Caballo,* like that of *Búfalos,* presents a dramatic departure from the baroque proliferation of Severo Sarduy, explored in chapter 2; interestingly, Echevarría also performs his own creation story and metamorphoses, where what is proper to a subject is consistently undermined. We see this at the opening of the novel as it describes its own genesis moment, "En el inicio no fue una palabra o frase el origen de este devenir. Ni siquiera un balbuceo. Pongamos entonces una imagen como el verdadero punto de partida."[114] The point of departure for this novel, or for this becoming, is another representation, despite its claims to being "una mujer real." "Solo quiero que trates de sobrellevar el mismo bochorno padecido por mí al interior de la imagen creada por esa mujer que me observa."[115] While the narrative voice fluctuates between the informal, *tú,* to the formal, *usted,* destabilizing the position of the interlocutor, what constitutes the interior of the narrative frame, or in this case "una imagen," who is being observed and described, and who, exactly, is framing or narrating the image, is thrown into a Borgesian game of mise-en-scènes.

The appeal to the reader, "Solo quiero que trates de sobrellevar," is also indicative of the novel's tendency to deploy the second-person narrative voice, implicating the reader in a relationship with the text. If *Búfalos* asked us to swallow the novel, "trágame. Pero no me leas," *Caballo,* is asking us to endure, "sobrellevar," what the narrator suffers, "padecer." As such, the text asks that we identify and assimilate (already a form of eating, if unconsciously so), as one does in the consumption of a realist novel. However, here we are made aware of the artifice through metatextual references,

"Una suerte de tamiz la curaduría del lenguaje. Un filtro para decantar, de lo real, lo verosímil," and moreover, that the image depends upon our interiorizing, or hosting it.[116] Let us return to Robespierre for another example of how the novel insists on its own incorporation.

A chapter titled, "Breve conversación con Robespierre (diálogo donde el cerdo habla sobre el futuro)," opens with a scene of hospitality: "Suaves y pausados los golpes en la puerta, tan rítmicos. Es su forma de llamar, el aviso de su visita."[117] The narrator continues to describe the pig's behavior:

> Su manera de mirarme y olfatear, antes de cruzar el umbral y tumbarse en el living, me lleva a imaginar que busca hacerse puro plasma para entonces cruzar la órbita de mis ojos; una vez dentro de mí, caminaría en el mismo sentido del torrente sanguíneo; sí, esa debería ser la ruta, para luego llegar a mi cabeza y acostarse allí, tal como lo hace en el living. [. . .] Él, siempre olisqueando, olfateando allí donde no debía. En mí cabeza, por ejemplo. Del interior manaba algo, del interior de mi cabeza quiero decir; el cerdo, el maldito cerdo, lo podía oler. ¿Cómo no sentirse desnudo? ¿Cómo evitarlo? Quizá si no me lo tomara tan a pecho . . . quizá debía preguntarle cualquier cosa, sonsacarlo, o rogarle . . .[118]

The phrase "cruzar la orbita de mis ojos," is one of many instances where the novel references going inside the body; it also makes seeing—that sense considered to be detached from the corporeal—a point of touch and penetration. Let us recall here the contiguity between "ojo" and "culo" in *Búfalos*. The mind's corporealness is, similarly, underscored when the pig is said to smell inside of the narrator's head, "siempre olisqueando [. . .] en mi cabeza [. . .] lo podía oler." "Hacerse puro plasma," gives the image—conventionally conceived as immaterial or abstract—a tangible materiality, which then becomes a torrent of blood in the body, "un torrente sanguíneo," not unlike the digestive process of meat. The description "caminaría [. . .] para luego llegar a mi cabeza y acostarse allí, tal como lo hace en el living," transforms the interior of our imagination into the living room of a home, a site of hospitality. The narrator, however, is not master of this house, nor we as readers. He feels invaded and shame; there is nothing exclusively or properly his, as his thoughts are not immune to the presence of the Other. The narrator and, by extension, we the readers, are hostage to the pig. Like Robespierre, the well-seasoned meaty text "[se] hace puro plasma" and a torrent of blood in our bodies.

The Politics of Cosmonauts and Generals

Above I described differences of gender, race, and age, in the novel as accessories or accoutrements to unnamed characters. Accordingly, I also described the shifts between narrative voice and perspective as a textual transvestism, using the dated term because of its reference to dressing in the clothes of the opposite sex. That differences of gender, race, and age at times appear as attributes the narrator takes off and puts on is problematic. These social differences might be read as hallow complimentary forms in the novel for the sake of a metatextual construction. However, much like *Búfalos,* the novel underscores experiences of vulnerability, loss, and marginality that are not necessarily determined by inhabiting a recognizable social identity and, in so doing, works against a politics of representation and its facile co-optation. Moreover, while the distinctions between characters are at times formalistic, Cuban society's anti-Blackness, the Revolution's assumed teleological gains, and its binary grammar of "dentro de la Revolución, todo; contra la Revolución, nada" are implicitly, if not scathingly, critiqued.[119]

Whereas *Búfalos* is almost impossible to situate, *Caballo* gives its readers exact coordinates, "Cuba./ La Habana./ Centro Habana./ San Leopoldo."[120] And if *Caballo's* engagement with racial and gender differences leaves much to be desired in the way of legible politics, the novel makes explicit references to Cuban contexts, historical events, and figures that demand from its readers socio-political reflection. In a chapter titled "Materva," the narrative describes an outdoor line of people waiting for the cold gassy beverage, "[l]a fila avanza, frente al mostrador describe una curva, como si en la ardiente acera hubiese un hueco, charco, o la disposición de algún perro callejero. Hay un hombre en la acera; tendido, breve, negro."[121] The narrative goes on to describe the man as wearing torn, stained, and dirty clothes. Apparently unhoused and sleeping in a public space, the man is treated as "un hueco," a hole, or a pit, people avoid so as not to risk falling in. The vulnerability and abandonment his body communicates is too much for some to register. As the line moves around the man's body, "hay quienes apenas reparan en aquello que los obliga a correrse."[122]

Never missing an opportunity to interiorize—or as with the *Matrioska,* find another doll within a doll—the narrator claims to have heard the Black man say the name of a woman in his sleep. The narrator then speculates as to the what the woman looks like and what she might be doing in the man's dream, "¿Qué estaría haciendo, en el sueño del hombre, ese cuerpo con el cuerpo del hombre?"[123] The reader must sift through various frames: the narrator imagining the woman, as she is being imagined in the dream of the man. This is one of the ways the novel plays with incorporation—a subject is perceived from/within the body of another, or quite simply the woman is inside the man's dream—and destabilizes the positions between subject and object/other. By playing with who is imagining and whom is being imagined, the text obfuscates the frontier between the two and gestures toward an infinite hospitality (Derrida). In other words, what is "good" cannot be institutionalized or morally coded with such fluid and porous boundaries between Subject and Other. Revolutionary ethos, by contrast, calls for an unambiguous commitment, "dentro la Revolución, todo."

In contradistinction to the anonymous and unhoused Black man, we have mention of Arnaldo Tamayo Méndez, the first man of African heritage to have gone into outer space, as part of the narrator's biographic memory. "Vi el rostro de Tamayo dentro de un casco [. . .] conservo un modelo de la Soyuz [. . .] y en mi memoria el negro rostro sonriente de Tamayo el Teniente Coronel en la pecera—."[124] In the novel's characteristic doubling, the narrator makes mention of another famous Arnaldo, General Ochoa who fought in Angola:

> ¿Para Tamayo y Ochoa las dos patrias serían las mismas, es decir, se llamarían igual, vista desde la negra cúpula donde, dicen, flotaba en una nave soviética el cosmonauta, o vista desde la negra África donde el General, dicen, desde su vehículo militar soviético hacía de las suyas con marfil, piedras preciosas, cocaína? Pensar Cuba. Pensar La Noche. Desear Cuba. Desear La Noche.[125]

While Arnaldo the cosmonaut would represent the progress the country had made in terms of racial equity, alongside its technological and scientific advancements, Arnaldo the General would represent Cuba's commitment to fighting alongside the African nation. Both however are done using Soviet vehicles in a Cold War landscape. The hope that Arnaldo the cosmonaut inspired in the narrator to study astronomy would be short lived, as that program would be eliminated from high school curriculum. Instead of learning the names of asteroids and planets, the narrator describes being taught, "los fundamentos del Marxismo-Leninismo."[126] The international comradeship between Cuba and Angola would be marked by Arnaldo the General's extraction and trafficking of marble, diamonds, and cocaine, suggestive of neocolonial relationships. Ultimately, these two military, internationally renowned Cuban Arnaldos did not make the island a more hospitable place toward the anonymous Black man sleeping on the sidewalk.

Within the same pages of the two Arnaldos, the text reminds its readers of the Mariel Boatlift, a spectacularly inhospitable event on the island. Months before the Soyuz launched into space in October 1980, a bus crashed into the gate of the Peruvian embassy in Havana. What began on April 1, 1980, with six Cubans seeking asylum would lead to the mass exodus of over 125,000 people. The narrator recounts taunting those that wanted to leave, "yo, en las tardes, lanzaba huevos y fango a las fachadas de quienes habían en su destino una embarcación."[127] This was not an isolated or idiosyncratic response, but the result of government mobilization to vilify those that were leaving. The state response was to treat those fleeing as undesirable criminals, deploying terms like *gusanos* to symbolize their unworthiness. The failed incorporation and purging of these so-called counterrevolutionary people and their devaluation, as *vidas que no valen la pena,* to use Robespierre's formulation, is symptomatic of the Revolution's moral hubris and exclusive binary grammar.

Intertwined in these historical events are repeated references, like a choral refrain, to one of José Martí's poems written in exile and published posthumously. In the passage cited above, the phrases "Pensar Cuba. Pensar La Noche" are from Martí's "Dos Patrias," that opens with "Dos patrias tengo yo: Cuba y la noche./ ¿O son una las dos?"[128] The poem has a dialogic structure that couples the poetic trope of the nocturne with an empirical political statement, his claim to Cuba as his nation, then still a colony of Spain.[129] "By evoking the night, [Martí], asserts that he goes beyond the physical senses [. . .] he finds himself in an alternate reality or dimension while viewing this dream," where Cuba appears as a grieving, but also erotic, widow, as she holds a red carnation that doubles as the poet's literal heart.[130] As we've seen, Echevarría similarly deploys a complimentary duality in the structure of the novel—as opposed to the mutually exclusive binary grammar of the Cuban state—particularly in the conveying of historical factums and literary dreamscapes, or grief and desire.[131] Like Martí, Echevarría also gestures toward the transformative and creative potential of the literary; the novel, after all, opens with a creation scene and demands of its readers imaginative gymnastics where the perceptible boundaries dissolve. However, Echevarría departs from the so-called Cuban apostle in a very significant way and, in so doing, from one of the Revolution's moral tenets.

In the dramatic realization that the carnation is his heart, the poetic voice in Martí's "Dos Patrias" states "Ya es hora/ De empezar a morir."[132] This call to self-sacrifice for the sake of the nation is reiterated in the Revolution's motto, "patria o muerte." As we saw with Ismael in *Búfalos, Caballo* also draws upon the figure of the ex-military. In *Caballo,* the narrator's father is described as "La seguridad del Estado, es decir, un soldado de la Patria," as well as "un ex militante del Partido [. . .] ex soldado de la patria."[133] State and fatherland mean two different things and yet here they are conflated, implicitly calling out the Cuban government's false equivalence between patriotism and the interests of the state and the party. Echevarría, moreover, challenges the notion that dying is ever glorious:

> ¿Usabas la pañoleta con un firme nudo corredizo a una pulgada de la blanca piel de tu cuello? ¿A quién mirabas cuando en la estrofa del himno de guerra, entonado en la mañana, llegabas a ese verso donde se habla de una muerte gloriosa? ¿Es cierto que la muerte, según la condición en que muera, puede catalogarse como gloriosa? [. . .] ¿Morir por la patria es vivir?[134]

In dialogue with the middle-aged white woman, the narrator recalls the symbolism of school uniforms and hymns. The question, "¿A quién mirabas cuando [. . .] llegabas a ese verso donde se habla de una muerte gloriosa?" powerfully insists on an ethics of the Other over blind sacrifice for the nation, as it calls upon the face of a singular and thus irreplaceable life. "¿Morir por la patria es vivir?" further challenges the logic of sacrifice, in which one's death is redeemed in the hypostatic union of the nation. Whether it's dying in Iraq or in Angola, Echevarría undermines state rhetoric and mechanisms that make lives disposable for the grand narrative of a metaphysical nation or a utopic community.

Corpses, Exhumation, and Reading

Caballo con arzones is replete with corpses. Some are animate like the neighbor who committed suicide and his wife, "cadáver lozano." Some cadavers are more ordinary like the narrator's grandmother lying on her bed, "mustia y rígida."[135] In one vignette, the narrator considers a compositional arrangement for a photograph in which his ex-military father's cancer-ridden corpse is staged alongside his own living body.[136] And in another, the narrator dreams of his father and of a cadaver in its coffin sunbathing, stretched out like an island, following a military procession.[137] Some corpses are fetuses that did not make it to term, "¿Es el feto—sanguinolento cadáver—un hijo?," or fetuses that were malformed, "Agustín fue solo un nombre para un amasijo de carne muerta," twin to the surviving "Pablo bestezuela tierna Síndrome de Down."[138]

If we recall Nancy's "Corpus," in which he deconstructs a Christian metaphysics of soul and body, alongside our reading of imperfect bodies in *Búfalos,* then we can interpret the dead and misshapen bodies that populate *Caballo,* as working against a sacrificial, or substitutive, logic where one body can subsume, or stand in for other bodies.[139] Indeed, the narrator states that there is "un fallo, el error, un error en la noción de sacrificio, calvario y resurrección."[140] By arranging bodies that are alive alongside those that are dead, having some cadavers be "heathly," while others exhibit "*rigor mortis,*" having talking, philosophizing pigs, and having characters' distinctiveness rest on an inventory of physical attributes, the novel renders inoperative the metaphysics of incarnation, where there is a one-to-one correspondence between a physical body (or representation) and an immaterial ideal.[141] In other words, the organizing structures or models that would determine which citizens are worthy of staying and being protected and which warrant abandonment and exile, come under attack when corpses can sunbathe, when "un amasijo de carne muerta" is named and mourned, or when sleeping unhoused men have rich interior lives.

Like *Búfalos,* the remains of the dead also figure prominently here. The narrator twice attends the exhumation of a relative's remains at the Cementerio de Colón in Havana, as they will be relocated to a common grave. While such an act might be considered sacrilegious, it takes on a bureaucratic efficiency:

> <<Extraer los huesos>>, vaya frase . . . Ese *performance,* tan impúdico, es una operación repetida casi con exactitud. Porque los restos serán acomodados luego en los osarios. Pequeños cajones grises, en su interior un cuerpo despiezado. De haber alguna diferencia, si existe alguna, solo es achacable a ese cuerpo tan próximo al fin sosegado transcurrir de su muerte. El cadáver de un hombre como la condición postrera de todo hombre. Pero cualquier hombre no es un cadáver cualquiera. Mi abuela muerta no es tu abuela muerta. Mi hermano muerto no es la condición postrera de tu hermano vivo.[142]

This "*performance,*" gives rise to the reflection that a corpse is simultaneously anonymous, common, and absolutely singular. However, this singularity comes in the possessive adjective "mi abuela," "mi hermano"; in other words, the singularity is in relation to other people, and only ever in relation to Others. Despite its efficient and uniform compartmentalization—"repetida casi con exactitud [. . .] acomodados [. . .] [en] [p]equeños cajones grises"—we can connect this scene to that of the mourning elephants in *Búfalos*. The ritual act of attending to the bones of our deceased points not only to shared biological material between humans and elephants, but also to shared finitude. The communication of death and the eventual disintegration of the body, of becoming common and anonymous, reveals our interdependence and bare material needs, which counter narratives of a sublime or glorious death.

Interestingly, within this chapter of death and exhumation there is a passage that most emphatically underscores the incorporation of the reader by the writer and vice versa. As the narrator describes the setting of his grandmother's death, he directs himself to his interlocutor, or more precisely to us, his readers:

> No solo llevo el hilo conductor de este pasaje . . . <<Hilo conductor>> . . . vaya frase.
>
> Tan pronto tu mirada logre divisar los bordes de cada objeto podrás definir el contorno de mi cuerpo.
>
> Estaré muy cerca de ti, tan cerca que podrás sentir cómo te hablo al oído, cómo me atrevo a ir un poco más allá, es decir, a cruzar los límites de tu cuerpo, adentrarme en ti hasta diluirme en tu libre fluir de la conciencia. Demorarme allí, entender, de ese torrente, cuanto crees ver y lo que ves, y deslizar allí una palabra que altere tu punto de vista, inocular una frase que consiga sedimentar ese cambio.[143]

The narrator goes so far as to insert his interlocutor into the scene of his grandmother's room where he observes his mother mourn over, and arrange, his grandmother's dead body. "Pero has decidido hacerte a un lado, tu reflejo [en los tres espejos] alteraría esta historia que te incluye en tanto testigo, o mejor: eres una suerte de interlocutor pasivo."[144] Passive or not, our reading of the text and visually imagining the scene, "Tan pronto tu mirada logre divisar los bordes de cada objeto," not only inserts us in the room, but also necessarily makes us hosts to the "<<hilo conductor>>" and the contours of the narrator's body, "podrás definir el contorno de mi cuerpo." The narrator first whispers in our ears, then enters our bodies, "adentrarme en ti hasta diluirme en tu libre fluir de la conciencia," possessing or infecting our conscious thoughts. In reading/hosting the text, we are forever transformed; the narrator "desliz[a] allí una palabra que altere tu punto de vista, inocul[a] una frase que consiga sedimentar ese cambio."

Notably, the chapter is titled "Brizna," which means a blade of grass or a strand, thread, or fiber. We can connect *brizna* to the narrator's thread, his "hilo conductor." As a fiber, *brizna* might also refer to the remains of the dead; every strand is precious and meaningful to those who are mourning that corpse. The fiber might even be a remainder left out from the uniform compartments of the "[p]equeños cajones grises," an irreducible and non-identifiable part.[145] In *Búfalos,* Ismael's call to smell the bones "sin saber" prompted us to elaborate a practice of reading as an "unknowing relating" (Colas). Here the descriptions of exhumation, framed by the above passage in which the reader evidently incorporates and is incorporated, suggest that writing is a corpus/corpse (Nancy), a body to be exhumed and consumed. And as a corpse, writing is only ever meaningful in relation to other bodies; it is not a physical incarnation of an already existing idea. It's a dead body, yet animate, like a healthy sunbathing cadaver.

Smelling Suicide Letters

In addition to its many cadavers, the narrative foregrounds a series of textual and visual objects: "un cuaderno pequeño, hermoso, de tapa dura. Un moleskin," "un álbum de fotografías," "pequeñas cartulinas blanquinegras," "cartas y varias fotos," "una libreta de escolar sencillo," "cuaderno de apuntes," an email, a suicide note, a "máquina fotográfica," an "estilográfica," "hojas rayadas," digital folders with archived porn, "una carta mensual," and a plethora of references to other texts and authors, as most chapters have one or more epigraphs.[146] The *cuaderno* as a recurring object, and various references to the tools and practices of writing is another point of touch between *Caballo* and *Búfalos.* Writing, like Ismael's glass eye or Amanda Carter's false teeth, appears as another prosthetic, a material, technical, and exterior device, that cannot be said to represent a subject's thoughts. Cary Wolfe points out that if we pay attention to the social and "cultural complexities of such devices [e.g., an email, a photo album, or a journal], then in what sense can the internal psychic states [. . .] call[ed] 'our thinking' be said to be 're-presented.'" A diary, for instance, already assumes a convention, a genre; it will be read in relation to other diaries and people's expectations of what diaries do. My diary may be an extension of me, like a detachable part, but it cannot stand in for me. Wolfe continues, "there can be no 're-presentation' of 'our' thinking in language because the meaning of an utterance is always subject to differential interpretation, an interpretation that itself takes place within multiple imbedded protocols, traditions, conventions and so on."[147]

If writing is a technicity that does not correspond with a metaphysical state or a distinct human consciousness, Echevarría's texts, as we've seen, also underscore its animality. In *Búfalos,* Amanda, who gifts Ismael a poem, is observed to always have a notebook when she is at the Albatross bar. Amanda explains, "no es un diario lo que estoy escribiendo—en sus manos tenía el cuaderno—. Es una jaula . . . eso, una jaula."[148] Given that creative production is presented as a becoming-beast in *Búfalos,* "[u]na estampida, una verdadera estampida,"[149] imagining the *cuaderno* as a cage is another indication of how Echevarría's texts not only undermine the pretenses of civilized society, but also the assumptions of what distinguishes human animals from nonhuman animals.

In *Caballo con arzones* writing as animal also comes to fore. In a chapter titled, "La nota," the narrator describes what *los suicidas* do before self-annihilation: "Arañan un pedazo de papel con el entintado aguijón de un bolígrafo o el oscuro colmillo de grafito."[150] Rather than describe the suicide as "writing," with its implicit production of intelligible discourse, the suicide "scratches" a piece (as opposed to a sheet) of paper, as an animal might mark its territory. The inked "sting" of a ball point pen, and graphite "fang" further highlight the predatory animality of writing. Accordingly, we as readers should also relate to the marks on the page like animals, using our corporeal senses: "[t]endríamos que acercar el oído al trozo de papel; allí estarían los últimos sonidos, las últimas imágenes, el último sabor, el olor último que el suicida sintió."[151] What constitutes writing is further destabilized and made beastly when the narrative later implicitly suggests that the suicide note is not a note per se, but the dead and sexually abused body of the suicide's adolescent daughter.[152] Again here we have the assimilation between a text and body to be exhumed, investigated for traces, and mourned for a singularity (or original meaning) that cannot be recovered. Like Amanda Carter's bruised face—"Tu cara es un maldito poema"—the injured body is a text.[153]

Another textual object arrives in the form of an email from someone unknown to the narrator. The text of the email in italics reads like a response to a personal ad with awkward sentence structure. The narrator interprets it as follows:

> Sus palabras tienen el aliento del mensaje escrito por un náufrago. Una suerte de alarido, de llamada. [. . .] Debería responder [. . .] *a pesar de la enrevesada redacción entiendo tu mensaje.* [. . .] *pero al puerto equivocado.* [. . .] Irse a la cama con el rostro de una mujer y sus palabras aparentemente calmas, gravitando dentro de las paredes de mi cabeza. Una mujer aferrada con todas las uñas a un *software translator* y a un mensajero electrónico (emphasis in the original).[154]

That her words "tienen el aliento" and that she clings "con todas las uñas," even if to a sophisticated piece of technology, presents writing as corporeal and savage. The description of going to bed with the image of her "dentro de las paredes de mi cabeza," reiterates the interiorization and hosting the novel characteristically foregrounds. What is also notable about this passage is the woman's imagined call for help, "[u]na suerte de alarido, de llamada" and that the message was sent, "*al puerto equivocado.*" The use of the software translator and the letter's arrival to the wrong recipient underscore the impropriety of writing; your words are never exclusively yours nor your addressee's. Nevertheless, that call to the Other, that need of the Other, is communicated: "*a pesar de la enrevesada redacción entiendo tu mensaje.*"

Responding to messages from unknown senders is repeated in the monthly letters the narrator receives, initially by accident as well:

> Aquella muchacha confesó en la tercera carta que <<mis descuidos>> la intrigaban—erotizaban—. El pegamento de los sobres, decía, no era resistente, mis manos dejaban grasa en los pliegos de papel, había migas, tachaduras—tinta negra, tinta azul—, incluso fantaseaba con <<mis>> cabellos y la picadura del cigarro.[155]

The description of what arouses "aquella muchacha" apparently has nothing to do with the content of the letter, but rather its corporeal traces, unintended marks like greasy fingerprints, or that which has been made illegible, "tachaduras." Writing here operates like traces that can be investigated or exhumed despite the author's intentions. What is proper to the author is further put into question, as we see the possessive adjectives in quotation marks. The passage also underscores the call to the Other that writing necessarily demands. The narrator later states, "[d]epositar las oraciones como ríos de sangre redactadas para mí. [. . .] En la última línea de sangre pidió, casi en un ruego, que no dejara de escribirle."[156] The trope of letter writing, which we see in both *Búfalos* and *Caballo,* implies an addressee and a response; it stages the need of and, therefore, inassimilable debt to the Other. The conditions for writing here, in other words, are vulnerability and the desire to survive; writing is like a blood transfusion ("ríos de sangre").

The narration not only provides ekphrasis of the textual and visual objects, but it also narrates their content. In fact, descriptions of what is written in the journals or photographed in black and white pictures are a significant portion of the narrative. Hence, the Borgesian mise-en-scènes we described earlier. The word "encuadre" appears often to mark the compositional frame of a picture or that of a narrated scene, and yet it is often unclear what exactly coincides within said visual or textual frame. For instance, in one chapter where the narrator describes the contents of his father's journals and a set of eight pictures it becomes unclear at times to whom the narrative voice belongs—the father's or the son's—and whether what is being described is the journal entry or the picture or the narrator's imaginative elaboration of them. To use Amanda Carter's description, it is unclear for the reader what is inside the *jaula* and who is conducting the narrative thread, "el hilo conductor." As I've suggested, these indistinctions between who is representing and what is represented, or between who is eating and what is being eaten, collapse distinctions between Subject and Object/Other. Such a collapse calls for an infinite hospitality.

Cannibal Conclusions

In *Búfalos camino al matadero* Amanda Carter gifts Ismael a poem, which appears in the body of the text in italicized font. The verses of this poem are reproduced in the prose/poetic lines of *Caballo con arzones* under the chapter titled "Diente de león." The narrative/poetic voice describes herself levitating above her body, "[a]bajo, en la fría losa, esa otra parte de mí, tendida." Like a dandelion, the weightless body floats above the interior of an apartment after a domestic violent fight. The poem's reappearance, slightly different, in Echevarría's later novel calls attention to the practice of writing and produces textual bodies that are not discrete or "well-organized" (Aristotle) but are rather like the starfish of which Ismael dreams; a piece might break off here or there and reconfigure into something else. The content of the poem, meanwhile, brings us to the suffering of the body and the impossibility of "[d]esprenderse de la carne, el moretón, el llanto."[157]

Where the characters in *Búfalos camino al matadero* were socially dead, "como si fueran camino al matadero,"[158] many of those in *Caballo con arzones* were already dead; they had already committed suicide or been ravaged by cancer. Where the former foregrounded the figure of the animal to such an extent, so as to destabilize its semiotic referent, the latter arguably went further and made the animal a philosophizing protagonist. In either case, we observed Ahmel Echevarría challenge the assumptions of humanism and its symbolic economy. In so doing, both novels lead us to question social models and values that would determine certain individuals as not having futures, making them disposable lives. Furthermore, through the figure of the ex-military, Echevarría questions the logic of sacrifice and the Cuban national rhetoric of a heroic and glorious death. Much like Portela's *El pájaro: Pincel y tinta china* and Ponte's *La fiesta vigilada,* Echevarría's novels present writing and reading as a means to survive, as a way to highlight our interdependence. Through writing and reading, Echevarría dismantles traditional conceptions of a coherent, autonomous, and independent subject.

Ismael's plea, "trágame. Pero no me leas" allowed us to formulate a practice and ethics of writing/reading as cannibalism. As such, writing/reading is not an elevated humanistic practice that demonstrates mastery over our bare material needs; reading/writing is not a static representation of so-called human triumph; reading/writing is the ingestion of the Other; it is mutual transformations, mutual blood transfusions, where neither writer nor reader are the same after. Through its various narrative frames and allusions to incorporation, *Caballo con arzones* allowed us to continue imagining writing/reading as a form of eating and hosting. The scenes of exhumation and attending to the remains of the dead further underscored the corporeality of writing.

The broader political implication of making literature meat is a destabilization of how society distributes and values bodies. Let us recall that phonetic writing, from a Eurocentric perspective, is the sign par excellence of civilization and that colonialism was imagined and justified as a civilizing project. In insisting that writing, art, and culture more generally, is beastly, animal, that it emerges from that which we share—vulnerability, suffering, empathy—and not that which makes us exceptional, Ahmel Echevarría is, at least implicitly, subverting a logic and system of organization that has justified the exploitation, sacrifice, and consumption of some bodies for the sustenance of others. The indistinctions Echevarría produces—

between flesh to be nourished and flesh to be consumed—challenge models of membership and an instrumentalizing logic that renders some bodies as exploitable material resources.

In the chapter that follows we will continue to explore the theme of hospitality through Portela's novel *Cien botellas en una pared* (2002) and the ICAIC produced film *Fresa y chocolate* (1993). Through the trope of inoculation, we will also continue to explore incorporation and the transformation of the body politic. We will even meet a cannibal.

5

The Body Politic and Immunitary Spaces

Hospitality and Friendship in *Fresa y chocolate* and *Cien botellas en una pared*

In the preceding chapters the focus has been on aesthetic strategies of opacity and impenetrability, rendering the identification of subjects, symbolic decoding, or the reproduction of a cohesive, linear narrative difficult, if not impossible. Antonio José Ponte, Ena Lucía Portela, and Ahmel Echevarría, as we saw in chapters three and four, largely forgo conventions of plot and character development. The bodies of their novels are fragmentary, at times disjointed, assembled from other cultural works like prosthetic limbs or parasitic appropriations. Barring its readers entry through dense and poetic intersecting narrative threads, Portela's, Ponte's, and Echevarría's texts might be charged with inhospitality. Indeed, if the conventions of hospitality require an immunitary space of which the host is master,[1] hospitality in the context of Ponte's inhabited ruins is then impossible, since the distinctions between what is proper and improper, or private and public, are obscured. With the crumbling of facades, the boundaries between interiority and exteriority collapse. In Portela's *El pájaro: Pincel y tinta china,* conventional hospitality is also foreclosed, as no space appears to be impervious to contamination, or the arrival of an uninvited guest that slips through under the door.[2] Echevarría's novels, with their references to ingestion ("Trágame. Pero no me leas.") and complex narrative frames that create indistinctions between who is the speaking subject and what is being represented, gesture toward an infinite hospitality. In other words, a hospitality whose limits and roles cannot be determined, or as Jacques Derrida explains, "One eats him regardless and lets oneself be eaten by him."[3] By contrast, the primary works of this chapter, the film *Fresa y chocolate* (1993) and a later novel by Portela, *Cien botellas en una pared* (2002), offer its viewers and readers a seemingly more traditional hospitality, that is to say transparent access to volumetric characters and plot development.

The wide appeal and commercial success of Tomás Gutiérrez Alea's 1993 film, *Fresa y chocolate,* is in part due to its adoption of the popular genre of melodrama. With clear protagonists and antagonists and an unambiguous plot, the producers of this film are no doubt hospitable to its audience. In fact, the paradigms of hospitality and friendship provide useful frameworks with which to analyze the film's narrative. Staged predominantly in a character's home, the drama of the film unfolds in the development of the unlikely friendship between a homophobic, militant communist and a gay, suspected counterrevolutionary. As such, *Fresa y chocolate* responds to the call of incorporating those who had been excluded by the Cuban Revolution, specifically its gay citizens. Its gay protagonist, Diego, is a sympathetic character, made consumable to a large audience and allegorically assimilated to the Revolution's narrative.

While my readings of other texts and images have worked to undo the metaphorical use of the body as a discrete organism, in turning to *Fresa y chocolate* and *Cien botellas en una pared,* I also now turn to the trope of the body politic. Doing so allows me to complicate the imagined unity of the nation or that of a shared identity and its attendant politics of assimilation, consumption, and seamless incorporation. Drawing from Roberto Esposito's conceptualization of "immunitas,"[4] as both a political and biological structure that includes by excluding and vice versa, I consider the dynamics of friendship and hospitality in these two works through a corporeal lens, once again bringing to the foreground relationships of interdependence, as well as fluid subjectivities.

In his text *Of Hospitality,* Derrida demonstrates how the lines between host and guest, hostage and hostile intruder are easily crossed. We see this in *El pájaro: Pincel y tinta china* when Fabián as "master" of the home rapes and tortures his guest, Camila. Although states of porosity and precariousness are heightened in Portela's *El pájaro,* Ponte's, and Echevarría's novels, these conditions are not exclusive to their contexts but always present, albeit by different degrees, in conventional modes of hospitality. In opening one's home to the foreigner, that space is no longer impervious. And were one to abide by the law of absolute hospitality, as Derrida argues, the host is in a relationship of unconditional obligation to the guest, paradoxically rendering the host hostage and collapsing the roles between host and guest.[5] While the larger narrative of *Fresa y chocolate* advocates for a politics of incorporation, paying close attention to expressions of vulnerability, dissymmetry, and irreducible difference, I aim to show how the film unworks the notion of community as a sovereign body made up of equal parts, and gestures toward an ethics of hospitality that demands risk, discomfort, and becoming Other. Betrayals and disguised intentions between the two friends place them in danger of political persecution and exclusion from their respective communities. In my reading of *Fresa y chocolate,* the insecurity that hospitality and friendship necessarily entail provides a means for an extra-institutional and non-official ethico-political practice.

Portela's *Cien botellas en una pared,* published nine years after the release of *Fresa y chocolate,* has also received significant critical and commercial attention; it too falls within a popular genre, that of detective fiction.[6] While *Fresa y chocolate* is considered a pivotal moment in Cuban cultural production for representing a gay man favorably, critics similarly consider *Cien botellas en una pared* "trailblazing" in its visibilization of female same-sex desire.[7] Although its commercial success cannot be compared to that of *Fresa y chocolate,* the novel has been translated into English, garnered numerous awards, and the Spanish edition to which I refer is a later one from Stockero, 2010. This version, edited by Iraida H. López, includes a substantial bibliography of secondary sources. Despite its wide appeal and greater accessibility, *Cien botellas* is by no means a conventional novel, as this chapter will underscore. The Stockero edition, for instance, includes new footnotes from Portela, extending the body of the text in a baroque proliferation. It is, however, far less impenetrable than her earlier novel *El pájaro: Pincel y tinta china.* As such, *Cien botellas* has generated characterological readings of the text, where questions of identity regarding gender, sexual orientation, and ethnicity have been explored in articles such as, "La mujer negra, lesbiana y punk en Cuba: la representación de La Gofia en *Cien Botellas en una pared* de Ena Lucía Portela," by Lucinda Anna Smith (2021).[8] *Cien botellas* is rich with representations of non-normative subjectivities; in fact, almost all the characters are queer in one way or another. In addition to its representations of marginalized subjects, the novel offers detailed portraits of Havana during the nineties, leading scholars to analyze the city as a protagonist in the text.[9] Like *Fresa y chocolate,* the novel stages friendship and hospitality to question dominant subject models in a post-Soviet context. The two works even share similar immunitary spaces, apartments in Havana that have been affectionately named by their protagonists.

Notwithstanding, if *Fresa y chocolate's* directors still aimed to work within the telos of the revolutionary narrative, Portela's novel holds no reverence for it and works against any and all grand narratives. Perhaps what is most distinctive about the novel is its sardonic humor and parodic representations, leaving nothing unscathed. In our treatment of the novel, we will look at the dynamics of friendship and hospitality among the various characters and consider how these relationships challenge classical paradigms. However, instead of focusing on how certain marginalized subjects are represented, as previous scholars have done, our attention will focus more on the composition of the text and how the authority of the writer is consistently undermined. Put otherwise, the novel expresses a hospitality and friendship toward its readers, by which the historical power and prestige of the book are subverted. In this regard, Portela allows us to pick up where we left off with Echevarría. The two authors challenge the pretenses of what constitutes writing, civilization, and the accomplishments of the Revolution, through allusions to becoming-nonhuman and foregrounding vulnerable and unideal subjects. In this chapter, "The Body Politic and Immunitary Spaces: Hospitality and Friendship in *Fresa y chocolate* and *Cien botellas en una pared*," we will see how Cuban cultural producers insist on a "vital relationship with the Other."[10]

Supermachos and Melodrama

"¿Por qué tú eres así?" The question upsets; it is taken offensively, as a rejection of his lifestyle. It is his friend and guest that poses the question and later follows it with an accusation: "tú no eres revolucionario." In this scene from *Fresa y chocolate* the disdain the militant student, David, expresses toward the effeminate mannerisms, or "monerías," of his friend Diego, in part reflects a historical machismo inherited from the Spanish and cultivated in Cuban national identity formation since the late eighteenth century.[11] However, for the interests of this chapter, I would like to point to another source of intolerance toward the feminine and accentuated gestures that Diego so emphatically exhibits from the start of the film. While many have looked to Cuba's postrevolutionary militarization as a cause of its hyper-masculinity,[12] I would add, alongside critics such as José Quiroga, that the figure of the homosexual presents an unassimilable excess to the ends of totalizing nation-building.[13] With the Revolution's promise of "El hombre nuevo," the birth of a new generation whose sense of civic obligation would surpass the pursuit of pleasure,[14] where would non-reproductive sexual behavior fit within the telos of this utopic project? If the institutionalized discrimination of gays served as a means to persecute political dissidents, designating their conduct as improper or counterrevolutionary,[15] I suggest that in associating the figure of the homosexual with decadence, spectacle, and extravagance—as indicated by the laws designed to persecute them, for example, "Ley contra la extravaganza" and "Ley contra la vagancia"[16]—this figure represents an unproductive expenditure,[17] a certain baroque aesthetic that is antithetical to the aims of monolithic communal projects—especially one that had become increasingly Sovietized[18]—and the establishment of a national subject. This becomes all the more evident when we consider that the 1960s labor camps designed to rehabilitate homosexuals, religious believers, and those deemed antisocial were called *Unidades Militares de Ayuda a la Producción.*[19] Indeed, the effort of making the figure of the homosexual a productive member of the community through forced labor and later attempts to incorporate this figure within the national narrative through representations, such as *Fresa y chocolate,* are symptomatic of reading nonheteronormative modalities of sexuality in excess to national unity. The confinement of gay citizens within the UMAPs not only implied they were unproductive, but also a contaminant to society. The medical discourse that circulated within the camps pathologized homosexuality as an incurable disease and societal reintegration was sought through the disciplining of "ostentatious" behavior, rules of comportment, and quota requirements.[20] *Fresa y chocolate's* deployment of the codified and accessible genre of melodrama, might be seen as another form of disciplining the figure of the homosexual making what presents a threat to the integrity of the body politic consumable to even its more *machista* audience.

Critics familiar with Tomás Gutiérrez Alea's experimental films, in which confrontational techniques, decentered narratives, and the use of collage demand an active viewership, were quick to note the stylistic shift *Fresa y chocolate* presented within his corpus. Having a straightforward narrative structure, clear protagonists and antagonists, and no Brechtian interruptions of the filmic illusion, *Fresa y chocolate* has been described as overly demonstrative and comparatively less complex.[21] In interviews, both Gutiérrez Alea and Juan Carlos Tabío, with whom he co-directed the film, have accredited its "universal" appeal to its denunciation of intolerance and promotion of the "comprehension of difference."[22] With regard to his stylistic shift, Gutiérrez Alea explains he felt the imperative to reach the largest audience possible and celebrates the accomplishment of doing so noting, "I've seen people you could call *supermachos* who left the film crying. If you cry, it's because you identify with Diego, who is not a macho. That's very important for me."[23] Although Gutiérrez Alea calls for the "comprehension of difference," the cathartic experience he holds dear entails a process of assimilation and, tellingly, he elaborates that in his adaptation of Diego's character from Senel Paz's short story, he left out the exaggerated effeminate behavior of the "loca" or "homosexual escandaloso" so that more viewers could self-identify with Diego.[24] In response to this image of the gay man made palatable, queer theorists have critiqued the film's attempts to domesticate the homosexual, neutralizing its oppositional charge.[25]

Notwithstanding the film's melodramatic structure and directorial aims to make its characters identifiable, in this chapter I will sustain my attention on interactions and visual components that remain extraneous to a project of incorporation and its presumptive elimination of a threat to national unity. If, on the level of the larger narrative, Senel Paz's script realized by Gutiérrez Alea and Tabío's direction advocates for a politics of assimilation, I suggest there are aspects of the film that signal irreconcilable differences—for instance, Diego's devotion to the Virgin Mary and David's dialectical materialism—and, in so doing, challenge the notion of community as a shared property or identity. Returning to the scene referenced above between Diego and David, I would like to take this confrontation where penetrating gazes intersect as an instance of friendship that questions the unity of the subject and provokes a self-othering. In the exchange of verbal jabs and unsettling stares, the staging of friendship here entails a vulnerability and risk that calls for an ethics of hospitality toward the foreigner and potential enemy. Set in 1970s Cuba, a political context of high vigilance and self-policing,[26] the interior of the home becomes a site for ethico-political practice, and personal interactions acquire the revolutionary significance of public demonstrations.

Philosophies of Friendship

In its Greco-Roman formulations, friendship is conceived as a filial bond established through similitude. Aristotle tells us that just as a father loves his son, or a brother loves another, friends love each other for being "other selves of theirs . . . having grown from the same sources."[27] Cicerón would later write, "él que mira a un verdadero amigo, mira, por así decir, un modelo de sí mismo."[28] With its self-identical subjects, the paradigm of classical friendship produces an aesthetic of harmonious geometry, achieving equilibrium through mutual reciprocity. For Aristotle the balance between giving and receiving is essential. And yet, as Derrida underscores in the *Politics of Friendship*, within this very model of reciprocity there is an irreducible dissymmetry.[29] Curiously, while Aristotle valorizes mutuality, he also argues that it is preferable to love than to be loved, to give than to receive. In his reading of these passages, Derrida argues, "The friend, the being-friend . . . is to love *before* being loved. . . . What is proper or essential to friendship, can be thought and lived without the least reference to the be-*loved,* or more generally to the *lovable* . . ."[30] Accordingly, friendship becomes an imperative to love without the expectation of it being corresponded, a unilateral act without measure. If we consider friendship not between identical or exemplary beings, if we depart from a filial model, this allows us to avoid the trap of producing centric structures—androcentric, phallocentric, or anthropocentric—and their inevitable exclusions. Moreover, recalling that for thinkers such as Cicerón the ideal friend is confident, virtuous, wise, and totally self-sufficient, the model exemplary friend is thus an absolute and immutable figure: having no need of or reliance to something outside of himself, he is invulnerable to an Other.[31]

Gilles Deleuze and Félix Guattari offer another useful reading of classical friendship and point to a necessary departure from its paradigm. Greek philosophy, they observe, emerged not from hierarchal or vertical relationships but from the horizontal interconnections that are formed in the society of friends, the society of equals.[32] And among these friends, there are rivalries, opinions, and antagonisms—the very stuff that generates concepts. As the persona of thought, the figure of the friend comes to signify a division within thought itself: "Thought needs the thinker-as-friend to actualize the concept. . . . Thought and thinker become claimant and rival and vice versa."[33] For Deleuze and Guattari, friendship as a splintering, or difference, continues to be the condition for the exercise of thought. However, after the catastrophe of totalitarian states, after the shame of Auschwitz—in a statement that markedly departs from the above quote by Cicero—they write, "friends can no longer look at each other, or each at himself, without a 'weariness'. . . ."[34] Friendship can no longer be "a simple rivalry" or a contest among equals for it is those selfsame homosocial institutions that led to incalculable atrocities.[35] As such, friendship and thought must "mutate": "After an ordeal too powerful . . . [there are] not two friends who communicate and recall the past together but, on the contrary, who suffer an amnesia or aphasia capable of splitting thought, of dividing it in itself. Personae proliferate and branch off . . ."[36] The shame that follows these catastrophes, "the shame of being human," does not arise from feeling "responsible for the victims but responsible before them."[37] If we consider that shame indicates feelings of inadequacy and constitutes an affront on dignity,[38] then Deleuze and Guattari's call for a new friendship is not only one that makes the relation between identical subjects untenable but insists on an insufficiency and "a vital relationship with the Other."[39]

Following Deleuze and Guattari's lead, I want to suggest that the legacy of the 1960s forced labor camps in Cuba, which worked to excise all that did not correspond to the exemplary revolutionary subject, compels us to consider alternatives to traditional models of friendship based on similitude and shared interests. Indeed, the shame of this legacy demands rethinking friendship in such a way that does not reiterate institutional collectives or social memberships. Against an androcentric model that produces exclusive allegiances and insists on mutual reciprocity,[40] the depiction of friendship in *Fresa y chocolate,* as we shall see, inverts classical norms, placing difference, vulnerability, and relations of dissymmetry at the foreground. The mutation and proliferation of personae Deleuze and Guattari observe "after an ordeal too powerful" is also operative in the film.

Incorporating *las locas*

Based on Senel Paz's story "El lobo, el bosque y el hombre nuevo," *Fresa y chocolate* presents us with a friendship between a young militant communist, David, who claims he only believes in dialectical materialism, and Diego, an older man who describes himself as "maricón," "religioso" "[y con] problemas con el sistema."[41] Produced in 1993 by the Cuban film institute, the film was lauded for its criticism of the state's rejection of its gay citizens.[42] The film not only aims at integrating this excluded community, but also a body of cultural production that had been stigmatized as superfluous to the Revolution's project. References to José Lezama Lima and his baroque novel *Paradiso* abound in the film.[43] However, alongside the praise, other critics have dismissed the significance of the film's political critique as too little, too late—never explicitly apologizing for the state's incarceration of gays and dissidents in the labor camps.[44] Emilio Bejel, among others, has pointed to the film's heteronormative ending, where David hooks up with Diego's neighbor Nancy, in the place of offering "a more committed gay politics."[45] Significantly, Diego's character "is from a social class inherently opposed to the film's basic ideology" and has "internalized some of the other prejudices of the society that discriminates against him."[46] He is, in Bejel's reading, racist, Eurocentric, and fetishizes high art, all of which "prevent [the film] from becoming a full blown treatise on the repressed."[47]

José Quiroga and Arnaldo Cruz-Malavé offer strong critiques of the film in its effort to incorporate the figure of the homosexual through the construction of a national allegory. Quiroga aptly posits that the film produces a typology of characters where the figure of the homosexual is subsumed in the larger narrative of the Revolution, legitimated as the nation's cultural producer, or the one who "bear[s] culture from one generation to the other."[48] Diego is not only stereotypically gay with effeminate and dramatic overtures, he is seen in a "positive light," as Quiroga says, and imparts to David a much needed education on national and international artists: María Callas, John Donne, and Lezama Lima to name a few. And not unlike Emilio Bejel, Quiroga also observes that Diego is "a conservative culture queen."[49] Drawing from Néstor Perlongher's essay "La desaparición de la homosexualidad," Quiroga succinctly states, "Si la sociedad no ha podido acabar con las locas, lo que resta entonces es incorporarlas."[50] He cautions against identitarian politics and the aims of making marginal figures visible in ways that are easily consumable by a dominant public, ultimately rendering these figures knowable and unthreatening.[51] Looking at Tomás Gutiérrez Alea's filmography, Quiroga explains that *Fresa y chocolate* serves as another progressive marker in the Revolution's teleological narrative. If *Memorias del subdesarrollo* (1968) addressed class-consciousness, *Fresa y chocolate* does the work of erotic liberation. For all its critique of the state, the film operates within the Revolution's dialectic.[52]

In a similar vein, Arnaldo Cruz-Malavé demonstrates how the homosexual in *Fresa y chocolate* represents an allegorical restitution. In his reading, the film and Paz's story aim to incorporate the error of the Revolution as part of the formation of a national subject.[53] The young communist David is no longer homophobic thanks to Diego's tutelage and comes to represent the new revolutionary man. In what Cruz-Malavé sees as a Christian *telos* in Che Guevara's promise of *el hombre nuevo,* the Revolution's initial rejection and persecution of gays is subsumed as an originary sin, or necessary transgression, in a narrative of redemption.[54] Citing a well-known phrase by Antonio Pérez, Cruz-Malavé illustrates the logic of incorporation in another way: "Sólo los grandes estómagos digieren veneno."[55] Calling to mind the process of inoculation, I want to suggest that perhaps Cruz-Malavé's and Quiroga's concern—the elimination of a threat posed by an oppositional figure through its integration—may better be understood and also complicated through the metaphor of the immunitary mechanism.

Before engaging with immunization's contradictory nature, we could say that on a characterological level, David has been inoculated by Diego; he is no longer threatened by gay men while Diego, forced into exile, is excised and disappeared from the body politic.

Inclusion through Exclusion

In a description that links its biological and political significations, Roberto Esposito writes of the immunitary logic:

> Evil must be thwarted, but not by keeping it at a distance from one's border; rather, it is included inside them. The dialectical figure that thus emerges is that of exclusionary inclusion or exclusion by inclusion. The body defeats a poison not by expelling it outside the organism, but by making it somehow part of the body.[56]

Significantly, Esposito tells us "This homeopathic protection practice—which excludes by including and affirms by negating—does not consume itself without leaving traces on the constitution of its object."[57] As Cruz-Malavé himself notes at the very end of his essay, despite attempts, it would be impossible "depurar el excedente homosexual de la nación, de devorarlo, de despedirse de él."[58] Remembering that the early 1990s was an especially vulnerable time for the Castro government with the dissolution of the Soviet Union, some have considered the film's production as a strategy to redeem the country's image abroad.[59] If *Fresa y chocolate* aims at immunizing the body politic by allegorically incorporating the figure of the homosexual, given "the structurally aporetic character of the immunitary process,"[60] I suggest the film inadvertently affirms this figure's oppositional charge. Put differently, in trying to vaccinate the body politic against the poison of the Revolution's error, the film affirms what it never explicitly addresses, the legacy of the camps and the institutional discrimination against gays.

Immunitas is an especially productive metaphor to understand the context within which friendship happens in the film. In its effort to protect the integrity of the body from an outside, or the limits of an identity from foreign incursion, Esposito explains, "immunity is a condition of particularity: whether it refers to an individual or a collective, it is always 'proper,' in the specific sense of 'belonging to someone' and therefore 'un-common' or 'non-communal.'"[61] Recalling that individuals were sent to the UMAPs for "im*proper* conduct," the camps may be interpreted as trying to preserve a collective identity, to maintain the boundaries of its properties in the most violent defense of an immunitary impulse. In the film, the perceived threat of a foreign incursion, specifically US imperialism, is made evident when David's friend Miguel exclaims "el enemigo está a 90 kilómetros." It is perhaps no coincidence that Diego's suspected counterrevolutionary art exhibit is linked with a foreign embassy. More accurately, it is Diego's supposed dealings with a foreign embassy that compel Miguel and David to investigate him. Recounting his initial encounter with Diego, David says: "Primero me enseñó unos libros extranjeros. . . . El tipo tiene la casa llena de cosas raras, unas esculturas rarísimas . . . Quieren [él y su amigo] hacer una exposición y una embajada lo va a ayudar." To which Miguel responds, "¿Una embajada? ¡Coño, David eso sí es grave!"

In an early scene, when David looks out the window of a cheap motel room, where he expects to finally sleep with his girlfriend, he sees a CDR billboard, signaling that even private spaces do not escape this penetrating surveillance. The Committees for the Defense of the Revolution provide another manifestation of an immunitary impulse, as Ted Henken explains, these were "neighborhood-based organizations . . . intended to monitor potential dissidents and pass information on to state security, further consolidating government power by turning the entire population into informants."[62] The fact that these are neighborhood-based organizations does not negate their non-communal operations, for as we shall see *immunitas* and *communitas* are inextricably linked. What I would like to highlight about this context is its high level of vigilance and inevitable paranoia,[63] which make a friendship like the one that develops between David, a card-carrying communist, and Diego, a religious fag, not only unlikely but, as I aim to demonstrate, especially risky.

Reiterating this sense of surveillance, references to "la vigilancia" become a common refrain throughout the film. All three main characters at some point remind the other not to say certain things out loud, or raise the volume of the music to mask their conversation. Before entering Diego's apartment for the first time, Diego pulls David under the stairs presumably to hide from "la vigilancia" about to cross their path and who happens be singing the verse, "yo perjudico tu reputación." As we later discover, this in fact is Nancy, Diego's black-market dealing neighbor and good friend. Nonetheless, this scene frames the gesture of hospitality that follows within a context of neighbor informants. Upon entering the apartment, Diego makes clear its desired exclusivity, "Bienvenido a la guarida. Este es un lugar donde no se recibe a todo el mundo." "La guarida," Diego's name for his apartment, has been associated to the proverbial closet, generating readings of the film as "la salida de la guarida."[64] Drawing from its significations—den, hide out, refuge, or cover—I would like to read "la guarida," as an immunitary space, or an attempt thereof.

La guarida: Johnnie Walker, Marilyn Monroe, and El Che

As viewers, we rarely see the apartment from a comfortable distance; the camera is placed from the actors' perspective, providing us with intimate and partial views of the sunlit space, brimming with objects. The building's architecture is classic baroque and the interior of the apartment exhibits an array of mix-matched antique furniture, patio fold out chairs, art works, cultural memorabilia, and religious iconography. Music is almost always playing. Objects from abroad, others off the street, like a fragment of an elaborate wrought iron gate—a quintessential Cuban architectural fixture—form an assemblage of personal identitarian markers that act as a boundary between him and the outside. Diego has, in effect, created a visual and sonic enclosure. And yet in bringing these objects within the walls of his apartment, he is producing a contact with the outside. Doors are notably left unlocked; we see Nancy and David come in and out of Diego's apartment unannounced. When Diego sits by his typewriter to compose a letter—his act of parrhesia[65] against government censorship—he is exposed through a large open window. Drawing once again from its aporetic structure, Esposito provides us with an apt description to think through this immunitary space:

> [T]he *clivage* that at the same time juxtaposes and connects immunity and community, mak[es] one not only the contrasting background for the other, but also the object and content of the other [. . .] Immunity as a private category, only takes relief as a negative mode of community [. . .] Immunity, in short, is the internal limit which cuts across community, folding it back on itself in a form that is both constitutive and deprivative: immunity constitutes or reconstitutes community precisely by negating it.[66]

Following Esposito's logic, in trying to create a personal sanctuary, Diego initiates a boundary, a point of touch between the private and the public, or *immunitas* and *communitas*. Significantly, la guarida, as an enclosure, is nowhere near sealed, but dynamic and porous. We may read the composition of the apartment as expressing what Esposito has described as, "immunity in a nonexcluding relation to its common opposite," "a conception of individual identity . . . [where] the body is understood as a functioning construct that is open to continuous exchange with its surrounding environment." In other words, identity and the body are not conceived as closed and monolithic units.[67] Alongside items that would bring Diego's revolutionary loyalty into question, such as bottles of Johnnie Walker ("la bebida del enemigo") and images of Marilyn Monroe, are photographs of national Cuban icons.

This nonexcluding relation is perhaps best expressed in the shrines to the Orishas and La Virgen de la Caridad we find in both Diego's and Nancy's apartments. As the art historian Donald Cosentino has noted, almost any object may be appropriated and converted into a sacred icon in the process of Afro-Atlantic altar making; that is, new objects may always be incorporated into the spaces of these altars.[68] This aesthetic—accumulative, proliferating, and unrestricted—is reiterated not just in the building's baroque architecture,[69] but also in the arrangement of Diego's apartment. We see this especially when David adds photographs of Fidel and El Che to one of Diego's displays on a wall. Ideologically incompatible as they may be with the Virgin Mary and pictures of Julián del Casal, at the level of the composition, these additions are easily accommodated. I suggest that when David places these images alongside Diego's other objects we have what Tom Roach calls "non-dialectical mingling."[70] We will return to this concept in more detail further ahead. Suffice it to say that the ethos expressed in these arrangements is one of hospitality to the foreign Other.

It is in Diego's apartment, "llena de cosas raras" and where national and international cultural objects cohabitate that the large majority of the film is shot. Staging the friendship that develops within the conventions of hospitality, Diego and David are both placed in vulnerable positions. Foregrounding this perilousness, David first refuses Diego's invitation: "Yo no voy a casa de gente que no conozco." Crossing the lines between host and guest, hostage and hostile intruder,[71] the first time David enters Diego's home it is due to a trick, a bet between Diego and his friend German; the second time, David enters with the intention of covertly investigating and reporting Diego to the authorities. While the conventions of hospitality would in principle require an immunitary space of which the host is master,[72] in opening one's home to the foreigner that space is no longer impervious. This precariousness is made all the more palpable in the film, not only because of the CDR's presumed monitoring, "violating the inviolable" principle of the home,[73] but also because the roles of host and guest are initially performed by Diego and David with ulterior motives.

Tocar la tecla que no se podía tocar: The Shame of Becoming Other

Whereas for Cicero virtuousness, transparency, and self-sufficiency are the defining features of an exemplary friend,[74] in *Fresa y chocolate,* disguised intentions, moments of weakness, desire, and need are the engines that propel friendships. In their first interaction at an open-air café when Diego takes a seat at David's table, David is visibly annoyed. He gestures to switch seats but finds himself corralled. Diego, with his many shopping bags and effeminate mannerisms is perceived as an intruder, an uninvited guest in this public setting. Undeterred, Diego makes a spectacle of savoring his strawberry ice cream, complains about the country's status quo, and invites David to his house on the pretext of lending him some hard-to-find books. Just before this encounter we see Diego walking with German. When the two see David they exchange looks that suggest an understanding. These two like-minded friends conspire together. And when Diego finally approaches David we suspect a scheme. As the narrator in Paz's story, David says "Sentí como si una vaca me lamiera el rostro. Era la mirada libidinosa del recién llegado . . . y se me trancó la boca del estómago."[75] The expression of discomfort and exposure to the other's gaze are indicative of the friendship that will ensue. In this initial encounter David feels like hunted prey: "me di cuenta de que se trataba de una carnada, y no estaba dispuesto a morderla."[76] He refers here to the contraband books Diego has deliberately removed from his bag to call his attention. What begins as bait will later become gifts. Notably, David's references to ingestion, with mention of his stomach, bait, and biting, can be linked back to our reading of incorporation and inoculation operative in the film.

Behind all the dissimulation and pretext, there is a genuine desire on Diego's part to know David. This desire of course is not mutual, but unilateral. We learn, especially in Paz's story, that Diego has admired David since long ago when he saw him perform on stage in a production of Ibsen's *House of Dolls.* Although the production as a whole was a fiasco, David's acting and improvisation were very good. Nonetheless, when Diego makes a reference to the play, David tells his readers "de haber sabido el efecto que me iban a producir sus palabras, Diego hubiera evitado aquel lance. Tocó la tecla que no se podía tocar."[77] For David, his participation in the play is associated with profound humiliation and he finally accepts Diego's invitation to go to his house in order to recover photos that Diego claims to have taken of the performance. David explains, "Eso fue lo peor, la lástima con que me aplaudieron. . . . [I]luminado por los reflectores, rogaba con toda mi alma que se produjera un efecto de amnesia total sobre todos . . . y que nunca, jamás, *never,* ¿me oyes, Dios?, me encontrara con uno de ellos, alguien que me pudiera identificar."[78] Curiously, in this moment of desperation, the militant atheist appeals to god and uses the language of the enemy. As we shall see, calls to gods and saints that seem to go un-responded will be a recurring device throughout the film.

Although the friendship between the two has not yet developed, there are various aspects of these initial encounters I would like to highlight as they signal a different friendship to come. That Diego's interest in David should be his creative talent works against classical models where shared moral values are considered the bonds between friends.[79] As a "culture queen" (Quiroga) Diego would predictably esteem artistic talent above all else; however, it bears considering that for Plutarch acting is the craft of the adulator not the exemplary friend.[80] Significantly, what Plutarch finds threatening about the adulator's mimetic skills is the malleability of his or her subjectivity, the ability to adapt and transform. And, in so doing, the capacity to transform destabilizes meanings and commonly held beliefs.[81] In a complete inversion of these values, I suggest that is precisely what Diego and David's friendship brings about: instability and transformation. When Diego sits at David's table at the open-air café and addresses him as "compañero Torvaldo," Ibsen's lead character, we may read this moment as "solicit[ing] a becoming."[82] In her text *Precarious Life,* Judith Butler formulates subjectivity in relation to an Other; it is the address and the request to be recognized that initiates a new sense of self.[83] Not only is one's sense of self constituted in the encounter but, consequently, questioned, made vulnerable: "It is also to stake one's own being, and one's own persistence in one's own being."[84] The fear "of becoming foreign to oneself"[85] is perhaps expressed when David repeatedly says "no soy yo" to Diego's claim, "Yo a ti te conozco. Te he visto muchísimas veces." Removing his Communist Youth Union ID from one front pocket to the other, David insists on being identified in a particular way. And yet when Diego asks him "¿Te interesa Vargas Llosa?" David reveals to the reader that he was in fact more than curious about this notoriously critical author of the Revolution, "Yo estaba loco por leer su última novela."[86] Against the persona of an obedient and loyal revolutionary who would abstain from reading such contraband books, Diego instigates and calls forth the possibility of an Other self, "Lo forras, viejo. Ten imaginación."

Remembering that for Derrida what is proper to friendship "can be thought and lived without the least reference to the be-*loved*, or more generally to the *lovable*,"[87] I want to highlight that the initial link between David and Diego is a shared sense of shame. Diego later confesses that his experience as an audience member at David's performance was, "la vergüenza más grande que he pasado en mi vida. . . . No hallaba cómo esconderme en la butaca, la mitad del público rezaba por ti . . . Por eso fuimos tan pródigos en los aplausos."[88] In Barbara Cassin's definition of the word, *vergüenza* implies a failure to fulfill a duty. To feel shame one must first have a sense of commitment and obligation. We might describe Diego's vergüenza for David as "vergüenza ajena," which "captures the feeling of shame that is experienced in the face of the incompetent or inadequate conduct of another person."[89] Cassin continues,

> The feeling of shame in this case has nothing to do with the subject's actions, for he or she has not done anything and cannot feel responsible or be held guilty. It is precisely because there is no direct relation to the person for whom one feels shame that the sentiment of *vergüenza* exhibits and constructs a tie. *Vergüenza* in this instance helps build a sense of community.[90]

Drawing from this definition, what Diego and David share even before their first interaction is an experience of inadequacy and an instance of community that has nothing to do with the security of belonging or a shared identity.

When David is recognized by Diego as the actor in the play, something which he desperately wished would never occur, he is placed in a vulnerable position, obligated to recall aspects of himself he had repressed in favor of his identity as an engineering student. After all, performing foreign plays is no way of serving the Revolution. In a later scene when Diego asks David why he is studying engineering when what he really wants to do is write, David responds that he owes it to the Revolution. Pursuing a vocation that is "unpurposive" would mean failing on his obligation to be a productive member. More importantly, recognizing this desire or potential self would mean becoming Other. In effect, Diego's words are like a "lance." The touching of "una tecla que no se podía tocar," will occur more than once in the trajectory of their friendship. In one of the few scenes where the camera pans back, we see Diego and David sitting across from each other listening to melancholic music. Moments of silence transpire between them as Diego adoringly stares at David, whose gaze is turned in the opposite direction, possibly avoiding direct eye contact. When their eyes finally do meet, following a comment Diego made about the affective quality of the music, David antagonistically asks Diego, "ven acá chico, ¿Por qué tú eres así?" What ensues is a series of questions that reproduce heterosexist myths of homosexuality as a medical condition that is treatable. Diego finds himself not only correcting these views but also defending his revolutionary commitment. Before asking him to leave, Diego does a parody of Cuban macho men and calls David "un comemierda." In the section that follows, I aim to show that these confrontational and unsettling exchanges might be understood as fulfilling "an ethics of discomfort."[91]

Non-Dialectical Mingling, Betrayal, and Discomfort

Drawing from Michel Foucault's late work, Tom Roach formulates a mode of friendship in which discomfort and estrangement realize an ethical imperative: "to annihilate identity [and] to transform the self and the friend."[92] Identities, we've seen, can produce exclusive communities and violent immunitary impulses. Roach's conception of friendship as "the space of the in-between . . . a zone of unbelonging, a property of the property-less"[93] allows us to imagine more fluid and transformative relations where coming together never coagulates into institutional bodies. He writes, "involving attraction and resistance . . . a friendship resists dialectical fusion in favor of non-dialectical mingling."[94] Collapsing the distinction between friend and enemy, Roach valorizes the act of betrayal, as it forces one to rethink their sense of self and produces a distance between friends that would prevent a fusion, or the Other being reduced to the Same. For Foucault, Roach explains, the concept of friendship "is anything but utopian":

> Betrayal, distance, brutal honesty, indeed, an impersonal intimacy founded on estrangement are its making. [. . .] This is, to be blunt, the shit of friendship. When the most troubling aspects of relationships become the very foundation of a friendship, however, new subjective, communal, and political forms can be imagined. [. . .] The friend-enemy dichotomy, which holds considerable sway in the philosophical canon from Aristotle through Carl Schmitt, is shattered when the betrayal of secrets is part and parcel of friendship. In this sense, the

true friend—the friend who will push one beyond historically determined identity, the friend who will help another think and relate differently—is the betrayer.[95]

What betrayal affords is the discovery that I am other. This is critical for Foucault whose interest in "care of the self" as practiced by the Greeks provided a way to work against current identitarian or "out politics," while attending to an ethos, or a way of life on an individual level.[96] In the same way that Néstor Perlongher and later José Quiroga were concerned with the "disappearance of the homosexual," Foucault saw coming-out-politics and its aims of self-discovery as working within the medicalization of sexuality and the institutions of biopower.[97] For him, care of the self "is the care of the activity and not the care of the soul-as-substance."[98] Care of the self is an aesthetic approach that does not assume there is anything to reveal about the self, but rather something that is wholly constructed through a principle of activity.[99] Friendships can facilitate these activities; push one away from their presumed sense of self to adopt other ways of being, other ways of life.[100]

Returning to the heated scene between Diego and David we can see here not just a discomfort, but also a betrayal. In response to Diego's expression of pathos with regard to the affectivity of the music, and thus at a moment of exposure and emotional vulnerability, David betrays Diego's friendship and hospitality by trying to provoke him with heterosexist comments. The dialogue that ensues—each accusing the other of "monerías" and "payaserías"—demonstrates the performative and fictive quality of their self-representations. In addition to this confrontation, there are a series of deceptions and betrayals that carry a great risk and destabilize the binary between friend and enemy. As he later confesses, Diego befriends David as part of a bet he makes with his friend German to lure and seduce him. David, we know, returns to Diego's house on the pretext of friendship as part of his strategy with Miguel to investigate and denounce him to the state. These betrayals never come to full fruition. However, had David completed his mission to report him for presumably working with a foreign embassy, as Miguel had instructed him, we learn that Diego could have faced a 15-year prison sentence. And though Diego had already jeopardized himself with his letter protesting the censorship of German's art exhibition, it is possible to imagine that Miguel's inquiries into Diego might have led to his forced exile. David's decision not to report Diego places him in a precarious position, as Miguel threatens to have him kicked out of school for colluding with an enemy. The threat of being exposed and reported to the authorities is reiterated in the various immunitary gestures referenced above. The film's allusions to the CDR suggest that the presumed inviolable space of the home is transgressed, making hospitality politically dangerous. In her treatment of friendship, Leela Gandhi explains that for friendship to have an ethical capacity it requires taking a risk: "the risk to become foreign to 'one's own' and above all to oneself." Friendship with a foreigner (or in this case someone outside of one's social milieu) is "unquestionably political . . . involving the potentially 'agonizing' risk of self exile."[101] For Gandhi, an ethico-political friendship is "extra-institutional"; it does not valorize the "relation of same with same" nor "privileges commitments to those who are either 'proximate' 'given' or in some inalienable way 'our own.'"[102] In effect, hospitality, risk, and exile are the defining features of an ethics for Gandhi, all of which, as we have seen, are operative in *Fresa y chocolate.*

The risk of becoming foreign to one's own is, perhaps, best exemplified in the distance that develops between the original pairs of friends: Diego and German, and David and Miguel. These other friends with whom Diego and David conspire each represents the identitarian community that corresponds to them at the beginning of the film; these are friendships based on similitude. Through David and Diego's friendship, one marked by instances of deception, betrayal, and discomfort, both characters transform and adopt different personas. David, as the narrator of Paz's story becomes a writer (as opposed to an engineer) and Diego is now referred to as "la Loca Roja" by his former friends. Notably, at the end of this story both Diego and David have produced texts. Although Diego always insisted on his revolutionary commitment, it is nonetheless surprising that it should be his text (the letter protesting censorship) that is the explicitly political one and David's a work of fiction—given that Diego is the "conservative culture queen" (Quiroga) who values art for art's sake and David the dialectical materialist.

A Matter of Honoring the Gods: Gifts, Debts, and Failings

David privileges his friendship with the "enemy" of the state over his commitments to Miguel and his obligation to report counter revolutionaries. In so doing, David fails to reciprocate on his debt as a benefactor of the Revolution. He fails to complete the mission that Miguel adamantly claims is his duty above all else. These failures to reciprocate or dissymmetrical exchanges, as I have been pointing to throughout this chapter, are staged on another level of the film. Much like David's plea to god in Paz's story "¿me oyes, Dios?," in the film we see Diego and Nancy regularly make appeals to the various Virgins and Orishas assembled in their home. Diego and Nancy will ask for favors, share intimate details, joke, reprimand, beg, and threaten these deities in such a way that reproduces the same conversations the friends have among themselves. Of course, these are monologues since the statues never respond. And in this regard the relationship with these statues is completely unilateral. Although Aristotle valorized mutual reciprocity, he also recognized instances where this is not possible: "Where it is a matter of honouring the gods or one's parents . . . no one could ever render them the honour they deserve. . . . [T]he son must repay the debt he owes, and since there is nothing he can do that is worthy of the benefits he has already received, he is always a debtor."[103] Accordingly, Diego and Nancy are always in a relationship of dissymmetry with these Virgins and Orishas, unable to ever adequately repay the debt they owe for their existence. It is significant that what surrounds the space of hospitality are these figures, to which we are forever indebted and vulnerable to their whims. Nancy and Diego are often seen making offerings of flowers, drinks, food, and candles to the statues. We also see these same offerings made between the three friends. I suggest that in the same way that Nancy and Diego are in a relationship of incommensurable debt to the gods, as Aristotle would have it, following Butler, the three friends, whose subjectivities are constituted in the encounter, are always in a relationship of incommensurable debt to each other. Recalling Derrida here too, friendship is an imperative to love without it being corresponded, a unilateral act without measure. The inability to ever adequately return the favor—be it David's donation of his blood to save Nancy's life after having attempted suicide, or Diego's invaluable tutelage—is what makes community. It is in the debt, the owing of the gift, where community happens.[104]

"Puta de mierda" or What Remains in Excess

If *Fresa y chocolate* aims to incorporate the figure of the homosexual through a national allegory, there are aspects of this film that remain in excess to any totalizing narrative. The film may do the work of sexual liberation, but the question of religious faith—evoked in the film through the ubiquitous statuettes and offerings—remains outside the telos of a Marxist-Leninist project. These statuettes and offerings, moreover, are reminders of debts that may never be adequately repaid, reminders of insufficiencies and excesses that make a "society of equals," or the symmetry of mutual reciprocity and unity under shared identity, untenable. Significantly, the character of Nancy, who is not in Paz's short story, referred to affectionately by Diego as "puta de mierda," is not easily subsumed within the Revolution's dialectic. Nancy provides a counter figure to David's first girlfriend who feigns purity and prudishness when they are about to have sex, and hypocritically marries someone for financial stability. In contradistinction, Nancy is sincere in her courting and financially self-sufficient. In this respect, her character works within the narrative of progress, inverting gender stereotypes. However, Nancy generates income through the black market. And when Diego asks her to sexually initiate David, she responds "ya no hago eso," allowing us to suspect she has also sustained herself as a sex worker. While some have dismissed the relationship that develops between Nancy and David as a heteronormative ending,[105] I offer that there are provocative aspects about their pairing. She is not only a criminal according to the state; she is religious and notably older than David. Most significantly, she has attempted to take her own life on various occasions. Nancy's character makes visible those lives unincorporated by the Revolution. Her illegal, monetary self-sufficiency puts her outside the economy of debt and obligation between citizen and the revolutionary state and, at the same time, she expresses "a defective condition" and "incompleteness" (to use Esposito's words), a need and desire for the Other.

David's donation of blood to Nancy, as I suggested above, is indicative of an incommensurable gift of friendship. From a biological viewpoint, the transfusion also evokes contamination by a foreign body and, as such, the process of inoculation to which I have alluded throughout this chapter. The notion of being contaminated is further reiterated when Nancy claims "Dentro de mí hay una cosa limpia que nadie ha podido ensuciar." Although this statement might be interpreted as sustaining a part of the self that is immune, what I want to underscore about the exchange between Nancy and David is an interdependence and vulnerability that counters the hubris of the Revolution's impervious and heroically righteous New Man.[106] If the figure of the New Man represents a future community, a telos realized through the logic of sacrifice,[107] then the relationships in *Fresa y chocolate* bring to the fore a consubstantiality and an "irreducible and inoperative difference."[108] Given that queer theorists have strongly critiqued *Fresa y chocolate* as an attempt to neutralize the oppositional charge of the homosexual figure,[109] I have argued, through the logic of inoculation, that *Fresa y chocolate* affirms what it aimed to deactivate. In its desire to incorporate the figure of the homosexual, to immunize itself against the poison of the Revolution's error, it necessarily corrupts the integrity of the body politic. Moreover, we might also consider the film's failure to adequately address the legacy of the UMAPs, never explicitly apologizing, as indicative of the "amnesia or aphasia" that Deleuze and Guattari observe in the shame that arises not from feeling "responsible for the victims but responsible before them."[110]

Shifting our attention from how Diego may or may not be a consumable representation of gay men, to the dynamics of a post-classical friendship, has allowed us to find another politics at work in the film that does not reiterate selfsame models of community. Considering again Derrida's statement, "What is proper or essential to friendship, can be thought and lived without the least reference to the be-*loved*, or more generally to the *lovable*," Diego and David may be deeply flawed (or for that matter the film itself), but that does not negate the potential to tease from their relationship an ethics of friendship. In fact, it enhances this potential given that we are privileging what is inadequate and insufficient. In its representation of friendship and the risks it necessarily entails, Gutiérrez Alea's film points to experiences of insecurity and un-belonging as that which create the possibility for political transformation.

The Lettered Man and the Artful Liar

Like Diego and David, we can also say of Ena Lucía Portela's protagonist, Zeta, that she is deeply flawed, insecure, and does not correspond to the revolutionary model, nor even to a traditional feminist one, as she tolerates the physical and psychic abuse from her older male lover, Moisés. Describing herself through Moisés's eyes, Zeta illustrates the debasement she endures when she rhetorically asks "¿Acaso podía yo comprender una brizna de temas tan complejos y sutiles como el argumento de autoridad [. . .] o la skepsis de Pirrón, la gran duda? ¿Qué sabia una gorda culona de los estados de incertidumbre?"[111] This self-deprecating "gorda burra con estampa de puta francesa del siglo XVIII," "gorda subnormal y despatarrada en el suelo, con el rímel corrido, llorando lágrimas negras y haciéndose la víctima, la dama de las camelias,"[112] is our narrator and aspiring professional writer, whose sarcasm and biting wit has us laughing at, and simultaneously reflecting upon, horrifying events and social discriminations, such as fatphobia. From the start of the novel, we can see how the figure of the writer, or at least our narrator, is devalued—she is "despatarrada en el suelo"—and, at the same time, undeniably skillful with language. Like Portela's earlier novel, *El pájaro: Pincel y tinta china, Cien botellas en una pared* is often self-referential and contains a meta-text. Linda Roth, Zeta's best friend, is a successful professional writer currently working on her third novel titled, *Cien botellas en una pared,* about a double homicide.

Cien botellas is especially productive to read alongside *Fresa y chocolate,* as it also foregrounds post-classical friendships, hospitality, and nonheteronormative genders and sexualities. Although Zeta is in a heterosexual relationship, her upbringing by her gay bohemian father did not entail gender behavioral conditioning; no one told her as a child, "que esos eran juegos de varones."[113] Not surprisingly, the Zeta we see as an adult makes extra money as an auto-mechanic and does not have sexual hang-ups or notions of conserving her purity. She has an unapologetically voracious appetite for sex and food and most of her friends are queer women. The novel is framed as a detective story; but the eventual revelation of the two homicides is not necessarily what keeps the reader engaged. The novel takes us to the "antro[s] de los bajos," clandestine spaces where a "socito mío" will grant access to all sorts of illegal goods like marijuana or homemade alcohol. These spaces are immunitary pockets in the city where Havana's outcasts can commune, and illegal transactions can take place. The hints of black-market trafficking we see in Gutiérrez Alea's depiction of the 1970s (produced and screened in the context of the early 90s *Periodo Especial*) is in full swing in Portela's novel, which is set in the late 90s and includes "el negocio del cerdito," another apartment-raised pig like Robespierre in Echevarría's *Caballos con arzones,* only that Portela's does not speak and philosophize. That said, Portela will flirt with the limits between humans and animals, as she does in *El pájaro: Pincel y tinta china.* Later in the chapter we will consider some of the ways *Cien botellas en una pared* undermines the boundaries of the human.

When Diego responds to David's heterosexist comments with an exaggerated "Asere monina, ¿qué bola?" *Fresa y chocolate* offers a parody of macho performativity with potentially classist and racist undertones, given that the distinctly Cuban slang has Yoruba origins and is considered the vernacular of *la calle.* Ena Lucía Portela also showcases macho performativity, except that the target of her parody is the privileged white male elite. *Cien botellas en una pared* opens with a series of *if*-clauses, "Si algo lo irritaba sobremanera, si algo lo predisponía a la violencia y el homicidio," and adjectives, "rojo, rojo fuego, rojo hierro, llamaradas vibrantes," "enloquecido, con cuernos y cola, una sierpe, un basilisco, un dragón, el diablo en el infierno," to create for the reader "[t]remendo espectáculo," or an over-the-top fantastic image of a male patriarch becoming-beast.[114]

In her reading of the novel, Karen Christian succinctly describes Zeta's abusive lover, Moisés, when she says that he, "articulates the sexist view that women are by nature intellectually inferior to men," and cites the following passage mimicking Moisés's discourse, "'Las mujeres eran el colmo del mongolismo, ¿Quién las habría inventado? Eran muy brutas, las mujeres.'"[115] Christian sees Moisés's masculinity and sexism as so excessive, "with his repeated attempts to dominate through physical and psychological abuse," that ultimately, he "comes across not as a 'real man' but as a parody of masculinity."[116] I concur with Christian but want to take her analysis of parody further. While Moisés allows Portela to demonstrate how male essence is in fact a social construct, he also allows her to deconstruct other structures of power and the ways in which society assigns value and authority. Before discussing the dynamics of hospitality and friendship in the novel, in this section and in the next, I examine how Portela subverts authority, since doing so, I argue, is one of the significant ways the novel extends hospitality toward its readers.

Not only is his name biblical, but Moisés also looks like the Judeo-Christian god. With Greco-Roman bone-structure and "una bella barba plateada," he is "un señor adusto que ya bordeaba los cincuenta, alto y fuerte con aspecto de patriarca hebreo."[117] "Mi dios griego," as Zeta also refers to Moisés, used to be a brilliant jurist, "había alcanzado una magistratura en el Tribunal Supremo de la República. Hombre cultísimo y muy elocuente, le encantaba calzar sus discursos con latinajos."[118] There are significant parallels between Moisés and Fabián from *El pájaro: Pincel y tinta china,* "ese loco de rostro renacentista"[119] who translates ancient Greek texts and physically abuses Camilla. Both Moisés and Fabián present a rebuke to the Humanist intellectual. With Moisés, however, given his high position in the government, we can explicitly associate him with the Cuban state, as well as a more historical Latin American figure, that of Ángel Rama's *hombre letrado.* The colonial lettered man, if not an ecclesiast, was often a lawyer or other administrative bureaucrat that would justify his arguments using Latinisms.

In chapter 4, we discussed the prestige of phonetic writing and the printed book for the European imaginary at the time of colonization and its continued persistence as such. The lettered man was the ultimate symbol of civilization, while that of barbarism was the cannibal. Indeed, the absence of phonetic writing or allusions to cannibalism were often called upon as a justification for colonialism.[120] Returning to Rama's seminal text, *The Lettered City,* allows us to appreciate how the practice of writing was also essential in exercising and administering colonial power. "To advance the systematic ordering project [. . .] to facilitate the concentration and hierarchal differentiation of power, and to carry out the civilizing mission [. . .] the cities of Latin America required a specialized social group."[121] Rama explains that the letrados were "[e]mployed as bureaucrats in the service of absolute monarchies." They became indispensable in their capacity to shape symbolic languages in the service of those in power. As such, they themselves "became masters of power."[122]

During the colonial and post-independence periods, it was these same men that would craft the nation's political ideology, literature, and identity. Even later in the twentieth century with avant-garde movements, when those participating within the lettered city included minoritized subjects, Rama suggests that, genealogically, this social group was part of a tradition that had emerged alongside the colonizing project.[123] The historical ties between literary production and governmental power and policies, in other words, remained strong.[124] We can see this in the literary works that emerged after the Cuban Revolution up until the 1990s. Scholars describe the bulk of published work before the fall of the Soviet Union as canonizing "master narratives" and "epic nationalism."[125] The masculinist Cuban detective novel that involved officers of the state apprehending those that work against the law was the most popular genre. As Iraida López states in her prologue to the 2010 edition of Portela's novel, "En Cuba, la novela policíaca fue promovida por el Ministerio del Interior, organismo que a partir de 1972 premió aquéllas que propagaran la ideología prevalente."[126] Ponte's *La fiesta vigilada* makes clear the fate of those writers that would depart from the master narrative, when its protagonist's civic identity is erased.[127]

The sort of elitism and aristocracy one would associate with the early *ciudad letrada* is ironically found among Cuban literary critics as they forgo a Marxist analysis. Guillermina De Ferrari explains that in Post-Soviet Cuba, with the insolvency of national publishing houses and the extremely prohibitive prices of books published abroad, access to new literary work became limited "to an intellectual class [. . .] formed by a few closed social networks." Add to this exclusive circulation—manuscripts passed from hand to hand among friends and family—a criticism that ignores the material conditions of contemporary literary production, so as not to highlight the dire situation of the status quo and critique the revolutionary government.[128]

My aim is not to reiterate a Post-Soviet periodization or claim that Portela is writing outside the bounds of the lettered city. I do, however, want to explore how she parodies and undermines the figure of the writer. And, in so doing, to use Rama's words, "the systematic ordering project," its "hierarchal differentiation of power," and presumed "civilizing mission." References to the civilized and the barbaric, as inherited from colonial discourse, abound in the novel. Cuba, for instance, is assumed to be seen as "un país [. . .] subdesarrollado. Primitivo, silvestre," from the perspective of Spanish publishers.[129]

Returning to Moisés, having been part of the Tribunal Supremo de la República, we can read him as a figure of sovereignty, as he determined the limits and application of the law. As Zeta notes, "pues las sentencias de muerte sólo puede dictarlas el Tribunal Supremo."[130] In his last lectures, "The Sovereign and the Beast," where the relationship between sovereignty, law, and violence is explored, Jacques Derrida explains that, as the one who determines and enforces the law, the sovereign is positioned above the law. The sovereign can use forms of violence deemed illegal, such as putting to death, to enforce the law. In other words, the sovereign works outside the law, or breaks the law, in order to keep the law. This paradox positions the sovereign in a shared space with the beast, who is below the law but, nevertheless, also outside and not subject to the law. The shared space between sovereigns and beasts allows us to appreciate how tenuous the line is between animals and humans, or nature (beast) and artifice (sovereign).[131] More broadly, the connection between the two figures destabilizes ontological and ethical boundaries.[132] In *Cien botellas,* the former judge and likely sociopath can be read as Derrida's figure of the Sovereign Beast, as Moisés cruelly and repeatedly beats Zeta in her home. We even see him described as a "una sierpe, un basilisco, un dragón," at the start of the novel.[133] Were we to read Moisés as an allegorical reference to the Cuban state, Portela is then making a scathing critique about the state of the Revolution, its moral righteousness, and arbitrary application of the law.

If Moisés presents a critique of the Cuban state and the historical figure of the letrado with his erudite and esoteric deployment of Latinisms—Zeta acknowledges that "la mayoría de personas no tienen por qué entenderlos, están muy ocupados y carecen tiempo para buscar las traducciones"[134]—through the figure of Linda Roth, Portela demystifies the aura of the literary author and the prestige of the book. In a chapter where Zeta recounts the trials and tribulations of publishing abroad for Linda, the reader is made privy to the negotiations, transactions, politics, egos, and economics involved in the publishing of books. Most of all we are made aware of the material necessities of the author, with such mundane references to electricity and water bills. These needs, the whims of editors, the demands of the market, and personal spitefulness impact the content of Linda's books; in response to a dispute with a previous editor, "comenzó a escribir otra novela, muy sarcástica y aún más pesimista que la anterior."[135] To Zeta's statement, "Qué complicada puede ser la existencia de una escritora *de verdad,*" Portela adds a footnote with her own initials, ELP, so the reader knows it comes directly from her (or a fictional her, for what is "real" and what is "art" is destabilized through metatextual references), affirming Zeta's comment: "¡Vaya si lo es! Hasta ahora he publicado cuatro novelas, primero acá y luego en España, o si no a la inversa, ya que Cuba está out del mercado editorial hispanohablante, y con todas ellas, incluyendo *ésta,* ha habido alguna clase de jodienda."[136] By listing some of the material and political conditions, as well as petty squabbles, that determine the making of *Cien botellas en una pared,* Portela not only brings down the elevated figure of the writer and the book, but makes sure her own novel is recognized as part of a complex web of material interdependences.

In contrast to how Portela would have us see her novel, literature and art have traditionally been conceived in Euro-American thought as transcendent from bare material needs, or spiritually elevating. In the Kantian sense art should strive to be pure and disinterested, allowing one to contemplate universal forms, and in Che Guevara's 1964 essay, self-representation was human triumph over mere animal existence.[137] However, it is worth remembering that for some ancient Greek philosophers, artistic representation was considered fraudulent and ignoble.[138] Plato famously banned mimesis from the ideal city, arguing that it corrupts citizens, because it deviates from truth and reality. As one reader of Plato states, for the Greek thinker "all impersonation is deranged" and "weakens the rational impulses' control."[139] Earlier in this chapter we also noted that for Plutarch the craft of acting, to imitate and mold one's persona, to be able to adapt and transform, were considered threatening. Plutarch, thus, aligns the talents of the actor with that of the adulator, as opposed to the exemplary friend.[140]

Moisés, it seems, holds a similar opinion as that of the ancient Greeks. What he most detests, and fears, is being duped by the illusion of fiction. According to Zeta:

> [M]i amante no leía novelas. Ni negras ni rosas ni de ningún otro color. ¿Qué imbecilidad era aquéllas? La novela en sí, a su juicio, era un género para tontos, mostrencos, verracos, mongoloides, gentecillas que se chupaban el dedo gordo del pie, que se mecían en el columpio de la idiotez con la necia esperanza de ser engañados algún día o, de ser posible, todos los días.[141]

Moisés refuses to be "engañado"; the Greco-Roman patriarch is no one's fool. Given his aversion to fiction, Zeta decides to recount the plot of Linda's latest novel as though she were reporting on an actual Havana crime heard through rumors. Moisés believes all of it, a testament to Zeta's storytelling skills, though she'll credit Linda and underplay her reinventions of the novel. Zeta claims, "no soy una mentirosa hábil, podrá calibrarse el alcance de la ficción de mi amiga, la enormidad de su talento para crear impresiones de realidad. Ella había logrado realizar el propósito que anunciara diez años atrás: convertirse en una consumada farsante, una sublime embustera."[142] For Zeta and Linda, what the writer and the novel do are much like what Plato and company disparaged: create impressions of reality, a farce, a lie, as opposed to inspire the contemplation of universal truths. Meanwhile Moisés,

> Me escuchó atento, inmóvil, sin pestañear, muy abiertos los grandes ojos negros. [. . .] aquella historia lo había atrapado. [. . .] Me asustaba muchísimo la posibilidad de que descubriese el engaño, de que me pescara tratando de pasarle gato por liebre. ¡Me había acusado tantas veces de embustera sin yo serlo! [. . .] Mas, por sorpresa mía y asombro del universo, Moisés me creyó las invenciones de Linda. Descontando algunas pinceladas folklóricas [. . .] encontró el caso perfectamente verosímil.[143]

Let us recall here that the language and techniques used to describe perspectival illusionism in pictorial representations, "take in" and "capture" were associated with the capacity to deceive and, in the case of decoys, to hunt animals.[144] Moisés is trapped, "atrapado"; he's been tricked by Zeta's (and Linda's) verisimilitude. And not incidentally, Zeta uses the animal metaphor of "pasarle gato por liebre." Literature then, is a craft, a techne, that makes you feel and think things that are false. Literature does more than that, of course. In the section that follows, we will see how Portela furthers another conception of writing and breaks with its historical associations to civility and authority.

El caníbal que untaba mayonesa

Although Zeta has had a university education and is versed well enough to provide her readers with translations of Latin and instances of homosexuality in the ancient Greek world, she consistently presents herself as uncivilized, beginning with her childhood: "me crié como los animalejos de bosque frondoso, a lo salvaje, a lo mataperros, a lo Huckleberry Finn. No guardo memoria de ninguna regla, ninguna prohibición, ningún tabú. Maloliente, piojosa y analfabeta, encantada de la vida."[145] Zeta, thus, creates the image of a romantic, Rousseau-like individual, unconditioned and untainted by society. With regard to her sexual partners, she claims, "Temo frustrarme y frustrar a algún pobre tipo, a uno de esos comunes y corrientes que tratan de mostrarse amables, cuerdos, civilizados,"[146] making clear her preference for the savage, while suggesting that the civil is normative and boring.

Unlike the figure of the letrado, Zeta finds the intellectual pretensions of prologues tedious, "es que me aburren, me dan sueño."[147] However, a good novel like Linda's she will devour, "En una sola noche devoré capítulo tras capítulo," underscoring her consumption of literature as something corporeally pleasurable. Further emphasizing her unrefined relationship to novels, Zeta says, "Me produjo un gran impacto, no tanto por sus excelencias literarias, que no pongo en duda, como por la terrible historia que cuenta."[148] Like our reading of Echevarría's novels in chapter 4, reading literature here is imagined as a transformative incorporation that is neither edifying nor transcendent. Zeta goes on to explain that it's the possibility, "*en la realidad*" [original emphasis], of such horrible stories happening in Havana that impact her, implicitly underscoring the verisimilitude, the illusionistic aspect of the narrative—that which Plato found fraudulent—as what she finds transformative.[149]

If her childhood presents us an image of a noble savage, in a parenthetical reference expressing her love of meat, Zeta goes so far as aligning herself with the character of the cannibal in one of Linda's stories, "yo, que soy muy carnívora, no tanto como el caníbal que untaba mayonesa, pero casi."[150] The idiosyncrasy of the mayo converts this figure with a long history in the Latin American imaginary into something comedic, or ridiculous, and also adds a culinary aspect to a practice considered savage. In response to Linda's self-outing, Zeta responds, "eres lesbiana, ¿y qué? Por mí, como si eres caníbal y untas mayonesa. No tienes que darme explicaciones. Yo te quiero igual."[151] We'll return to this expression of unconditional love;

for now let us note that Zeta again sympathizes with the cannibal and curiously assimilates his preference for human meat and mayonnaise to nonnormative sexual orientation.

The affinity between Zeta and the cannibal and the uncivilized becomes more explicit in the following passage where she is eating meat at a restaurant, during intense scarcity in Cuba, with Linda, who is a vegetarian:

> Podrá parecer una barbaridad, un atavismo, una salvajada, pero lo cierto es que, después de tanto ayuno [. . .] casi me provoca un orgasmo [. . .] Soy así, primitiva, pantagruélica, miembro de la horda. [. . .] la mera visión de un buen filete choreando sangre puede llegar a convertirse en un espectáculo dantesco [. . .] ella me miraba como los cervatillos a los leones: con horror. [. . .] Supongo que eso (lo de la cuerda floja) nos ocurre a todos los seres humanos, incluso todos los seres, sólo que el hambre lo hace más evidente, más descarnado.[152]

Zeta leaves no adjective associated with the uncivil out; she describes herself as barbarous, atavistic, savage, primitive, excessive, and even part of a horde, like Ismael's *manada* in *Búfalos camino al matadero.*[153] The spectacle in Dante's *Inferno* that Zeta likely refers to is one of cannibalism; in Canto 33 a starving and grieving father eats his dead children. The reference is fitting giving Zeta's assertion that hunger makes the precariousness of life, "lo de la cuerda floja" more brutally evident, "más descarnado," the past participle of *descarnar* which means to remove flesh/meat. Given the scarcity of food that Zeta has had to endure coupled with her carnivorous predilection and love of life, her voracious consumption of steak makes her appear as a predator to Linda. As a vegetarian, Linda would be the moral eater. However, recalling Derrida's "Eating Well," Zeta's recognition of the precariousness of life and the undeniable needs of the body, expresses an interdependence, or what we have been referring to as an ethics of the Other.[154]

Zeta's love of food and sex, to consume and take in the world—both are forms of incorporation—might be the reason she is such a good writer. Recalling our discussion of Gregory Bateson and Rosi Braidotti,[155] it is Zeta's territorial interdependence and empathy, what she shares with the animal, that allows her to write with such grace. Incidentally, in the citations that follow, we will see how Zeta is continuously assimilated to the nonhuman: "bicharraco," "microbio," "araña pelúa," "un virus." Zeta consistently positions herself in opposition to the traditional *letrado* or what writing has historically stood for in the Latin American imaginary: refinement, enlightenment, authority, and power. From Moisés's viewpoint, Zeta describes herself as follows: "Yo era, en resumen, la criatura más despreciable que él hubiera conocido en su vida. Un corpúsculo de la franja solar, un microbio indigno de ser tomado en cuenta. [. . .] Como si fuera una araña pelúa"[156] "En resumen," she is virtually worthless. And from the perspective of her best friend, Linda, "una escritora de verdad,"[157] Zeta is pathologized and disparaged: "Lo mío era patológico. Una especia de trauma en el cerebelo, un virus. [. . .] Algo lastimoso, abyecto, patético. Mujercita de basura. Qué asco."[158] Even her name is a reference to her worthlessness: "<<Eres una zeta, ¡letra inútil!>>"[159]

Equated with most abject and useless, Zeta narrates from a position that does not presume authority or penetrating knowledge. She has a circuitous, meandering way of getting to her point. The reader feels as though she is in conversation with an unpretentious friend who has the luxury of time and allows herself long tangents and adjectives and modifying clauses galore. As such, Zeta's style is antithetical to Aristotelian logic and reflects a baroque aesthetic. According to another character responding to one of Zeta's oral stories, what was funny, "no radicaba tanto" in the content of what she was reporting, but rather "[su] forma carnavalesca de hacer el cuento." Zeta was "uno de los bicharracos más divertidos de La Habana. Capaz de levantarle el ánimo a cualquiera."[160] Returning to the image of Moisés becoming a fantastic beast, we can see the carnivalesque: "rojo, rojo fuego, rojo hierro, llamaradas vibrantes," "enloquecido, con cuernos y cola, una sierpe, un basilisco, un dragón, el diablo en el infierno."[161] Through additive and hyperbolic language Portela undermines figures of power. Even Zeta's assimilation to a corpuscle, a microbe, a virus, and trash is so exaggerated it parodies her devaluation.

Although in Rama's analysis, a baroque sensibility permeated the *ciudad letrada,* as it was the dominant style of the colonial era,[162] considering a baroque aesthetic within the context of the Cuban Revolution as we've seen takes on a different political valence. Eloy E. Merino explains that "la visión barroca ante la vida, de exceso, [fue] reputada tradicionalmente de femenina, contra una austeridad, de tirante contención masculina, que la Revolución auspicia en sus abanderados."[163] Moreover, the UMAPs and the laws designed to persecute gays are in essence anti-baroque as they promote utilitarianism and uniformity. As I suggest in my analysis of *Fresa y chocolate,* that which remains in excess, or is unproductive, challenges a heteronormative ethos of re/production. Zeta's association to fluid and viscous things—"choreando sangre, rímel corrido, llorando lágrimas negras," or even the cannibal's mayo—not only aligns her with the abject, but also with that which remains in excess to the body, that which escapes the discreet contours of the body. The excessive adjectives and carnivalesque exaggerations, moreover, place her in diametrical opposition to the directness of Linda's prose.[164] Where Linda's stories can be recounted without much being lost, *lo divertido* of Zeta's story lies in the form, in that which cannot be synthesized and reproduced.

Zeta not only meanders—starting with one scene and then following a tangent for almost an entire chapter before returning to that initial scene—she also expresses an epistemological humility. In her recounting of how she met Linda's girlfriend, Alix, and Moisés on the same day, Zeta says:

> Pero no nos hagamos ilusiones. Conocer, lo que se dice conocer, en el sentido de que alguien nos revele *todos* sus secretos, sus mecanismos y resortes ocultos, sus complejos y frustraciones, sus más recónditos anhelos, de que alguien se despoje ante nosotros no solo de la ropa, sino también de la piel, músculos, órganos, hasta quedar en puro esqueleto, hasta volverse previsible, no llegué a conocer a ninguno de los dos. En realidad nunca he llegado a conocer a nadie de esa manera. [. . .] Ni siquiera mí misma. Estos retratos no son más que aproximaciones. Ora nítidas, ora borrosas. Fragmentarias siempre.[165]

If there are truths that literature can unveil, then maybe one is the illusion of knowing, the illusion that one could ever remove enough layers and reach some kernel of essence. Through the absurdity of removing of skin and bones, "no solo de la ropa, sino también de la piel, músculos, órganos, hasta quedar en puro esqueleto," Portela suggests the absurdity of ever becoming "previsible." *Previsible* means predictable, that you can see it before it happens. Curiously, its prefix and root literally translate to pre-visible, which we could take to mean before representation. The impossibility of seeing through someone, of reaching some hard truth, is reiterated when Moisés complains about people observing him,

> como si tuvieran rayos X en los ojos. Como si pudiesen *ver* a través de la materia opaca, divisar lo oculto, distinguir formas en la oscuridad de lo profundo, cuando en realidad no veían más que allá de sus estúpidas narices [. . .] como si le radiografiaran el cerebro, las ideas, los pensamientos a través del cráneo.[166]

The sarcastic assimilation to the technology of radiography and its presumption of making the interior of the body transparent implicitly coincides with Foucault's critique of coming-out-politics, its medicalization of sexuality, and assumptions of there being an essential subjectivity to discover.[167] In the removal of clothes and skin that Zeta lists and Moisés's reference to X-raying his brain and thoughts, Portela also brings us back to the concept of impenetrable materiality, which we explored in chapters one and two.[168] Impenetrable materiality refers to the notion that under every layer, inside every cavity, there is another surface, another exterior, another point of touch. In other words, there is no absolute inside that is not already in relation to something else. When Zeta says she doesn't even know herself completely, "Ni siquiera mí misma," we can understand this through Butler's notion of subjectivity, discussed earlier in the chapter, as constituted in relation to an Other: "To ask for recognition, or to offer it, is precisely not to ask for recognition for what one already is. It is to solicit a becoming, to instigate a transformation, to petition the future always in relation to the Other."[169] Because of this relation and future becomings, the self is never static and, therefore, never fully knowable.

"La esquina del martillo alegre" and Other Comm/Immunitary Ecosystems

Zeta's fluid and seemingly disordered narrative, where various threads branch off to other histories and characters, and the text's suggestion that subjectivity has no immutable interiority, are reiterated in the cavernous and boisterous spaces of the novel. In my analysis of Diego's apartment, *La guarida*, I underscored its porosity and accumulative composition, as instances of "non-dialectical mingling" (Roach) and "immunity in a nonexcluding relation to its common opposite" (Esposito).[170] In creating a sanctuary, a visual and sonic enclosure that expresses and holds what he values, Diego also instantiates community, a border, or point of touch with the outside. "[T]he *clivage* that at the same time juxtaposes and connects immunity and community, mak[es] one not only the contrasting background for the other, but also the object and content of the other."[171] As such, *La guarida* is by no means impervious to the risks of hospitality. *Cien botellas* is also largely set within interior spaces where marginalized figures, illegal transactions, and non-normative behavior can operate with a certain degree of immunity. The difference being that Portela's rooms have a heightened porosity and, therefore, precariousness. One of the key spaces of the novel, the site of hospitality and the double homicide, is Zeta's apartment in the residential Vedado neighborhood in Havana. In a decaying mansion whose rooms have been converted into smaller apartments—recall Ponte's trugadors from *La fiesta vigilada*—Zeta battles against the noise that penetrates the walls of her home. Euphemistically called "La esquina del martillo alegre," Zeta's building is an ecosystem enveloped in the din of hammers, yelling, and loud music, where mostly hostile inhabitants continuously try to carve out new immunitary spaces.

The neighborhood, El Vedado, which was built for Havana's most wealthy in the late nineteenth and early twentieth centuries, could serve as a model for Rama's ordered colonial city. Organized into uniform grids, rectilinear, parallel streets, and wide avenues, El Vedado corresponds to a "rationalizing vision of an urban future" to meet the systematizing and administrative needs of imperial enterprise and capitalism.[172] In the interior spaces of *Cien botellas,* rationalization, order, and authority get thrown out the window, quite literally, as we shall later see. Not only do Zeta's neighbors disapprove of classical music—they almost kill her for blaring Mozart one day—the building itself is a classicist's nightmare:

> [D]esde que nací habito en un palacete del Vedado que es una joya arquitectónica, un monumento a la extravagancia, un prodigio de retazos y parches y costuras, un Frankenstein ecléctico según la moda de 1926 y hecho una ruina según la moda del año en curso. [. . .] [Tiene] un tejado colonial, entre vitrales neogóticos, arcadas románticas, balaústres barrocos, rejas art nouveau y columnatas griegas de distintos órdenes. El observador más o menos entendido en arquitectura se rasca la cabeza: no logra explicarse como es que faltan el minarete mudéjar, la cúpula bizantina y la pirámide egipcia.[173]

This "Frankenstein" of a building—an apt description since it also refers to a living body—is an affront to the masculine austerity of the Revolution, as well as any ordering system. The palace is a configuration of the most diverse styles, a body made up of mismatched parts. As the next citation shows, it has also become increasingly vulnerable.

The building has endured so many transformations, "tan brutales," in the past century, Zeta finds it remarkable it is still standing. She explains,

> Cualquier día se desploma, con estos huracanes tropicales . . . vivir por ver. Por lo pronto, el techo se filtra y suelta boronilla, pedazos de estuco. He pensado en usar un casco de construcción, por si acaso, no vaya a ser que un día se me estropee el cráneo. También hay grietas en los muros. Grietas verticales, de las peligrosas. En temporada ciclóni-

ca en el agua entra por todos los lados (excepto la por la pila, claro) y mi vida se llena de palanganas y cubos destinados a cazar goteras.[174]

Zeta's home offers so little protection it might even be the cause of her death as she worries about being struck in the head by a piece of debris. With so many cracks, the outside easily seeps in, and not just water, but the "toc toc toc por aquí, toc toc toc por allá," "una epidemia de martillazos." "El toc toc toc es un absoluto, una presencia fija," because of the incessant partitioning of rooms within the existing building to make space for new arrivals. "La ciudad crece hacia adentro, se torna densa, una colmena, un avispero."[175] This wasp nest is not the image of order and civility, nor does it smell like it: "el solar huele a jungla, a naturaleza agreste, a salvajismo."[176] As for Zeta's "cuartico en miniatura con una ventana descomunal" (we can read the giant window as another indication of the room's porousness), it is certainly not the room of one's own that Virginia Woolf had in mind: "una habitación propia, un refugio apartado del mundo ruido, un lugar donde encerrarse a solas con la voz interior, el espacio vital imprescindible para que cualquier escritora lo sea."[177] In addition to the non-stop hammering, Zeta provides a long list—a seemingly unending sentence that spans two pages—of Cuban Salsa and Timba bands, various animal sounds, and the yelling of her neighbors, "palabritas vernáculas, expresiones folklóricas y demás estridencias," reproducing for the reader a dense and entangled web of sounds.[178] Zeta is by no means sovereign of an immunitary space. Nevertheless, she writes this narrative and plays the role of host at least twice.

The lack of an immunitary space of which the host is master, where one might be alone with "la voz interior," is also expressed in the composition of the text. In the 2010 Stockero edition, Portela adds footnotes and parenthetical explanations to those from the first edition. Typically, footnotes carry an academic authority as they come from an editor or the author to illuminate the text. In this edition there are asterisk footnotes marked "Noticia de Zeta," numbered footnotes, possibly from an editor, often with definitions from *Diccionario de la lengua española,* and parenthetical add-ons from Ena Lucía Portela, as "ELP." Like Zeta's lists of adjectives and modifying clauses, these footnotes accumulate. In an expression of excess or unproductive expenditure, they elaborate upon elaborations, sometimes occupying more space on the page than the body of the text. As such, they undermine the authority and the limits of the novel.

The parenthetical asides, moreover, are written in an informal language with irreverence and humor. Following a serious and standard biographic description of Anna de Noailles in note #71, ELP adds information that reads like salacious gossip, "Se dice que esta señorita tenía un ego sumamente hipertrofiado. Tanto que no soportaba que ningún hombre se enamorara de ninguna mujer que no fuese ella."[179] With regard to the Greek philosopher Pirrón de Elis, "era tremendo jodedor."[180] It's as though Portela were making confidants of her readers. In this respect, the text performs a hospitality and friendship toward the reader and, in that same gesture, parasitically undermines the boundaries of the text. Perhaps because of the noise that Zeta must endure, there is not just Zeta's voice, but the reader suspects that maybe Linda has sneaked into the text since she is the "professional," writing a novel by the same name, there is an editor's voice and there is "ELP," Portela, or a fictionalized version of herself. Whatever power and authority the *letrado* held in his masterful manipulation of symbols is destabilized through Portela's metatextual hospitality and friendship.

It is not surprising that Zeta would be a hospitable narrator, allowing space for these editorial interventions, and offering, for example, explanations for Moisés's and Linda's esoteric statements, for she is generous to a fault, sarcastically called by Linda "Santa Zeta del Vedado."[181] Her first significant act of hospitality is allowing Moisés, who had apparently been unhoused, to live with her after he sexually assaulted her in a park. This hosting results in a physically and psychically abusive relationship, from which Zeta seems incapable of extricating herself. The second significant act of hospitality involves Zeta inviting Alix, who had also become unhoused, to live with her. At this point, Alix is Linda's ex-girlfriend and persona non-grata. Alix, who gave Zeta an uneasy feeling from their first meeting and has been unkind to her, is by all accounts an enemy. As Zeta's best friend, Linda considers Zeta's hosting Alix a betrayal and cuts off communication with Zeta. Zeta not only defaults on her obligation to Linda as a loyal friend, but also puts herself at considerable risk since Alix does not appear to be a stable person. Zeta explains that her acts of benevolence come from the need to "quedar lo mejor posible conmigo misma":

> Quizás por ese motivo, por seguir los dictados de mi conciencia católica y apostólica y habanera (y estúpida a juicio de mi amiga), fue que me acerqué a Alix en el portal de La Pelota y le ofrecí ayuda. No veía por ningún lado la gitana taciturna que me empujó en el trigésimo cumpleaños de la Gofia, ni a la pesada que me llamaba <<gorda socarrona>>, ni a la salvaje que por poco mata a Linda, ni a la loquita que le plantó una pizza en la cara a Chicha la Mofeta. Sólo veía a una

> muchacha desvalida, andrajosa, tiznada, flaquísima, con marcas de golpes en la cara y en los brazos, con los ojos ardientes de la fiebre y casi irreconocible en su devastación.[182]

Given Alix's past behavior, Zeta could have reasonably, "virado la espalda y ya, como hubiese hecho cualquier persona medianamente cuerda."[183] Instead, Zeta sees a person who is vulnerable and helpless. I read Zeta's compassion toward Alix as an expression of friendship without the expectation of it being corresponded, as a unilateral act without measure (Derrida).[184] Zeta's willingness to suffer estrangement from Linda for the sake of offering Alix shelter and care is indicative of her willingness to "risk to become foreign to 'one's own'" (Gandhi).[185] It is significant that Zeta's description of Alix is framed as a perception of her, "No veía [. . .] Solo veía," reiterating the notion that people's subjectivities are representations, capable of transforming in relation to others. At the very least, the wording suggests that Zeta does not allow previous perceptions of Alix to stop her from seeing someone in need. I'll return to the implications of her compassion and hosting an enemy further ahead.

Another interior space in the novel, which has been read as an "almost" gay feminist "utopia,"[186] illustrates the contradictions of hospitality and community. A friend of Linda's, and eventually Zeta's, is Gofia, "la mujer negra, lesbiana y punk."[187] Gofia and one of her lovers become notorious for hosting parties at their apartment in Centro Habana with a sign that reads "No se admiten machos ni otros animales apestosos."[188] Here we have a perfect example of the aporia of communitas and immunitas. In trying to create a space that is inclusive to non-normative genders and sexualities, a space that is safe from the discrimination of heterosexism, the effort necessarily involves an exclusion and with it a similar deployment of dehumanizing verbiage. It also demands that the hosts put themselves at risk: "Así, la Gofia y Mari la Roja recibieron improperios, amenazas, actas de advertencia, un par de multas, incluso fueron detenidas una vez, acusadas de [. . .] perturbar la tranquilidad."[189] Furthermore, in trying to be a space that is as inclusive as possible of all marginalized subjectivities, the party results in being a potentially dangerous space where individuals self-censure political speech in case of who might be listening:

> Se cuidaban mucho de no hablar de política, por más que alguien las provocara. No sólo porque la política no les interesaba en lo más mínimo, porque les parecía un tema propio de machos y otros animales apestosos, sino también porque en una fiesta donde entra cual-

> quiera, entra efectivamente *cualquiera*. Siempre hay un ojo que te ve y las paredes tienen oídos [original italics].[190]

Finally, there are "amigas y enemigas," jealousies, scorned lovers, and petty rivalries at these parties of presumably selfsame individuals. Ironically, these amigas hurl at each other the worst heterosexist insults such as, "la polaca maricona y corrupta de menores."[191] In other words, there is no such thing as an absolutely impervious space, "[s]iempre hay un ojo que te ve y las paredes tiene oídos." Being inclusive necessarily involves risk, allowing whoever may appear at the door to enter the party, whereas trying to protect the community—from "machos y otros animales apestosos"—necessitates anti-communal actions, the immunitary response of excluding dangerous foreign bodies.

A Totalitarian (Feminist?) Friend

Linda Roth, "traductora y novelista, futuro Premio Nobel," is often referred to as "una gran tipa, una mujer excepcional."[192] In addition to her professional success, Linda has also inherited a spacious apartment; she's savvy, daring, and seemingly emotionally and physically invulnerable. She's not even afraid of Moisés, "él sería grande y fuerte, pero ella tenía sus mañas y un hierro (¿descargado?) en la cartera." Should Zeta ask for help, Linda would come to her rescue "igualitica que Supermán."[193] Linda is also brutally honest; she will tell you what she thinks even if it causes you injury. Recalling that for Cicerón the ideal friend is confident, wise, totally self-reliant, and transparent,[194] Linda would be exemplary; she has no need of or reliance to anyone outside herself.

In fact, Linda is so concerned not to take advantage of Zeta that she is incapable of accepting gifts from her, whether it's a pair of tacky boots or Zeta's expression of unconditional love. "¿Cuánto pedía yo por [las botas]? Yo no pedía nada. Qué pedir ni pedir. Se las obsequiaba de todo corazón [. . .] [pero Linda] insistió en pagarme los chirimbolos [. . .] Yo era muy manirrota, desprendida, dispendiosa, despilfarradora, en resumen, una calamidad. No iba ella a aprovecharse de mis defectos."[195] Rather than accept Zeta's generosity and be in her debt, Linda responds to the offer with a recitation of Zeta's defects. When Zeta tells Linda "Yo te quiero igual," to her coming-out, Linda not only makes fun of her for using the word "lesbiana," "¿Y esa palabra tan fina, de dónde la sacaste?" she also berates her for being "empalagosa."[196]

The irony is that Linda, as the strong independent feminist, is often as oppressive and totalitarian as Moisés. As Zeta observes, "Lo curioso de todo este asunto, al menos para mí, es que Moisés también participaba de la intransigencia de mi amiga, de su carácter de halcón."[197] What's more, Linda's pretended brutal honesty is as discriminatory and abusive as Moisés':

> Que si la imbécil, que si la víctima, que si las mujeres de los países islámicos. Me había tratado muy mal, casi con el mismo desprecio que Moisés, como si yo fuera una cucaracha o algo así. Y peor es que yo la quiero muchísimo, más que a nadie. Que tengo muy en cuentas sus opiniones y, por tanto, *me sentía* cucaracha. No molesta, sino triste. Una cucaracha triste. Qué patético (emphasis in original).[198]

Linda pathologizes Zeta for being unable to end the relationship and kick Moisés out. However, as Zeta and the reader come to realize, Zeta's addiction to Moisés is not unlike Linda's addiction to Alix, that is, the addiction of blindly falling in love with the illusion of someone. Just as Moisés is for Zeta "el tipo que más me ha gustado en la vida," for Linda, "jamás encontró a nadie [. . .] que le gustara tanto como la muchachita del pelo negro."[199] The text suggests a parallel between the desire and lack of self-control that Linda displays toward Alix—"Linda se había quedado hipnotizada, embobecida, lela, muy distinta de sí misma"[200]—despite her independence and self-discipline, and that which keeps Zeta with Moisés. It's an addiction and madness to which anyone can fall victim. But Linda never manages to realize this or express empathy. Instead, she cruelly berates Zeta for being cowardly. I suggest that Linda as an exceptional woman, as a "superman," is a female version of the classical Greek exemplary friend, or even *el hombre nuevo,* a heroic and impervious figure. Portela demonstrates how such an ideal, such an archetype, is hegemonic and oppressive. She makes Zeta feel "cucaracha."

Ultimately, it was not Linda who saves Zeta from Moisés. The hospitality and friendship that Zeta extends to Alix involved risk and estranging herself from her community. Her friends considered it reckless, and yet, in hosting the enemy Zeta was rewarded with the greatest gift. Alix manages to trick Moisés into falling out of the giant window and, in his fall, takes down Poliester, a neighbor who played a cornet horribly and constantly. Hosting the enemy resulted in the double homicide, which was a blessing: it eliminated Moisés, the Sovereign Beast, former magistrate, and domestic abuser, along with one of the worst sonic nuisances. In hosting the enemy, Zeta paradoxically made her home safer and quieter. We can also speculate that it is because of this hosting and double homicide that Zeta is compelled and able to write the narrative we read. As such, the novel, in its compositional form as accumulative and inclusive (recall its seemingly endless sentences and proliferating, multivocal footnotes) and in its character and plot development, gestures toward an ethics of hospitality; it underscores a vital relationship to the Other. The novel demonstrates that being hospitable demands risk; however, it does not prescribe hospitality as an absolute moral, for Zeta's first hospitable act was toward Moisés. We can read Zeta's compassion, which is at the same time a betrayal to Linda—"Porque aquello era una traición, una sórdida puñalada por la espalda"[201]—as indicative of Roach's "shit of friendship" and more broadly of an ethics toward the Other that is not morally righteous. In this manner, Portela is also working against the moralism and idealism of the Cuban Revolution, which was reflected in the popular genre of the detective novel where the state apprehends the criminal. In *Cien botellas* these distinctive roles—of good guys and bad guys or amigas and enemigas—are collapsed. Its protagonist-narrator is flawed and "uno de los bicharracos más divertidos de La Habana. Capaz de levantarle el ánimo a cualquiera."[202]

Hospitable Conclusions

Untying the concept of community from its historical association to the semantics of *proprium,* it is from a sense of debt, the absence of a property, the negative, or to use his word, the concave, that Roberto Esposito aims to engage the notion of community. His text, *Communitas,* answers the call of philosophers, such as Jean-Luc Nancy and Maurice Blanchot, who argue for the exigency of rethinking community not as a work, a unified, or coherent body of subjects but through its incongruousness, its exposure to loss and the sharing of mortality. If community has been misconceived as a fullness, an interiority, the unity of individual subjects forming a larger subjectivity, he insists that what we have in common "is an otherness that withdraws us from our subjectivity."[203] Honing in on its etymological implications of gift, obligation, and duty, *communitas,* Esposito demonstrates, is calibrated on a "'debt,' 'guilt,' 'failing,'" and thus expresses "a defective condition" and "insurmountable incompleteness."[204]

In *The Inoperative Community,* Nancy explains that the failure of communist projects wasn't that its ideals were betrayed, but that its main ideal was problematic: "human beings defined as producers . . . human beings defined at all."[205] He presents the humanist archetype of the indivisible self as a totalitarian form since its articulation can only be achieved through a work of death. That is, the desire for immanence, an interiority without relation—the closure of the absolute—or communion of individuals within a mystical body, or head of state—calls for the "the extermination of the other," as it seeks to eliminate all that is extraneous to its circumscribed identity.[206] Through his reading of Martin Heidegger's "being-with," Esposito arrives at the conclusion that community *is*, it is existence, ontological, that is to say, community is not something that was lost, to be recovered, or a teleological end, but the awareness that I am insufficient, that "I owe you."[207]

Fresa y chocolate and *Cien botellas en una pared* both respond to an immunitary purging of those that threaten the national body or the community ideal, specifically the historical marginalization and persecution of non-heterosexual Cubans. Both film and novel have been applauded for making visible those who have been omitted and erased from the national discourse. However, what I have underscored in my analysis of these two works is not the positive representation of these subjectivities and their consequent inclusion in the national imaginary. Rather, I have aimed to underscore a shared "defective condition" and "insurmountable incompleteness" that their stories make evident, precisely that which does not lend itself to becoming an archetypal model against which others can be measured. Linda might be a gay woman, but that doesn't make her any less hegemonic than the patriarchal ex-magistrate.

Representations, moreover, are easily co-opted by the establishment in cynical ways that do not address lived material disparities. Today, fortunately, queer Cubans face a very different legal status than did our fictional Diego in the early 70s. Homosexuality was decriminalized in 1979 and in 2010 Fidel Castro apologized for the persecution of gay citizens and the grave injustices they endured. Today, there are institutions, such as the Federación de Mujeres Cubanas (Federation of Cuban Women) and the Centro Nacional de Educación Sexual (National Center of Sex Education), advocating for the rights and representation of women, queer, and trans Cubans. However, as many artists and activists claim, these establishment institutions have also absorbed and silenced smaller activist independent groups and have stopped short of advocating for the legalization of gay marriage and the criminalization of same-sex discrimination.[208] These institutions, moreover, operate in paternalist ways, "setting the terms of engagement," and have been deployed to save face internationally.[209] As Jonathan Dettman explains,

> It would be shortsighted to think that the state cannot incorporate and control non-heterosexual bodies, symbols, and discourses. [. . .] While many of the changes in Cuba's sexual and reproductive politics are welcome, the about-face can be seen as an attempt to "pinkwash" the revolutionary government's history of repression of gays and to legitimize itself in the eyes of the international order, where according to Negrón-Muntaner, gay rights have become a "litmus test" of civilization.[210]

Indeed, the litmus test of civilization is itself questioned and challenged in *Cien botellas en una pared.* If Gutiérrez Alea's Diego was a "conservative culture queen" (Quiroga), Portela's Zeta consistently refuses the authority and prestige of being a writer. While her assimilation, as well as other characters, to the nonhuman, is at once a reflection of how she is devalued, made to live in and survive inhospitable, or dehumanizing, conditions, the novel also puts into question what constitutes the human and whether the nonhuman is any less worthy of dignity. Zeta, as we've mentioned, also had her apartment-raised pig—a trend that developed to stave off starvation. In naming her pig, Zeta comes to realize and express the arbitrariness of what determines the distinctions between bios and zoē, "Mi cerdito respondía al nombre de Gruñi, al cual añadí mis apellidos en un arranque de afecto maternal. He ahí el primer error: ponerle nombre. [. . .] Porque nombrar es individualizar. Nombre equivale a espíritu, a personalidad propia. A lo que debe cuidarse, pues de algún modo es único e insustituible."[211] In other words, what distinguishes pigs to be anonymously consumed from those to be cherished is simply the act of naming. Thus, the spirit, the singularity of a being is in the name, in the way we choose to relate and recognize that being, rather than something inherent and immutable about that body. Zeta's recognition of Gruñi's un-substitutable singularity is the ultimate gesture of hospitality and friendship.

Coda

Corporeal Readings of Cuban Literature and Art: The Body, the Inhuman, and Ecological Thinking opens with Roberto Diago's black paintings of Black skin. I would now like to close with another series that equally insists on exteriority and the formal qualities of a canvas, or so it would seem. The photographic series, titled *El dibujo, la escritura, la abstracción* (1997–2012), by the contemporary Cuban artist Carlos Garaicoa, might at first appear like large non-objectivist paintings. As a series, the rows of color photographs, each measuring approximately 6 × 5 ft., recall the Color Field compositions by the "abstract expressionist" Mark Rothko and the gestural oil scribbles of Cy Twombly. And yet, these are in fact photographic images printed on glossy paper that show no traces of manipulation of the medium; in their high-resolution, they remain true to the technology of the camera. If these images are not the result of painterly abstraction, what then has Garaicoa made the subject of the lens's sharp focus, of the camera's viewfinder, that tiny window through which the photographer sees and frames? Each of the rectangular photographs in this series provides a frontal view of a wall, a roughened architectural exterior with stains, fading and peeling paint. Having no other figures or horizon line to partition the compositional space and situate the viewer's gaze, the images lack a dominant or centralized focal point. It would seem the sole function of each photo is the cataloguing of a single datum: an impenetrable material surface, bearing nondescript marks, textures, and colors.

Turning our attention to a piece titled *La abstracción VI, Blood Wall,* we find smudges of burnt sienna and ochre—earthy, organic colors that do indeed resemble blood. An amorphous darker cloud at the top right—possibly a soot stain—appears like the specter of a previous fire. The smooth glossy surface of the photographic paper displays rough textures, as the precision of the lens allows us to detect a minutia of lines, scratches, incisions, fine and coarse, almost imperceptible marks, traces of impact,

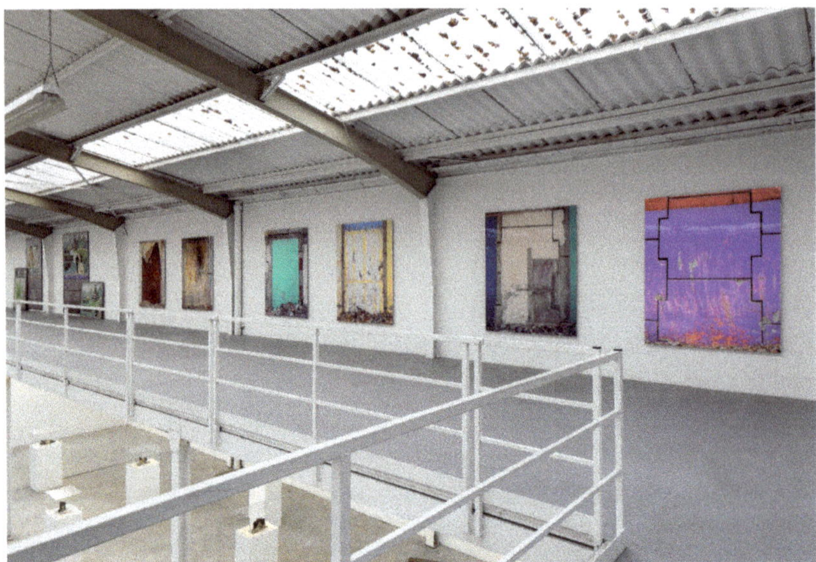

Figure 9. Exhibition view of Carlos Garaicoa's series *El dibujo, la escritura, la abstracción* (1997–2012) at "L'Optimiste" in Les Moulins, Galleria Continua (Paris) in 2012. Courtesy of the artist and Galleria Continua. Photography by Oak Taylor-Smith. © 2023 Artists Rights Society (ARS), New York / VEGAP, Madrid.

deterioration, and duration. Recalling Roberto Fabelo's paintings on embroidered silk, in the shallow space of the composition, there is a depth at the surface. As a vertical plane we are drawn to its incisions like the traces of a writing; however, that writing is no longer legible. Invisible, unreadable histories are made palpable. Ochres, scratches, soot stains, and marks of impact betray a violence and a material decay that evokes corporeal vulnerability.

There are tensions in Garaicoa's photographic series I find analogous to the kind of irresolute engagement I have sustained in my treatment of literary and visual work from Cuba. There is a tension between the dense, resistant opacity of the walls and the viewer's desire to recognize, identify, and make sense of the photographs, a tension between the seemingly unmediated raw data the camera records and compositions which approach the condition of language and art, as "dibujo," "escritura," and "abstracción." There is a tension between the aesthetic seduction of the walls' abstraction and the lived materiality of which those walls are co-constitutive. Against the tiny window of the camera and its promise of seeing through,

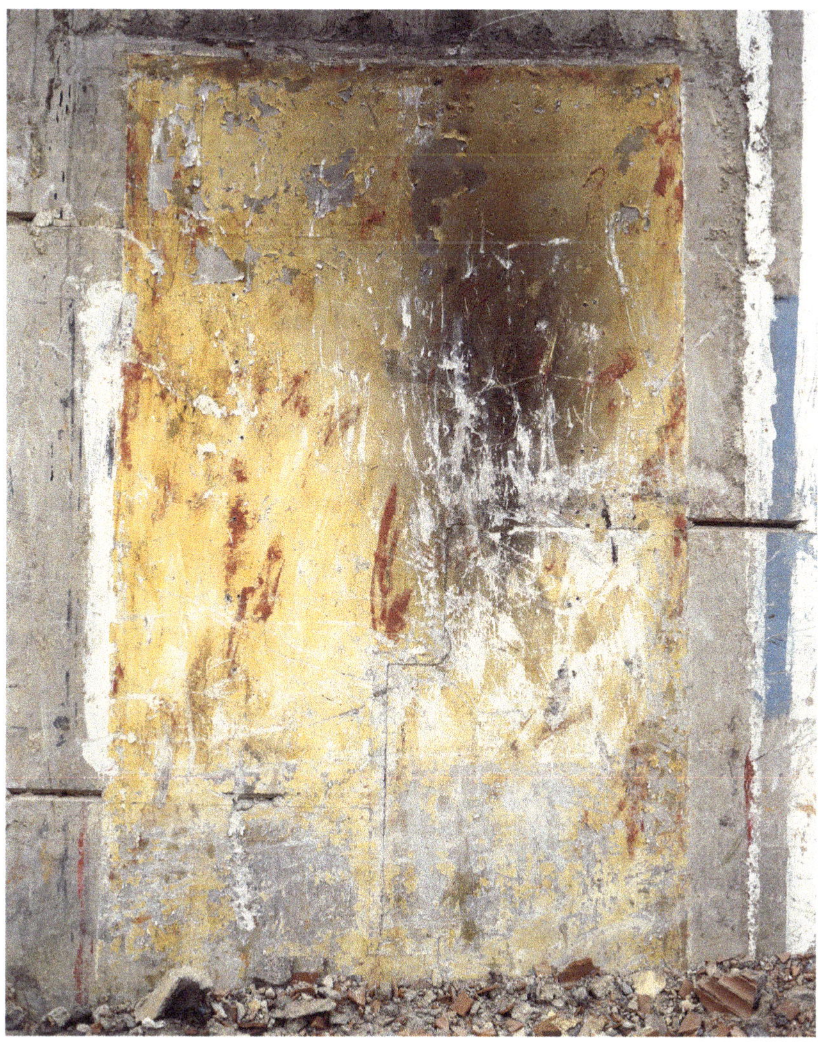

Figure 10. *La abstracción VI, Blood Wall* by Carlos Garaicoa from his series *El dibujo, la escritura, la abstracción* (1997–2012). Photograph 6 × 5 ft. Courtesy of the artist and Galleria Continua. Photograph by Carlos Garaicoa. © 2023 Artists Rights Society (ARS), New York / VEGAP, Madrid.

of capturing, and rendering static, Garaicoa obstructs our view; we are left facing walls with un-exhaustive creative potential.

At the bottom of *Blood Wall* we see a rim of rubble. Garaicoa, much like Antonio José Ponte, has made Havana's ruins a focal point of his work. We might consider *Blood Wall* as a visual correlate to Antonio José Ponte's statement, "las ruinas son arquitectura torturada,"[1] a statement which attributes sensation and feeling to what is conventionally perceived as inanimate. Taken between 1997 and 2012, Garaicoa's photographs document the city's architectural disrepair, representations of which are now a common trope, synonymous with the economic crisis of the 1990s. Following Ponte, the ruins are a testament of a criminal and violent negligence—a culpability he assigns to the Cuban government.[2] However, Garaicoa's series, *El dibujo, la escritura, la abstracción,* with its decentralized compositions, absence of figures, and indecipherable marks, works against facile identifications or the elaboration of linear, cause-and-effect narratives.

The framing or transformation of damaged and discarded materials, in such a way that resists instrumentalization, is seen throughout the contemporary Caribbean archipelago. In the artwork of Puerto Rican Eduardo Lalo, we find poetic photographs of debris and illegible city signage;[3] in Virgin Islander La Vaughn Belle's beautiful collages we can trace the fragments of ruined paper she repurposed from works damaged during Hurricane María,[4] and in Dominican Tony Capellán's installations we are confronted with trash he collected from the seashore: Detergent bottles, sandals, and hairbrushes seduce the viewer through harmonious color arrangements and a density of plastics that shimmer and refuse to disappear.[5] All of these are instances of material transformations where systems of meaning and value are upended. More specifically, these transformations are a rebuke to an international economic order that not only ruins landscapes, but also renders individuals as disposable.

The ecological and new materialist lens that *Corporeal Readings* adopts necessarily calls for a more expansive analysis that goes beyond Cuba. Future projects that attend to these Caribbean aesthetic trends, in which discarded materials are reanimated, soliciting alternative registers of sensibility, have the potential to challenge ontological hierarchies imposed by the global north and its ethos of productivity. Such projects might also contribute to recent discussions on the value of aesthetics, and whether arts and letters do or do not come to the aid of our planetary crises. Recently in major US and British media outlets, such as the *British Broadcasting Corporation, The New York Times, The Chronicle of Higher Education,* and *The*

New Yorker, numerous articles question the purpose of the Humanities disciplines, and speculate as to their demise.[6] Given the drastic funding cuts to the arts and a corollary decrease in college students majoring in non-STEM fields internationally, their future—judging by these metrics—do indeed look bleak. In the face of such underestimation by the dominant culture and economic forces, scholars appeal to their political and social impact and, as such, activist disciplines like ecocriticism have superseded traditional specializations like British Romanticism. John Guillory's 2022 book *Professing Criticism* rightly calls out the inflated claims of leading social change and the "political surrogacy" of literary critics. Relatedly, there are articles that challenge the positive effects of climate fiction, debating whether consuming such works results in environmental activism or apathy. Meanwhile, proponents of the so-called Postcritical turn argue that the ambivalence and opacity of some texts and criticism are unhelpful and advocate for transparent and uncomplicated readings.[7]

The Cuban cultural producers discussed in this book offer an alternative to these debates, which are often reductive. Their work suggests that the most powerful and transformative aspects of creative production are irreducible to didactic instruction or a recognizable political project. In other words, the impacts of creating and consuming creative work cannot be measured and weighted. Engaging with Caribbean arts, letters, and sounds more broadly, as well as Afro-diasporic cosmologies, in which visible and invisible worlds are interconnected and ritual is not merely symbolic but perceptibly transforms environments, will no doubt provide ways to relate to the world that bypass Euro-US metrics of productivity and morality. I want to suggest, alongside these creative producers, that it is in the enchantment, in the awe and joy and even the discomfort, opacity and confusion—experiences that are unproductive—that can stretch the limits of what is possible. Caribbean writers and artists point the way to fantastic ontologies, virtual potentialities, unthought alternatives.

In attending to the construction of Severo Sarduy's sentences—to the comma that both separates and brings together "frozen orchid" and "asthmatic bishop"—*Corporeal Readings of Cuban Literature and Art* does not read them as representations of transformations. *Corporeal Readings,* instead, reads them as zones of indeterminacy in which the reader must sustain an imaginative doing and undoing from one word to the next; *Corporeal Readings* reads his sentences as the site of transformation. Nicolás Guillén's rhythmic and sonorous verses are not merely representations of Afro-Cubans, they are incantations. Like the percussion of drums that call forth the mounting of an Orisha, Guillén's eight count beat possesses its readers; we become vehicles of Black Cuban speech. Antonio José Ponte's talking trash is not an allegory, it is also more than vibrant, it is fabulous. Ahmel Echevarría's Robespierre does, indeed, enter our blood stream; we are hosts to this well-seasoned philosophizing pig. Ena Lucía Portela's narrator, Zeta, befriends us and makes us accomplices in her black noire; we are not fools for falling for the trick of fiction. The illusion matters.

In sustaining our attention on the materiality of Cuban writers and artists' "human-cultural-production" we have located a vibrancy, a vibration, in the very grammar of their texts and the cross-hatching of their images. The fantastic transformation of Cobra's skin or Fabelo's roaches is not an immaterial idea but has material body that transverses and impacts other bodies. That is, the fabulous elements of these literary and visual works are no less positively material than the discarded trash, electrical storms, and marine polyps to which new materialists have turned. When Stacy Alaimo calls on her readers to acknowledge "the often unpredictable and unwanted actions of human bodies, nonhuman creatures, ecological systems, chemical agents, and other actors,"[8] I suggest we add to that list texts, images, sounds, and the cosmologies and imaginaries that also intermesh and touch our skins.

NOTES

Introduction

1 Brochure essay for the exhibition at the Halsey Museum of Contemporary Art.
2 I'm drawing from Deleuze and Guattari's notion of becoming-animal, which I specifically engage in chapter 2. However, I have chosen becoming-beast because of its antinomy to the civilized subject, as well as specific references to behaving beastly in Ahmel Echevarría's novels discussed in chapter 4.
3 In his reading of Francis Bacon's work, Gilles Deleuze makes a distinction between work that produces an intelligible narrative, in which the viewer can walk away with knowable content, and work that creates sensation or affect in the body. *Francis Bacon: The Logic of Sensation*, translated and with an introduction by Daniel W. Smith, afterword by Tom Conley (Minneapolis: University of Minnesota Press, 2003) 31, 32.
4 United Nations Chronicle, "The Legacy of Slavery," https://www.un.org/en/un-chronicle/legacy-slavery-caribbean-and-journey-towards-justice, accessed February 8, 2023; PBS, "Traces of the Trade," https://www.pbs.org/pov/films/tracesofthetrade/.
5 Elizabeth M. DeLoughrey, Renée K. Gosson, and George B. Hadley, (eds.), *Caribbean Literature and the Environment: Between Nature and Culture* (Charlottesville: University of Virgina Press, 2005), 48.
6 Antonio Benítez-Rojo, "Sugar and the Environment," in *Caribbean Literature,* 45.
7 Benítez-Rojo, "Sugar and the Environment," 44.
8 Benítez-Rojo, "Sugar and the Environment."
9 María A. Cabrera Arús, "The Material Promise of Socialist Modernity: Fashion and Domestic Space in the 1970s," in *The Revolution from Within: Cuba, 1959–1980*, edited by Michael J. Bustamente and Jennifer L. Lambe (Durham: Duke University Press, 2019), passim.
10 Tara Phillips discusses 1990s food lore in "Residuos Cubanos: The Aesethetics and Politics of Virgilio Piñera's 'La carne' and 'La cena,'" in *Undisciplined Cuba,* edited by Christina M. García with Mrinalini Tanka and Yairamaren Maldonado, forthcoming. The fan is cited in Elliott Mackie, "Ernesto Oroza's Technological Disobedience project celebrates Cuban ingenuity," *Assemblepapers* (2017), https://assemblepapers.com.au/2017/04/28/technological-disobedience-ernesto-oroza/.
11 Ernesto Oroza in interview with Elliot Mackie in "Ernesto Oroza's Technological Disobedience."
12 Mackie, "Ernesto Oroza's Technological Disobedience."

13 Coco Fusco, "The Artist as Hostage: Luis Manuel Otero Alcántara," *e-flux* (May 21, 2021), https://www.e-flux.com/announcements/398535/coco-fusco-in-e-flux-journal-the-artist-as-hostage/.

14 Lillian Guerra, "What to Know about the Ongoing Protests in Cuba," by Nicci Brown, *University of Florida News* (November 23, 2021), https://news.ufl.edu/2021/11/from-florida-episode-11/?fbclid=IwAR1Gi1F37Xs4Q0uFq3qJ1mWnFZ0m58MTNaG-R9K30XMm0GpgwS6b7nqn34c, accessed August 25, 2022.

15 Fusco, "The Artist as Hostage."

16 Coco Fusco, "Artists in Cuba Spearhead First Major Protests in Decades," *NACLA* (December 14, 2020) https://nacla.org/news/2020/12/14/artists-cuba-spearhead-first-major-protest-decades.

17 Guerra, "What to Know about the Ongoing Protests in Cuba."

18 Fusco, "The Artist as Hostage."

19 I'm specifically referring to the *Unidades Militares de Ayuda a la Producción*. See Abel Sierra Madero's interview of Dr. Lillian Guerra, a psychologist who participated as a researcher and in the presumed rehabilitation of "anti-social" citizens in the UMAP camps. "Lo de las UMAP fue un trabajo 'top secret': Entrevista a la Dra. María Elena Sol Arrondo," *Cuban Studies* 44 (2016).

20 See "De testimonios y de reos: Biopolítica y Revolución. El seropositivo cubano," (2015), where Mirta Suquet Martínez explains how Cuban Revolution's strong public health policy (and its corresponding moral codes) manifested itself in the medicalization of the New Man as an immune man, 303. See also Marta Hernández Salván, *Mínima Cuba: Herectical Poetics and Power in Post-Soviet Cuba* (Albany: SUNY Press, 2015), 48, 49.

21 Nancy Burke, "Precarity in the Time of COVID-19: Aging Housing and Aging Population in Cuba," *Global Perspective* 2, 1 (2021), 5.

22 Guerra, "What to Know about the Ongoing Protests in Cuba." See also Ariana Hernández-Reguant, Susannah Rodríguez Drissi and Carlos Juárez, "Anti-Governmemnt Protests in Cuba," *Think Tech Hawaii*, July 16, 2021, https://thinktechhawaii.com/anti-government-protests-in-cuba-global-connections/.

23 Guerra, "What to Know about the Ongoing Protests in Cuba."

24 Burke, "Precarity in the Time of COVID-19," 5.

25 Rachel Price, *Planet/Cuba: Art, Culture, and the Future of the Island* (London and New York: Verso Books, 2016), 4.

26 Price, *Planet/Cuba*, 21.

27 Price, *Planet/Cuba*, 9.

28 Although the focus of the book is contemporary cultural production, Price draws upon a history of environmentalism that emerged with colonial deforestation, ecological essays published in the 1930s, as well as artists from the 70s and 80s. Price, *Planet/Cuba*, 34–37.

29 In my formulations of material and territorial interdependence I am drawing from Jane Bennett's *Vibrant Matter: A Political Ecology of Things* (Durham: Duke University Press, 2009) *and* Rosi Braidotti's *Metamorphoses: Towards a Materialist Theory of Becoming* (Malden: Blackwell Publishers, 2002). In *Vibrant Matter*, Bennett aims

"to detach materiality from the figures of passive, mechanistic, or divinely infused substance," and argues, "vibrant matter is *not* the raw material for the creative activity of humans or God," xiii. Her book challenges anthropocentrism and calls for an attentiveness to "the capacity of things [. . .] not only to impede or block the will and designs of humans but also to act as quasi agents or forces with trajectories, propensities, or tendencies of their own," iii.

30 See note 29.

31 Edward J. Kormondy, "A Brief Introduction to the History of Ecology," *The American Biology Teacher* 74, 7 (2012), 441.

32 Cheryll Glotfelty qtd. in *The Latin American Ecocultural Reader*, edited by Jennifer French and Gisela Heffes (Evanston: Northwestern University press, 2012), 14.

33 Glotfelty qtd. in *The Latin American Ecocultural Reader.*

34 Laura Barbas-Rhoden, *Ecological Imaginations in Latin American Fiction* (Gainesvillle: University Press of Florida, 2011), 5.

35 French and Heffes, (eds.), *The Latin American Ecocultural Reader,* 5.

36 Héctor Hoyos, *Things with a History: Transcultural Materialism and Literatures of Extraction in Contemporary Latin America* (New York: Columbian University Press, 2019), 27.

37 Hoyos, *Things with a History*, 3.

38 Piñera qtd. in Thomas F. Anderson, *Everything in Its Place: The Life and Works of Virgilio Piñera* (Lewisburg: Bucknell University Press, 2006), 152.

39 Phillips, "Residuos Cubanos."

40 See note 38.

41 Michael Wiedorn, *Think Like an Archipelago: Paradox in the Work of Édouard Glissant* (Albany: State University of New York Press, 2018), xiv, xv.

42 Wiedorn, *Think Like an Archipelago*, xxvii, xxviii.

43 Anna Reckin, "Tidalectic Lectures: Kamau Brathwaite's Prose/Poetry as Sound-Space," *Anthurium: A Caribbean Studies Journal* 1, 1(2003), 1.

44 Juan Duchesne Winter, *Caribe, Caribana: Cosmografías literarias* (San Juán: Ediciones Callejón, 2015), 14–16.

45 Juan Carlos Quintero Herencia, *La hoja de mar (:) Efecto archipiélago I* (Leiden: Almanera, 2006), 34.

46 Qtd. in Wiedorn, *Think Like an Archipelago,* 10.

47 Gregory Bateson, *Steps to an Ecology: Collected Essays in Anthropology, Psychiatry, Evolution, and Epistemology* (London: Jason Aronson, 1972), 145–152.

48 Samantha Frost, "The Implications of The New Materialisms for Femenist Epistemology," in *Feminist Epistomology and Philosophy of Science: Power in* Knowledge, edited by H.E. Grasswick (London and New York: Springer Netherlands, 2011), 79.

49 Jean-Luc Nancy, *The Inoperative Community*, edited and translated by Peter Connor, Lisa Garbus, Michael Holland, and Simona Sawhney (Minneapolis: University of Minnesota Press, 1991), 21.

50 Antonio José Ponte, *Un seguidor de Montaigne mira La Habana & Las comidas profundas* (Madrid: Editorial Verbum, 2001), 58–59. See also Rita de Maeseneer, *Devo-*

rando a lo cubano: Una aproximación gastrorítica a textos relacionados con el siglo XIX y el Período Especial (Madrid: Iberoamericana—Vervuert, 2012), 248–249.

51 As we shall see in chapter 1, some critics of Guillén's *Motivos de son* dismissed its aestheticism as a cynical incorporation of Black Cubans, a way to diffuse racial tensions without addressing lived material disparities. Similarly, critics of the 1993 film *Fresa y chocolate* (see chapter 5) dismissed the film as trying to eliminate the challenge that marginalized figures posed to national unity, by allegorically including them in the national imaginary.

52 Denise Ferreira da Silva, "Hacking the Subject: Black Feminism and Refusal beyond the Limits of Critique," *philoSOPHIA* 8, 1 (Winter 2018), 24.

53 In his essay, "Racism as Universalism," Etienne Balibar writes, "no definition of the human species, or simply the human—something which is so crucial for universalism, or universalism as humanism—has ever been proposed which would not imply latent hierarchy. This has to do with the impossibility of fixing the boundaries of what we call 'human,' or fixing the boundaries within which all human beings could possibly be gathered." *Masses, Classes, Ideas: Studies on Politics and Philosophy After Marx*, translated by James Swenson (London: Routledge, 1994), 197.

54 *El hombre nuevo* refers to Che Guevara's seminal essay "El socialismo y el hombre en Cuba" (1965). The terms *gusano* and *escoria* were used to stigmatize those who would want to exile, especially during the 1980 Mariel Boatlift, when over 125,000 Cubans left the island. Jorge Duany, "Neither Golden Exile nor Dirty Worm: Ethnic Identity in Recent Cuban-American Novels," *Cuban Studies* 23 (1993), 168.

55 Guillermina De Ferrari, *Community and Culture in Post-Soviet Cuba* (New York: Routledge, 2014) 1.

56 De Ferrari, *Community and Culture*, 23. Jonathan Dettman, "Literature as Reproductive Labor in Post-Soviet Cuba," *Chasquí* 47, 2 (2018), 101. Price, *Planet/Cuba*, 4.

57 Ahmel Echevarría, *Búfalos camino al matadero* (Santiago: Editorial Oriente, 2013), 98.

58 Dettman in "Literature as Reproductive Labor in Post-Soviet Cuba," 109.

59 Nancy, *The Inoperative Community*, 3.

60 UMAP is the acronym for Unidades Militares de Ayuda a la Producción, the 1960s labor camps designed to rehabilitate homosexuals, religious believers and those deemed anti-social. See Ted Henken, *Cuba: A Global Studies Handbook* (Santa Barbara: ABC-CLIO, 2008), 248.

61 Fidel Castro, "Palabras a los intelectuales," in *Política cultural de la Revolución Cubana* (La Habana: Editorial de Ciencias Sociales, 1977). It is in this speech where Castro famously stated "dentro de la Revolución, todo; contra la Revolución, nada."

62 Fred Moten, *In the Break: The Aesthetics of the Black Radical Tradition* (Minneapolis: University of Minnesota Press, 2003), 12.

Chapter 1. Reading as Touching

1 María Golán, "El grotesco popular en la obra de Nicolás Guillén: Motivos de son," in *Nicolás Guillén: Hispanidad, vanguardia y compromiso social*, edited by Matías Barchino, and María Rubio Martín. (Cuenca: Ediciones de la Universidad de

Castilla-La Mancha, 2004), 303. Golán posits that Guillén's stereotypical characters are ironic critiques, intentionally drawn from popular theatrical shows, 330. See also Roberto González Echevarría, "Guillén as Baroque: Meaning in Motivos de son," *Callaloo* 31 (Spring, 1987), 311. However, it was not the general consensus that these characters were ironic adaptions. While some readers, as I will note ahead, found these poetic speakers to be (non-ironic) offensive stereotypes of Black Cubans, others like Nancy Morejón in a 1972 essay, considered them audacious for representing Black working-class archetypes, "Su obra: Introducción," https://www.cervantesvirtual.com/portales/nicolas_guillen/su_obra_introduccion/.

2 Nicolás Guillén, *Obra poética 1920–1958, tomo I* (La Habana: Instituto Cubano del Libro, 1972), 103. All citations of *Motivos de son* are taken from this edition.

3 Guillén, *Obra poética*, 105.

4 Guillén, *Obra poética.*

5 Golán provides a good summary of the initial reception of *Motivos de son* in her essay, "El grotesco popular." See also Andre Guridy, *Forging Diaspora: Afro-Cubans and African Americans in a World of Empire and Jim Crow* (Chapel Hill: University of North Carolina, 2010), where he explains that representations like those in *Motivos,* which "foregrounded . . . the cultural practices and the material conditions of the working classes," were "shunned by aspiring-class and elite blacks." These representations "challenged the tenets of racial respectability touted by black institutions," 118. Along similar lines, see Thomas Anderson, *Carnival and National Identity in the Poetry of Afrocubanismo* (Gainesville: University Press of Florida, 2011), 4, and Vera Kutzinski, *Sugar's Secrets: Race and the Erotics of Cuban Nationalism* (Charlottesville: University Press of Virginia, 1993), 152.

6 Guridy, *Forging Diaspora,* 118.

7 Adriana Tous, *La poesía de Nicolás Guillén* (Madrid: Ediciones Cultura Hispánica, 1971), 111.

8 Ángel Aguirre, "Elementos Afronegroides en dos poemas de Luis de Góngora y Argote y en cinco villancicos de Sor Juana Inés de la Cruz," *Atti del Convegno di Roma* 1 (March, 1995), 296–298. Aguirre specifies that with Sor Juana Inés de la Cruz, by contrast, the reproduction of Black voices is not meant to be parodic but instead to demonstrate their religious devotion to Catholicism, 307.

9 Luis Palés Matos, *Tutún de pasa y grifería* (San Juán: Editorial de la Universidad de Puerto Rico, 1993), 95–96. José Zacarías Tallet, "La rumba" (Buenos Aires: Biblioteca Virtual Universal, 2003).

10 José Quiroga describes the characters in *Motivos de son* as speaking "without mediation or contextual setting on the page. No scene is described: these are actual performances that use the black rhythmic idioms of the *son.*" "Spanish American Poetry from 1922 to 1975," in *The Cambridge History of Latin American* Literature, vol. 1, edited by Roberto González Echevarría and Enrique Pupo-Walker (Cambridge: Cambridge University Press, 1996), 336.

11 I am borrowing this term from an article by Santiago Colas, "Toward an Ethics of Close Reading in the Age of Neo-Liberalism," CR: The New Centennial Review 7, 3

(2007), that has been very influential in my thinking of reading, as a practice and its ethical implications.

12 Severo Sarduy, "Pintura y Revolución," *Revolución* (January 31, 1953), 14.

13 Sarduy, "Pintura y Revolución."

14 Castro, "Palabras a los intelectuales."

15 Mercedes Sarduy, *Severo Sarduy: Cartas a mi hermana en La Habana* (Coral Gables: Severo Sarduy Cultural Foundation, 2013), 73.

16 Lucía Guerra, *Ciudad, género e imaginarios urbanos en la narrativa latinoamericana* (Santiago: Editorial Cuartopropio, 2014), 255. Roberto González Echevarría, (ed.), "Introducción," *De donde son los cantantes de Severo Sarduy* (Madrid: Cátedra, 1993), 20, 21.

17 González Echevarría, *De donde son los cantantes,* 20.

18 González Echevarría, *De donde son los cantantes,* 11.

19 Moten, *In the Break,* 32–33.

20 Moten, *In the Break* , 35.

21 Moten, *In the Break,* 12.

22 Nicolás Guillén, *Sóngoro cosongo* (1931), in *Obra poética 1920–1958,* tomo I (La Habana: Instituto Cubano del Libro, 1972), 111–132.

23 Jacques Rancière, *The Politics of Aesthetics: The Distribution of the Sensible*, edited and translated by Gabriel Rockhill (London: Bloomsbury, 2004), 10. "There is [. . .] an 'aesthetics' at the core of politics. [. . .] This aesthetics [. . .] can be understood [. . .] as the system of a priori forms determining what presents itself to sense experience. It is a delimitation of spaces and times, of the visible and invisible, of speech and noise. [. . .] Politics revolves around what is seen and what can be said about it, around who has the ability to see and the talent to speak, around properties of spaces and the possibilities of time."

24 Julio Ramos, *Desencuentros de la modernidad en América Latina: Literatura y politica en el siglo XIX* (Cuidad de México: Fondo de Cultura Económica, 1989), 237. Kutzinski, *Sugar's Secrets,* 5. See also José Enrique Rodó, *Ariel,* translated by Margaret Sayers Peden, foreword by James W. Symington and prologue by Carlos Fuentes (Austin: University of Texas Press, 1988).

25 Anderson, *Carnival and National Identity,* 8–9.

26 Anderson, *Carnival and National Identity,* 7.

27 Kamau Brathwaite, "The African Presence in Literature," *Daedalus* 103, 2 (Spring 1974), 75.

28 Guillermo Cabrera Infante's prologue to Natalio Galán's *Cuba y sus sones* (Madrid: Artegraf, 1997), XII.

29 Brathwaite, "The African Presence in Literature," 73.

30 The citation is from the title of Brathwaite's essay and refers precisely to the aims of his analysis.

31 Brathwaite, "The African Presence," 79.

32 Brathwaite, "The African Presence."

33 Kutzinski, *Sugar's Secrets,* 143, 145.

34 Michael Dash, *The Other America: Caribbean Literature in a New World Context* (Charlottesville: University Press of Virginia, 1998), 72.
35 Dash, *The Other America,* 76.
36 Kutzinski, *Sugar's Secrets,* 143.
37 Richard Jackson, *Black Literature and Humanism in Latin America* (Athens: The University of Georgia Press, 1988), 26. See also René Depestre's "Aventuras del negrismo en América Latina," *América Latina en sus ideas*, edited by Leopoldo Zea (Mexico D.F.: Editorial Siglo XXI, 1986)
38 See Kutzinski, *Sugar's Secrets,* and Dash, *The Other America.*
39 Miguel Arnedo-Gómez, *Uniting Blacks in a Raceless Nation: Blackness, Afro-Cuban Culture and Mestizaje in the Prose and Poetry of Nicolás Guillén* (Lewisburg: Bucknell University Press, 2016), xxii.
40 Arnedo-Gómez, *Uniting Blacks in a Raceless Nation,* xiii. Arnedo-Gómez refers specifically to Kutzinski's *Sugar's Secrets* and Robin D. Moore's *Nationalizing Blackness: Afrocubanismo and Artistic Revolution in Havana, 1920–1940* (Pittsburgh: University of Pittsburgh Press, 1997).
41 Arnedo-Gómez, *Uniting Blacks in a Raceless Nation,* xxvii.
42 Florit and Jiménez's 1968 reading cited in Luis Duno-Gottberg, *Solventando las diferencias: La ideología del mestizaje en Cuba* (Madrid: Iberoamericana-Vervuert, 2003), 85. Jorge Ruffinelli echoes this in his description of the poems as a superficial engagement with Blackness, *Poesía y descolonización: Viaje por la poesía de Nicolás Giullén* (Xalapa: Universidad Veracruzana, 1985), 19.
43 Morejón, "Su obra: Indroducción."
44 Jackson, *Black Literature and Humanism in Latin America,* 26.
45 Duno-Gottberg, *Solventando las diferencias,* 95–97; Kutzinski, *Sugar's Secrets,* 151–154.
46 Ruffinelli, *Poesía y descolonización,* 19; Tous, *La poesía de Nicolás Guillén,* 111.
47 González Echevarría, "Guillén as Baroque," 313; Anderson, *Carnival and National Identity in the Poetry,* 80.
48 Arnedo-Gómez, *Uniting Blacks in a Raceless Nation,* 71.
49 Arnedo-Gómez, *Uniting Blacks in a Raceless Nation*, xx, 71.
50 I'm using Fred Moten's phrasing cited in the introduction to this chapter. See note 19.
51 José Martí, "Nuestra América," *La Revista Ilustrada de Nueva York* (United States, Januray 30, 1891), 134, 137.
52 Ramos, *Desencuentros de la modernidad,* 239.
53 Martí, "Nuestra América," 138.
54 Kutzinski, *Sugar's Secrets,* 6.
55 Kutzinski, *Sugar's Secrets*, 5.
56 Fernando Ortiz, *Cuban Counterpoint: Tobacco and Sugar*, translated by Harriet de Onís (Durham: Duke University Press, 1995), 98.
57 Ortiz, *Cuban Counterpoint,* 101, 103.
58 Martí, "Nuestra América," 133.
59 Juan Martínez, *Cuban Art and National Identity: The Vanguardia Painters, 1927–*

1950 (Gainesville: The University Press of Florida, 1994), 72–75. The word "cóctel" comes from Guillén's prologue cited above and "ajiaco" is taken from Fernando Ortiz quoted in Martínez' text.

60 Stephan Palmié's recent treatment of Fernando Ortiz's conceptualization of transculturation and the metaphor of *ajiaco* offers a sustained and nuanced analysis of these terms where they do not operate as simply processes of assimilation, but instead as a means of working "against the metapragmatics of essentialist racial taxonomizing." Most notably, what distinguishes the *ajiaco* dish, at least in theory, is its non-recipe and capacity to include any ingredient on hand. I would, however, add that ultimately the metaphor still implies a logic of incorporation. And that as a metaphor it operates as a stand-in or representation of what would otherwise be irreducible singularities. "The Cuban factors: Reproductive biology, historical ontology and the metapragmatics of race," *Anthropology* Theory 16, 1 (2016), 4. Along these lines, Duno-Gottberg looks at *ajiaco* and transculturation as part of a national imaginary that aimed to represent Cuban identity through an ethnic synthesis, generated by intellectual elites in their desire to eliminate internal conflicts and the threat of racial war. *Solventando las diferencias,* 20.

61 I am using these terms abstractly in order to consider the homogenizing and exclusionary tendencies that arise in a politics of incorporation/assimilation and how that politics is symptomatic of a particular conceptualization of community. Arnedo-Gómez has aptly argued, when considering the deployment of terms, such as *mestizaje* and transculturation, within their specific socio-cultural contexts, these terms operate in far more complex and contradictory ways, *Uniting Blackness,* xxvi.

62 Roberto Esposito, *Communitas: The Origin and Destiny of Community*, translated by Tomothy Campbell (Stanford: Stanford University Press, 2010), introduction, passim.

63 Nancy, *The Inoperative Community,* and Maurice Blanchot, *The Unavowable Community*, translated by Pierre Joris (Barrytown: Station Hill Press, 1988).

64 Esposito, *Communitas,* 10.

65 Guillén, "Prólogo," *Sóngoro cosongo,* 132.

66 Mladen Dolar, *A Voice and Nothing More,* edited by Slavoj Žižek (Cambridge: The MIT Press, 2006) 15.

67 Kutzinski, *Sugar's Secrets,* 180.

68 Julio Ramos, "Descarga acústica," *Papel Máquina* 2, 4 (2010), 61. My translation from Spanish.

69 Vladimir Jankélévitch, *Music and the Ineffable,* translated by Carolyn Abbate (Princeton: Princeton University Press, 1983), 1.

70 Carolyn Abbate, "Music—Drastic or Gnostic?" *Critical Inquiry* 30 (2004), 517.

71 Andrew Bowie, *Music, Philosophy, and Modernity* (Cambridge: Cambridge University Press, 2007), 11.

72 Doris Sommer, "Ethical Asymmetries: Learning to Love a Loss," in *The Ethics of Latin American Literary Criticism: Reading Otherwise*, edited by E. Zivin Graff (New York: Palgrave Macmillan, 2007), 188–189.

73 Abbate, "Music—Drastic or Gnostic?" 509.

74 Jankélévitch, *Music and the Ineffable*, 19.
75 González Echevarría, "Guillén as Baroque," 313.
76 Anderson, *Carnival and National Identity*, 80.
77 Anderson, *Carnival and National Identity*.
78 Anderson, *Carnival and National Identity*.
79 González Echevarría, "Guillén as Baroque," 314.
80 Moten, *In the Break*, 12–15. Italicizing the *mater* in *mater*iality, Moten links materiality to maternity in order to underscore the generative, reproductive performativity of Black aesthetics, as opposed to an originary, historical property that can be identified and recovered. Significantly, the maternity in materiality animates it and undoes distinctions between spirit and matter.
81 Karl Marx, *Capital: A Critique of Political Economy*, vol. 1, translated by Ben Fowkes (London: Penguin Books, 1990), 176.
82 Moten, *In the Break*, 8–12. Marx's fictional scenario of speaking commodities is meant to show the absurdity of assuming that commodities have inherent value; (exchange) value is determined only through human sociality, that is, given from an outside. Moten takes the figure of the slave who speaks/shrieks (and its recordings in Black artistic production) as an instance that disproves that theory and an entire science based on the dichotomy of the material and the immaterial, inside and outside. The impassioned shriek of the slave, the phonic irruption of the commodity and its re-generations in Black performances "embodies the critique of value, or private property, of the sign" and disrupts the law of equivalence, semiotics, or any other such sciences of universals.
83 Moten, *In the Break*, 5–6.
84 Thom Donovan, "A grave in exchange for the commons: Fred Moten and the resistance of the object," *Jacket2* (April 2011) http://jacket2.org/article/grave-exchange-commons.
85 Moten, *In the Break*, 26.
86 Simon Gikandi's "E. K. Brathwaite and the Poetics of the Voice: The Allegory of History in *Rights of Passage*," in *The Critical Response to Kamua Brathwaite*, edited by Emily Allen Williams (Westport: Praeger, 2004), 16.
87 Glissant quoted by Gikandi in "E. K. Brathwaite," 16. See also Édouard Glissant's *Caribbean Discourse: Selected Essays*, translated by Michael Dash (Charlottesville: University Press of Virginai, 1996), 120–130. Here he argues in favor of "opaque" strategies as a way to defy "a universalizing and reductive humanism," 133.
88 Gikandi, "E. K. Brathwaite," 16.
89 In addition to González Echevarría and Anderson, see José Piedra, "From Monkey Tales to Cuban Songs," in *Sacred Possessions: Vodou, Santería, Obeah, and the Caribbean*, edited by Margarite Fernández Olmos and Lizabeth Paravisini-Gerbert (New Brunswick: Rutgers University Press, 1997).
90 See note 27.
91 This is not to suggest that there is a void or an empty signifier, but rather, in thinking opacity or impenetrability, to undo the opposition and correspondence between

signifier and signified and the negative dialectic through which meaning is produced, to challenge the privileging of the signified.

92 Ruffinelli, *Poesía y descolonización,* 19; Dash, *The Other America,* 76.

93 Guillén, *Obra poética,* 103.

94 Guillén, *Páginas vueltas,* 83, quoted in Ruffinelli, *Poesía,* 50.

95 Tous, *La poesía de Nicolás Guillén,* 121. Ruffinelli, *Poesía,* 22.

96 See note 1.

97 Ruffinelli, *Poesía,* 51. Duno-Gottberg also notes that the musical instrument of the bongó, as a double drum, operates as a single, unifying voice of Blacks and Whites, while "Balada de los dos abuelos," annuls the confrontation between Blacks and Whites, *Solventando las diferencias,* 97. Following Duno-Gottberg's reading, not only is a binary symmetry of ancestors formulated in these poems, but lived material tensions are effectively dissolved.

98 Guillén, *Obra poética,* 103.

99 In the following pages I will elaborate further on the ironic adaptation of these codified stereotypes and how doing so consciously insists on a surface or inaccessibility.

100 Guillén, *Obra poética,* 108.

101 Guillén, *Obra poética,* 107.

102 Antonio D. Tillis, "Language as Vernacular, Cultural Performance in Black Communities in Cuba and the USA," *Estudos Anglo Americanos* 39 (2013), 152.

103 Emily Maguire, *Racial Experiments in Cuban Literature and Ethnography* (Gainesville: University Press of Florida, 2011), 104. Here she is drawing from Jorge Mañach's 1928 essay *Indagación del choteo.*

104 Pablo Neruda, *Canto general* (1950) http://www.literatura.us/neruda/general.pdf, 420.

105 Maguire, *Racial Experiments,* 115.

106 Jankélévitch, *Music and the Ineffable,* 21.

107 González Echevarría, "Guillén as Baroque," 311.

108 Arnedo-Gómez, "*Motivos de Son,*" 92. "En la crítica sobre Guillén existe cierta tendencia a asumir que, al ser mulato, el poeta consiguió representar a los afrocubanos y su cultura de una forma más auténtica que otros poetas afrocubanistas, quienes al ser blancos no fueron capaces de representar al negro cubano «desde dentro» o desde una perspectiva interna. Sin embargo, la supuesta interioridad de la perspectiva de Guillén en relación a los sectores de la población afrocubana sobre los que se enfocaba el afrocubanismo no puede legitimarse en base a su pertenencia a dichos sectores."

109 In *Uniting Blacks in a Raceless Nation,* Arnedo-Gómez writes, "as the scholarship of Antonio Cornejo Polar demonstrates, the exteriority of a group of writers with respect to the human groups they write about does not by itself justify dismissing their literature as a superficial or inaccurate representation," xxi.

110 Cited above, Moten, *In the Break,* 26.

111 Guillén, *Obra poética,* 105.

112 See Martin Jay, "The Disenchantment of the Eye in Surrealism and the Crisis of

Ocularcentrism," in *Visualizing Theory, Selected Essays from V.A.R. 1990–1994*, edited by Lucien Taylor (New York: Routledge, 1994).

113 Guillén, *Obra poética*, 104.

114 Fernando Ortiz, "Los últimos versos mulatos," 334, cited in Tous, *La poesía de Nicolás Guillén*, 123. My translation to the English.

115 Jean-François Lyotard, Adam Krims, and Henry James Klumpenhouwer, *Music/Ideology: Resisting the Aesthetic: Essays* (Amsterdam: G + B Arts International, 1998), 24.

116 Maguire, *Racial Experiments*, 112.

117 Guillén, *Obra poética*, 110.

118 Guillén, *Obra poética*, 105.

119 Maguire, *Racial Experiments*, 113.

120 Fernández, *From Afro-Cuban Rhythms to Latin Jazz*, 28.

121 Fernández, *From Afro-Cuban Rhythms to Latin Jazz*, 26.

122 Robert Farris Thompson, *Flash of the Spirit: African & African American Art & Philosophy* (New York: Random House, 1983), Introduction, passim.

123 The more obviously incantatory and sonorous poem of Guillén's is "Sensemayá: Canto para matar una culebra" (1934). I do not address this poem here because it more easily lends itself to readings linking it to specific cultural practices and beliefs (e.g. see Anderson cited above). My interest in *Motivos* is its insistence on artifice and the inability to recover from its archaic cultural properties.

124 Velimir Khlebnikov, *The King of Time: Selected Writings of the Russian Futurism*, translated by Paul Schmidt. (Cambridge: Harvard University Press, 1990), 152–154.

125 Jankélévitch, *Music and the Ineffable*, xviii.

126 Jankélévitch, *Music and the Ineffable*, 1.

127 González Echevarría, "Guillén as Baroque," 314.

128 González Echevarría, "Guillén as Baroque," 313.

129 Fernández, *From Afro-Cuban Rhythms to Latin Jazz*, 36–37.

130 González Echevarría, "Guillén as Baroque," 314.

131 See note 72.

132 Sarduy in Joaquín Soler Serrano, "Severo Sarduy, a fondo," *A Fondo* de RTVE, Ministerio de Cultura, Expte no. 63. 158, 1976.

133 González Echevarría, *La ruta de Severo* Sarduy, 83.

134 José Ortega y Gasset, "La deshumanización del arte," *Obras Completas José Ortega y Gasset*, Tomo III, 368–376 (Madrid: Revista de Occidente, 1994), 368.

135 Ortega y Gasset, "La deshumanización del arte," 368–376.

136 Severo Sarduy, *Gestos* (Barcelona: Editorial Seix Barral, 1963), 13.

137 Vicky Unruh, *Latin American Vanguards: The Art of Contentious Encounters* (Los Angeles: University of California Press, 1994), 21.

138 Eva Hayward and Jami Weinstein, "Introduction: Tranimalities in the Age of Trans* Life," *TSQ: Transgender Studies Quarterly* 2, 2 (2015), 195.

139 Sarduy, *Gestos*, 32.

140 Serrano, "Severo Sarduy, a fondo."

141 Rolando Pérez, *Severo Sarduy and the Religion of the Text* (Lanham: University of

America Press, 1988), 27. See also Roberto Fernández Retamar, *Calibán: Apuntes sobre la cultura en nuestra América* (Ciudad de México: Editorial Diógenes, 1972), 71.

142 Jean-Luc Nancy, "Corpus," in *Thinking Bodies,* edited by Juliet Flower MacCannell and Laura Zakarin (Stanford: Stanford University Press, 1994), 24. This was first presented at a conference on the body organized by the International Association for Philosophy and Literature at the University of California Irvine in 1990.

143 Nancy, "Corpus," 21.

144 Nancy, "Corpus," 31.

145 Serrano, "Severo Sarduy, a fondo."

146 Serrano, "Severo Sarduy, a fondo."

147 Nancy, "Corpus," 17.

148 Nancy, "Corpus," 27, 28.

149 Here I am drawing from Jonathan Burt's reading of Deleuze and Guattari's theory of the cinema of the in-between, where he explains that images in film are "material and integral" to our everyday relations in his article, "The Aesthetics of Livingness," 10.

150 Nancy, "Corpus," 24.

151 Sarduy, *Gestos,* 37–38.

152 Bennett's theory of "vibrant matter" informs my reading of this vignette in Sarduy's text. I will discuss her book "Vibrant Matter" (2010) further ahead.

153 Sarduy, "Gestos," 22–23.

154 Julían Ríos (ed.), *Severo Sarduy,* Espiral/Figuras (Madrid: Editorial Fundamentos, 1976) 10. The quote "pintar con palabras" is from Sarduy in "Severo Sarduy, a fondo."

155 Sarduy, "Gestos," 27.

156 In his description of contemporary art works that use or refer to the bodies of animals, Steve Baker uses the phrase "obstinate thereness" to describe the presence of an animal and its resistance to ready-made concepts. I find the phrase to be an apt description for how Nancy invokes the body.

157 Nancy, "Corpus," 24.

158 Nancy, "Corpus."

159 Sarduy, *Gestos,* 7.

160 Sarduy, *Gestos,* 32.

161 Sarduy, *Gestos,* 18.

162 In her reading of the text, Guerra writes, "se presentan a través de una voz narrativa despojada de toda opinión y saber, como figura contratextual del narrador realista y su proverbial omnisciencia. Se trata, más bien, de una mirada anónima, despojada de toda subjetividad" *Cuidad, género e imaginarios,* 257.

163 Nancy, "Corpus," 25.

164 Sarduy, *Gestos,* 56.

165 Sarduy, *Gestos,* 14.

166 Sarduy, *Gestos,* 7.

167 González Echevarría, *La ruta de Severo Sarduy,* 92.

168 González Echevarría, *La ruta de Severo Sarduy,* 91, 92.

169 Sarduy, *Gestos,* 7.
170 Sarduy, *Gestos.*
171 Sarduy, *Gestos,* 50.
172 See note 158.
173 Nancy, "Corpus," 28–31.
174 Nancy, "Corpus," 18.
175 Bennett, Vibrant Matter, viii
176 Bennett, Vibrant Matter, xvi.
177 Bennett, Vibrant Matter, viii.
178 Bennett, Vibrant Matter, xiii.
179 Gabriel Giorgi, *Formas comunes: Animalidad, cultura, biopolítica* (Buenos Aires: Eterna Cadencia Editora, 2014), 26.
180 Bennett, Vibrant Matter, 13.
181 Ian James, *The Fragmentary Demand: An Introduction to the Philosophy of Jean-Luc Nancy* (Stanford: Stanford University Press), 143.
182 James, *The Fragmentary Demand.*
183 Colas, *Toward an Ethics of Close Reading,* 173, 186.
184 Colas, *Toward an Ethics of Close Reading,* 184, 192.
185 Colas, *Toward an Ethics of Close Reading,* 173, 189.
186 Here I am drawing from Moten's treatment of racial difference as a material surplus and its continual reproduction, as the dominant culture tries to subordinate difference through appropriation. As I understand this, an example of such subordination through appropriation might be Modernist Primitivism (which influenced movements like *afrocubanismo*) in the work of artists such as Pablo Picasso. What in part made his art "avant-garde" was the appropriation of non-European forms made possible materially and rhetorically through colonialism. Considering that avant-gardism is couched in the notion of developmental history (and the presumed crossing of frontiers) puts it at odds, if not in opposition, to a Black politics. However, what Moten seems to insist on is that in this appropriation there is the (re)production of a surplus. Blackness and Black art is this surplus, an irreducible materiality, a material performative reproduction that is neither a property nor an object of knowledge. *In the break,* introduction, passim, 262.
187 Guillermina De Ferrari, "Embargoed Masculinities: Loyalty, Friendship and the Role of the Intellectual in Post-Soviet Cuban Novel," *Latin American Literary Review* 35, 69 (January–June 2007), 88.
188 Henken, *Cuba, 248.*

Chapter 2. Transmaterialities

1 Ovid, *The Metamorphoses,* translated into English prose by A.S. Kline (The Netherlands: Poetry in Translation, 2000), 9–11.
2 Ovid, *The Metamorphoses,* 12.
3 Elaine Fantham, *Ovid's Metamorphoses* (Oxford and New York: Oxford University Press, 2004), 6.

4 Karl G. Galinsky, *Ovid's Metamorphoses: An Introduction to the Basic Apects* (Berkeley and Los Angeles: University of California Press, 1975), 1.
5 For a list of transformations in *The Metamorphoses* from Ian Johnston's translation to the English (Arlington, VA: Richer Resources Publications, 2012) see http://records.viu.ca/~johnstoi/ovid/transformations.htm, accessed May 7, 2018.
6 Sarduy, *Cobra,* 20. All citations of the novel are taken from this edition.
7 The two works I am predominantly drawing from here, discussed in more depth in chapter 1, are Nancy's "Corpus," in *Thinking Bodies* and Bennett's *Vibrant Matter.*
8 Karen Barad, "Transmaterialities: Trans*/Matter/Realities and Queer Political Imaginings," *GLQ: A Journal of Lesbian and Gay Studies* 21 (2015), 411.
9 Ovid, *The Metamorphoses,* 9.
10 While this term is taken from the fragment of Karen Barad's essay cited in the epigraph, Eva Hayward provides us with a useful elaboration on the significance of Trans* in "Introduction: Tranimalities in the Age of Trans* Life," cited in chapter 1. "Trans* foregrounds and intensifies the prehensile, prefixial nature of trans- and implies a suffixial space of attachment that is simultaneously generalizable and abstract yet its function can be enacted only when taken up by particular objects (though never any one object in particular): trans* is thus more than and equal to one. [. . .] The sticky tentacularity of '*' signals not the primacy of 'the human' [. . .] but the eventualization of life. If trans* is ontological, it is that insofar as it is the movement that produces beingness. In other words, trans* is not a thing or being, it is rather the processes through which thingness and beingness are constituted. In its prefixial state, trans* is prepositionally oriented—marking the with, through, of, in, and across that make life possible," 196.
11 Bennett, *Vibrant Matter,* xiii.
12 See note 2.
13 Barad, *Transmaterialities,* 395.
14 I am drawing from Gilles Deleuze's *Difference and Repetition,* translated by Paul Patton (New York: Columbia University Press, 1994) to better understand Barad's theorization of the virtual particles via QFT (214).
15 Barad, "Transmaterialities," 393, 395, 410.
16 W.J.T. Mitchell, "Illusion: Looking at Animals Looking," in *Picture Theory: Essays on Verbal and Visual Representation* (Chicago: University of Chicago Press, 1994), 342.
17 The single point perspective was typically placed at the eye level of someone who measured 5ft9in, since this was the average height of an Italian man in the 15th century.
18 Aristotle, *Poetics* (Chicago: Dover Thrift Editions, 1997), 15, 40.
19 Aristotle, *Poetics,* 15.
20 Alejo Carpentier, "The Baroque and the Marvelous Real," in *Magical Realism,* edited by Lois Parkinson Zamora and Wendy B Faris (Durham: Duke University Press, 1995) 92, 93.
21 See Severo Sarduy, *Ensayos generales sobre el barroco* (Buenos Aires: Fondo de Cultura Económica USA, 1987).

22 Mercedes Sarduy, *Severo Sarduy: Cartas a mi hermana La Habana* (Coral Gables: Severo Sarduy Cultural Foundation, 2013), 73.
23 Sarduy, *Cobra,* 47, 56.
24 Pedro de Jesús, *Imagen y libertad vigilada: Ejercicios de retórica sobre Severo Sarduy* (La Habana: Editorial Letras Cubanas, 2014), 71.
25 Sarduy, *Cobra,* 32.
26 Images for this series are reproduced in *Fabelo's Anatomy,* Museum of Latin American Art Long Beach exhibition catalogue (2014), 36.
27 Collado Otero, essay contribution to *Fabelo's Anatomy,* 36.
28 Ernesto Che Guevara, "El socialismo y el hombre en Cuba (1965)," https://www.marxists.org/espanol/guevara/65-socyh.htm#n*. Translations from the Spanish are mine.
29 See the book's introduction, note 20.
30 Guevara, "El socialismo y el hombre en Cuba."
31 Sarduy, *Cobra,* 12.
32 Sarduy, *Cobra,* 65, 66. More on this passage to follow.
33 Ovid, *The Metamorphoses,* 9.
34 Sarduy, *Cobra,* 11.
35 Sarduy, *Cobra.*
36 Peter Hallward, *Absolutely Postcolonial: Writing Between the Singular and the Specific* (Manchester: Manchester University Press, 2001) , 290.
37 Sarduy, *Cobra,* 66.
38 Emir Rodríguez Monegal, "Metamorphoses of the text," *Review 74: Focus on Cobra* (Winter 1974), *16.*
39 Monegal, "Metamorphoses of the text."
40 Sarduy, *Cobra,* 33.
41 Karen Barad, "Posthumanist Performativity: Toward an Understanding of How Matter Comes to Matter," *Signs: Journals of Women in Culture and Society* 28, 3 (2003), 802.
42 Sarduy, *Cobra,* 49.
43 See Rodríguez Monegal, "Metamorphoses of the text," and González Echevarría, "Rehearsal for Cobra," in *Review 74: Focus on Cobra,* Winter (1974), as well as Suzanne Jill Levine's preface to *Cobra* and *Maitreya* (Normal: Dalkey Archive Press, 1995). The four experimental painters, as well as the poem by Paz, appear in the novel. Sarduy, *Cobra,* 136, 229.
44 Philippe Sollers uses the metaphor of "pulverized rock" and "concentric vibrations" to describe this quality of layered, concentrated meanings of individual words in *Cobra* in "La Boca Obra," in *Review 74: Focus on Cobra,* Winter (1974), 13.
45 González Echevarría, "Rehearsal for Cobra," 41.
46 González Echevarría, "Rehearsal for Cobra."
47 Sarduy is cited in Enrique Márquez, "Cobra: De aquel oscuro objeto del deseo," *Revista Iberoamericana* 154 (enero-marzo 1991), 310.
48 See the *Review 74: Focus on Cobra,* Winter (1974) issue.
49 Suzanne Jill Levine, "Discourse as Bricolage," *Review 74: Focus on Cobra* (Winter

1974), 33. I would like to note that while Levine's analysis reproduces the negative dialectics of language, she concludes by associating *Cobra* to a Nietzschean affirmation which would correspond to the New Materialist notion of plenitude.

50 Márquez, "Cobra: De aquel oscuro objeto del deseo," 302.
51 Márquez, "Cobra: De aquel oscuro objeto del deseo."
52 Severo Sarduy, *La simulación* (Caracas: Monte Ávila Editores, 1982), 20.
53 For more on *lettericity,* see chapter 1, section "Writing, Painting, Matter," where I cite Jean-Luc Nancy.
54 In my allusion to malformed pearls I'm taking inspiration from the word "Barroco." Sarduy writes "del barroco perdura la imagen nudosa de la gran perla irregular—del portugués *barroco*—, el áspero conglomerado rocoso—del español *berrueco.*" *Ensayos generales sobre el barroco,* 149.
55 Sarduy, *Cobra,* 11.
56 Sarduy, *Cobra.*
57 Sarduy, *Cobra,* 16.
58 Sarduy, *Cobra.*
59 Sarduy, *Cobra,* 16–17.
60 Sarduy, *Cobra,* 21
61 Sarduy, *Cobra,* 26.
62 Sarduy, *Cobra,* 12.
63 See note 49.
64 Sarduy, *Cobra,* 59.
65 Daniel Miller (ed.), *Materiality* (Durham: Duke University Press, 2005), 1.
66 Sarduy, *La simulación,* 20. See also Pérez, *Severo Sarduy and the Neo-Baroque,* 4, 5.
67 Sarduy, *Cobra,* 11, 14.
68 Rolando Pérez, *Severo Sarduy and the Neo-Baroque Image in the Visual Arts* (West Lafayette: Purdue University Press, 2012), 4. Pérez is drawing from Sarduy's text, *La simulación,* which I cite in the section, "Cataloguing Cobra from Frozen Orchids to Asthmatic Bishops," note 52.
69 See Roland Barthes, *The Pleasure of the Text,* translated by Richard Miller (New York: Hill and Wang, 1975).
70 In Sarduy's text *La simulación,* transvestism is a self-effacement, a disappearance, like the insect's camouflage. It also is not an imitation of an already existing model, or determined reality, for there is no "woman," only ever an icon, or an "infinite irreality," 14. Sarduy's association of human transvestism to the insect is especially interesting to keep in mind when I turn to the work of Roberto Fabelo in the second half of this chapter. We will see how insects and their metamorphic potential figure prominently in his art.
71 Pérez, *Severo Sarduy and the Neo-Baroque,* "The (eccentric) transvestite figure demands to be read eccentrically, and in so doing it forces us—perhaps disturbingly—to move from our comfortable position to one that actively transforms us. Ethically and philosophically, Sarduy makes us take note that there is no such thing as an 'innocent,' normative position, but that instead every point of view reflects an aesthetic," 35.

72 Sarduy, *Cobra*, 11.
73 Sarduy, *Cobra*, 12.
74 Donna J. Haraway, *Simians, Cyborgs, and Women: The Reinvention of Nature* (New York: Routledge, 1991), 152.
75 "Severo Sarduy, a fondo." Also cited in chapter 1.
76 Sarduy, *Cobra*, 126.
77 Sarduy, *Cobra*.
78 Sarduy, *Cobra*, 61–62.
79 Sarduy, *Cobra*, 65.
80 Sarduy, *Cobra*, 62–63.
81 I'm drawing here again from Barad's notion of transmaterialities and QFT, discussed in the introduction of the chapter.
82 Terms such as "castration" and "conversion," as opposed to "Sex Confirmation Surgery" or "Transgender-Sex Reassignment," are used to be consistent with the historical context of the novel and the language in the text.
83 Sarduy, *Cobra*, 85, footnote.
84 Sarduy, *Cobra*, 106–108.
85 Sarduy, *Cobra*, 106.
86 Sarduy, *Cobra*, 115.
87 Teresa Brennan, *The Transmission of Affect* (Ithaca: Cornell University Press, 2004), 29. "A projection is what I disown in myself and see in you; a projective identification is what I succeed in having you experience in yourself, although it comes from me in the first place."
88 My use of the terms cosubstantial and enfleshment come from Elizabeth Povinelli, *Economies of Abandonment: Social Belonging and Endurance in Late Liberalism* (Durham: Duke University Press, 2011), 4.
89 Carpentier, "The Baroque and the Marvelous Real," 89–108.
90 Carpentier, "The Baroque and the Marvelous Real," 92–93.
91 Anthony Vidler, "The Smooth and the Rough: Surfaces Psychological and Architectural from Adrian Stokes to Rem Koolhaas," School of Criticism and Theory, Cornell, July 12, 2017.
92 Adrian Stokes, *Smooth and Rough* (London: Faber & Faber, 1951), 243.
93 Sarduy, *Cobra*, 30.
94 Sarduy, *Cobra*, 34.
95 See the introduction.
96 Sarduy, *Cobra*, 187.
97 Sarduy, *Cobra*, 190.
98 Sarduy, *Cobra*, 11.
99 Sarduy, *Cobra*, 190.
100 Sarduy, *Cobra*, 34.
101 Sarduy, *Cobra*, 196–197.
102 Steve Baker, *The Postmodern Animal* (London: Reaktion Books, 2000), chapt. 1, passim.
103 Baker, *The Postmodern Animal*, 54–61.

104 Baker, *The Postmodern Animal*. Clumsy suturing does not apply to all these artists; Thomas Grünfeld's pieces are seamless and very carefully constructed.
105 Baker, *The Postmodern Animal*.
106 Achille Mbembe, "Necropolitics," *Public Culture* 15, 1 (2003), 13–15.
107 Mbembe, "Necropolitics," 11, 17.
108 Baker, *The Postmodern Animal*, 19, chapt. 1, passim.
109 Gregory Bateson, *Steps Towards an Ecology of Mind: Collected Essays in Anthropology, Psychiatry, Evolution, and Epistemology* (London: Jason Aronson, 1972), 120.
110 Braidotti, *Metamorphoses: Towards a Materialist Theory of Becoming*, 139–142.
111 I'm borrowing the difference between figure and figurative from Steve Baker, 141.
112 Braidotti, *Metamorphoses*, 139, 140.
113 Bateson, *Steps Towards an Ecology*, 110.
114 Bateson, *Steps Towards an Ecology*, Introduction, passim.
115 Bateson, *Steps Towards an Ecology*, 114.
116 Bateson, *Steps Towards an Ecology*, 119.
117 Bateson, *Steps Towards an Ecology*.
118 Bateson, *Steps Towards an Ecology*.
119 Bateson, *Steps Towards an Ecology*, 108, 119.
120 Braidotti, *Metamorphoses*, 133.
121 Braidotti, *Metamorphoses*, 132, 133.
122 Braidotti, *Metamorphoses*, 133.
123 Braidotti, *Metamorphoses*.
124 Mbembe, *Necropolitics*, 14.
125 Mbembe, *Necropolitics*.
126 Ron Broglio, "'Living Flesh': Animal-Human Surfaces," *Journa of Visual Culture* 7, 1 (2008), 110.
127 *Fabelo's Anatomy*, 16.
128 As I suggested in the introduction of this chapter, the encyclopedia operates as a symbolic object of the Enlightenment, its predilection for scientific knowledge and classifications, and the modernizing projects it spawned, of which eugenics was just one of its outcomes. To tamper, then, with the authoritative knowledge of the encyclopedia and to illustrate human-animal bodies in a web of interconnections presents a challenge to a science of compartmentalization on which a necropolitics relies.
129 *Fabelo's Anatomy*, 16.
130 Giovanni Aloi, in his lecture "On a Wing and a Prayer: Butterflies in Contemporary Art," at the Natural History Museum in London, April 2014, describes the inherent violence in the production of natural science illustrations of butterflies and how the flattening of the butterfly serves our visual vantage point.
131 See note 101.
132 Mitchell, "Illusion: Looking at Animals Looking," 332–335.
133 Cary Wolfe, *Animal Rites: American Culture, the Discourse of Species, and Posthumanist Theory*, forward by W.J.T. Mitchell (Chicago: University of Chicago Press, 2003), 19, 20.

134 Nancy, "Corpus," 19.
135 Nancy, "Corpus."
136 For more on the in-distinction between human flesh and animal meat see James Goebel's essay on "Uncanny Meat," *French Journal of English Studies* 55 (2016).
137 Monica E. Kupfer, "Roberto Fabelo," *Art Nexus* 82, 128 (Septmeber/November 2011), 147.
138 Gilles Deleuze and Félix Guattari, *Kafka: Toward a Minor Literature* (Minneapolis: University of Minnesota Press, 1987), 7.
139 Deleuze and Guattari, *Kafka,* 13.
140 Braidotti, *Metamorphoses,* 118.
141 Deleuze, *Francis Bacon*, 32. In her book, *Surface: Matters of Aesthetics, Materiality, and Media* (Chicago: University of Chicago Press, 2014), Giuliana Bruno writes with regard to depth, "[T]he motion of an emotion can itself be drafted onto the surface, in the shape of a line or in the haptic thickness of pigment [. . .]. An affect is actually 'worn' on the surface as it is threaded through time in the form of residual stains, traces, and textures. In visual culture, surface matters, and it has depth. [. . .] On this material level [. . .] distinctions between inside and outside temporarily dissolve into depth of surface," 5.
142 Braidotti, *Metamorphoses,* 149.
143 Caridad Blanco de la Cruz, "Roberto Fabelo," *Art Nexus* 60, 5 (2006), 130.
144 David John Carton, "Giant Mutant Cockroaches," *Fotolibra*, http://www.fotolibra.com/gallery/533546/giant-mutant-cockroaches-havana, accessed July 7, 2017.
145 "Montaje de Sobrevivientes," *Museo Nacional de Bellas Artes,* 10 Edición de la Bienal de la Habana, Video, March 2009. http://www.youtube.com/watch?v=ZZVWmzY4sPY
146 Gabriele Schwab, "Haunting from the Future: Psychic Life in Wake of Nuclear Necropolitics," *The Undecidable Unconscious: A Journal of Deconstruction and* Psychoanalysis 1 (2014), 85–101.
147 "Montaje de Sobrevivientes."
148 Esther Katheryn Whitfield, *Cuban Currency: The Dollar and "Special Period" Fiction,* vol. 21. (Minneapolis: University of Minnesota Press, 2008), 143.
149 Ernesto "Che" Guevara, "El socialismo y el hombre en Cuba," cited in Arnaldo Cruz-Malavé, "Lecciones de cub*anía*: Identidad nacional y errancia sexual en Senel Paz, Martí y Lezama Lima." *Cuban Studies* 29 (Jan 01, 1999), 133.
150 In her analysis of *el hombre nuevo*, Marta Hernández Salván highlights an ethos of self-sacrifice and heroic righteousness in *Mínima Cuba: Heretical Poetics and Power in Post-Soviet Cuba* (Albany: SUNY Press, 2015), 48, 49.
151 In her dissertation chapter, "De testimonios y de reos: Biopolítica y Revolución. El seropositivo cubano," (Universidad de Santiago de Compostela, 2015) Suquet Martínez explains how Cuban Revolution's strong public health policy (and its corresponding moral codes) manifested itself in the medicalization of the New Man as an immune man, 303.
152 See Nancy's "Corpus" (cited above and in chapter 1) for a deconstruction of a Christian metaphysics and the unity of the sign and the body.

Chapter 3. Inhuman Writings

1 Ena Lucía Portela, *El pájaro: Pincel y tinta china* (Barcelona: Editorial Casiopea, 1998), 178.
2 I am drawing from Nancy, "Corpus," discussed in chapt. 1, section "Writing, Painting, Matter," note 158.
3 "Montaje de Sobrevivientes," *Museo Nacional de Bellas Artes,* Video, March 2009.
4 Schwab, "Haunting from the Future," 85–101.
5 Whitfield, *Cuban Currency,*143.
6 Antonio José Ponte, *La fiesta vigilada* (Barcelona: Editorial Anagrama, 2007) 187, 188. All translations from Spanish to English are mine.
7 Whitfield, *Cuban Currency*, 143. María Guadalupe Silva, "Antonio José Ponte: El espacio como texto," *Iberoamericana* 14, 53 (2014), 76.
8 Jean-François Lyotard, *The Inhuman: Reflections on time*, translated by Geoffrey Bennington and Rachel Bowlby (Stanford: Stanford University Press, 1991), 12.
9 Lyotard, *The Inhuman*, 18–19.
10 Maxwell Hearn, The Metropolitan Museum of Art History, Heilbrunn Timeline of Art History, Chinese Painting, https://www.metmuseum.org/toah/hd/chin/hd_chin.htm.
11 Hearn, The Metropolitan Museum of Art History.
12 Hearn, The Metropolitan Museum of Art History.
13 Hearn, The Metropolitan Museum of Art History.
14 Portela, *El pájaro,* 21, 38, 185.
15 Portela, *El pájaro*, 227.
16 Nancy, "Corpus," 28–31. The implications of this phrase are elaborated in chapt. 1, section "The Art of Assemblage."
17 For an exhaustive list of Portela's intertextual references in *El pájaro*, desacralization of the canon, and self-parody see Nara Araújo, "Erizar y diverter: La poética de Ena Lucía Portela," *Cuban Studies* 32 (2001), 61, 62.
18 Nancy, "Corpus," 24. *Lettericity* is discussed in chapter 1, section "Writing, Painting, Matter."
19 Lyotard elaborates his theory on the suffering of the unthought specifically with regard to the calligrapher, *The Inhuman,* 18–20.
20 Lyotard, *The Inhuman.*
21 Portela, *El pájaro*, 28.
22 Portela, *El pájaro*, 183.
23 Portela, *El pájaro*, 30.
24 Portela, *El pájaro*, 29.
25 Portela, *El pájaro*, 30.
26 Portela, *El pájaro*, 30, 31.
27 Odette Casamayor-Cisneros, "Incertidumbre resplandeciente. Breve incursión en la narrativa escrita durante la década durante del 90 en la Isla de Cuba," *Caravelle* 78 (June 200), 190. With regard to Portela's characters in *El pájaro*, Casamayor-Cisneros writes, "Ningún estigma es evidente en ellos y es difícil encontrar una lógica

cualquiera a su alejamiento del cuerpo social. En realidad, este extrañamiento no es bien definido. Se trata más bien de un flotar en sociedad, de un estar sin asumirlo realmente. [. . .] Esta literatura no pertenece a nada ni a nadie. Se pierde en ella toda noción de grupo."

28 Portela, *El pájaro*, 29.
29 See Aristotle, *Poetics*.
30 Guevara, "El socialismo y el hombre en Cuba," 1965, https://www.marxists.org/espanol/guevara/65-socyh.htm#n*. Discussed in the introduction to chapter 2.
31 Guevara, "El socialismo y el hombre en Cuba," 176.
32 Guevara, "El socialismo y el hombre en Cuba," 46.
33 Joseph S. Salemi, "Kalos Kai Agathos," *The Pennsylvania Review* (May 2009).
34 Portela, *El pájaro*, 73.
35 In second half of this chapter, section "Inhabited Ruins," Ponte will cite the philosopher George Simmel, who offers a theorization of cultural production as the transcendence of human spirit over nature, or mere material subsistence. For an analysis of the artist and the animal, as both participating in discourse and materially interdependent on a territory, see Braidotti, *Metamorphoses*, 132–133. Also discussed in chapter 2, section "Thinking Ecologically."
36 Castro, "Palabras a los intelectuales." Also cited in the introduction to chapter 1.
37 Portela, *El pájaro*, 22.
38 Portela, *El pájaro*, 146.
39 Portela, *El pájaro*, 32, 58, 106, 46, 195, 44, 138, 119, 39, 36, 37, 43.
40 Portela, *El pájaro*, 124.
41 Portela, *El pájaro*, 182. Lucian Taylor, ed., *Visualizing Theory*, xiv.
42 Portela, *El pájaro*, 131.
43 Chiara Bolognese, "El pájaro: Pincel y tinta china de Ena Lucía Portela: Escritura y cuerpo en escene," *Mitologías hoy* 10 (Winter 2014), 52. In her description of narrative strategies, Bolognese writes, "Queda claro que la autora nos confunde constantemente con las diferentes instancias narrativas: la voz del narrador es, según la situación, la de Emilio U, la de Fabián, o la de un narrador omnisciente extradiegético, de una narradora, o de un narrador metadiegético."
44 Mitchell, "Illusion: Looking at Animals Looking," 332–335.
45 Mitchell, "Illusion," 332–342.
46 By interdependence and territory, I mean both the material resources the writer depends on to subsist and write—Portela notes that the greatest challenge to writers in Cuba during the 90s was not the threat of censorship but the lack of paper—their situatedness historically and geographically, and literary tradition. Portela is cited by Iraida H. López in the prologue to *El Viejo, el asesino, y yo y otros cuentos*, edited by Iraida H. López (Doral: Stockero, 2009), vii.
47 Portela, *El pájaro*, 195.
48 Portela, *El pájaro*, 36, 37.
49 Portela, *El pájaro*, 37.
50 Bolognese, "El pájaro," 51.
51 Portela, *El pájaro*, 25, 26, 21.

52 Portela, *El pájaro*, 21.
53 Portela, *El pájaro*, 22.
54 Portela, *El pájaro*, 37
55 Portela, *El pájaro*, 39.
56 Portela, *El pájaro*, 37, 24, 22.
57 Portela, *El pájaro*, 37.
58 Portela, *El pájaro*, 43.
59 See chapter 1, sections "Writing, Painting, Matter" and "The Art of Assemblage."
60 See chapter 2, section "Cataloguing *Cobra* from Frozen Orchids to Asthmatic Bishops."
61 Douglas Harper, Online Etymology Dictionary, last updates August 29, 2023, https://www.etymonline.com/search?q=kaleidoscope.
62 Portela, *El pájaro*, 43.
63 Portela, *El pájaro*, 44.
64 Portela, *El pájaro*.
65 Portela, *El pájaro*, 64.
66 Portela, *El pájaro*, 72.
67 Portela, *El pájaro*, 47, 52, 53.
68 Giorgi, *Formas comunes,* 26. Also cited in chapter 1.
69 Giorgi, *Formas comunes*, 58.
70 Giorgi, *Formas comunes*, 62.
71 Giorgi, *Formas comunes*, 58.
72 Bolognese also reads the "el ciudadano modelo" as a clear allusion to Che's *hombre nuevo*, "*El pájaro*," 54.
73 Portela, *El pájaro*, 59.
74 Portela, *El pájaro,* 73.
75 Portela, *El pájaro*, 72.
76 Portela, *El pájaro*, 73.
77 Portela, *El pájaro*, 75.
78 Portela, *El pájaro*, 81.
79 Portela, *El pájaro*, 64, 72.
80 Portela, *El pájaro*, 63.
81 Portela, *El pájaro*, 61
82 See André Breton, "First Manifesto of Surrealism," *In Art in Theory 1900–1900: An Anthology of Chnaging Ideas*, edited by Charles Harrison and Paul Woods (Malden: Blackwell Publishers, 1992), 87–88.
83 Portela, *El pájaro*, 61.
84 Portela, *El pájaro*, 62, 63.
85 Nancy, "Corpus," 27, 28. Discussed in chapter 1, section "Reading as Touching."
86 Portela, *El* pájaro, 71. We might also interpret this desire to forget as Portela's own, given that she also experienced a series of neurological examinations before she was diagnosed with Parkinson's disease. In "Alas rotas" reproduced in *El Viejo,* Portela gives an account of her diagnoses and subsequent treatment, 123–127. Bolognese

also argues that Camila's paralysis is akin to the symptoms of Parkinson's, "El pájaro," 51.

87 Portela, *El pájaro*, 73.
88 Portela, *El pájaro*, 75.
89 Portela, *El pájaro*, 85.
90 Portela, *El pájaro*, 78.
91 Portela, *El pájaro*, 78.
92 Portela, *El pájaro*, 103.
93 Portela, *El pájaro*, 85.
94 See note 67.
95 Portela, *El pájaro*, 106.
96 Camila is again referred to after her escape from the hospital as "nuestro animalejo" and "nuestro bichito." Portela, *El pájaro*, 128, 129.
97 Portela, *El pájaro*, 74. Later the narrator states Camila, "optará por vivir durante algún tiempo," 246, and describes her as, "Muchacha viscosa hasta escalofrío, sobreviviente de prácticas brutales, radiaciones, anestesias, en cuya pancita o sueño de razón se engendraban monstruos," 261. In keeping with the art historical references and allusions to visuality, in this quote Portela imbeds a reference to Francisco Goya's 1799 engraving, "El sueño de la razón produce monstruos." More to the point, this reference also shows how the work of author is not transcendent, but interdependent on a territory, in this case networks of literary and visual culture.
98 Casamayor-Cisneros, "Incertidumbre resplandeciente," 190.
99 Cisneros, "Incertidumbre resplandeciente."
100 The story that Camila is read, from an anthology she is gifted at the hospital by Bibiana, is authored in the narrative by Emilio U and titled "La urna y el nombre: un cuento jovial." The story is in fact written by Ena Lucía Portela. In her reading, Bolognese notes that Camila's inexplicable recovery, "sin que haya una razón médica," follows her having been read the story and is, therefore, indicative of Portela's relating writing to life, or of writing providing the impetus to survive. "Escritura y cuerpo," 53.
101 Portela, *El pájaro*, 106.
102 Portela, *El pájaro*, 77.
103 Portela, *El pájaro*.
104 Portela, *El pájaro*, 102.
105 Roberto Fabelo's painting *Perla* discussed in chapter 2 also presents human bodies as edible meat. See also Goebel, "Uncanny Meat."
106 Giorgi, *Formas comunes*, 11–16. See also chapter 4, section "Meaty Bodies."
107 Portela, *El pájaro*, 102.
108 Portela, *El pájaro*.
109 Portela, *El pájaro*, 182.
110 Portela, *El pájaro*, 178.
111 Portela, *El pájaro*, 179.
112 Portela, *El pájaro*, 182.
113 Portela, *El pájaro*, 176.

114 Portela, *El pájaro*, 157
115 Portela, *El pájaro*, 156, 157.
116 Portela, *El pájaro*, 108, 109.
117 Portela, *El pájaro*, 132.
118 Portela, *El pájaro*, 107, 108.
119 Portela, *El pájaro*, 176.
120 Portela, *El pájaro*, 152, 153.
121 Portela, *El pájaro*, 160.
122 Portela, *El pájaro*, 119, 120.
123 Portela, *El pájaro*, 58.
124 Portela, *El pájaro*, 257.
125 Portela, *El pájaro*, 267.
126 Portela, *El pájaro*, 97.
127 Ponte, *La fiesta*, 31.
128 Ponte, *La fiesta*.
129 Ponte, *La fiesta*, 40–47.
130 See Adriana Kanzepolsky, "¿Yo no soy el tema de mi libro? *La fiesta vigilada* de Antonio José Ponte," *Abehache* 1–2 (2011) for a reading of how Ponte complicates the conventions of autobiography.
131 Ponte, *La fiesta*, 120, 121.
132 Ponte, *La fiesta*, 66, 126.
133 Ponte, *La fiesta*, 121.
134 Ponte, *La fiesta*, 66.
135 Ponte, *La fiesta*, 66, 67.
136 Ponte, *La fiesta*, 122.
137 Ponte, *La fiesta*, 65.
138 "Jean Paul Sartre no se equivocó al conjeturar que, de no existir los Estados Unidos de América, la revolución cubana se los habría inventado. La proximidad norteamericana (proximidad que es peligro) es incesantemente recordada en las alocuciones revolucionarias. Y, para un pensamiento así, La Habana es menos ciudad viva que paisaje de legitimación política," 204. See Rob Nixon, *Slow Violence and the Environmentalism of the Poor* (Cambridge: Harvard University Press, 2011). Within the context of Cuba we can point to the debilitating economic constraints imposed by the US embargo and (as per Ponte) the Cuban State's willful neglect to improve living conditions as forms of unspectacular violence. As we'll see further ahead, Ponte's account is also a testament to processes of social death in the form of criminalization, expulsion, and censorship. The above quote speaks to a politics of clearly defined antagonists; such a binary distinction (recalling here Castro's 1971 quote) produces a context of vigilance and policing.
139 Brad Evans and Henry A. Giroux, *Disposable Futures: The Seduction of Violence in the Age of Spectacle* (San Francisco: City Lights Books, 2015), 45, 46.
140 Néstor Almendros and Orlando Jiménez-Leal, *Conducta impropia* (Barcelona: Eagles Editorial, 2008).

141 Georges Bataille, *The Accursed Share,* Volume 1, 2 & 3, translated by Robert Hurley (Zone Books, 1993), 21.
142 Bataille, *The Accursed Share.*
143 See note 6.
144 Bataille, *The Accursed Share*, 25, 26.
145 Ponte, *La fiesta*, 127.
146 Ponte, *La fiesta*, 46.
147 Ponte, *La fiesta*, 33.
148 Ponte, *La fiesta*, 30, 31.
149 Ponte, *La fiesta*, 31.
150 Ponte, *La fiesta*, 30.
151 Ponte, *La fiesta*, 31.
152 Ponte, *La fiesta*, 65.
153 Ponte, *La fiesta*, 65, 66.
154 Ponte, *La fiesta*, 71.
155 Ponte, *La fiesta*, 174.
156 Ponte, *La fiesta*, 203.
157 Ponte, *La fiesta*, 48.
158 On the destructiveness of compartmentalization and mere purposive rationality see Bateson, *Steps Towards an Ecology of Mind:* 119, cited in chapter 2. For the concepts *cosubstantial* and *enfleshment* see Povinelli, *Economies of Abandonment.*
159 Ponte, *La fiesta*, 81.
160 Ponte, *La fiesta*, 73.
161 Ponte, *La fiesta*, 167, 168.
162 Ponte, *La fiesta*, 174.
163 Ponte, *La fiesta.*
164 Ponte, *La fiesta.*
165 Ponte, *La fiesta*, 148.
166 Ponte, *La fiesta*, 174. In addition to the novel, these processes and relationships are the subject of Ponte's short story, "Un arte de hacer ruinas," *Un arte de hacer ruinas y otros cuentos.* See Borchmeyer's 2006 documentary, *Arte nuevo de hacer ruinas*, which features Ponte. See also Whitfield's description of *solares* in texts by Pedro Juan Gutiérrez, where she describes them as "animated" by their inhabitants, *Cuban Currency*, 106.
167 Ponte, *La fiesta*, 164.
168 Ponte, *La fiesta*, 175.
169 Ponte, *La fiesta*, 148.
170 Ponte, *La fiesta*, 72.
171 Ponte, *La fiesta*, 145.
172 Ponte, *La fiesta*, 175,
173 Ponte, *La fiesta*, 28, 91, 15.
174 Ponte, *La fiesta*, 15.
175 Ponte, *La fiesta*, 161.
176 Ponte, *La fiesta.*

177 Ponte, *La fiesta*, 165.
178 Ponte, *La fiesta*, 166.
179 Ponte, *La fiesta*, 205–239.
180 Whitfield, *Cuban Currency*, 144.
181 Symptomatic of this compartmentalizing logic, we might recall, in addition to the 1960s forced labor camps (UMAPs), the Cuban state's involuntary quarantines for those infected with HIV in the 1980s.
182 Ponte, *La fiesta*, 239.
183 I want to thank George Allen for prompting me to consider the relationship between writing and the dwellers of the ruins.
184 Whitfield, *Cuban Currency*, 106, 107.
185 Bennett, *Vibrant Matter*, xiii. Also discussed in chapter 1, section "Vibrant Corpse."
186 Bennett, *Vibrant Matter*.
187 Bennett, *Vibrant Matter,* 4.
188 Ponte, *La fiesta*, 145.
189 Ponte, *La fiesta*.
190 Ponte, *La fiesta*.
191 Ponte, *La fiesta*, 173.
192 Bennett, *Vibrant Matter*, xvi.
193 Brizuela, "Sense of Place," 62.
194 See note 30.
195 See the book's introduction, note 20.

Chapter 4. Eat Me

1 Ahmel Echevarría, *Búfalos camino al matadero* (Santiago: Editorial Oriente, 2013), 98.
2 Echevarría, *Búfalos*, 99.
3 Echevarría, *Búfalos*, 98.
4 See chapter 1, section "The Logic of Incorporation."
5 This reading of Lezama Lima's use of the verb *incorporar* as *comer* and *templar* comes from Ponte's *Las comidas profundas*. The elaboration of what it implicitly refers to as "a metabolic process of change and corporeal expenditure" is my own. De Maesneer also includes an analysis of Ponte's reading of Lezama Lima in her book *Devorando a lo cubano*. Both texts are cited in the book's introduction.
6 For an analysis of *La noria*, see Mónica Simal, "*La noria* de Ahmel Echevarría Peré o la máquina contra el olvido," *Revista LETRAL* 18 (2017). For one on *Días de entrenamiento*, see Nanne Timmer, "Sujeto y comunidad: Voz, isla y muetre en la narrativa cubana del siglo XXI," *Mitologías hoy* 12 (Winter 2015). Emily Maguire includes an analysis of his short story "Cuba in Splinters" in "Temporal Palimpsests: Irrealism in Generation Zero's *Cuba in Splinters*," *Revista de Estudios Hispánicos* 2 (June 2017).
7 Rafeal Rojas, "Cuba la historia en rebanadas," *El Cultural* (Suplemento de La Razón)

338, December 2, 2022, 6–7, https://www.razon.com.mx/220211/cultural-338, accessed February 10, 2022.

8 In addition to not treating animals as symbolic stand-ins for a humancentric drama, or symbolic codes that presumes accesses to a deeper, more static being, a cartographic approach is horizontal, aesthetic, and attends to relationships, points of touch and transformations. See chapt. 2, section "Ecological Thinking."

9 Cristóbal Colón, *La carta de Colón: Anunciando el descubrimiento* (Barcelona: Linkgua Ediciones, 2007), domingo 4 de noviembre.

10 As late as the early twentieth century, United States propaganda made claims of cannibalism and primitivism for invading and occupying Haiti. They also claimed to bring civilization to Puerto Rico. See Dayan's essay "Vodoun, or the Voice of the Gods," in *Sacred Possessions,* as well as the 2020 documentary *Landfall* by Cecilia Aldarondo. Aside from these explicit deployments of the civilization/barbarism dichotomy, more generally what is globally recognized as development is a specific technological development, positivist views of the world, and participation within capitalist economies. Further ahead in this section, we see how Fidel Castro also deploys the concept and assumes technological advancement and a scientific education as the mark of progress.

11 For examples of the cannibal, as representative of the opposite of civilization, in addition to Columbus, see Bartolomé de las Casas, *Brevísima relación de la destrucción de las Indias*, edited by André Saint-Lu (Madrid: Ediciones Cátedra, 2003); Theodor de Bry's engravings printed in *Collected travels in the East Indies and West Indies* (1594), https://smarthistory.org/engravings-theodore-de-bry/.; Jan van der Straet's engraving, "Allegory of America" ca. 1587–89, https://www.metmuseum.org/art/collection/search/343845. For alphabetic writing as the sign par excellence of civilization, see Walter Mignolo, "On the Colonization of Amerindian Languages and Memories: Renaissance Theories of Writing and Discontinuity of the Classical Tradition," *Comparative Studies in Society and History* 34, 2 (Arpil 1992). See also Ángel Rama, *The Lettered City*, edited and translated by John Charles Chasteen (Durham: Duke University Press, 1996) which I will discuss in chapt. 5.

12 Cited by Mignolo, "On the Colonization of Amerindian Languages," 235.

13 Cited by Mignolo, *The Darker Side of the Renaissance: Literacy, Territoriality, & Colonization* (Ann Arbor: The University of Michigan Press, 2003), 45.

14 Adriana Johnson, "Precolumbian Writing Systems," Lecture at the University of California, Irvine, Summer, 2018.

15 In her lecture, "Precolumbian Writing Systems," Johnson provides an example of how important the book was to the European imaginary, particularly in its justification of colonialism, through the various historical accounts that circulated regarding the last Incan emperor Atahualpa's response to a book (possibly the bible) he was presented by a bishop. In one account he committed sacrilege by tossing the bible and in another he showed himself to be a barbarian for not understating how a text functions. Atahualpa's response to the book justifies colonialism as either a just war or a civilizing project. See also Seed, "'Failing to Marvel': Atahualpa's Encounter with the Word."

16 Contemporary anthropologists, such as José Barreiro, contest the long-held notion that the indigenous populations were totally destroyed in Cuba, identifying people and practices today of Taíno and Arawak origin in the eastern part of island. Nevertheless, the estimated population in Cuba at the time of the encounter, one hundred thousand, is significantly smaller than other Caribbean islands and the mainland. The physical attributes of Taíno towns, their social stratification and what they produced would also have appeared less monumental and complex relative to the Inca and Aztec cities the conquistadors later encountered. See Barreiro and Pérez de la Riva's entries in *The Cuba Reader: History, Culture, Politics*, edited by Aviva Chomsky, Barry Carr and Pamela Maria Smorkaloff (Durham: Duke University Press, 2003).

17 Jacqueline Loss, "Notes on Cuba, Taste, and Mobility," *The Global South* 13, 1 (Spring 2019), 45.

18 Loss, "Notes on Cuba."

19 An example of a novel that explicitly deploys the practice of cannibalism and provides a fascinating counterpart to *Búfalos camino al matadero* is *Cadáver exquisito* (Buenos Aires: Alfaguara, 2017) by Argentinian Agustina Bazterrica (2017). Where cannibalism (or more specifically cannibal reading) in my analysis of Echevarría presents us with an ethics of the Other, in Bazterrica it represents the opposite. Cannibalism in her novel is the result of a dystopic future, where animals have been completely eliminated because of a virus and humans are bred and farmed as meat. What both Echevarría's and Bazterrica's novels share is a critique of biopolitics, or the way in which societies determine which bodies are sacrificed and consumed and which bodies are protected. Both writers do this by presenting the human body as meat. Later in this chapter I will refer again to Esteban Echeverría's *El matadero* and the indistinctions he creates between human and animal bodies as a means to critique totalitarian state practices of the de Rosas government in nineteenth-century Argentina. If we also consider the Cuban Virgilio Piñera's 1944 short story *La carne*, where citizens self-cannibalize because of meat shortages, we can trace a literary tradition in which presenting the human body as meat has been used to critique totalitarian states. Virgilio Piñera, *Cuentos frios* (Buenos Aires: Editorial Losada, 1956). I am indebted to Tara Phillips's presentation, "The Politics and Aesthetics of Virigio Piñera's 'Carne'" at the Latin American Studies Association conference in May of 2022.

20 Maggie Kilgour, *From Communion to Cannibalism: An Anatomy of* Metaphors of Incorporation (Princeton: Princeton University Press, 1990), 7.

21 Echevarría, *Búfalos*, 11.

22 Echevarría, *Búfalos*, 72, 33.

23 Bataille cited by Jay, "The Disenchantment of the Eye," 15.

24 My reading is inspired by Jay's and Barthes's readings of Bataille's short pornographic and sado-masochist novel, *The Story of an Eye*, in which the eye no longer sees, having been enucleated from a priest and later inserted in the anus and vagina of the heroine. The novel "challenges the primacy of sight," and plays with metaphoric transformations. "The most notable series is that linked to the eye itself, which is

enchained with images of eggs, testicles and the sun [. . .] According to Barthes, none of these terms is given any privilege, none has any foundational purity [. . .] Thus, the time-honored function of the penetrating gaze, able to pierce appearances to 'see' the essences beneath, is explicitly rejected." "The Disenchantment of the Eye," 18.

25 This reading of Freud is made by Cary Wolfe in his book, *Animal Rites,* 2–3.

26 Echevarría, *Búfalos*, 72, 39, 80.

27 See chapter 2, section "Thinking Ecologically."

28 Giorgi, *Formas comunes*, 129.

29 Wolfe, *Animal Rites*, 8.

30 For instances of these historic practices, we have Augusto Pinochet's dictatorship in Chile and The Dirty War in Argentina. Patricio Guzmán's *Nostalgia for the Light* (New Wave Films UK, 2010) provides images of the camps and shows how these structures of compartmentalization are reused in different historic periods and governments. Manuel Puig's canonical *Kiss of the Spider Woman*, translated by Thomas Colchie (London: Vintage Books, 1991) provides a fictional analysis of biopolitical knowledge and discourse in Argentina.

31 For UMAPs see book's introduction, notes 19 and 20. For quarantines see introduction to chapter 2, and for the term *gusano* see the book's introduction and chapter 2, as well as the second half this chapter.

32 Consider here the Mariel Boatlift discussed in this chapter, section "The Politics of Cosmonauts and Generals."

33 Giorgi, *Formas communes*, 129–131.

34 Giorgi, *Formas communes*, 129.

35 Echevarría, *Búfalos*, 11.

36 Puig, *Kiss of the Spider Woman*, 166. See also Dayan's chapter in *Sacred Possessions* cited in note 10. The historian Lillian Guerra notes that the term zombie is often used in Cuban speech to express political demobilization. She also observes that the term zombie expresses a form of cannibalism. We might catalogue this form of social cannibalism under its negative anti-ethical practice. Guerra explains, "People also use the word zombie, *yo soy zombie*, which also means that we eat each other [. . .] we distrust each other so much that we cannibalize each other. We pull each other down." https://news.ufl.edu/2021/11/from-florida-episode-11/?fbclid=IwAR1Gi1F37Xs4Q0uFq3qJ1mWnFZ0m58MTNaG-R9K30XMm0GpgwS6b7nqn34c

37 Echevarría, *Búfalos*, 9.

38 For Deleuze and Guattari, the pack is key to understanding their concept of becoming-animal in large part because its formation is not based on filial, hereditary, or state relations. The pack does not cohere into a larger unified body; it does not share a common identity. As a field of relations, shared interests or desires, a pack is a temporary amorphous movement of multiplicities that proliferates through "contagion, epidemics, battlefields, and catastrophe." "Becoming-Animal," in the edited volume *Animal Philosophy: Essential Readings in Continental Thought* (London: Continuum, 2004), 90. See also chapter 2 for more on becoming-animal.

39 Echevarría, *Búfalos,* 10.
40 In chapter 1, I discuss Nancy's notion of "parts outside parts." See note 158.
41 Echevarría, *Búfalos,* 166.
42 Echevarría, *Búfalos,* 9.
43 Echevarría, *Búfalos,* 17.
44 Echevarría, *Búfalos,* 149.
45 Echevarría, *Búfalos,* 16.
46 The passages I cite from Blake and Baudelaire do not appear in the novel.
47 My reading here is informed by Burt's essay "The Aesthetics of Livingness," where he links the difficulty of speaking about animals to the difficulties or impossibility of interspecies communication. See chapter 1, note 149.
48 Echevarría, *Búfalos,* 105, 29, 39, 18, 24. In his book, *Why Look at Animals* (London: Penguin, 2009), the art historian John Berger explains (via Jean-Jacques Rousseau and Lévi-Strauss) that the first metaphor was very likely the word animal, 16.
49 Echevarría, *Búfalos,* 86, 45, 18, 81.
50 Echevarría, *Búfalos,* 20, 21.
51 Echevarría, *Búfalos,* 98.
52 In *The Shell and the Kernel: Renewals of Psychoanalysis, Volume 1,* edited and translated by Nicholas T. Rand (Chicago: University of Chicago Press, 1994), Nicolas Abraham and Mária Török, write, "So in order not to have to 'swallow' a loss, we fantasize swallowing (or having swallowed) that which has been lost, as if it were some kind of thing. Two interrelated procedures constitute the magic of incorporation: *demetaphorization* (taking literally what is meant figuratively) and *objectivation* (pretending that the suffering is not an injury to the subject but instead a loss sustained by the love object). The magical 'cure' by incorporation exempts the subject from the painful process of reorganization," 127.
53 This reading draws from Gabriele Schwab's analysis of Juan Saer's *El intenado,* a novel that explicitly foregrounds cannibalism, in her book *Imaginary Ethnographies: Literature, Culture, and Subjectivity* (Columbia University Press, 2012). Schwab describes the narrator's melancholy as another form of cannibalism. *Imaginary Ethnographies,* chapter 4, passim, "The Melancholic Cannibal." We will refer to Saer's novel later in the chapter.
54 Echevarría, *Bufalos,* 59, 60.
55 Echevarría, *Bufalos,* 19.
56 Echevarría, *Bufalos,* 19, 20.
57 Echevarría, *Bufalos,* 22, 80.
58 In chapter 5, section "The Lettered Man and the Artful Liar," I will refer to Immanuel Kant's notion of disinterested art, where the contemplating of art reveals universal forms, and Che's notion of self-representation as human triumph over nature. We can also consider Echevarría's insistence on art-from-the-wound as counter to the impervious *hombre nuevo,* discussed in chapters two and five.
59 Echevarría, *Búfalos,* 70.
60 Echevarría, *Búfalos,* 69.
61 Echevarría, *Búfalos,* 72.

62 Echevarría, *Búfalos*.
63 Echevarría, *Búfalos*.
64 Echevarría, *Búfalos*, 73.
65 Echevarría, *Búfalos*, 28.
66 See chapter 3, note 9.
67 See note 50.
68 Echevarría, *Búfalos*, 101.
69 Echevarría, *Búfalos*, 164.
70 Echevarría, *Búfalos*, 138.
71 I am drawing here from Nancy's deconstruction of a Christian metaphysics. See chapt. 1, section "The Art of Assemblage."
72 Aristotle, *On the Soul*, Book II.
73 Echevarría, *Búfalos*, 85, 10.
74 I am in debt to Isabella Vergara who suggested that writing in this text operates as a prosthetic limb.
75 Echevarría, *Búfalos*, 131.
76 Echevarría, *Búfalos*, 166.
77 Echevarría, *Búfalos*, 110.
78 Echevarría, *Búfalos*, 116.
79 Echevarría, *Búfalos*, 116.
80 Echevarría, *Búfalos*, 110
81 Cary Wolfe's synthesis of Freud's "Civilization and its Discontents" in *Animal Rites*, 2.
82 See chapter 1, note 11.
83 See chapter 1, note 183.
84 See chapter 1, note 184.
85 Echevarría, *Búfalos*, 73.
86 Oswald de Andrade, "Cannibalist Manifesto," translated by Leslie Bary, *Literary Review* 19, 38 (July–December, 1991), 35–47. Also see Susan Bassnett and Harish Trivedi's introduction, "Of colonies, cannibals and vernaculars," to *Post-Colonial Translation* (London and New York: Routledge, 1999) .
87 Andrade, "Cannibalist Manifesto."
88 Eduardo Viveiros de Castro, *Cannibal Metaphysics: For a Post-Structural Anthropology*, edited and translated by Peter Skafish (Minneapolis: Univocal Publishing, 2014), 143.
89 Citing Peter Skafish in his introduction to *Cannibal Metaphysics*, 12.
90 This articulation is a paraphrase from the introduction to *Cannibal Metaphysics*, 12, but the larger argument about the novel is drawn from Gaby Schwab's reading of Saer. Further in the chapter, I will discuss Jacques Derrida's conception of hospitality.
91 See Schwab's reading of Saer in her book *Imaginary Ethnographies*.
92 Echevarría, *Bufalos*, 96.
93 Echevarría, *Bufalos*.
94 Echevarría, *Bufalos*, 98.

95 Echevarría, *Bufalos*, 100.
96 Echevarría, *Bufalos*, 102.
97 Echevarría, *Bufalos*, 98, 99.
98 See notes 42 and 45.
99 Echevarría, *Bufalos*, 178.
100 Echevarría, *Bufalos*, 180.
101 Echevarría, *Caballo*, 36.
102 Echevarría, *Caballo*, 37.
103 Echevarría, *Caballo*, 37.
104 Lezama Lima's sumptuous banquet scene in *Paradiso* (1966) and his deployment of food imagery in *La expresión americana* (1957) are the most notable, also See Kulez's excellent article, "Eating (by) Oneself."
105 Ahmel Echevarría, *Caballo con arzones* (La Habana: Editorial Letras Cubanas, 2017), 37.
106 See note 97.
107 Derrida, "'Eating Well', or the calculation of the subject: An interview with Jacques Derrida," *Who comes after the subject*, edited by Eduardo Cadava, Peter Connor, and Jean-Luc Nancy (New York: Routledge, 1991), 115.
108 Kelly Oliver, "Derrida and Eating," in *Encyclopedia of Food and Agricultural Ethics*, edited by Paul B. Thompson and David M. Kaplan (Dordrecht: Springer Reference, 2014), 460.
109 Derrida, "'Eating Well,'" 115.
110 Derrida, "'Eating Well,'" 114.
111 See note 88.
112 Katia Viera, "Ahmel Echevarría: Diálogo desde su obra," *Recial* 8, 12 (2017), 3.
113 Echevarría, *Caballo*, 12.
114 Echevarría, *Caballo*, 9.
115 Echevarría, *Caballo*, 10.
116 Echevarría, *Caballo*, 12.
117 Echevarría, *Caballo*, 123.
118 Echevarría, *Caballo*, 123, 124.
119 See chapter 1, note 14.
120 Echevarría, *Caballo*, 12.
121 Echevarría, *Caballo*, 100.
122 Echevarría, *Caballo*.
123 Echevarría, *Caballo*.
124 Echevarría, *Caballo*, 173–174.
125 Echevarría, *Caballo*, 176.
126 Echevarría, *Caballo*, 174.
127 Echevarría, *Caballo*, 175–176.
128 José Martí, *Poesías Completas*. Prólogo y Notas de Luis Alberto Ruiz (Buenos Aires: Ediciones Antonio Zamora, 1975), 174.
129 Monica Simal also identifies references to Martí's "Dos patrias" in Echevarría's 2013

novel *La noria* and associates the dualistic structure in both authors in her article "*La noria*," 66.

130 Ryan Anthony Spangler, "Ninguna patria tengo yo: Cuba's Poetic and Political Redemption in José Marté," *Journal of Critical Southern Studies* 3 (Winter 2015), 79.

131 Not unlike *Búfalos, Caballo* also contains passages of love making and romantic affairs. The one character who has a name, La Percanta, the white woman who is presumably narrating as the Black man, was the Black man's father's lover. Part of the narrative entails the narrator's discovery of his father's letters and pictures of her.

132 Martí, *Poesías completas*, 174.

133 Echevarría, *Caballo*, 23, 17.

134 Echevarría, *Caballo*, 174.

135 Echevarría, *Caballo*, 73.

136 Echevarría, *Caballo*, 35.

137 Echevarría, *Caballo*, 35, "el cadáver parecía tomar el sol," "El cadáver estaba tendido bajo el cielo como suelen estar tendidas, al sol, las islas," 52–53.

138 Echevarría, *Caballo*, 18, 25.

139 Echevarría, *Caballo*, 35. See chapter 1, section "Reading as Touching," for discussion of Nancy's "Corpus."

140 Echevarría, *Caballo*, 74.

141 See chapter 1, section "Reading as Touching," for Nancy's deconstruction of a Christian metaphysics.

142 Echevarría, *Caballo*, 75.

143 Echevarría, *Caballo*, 72–73.

144 Echevarría, *Caballo*, 73.

145 See note 124.

146 Echevarría, *Caballo*, 65, 18, 34, 57, 147, 81, 94, 95, 160, 155.

147 Cary Wolfe, *What is Posthumanism* (Minneapolis: University of Minnesota Press, 2010), 35.

148 Echevarría, *Búfalos*, 87.

149 See note 63.

150 Echevarría, *Caballo*, 81.

151 Echevarría, *Caballo*.

152 Echevarría, *Caballo*, 82.

153 See note 56.

154 Echevarría, *Caballo*, 89, 90.

155 Echevarría, *Caballo*, 156.

156 Echevarría, *Caballo*.

157 Echevarría, *Caballo*, 113.

158 See note 45.

Chapter 5. The Body Politic and Immunitary Spaces

1 Jacques Derrida and Anne Dufourmantelle, *Of Hospitality* (Stanford: Stanford University Press, 2000), 25.

2 Recall the passage cited from Portela, *El pájaro,* 97, in the section "Inhuman Writings," of chapter 3, where the writer is imagined slipping under the door like a Christmas card, as well as allusions to the unvaccinated body of Camila, and of writing operating as something that contaminates.
3 See chapter 4, note 110.
4 In its biological and political signification, the term refers to the aporetic structure in which "[t]he body defeats a poison not by expelling it outside the organism, but by making it somehow part of the body." Roberto Esposito, *Immunitas: The Protection and Negation of Life,* Translated by Zakiya Hanafi (Malden: Polity, 2011), 8.
5 Derrida, *Of Hospitality*, 25.
6 For analysis of the novel as detective, crime, or *noir* fiction see Birkenmaier, "El linchamiento," 63–71. Also see Lopez's prologue to the Stockcero 2010 edition of the novel, "En torno a la novela negra: Poética y política en *Cien botellas un una pared*."
7 Karen Christian, "Beyond Essence: Performing Gender and Sexuality in Ena Lucía Portela's *Cien botellas en una pared*," *International Journal of Cuban Studies* 5, 2 (Summer 2013), 193.
8 See also Christian's article "Beyond Essence," cited above, as well as Ana Belén Martín Sevillano's "Violencia de género en la narrativa cubana contemporánea: Deseo femenino y masculinidad hegemónica," *Hispanic Review* 82 (Spring 2014).
9 See María del Mar López-Cabrales's "La Habana, una ciudad que nunca duerme. Género y escritura durante y despué del periodo especial," *Studies in Latin American Popular Culture* 27 (2007).
10 Here I am quoting Gilles Deleuze and Félix Guattari whom I will discuss further ahead. *What is Philosophy?*, transalted by Hugh Tomlinson and Graham Burchell (New York: Columbia University Press, 1994). See note 39.
11 Guillermo Cabrera Infante and Susan Sontag discuss the roots of homophobia in Cuba in Néstor Almendros and Orlando Jiménez-Leal's documentary, *Conducta impropia* (Barcelona: Eagles Editorial, 2008). See also Frances Negrón-Muntaner, "'Mariconerías' de estado: Mariela Castro, los homosexuales y la política cubana," *Nueva Sociedad* 218 (noviembre-diciembre 2008), 168.
12 Sontag, *Conducta impropia*, and Negrón-Muntaner, "'Mariconerías," 168.
13 In his book, *Tropics of Desire: Interventions From Queer Latino America* (New York: New York University Press, 2000), José Quiroga writes that the body of the homosexual "stands for an excess of signification" in Post-Cold war Cuba, 124.
14 Guevara, "El socialismo y el hombre en Cuba," cited in Arnaldo Cruz-Malavé, "Lecciones de cub*anía*: Identidad nacional y errancia sexual en Senal Paz, Martí y Lezama Lima," *Cuban Studies* 29 (1999), 133.
15 Sontag, *Conducta impropia.*
16 Sontag, *Conducta impropia.*
17 In his text *The Accursed Share* Volume I, Bataille uses the term unproductive expenditure to describe the consumption, waste, or expenditure of energy that does not operate within a productive or useful economy. He arrives at this concept in part by looking at the gift economies studied by Marcel Mauss. See chapter 3, section "Unproductive and De/composing Bodies."

18 Henken, *Cuba,* 246.
19 Henken, *Cuba*, 248. See also Abel Sierra Madero's "Lo de las UMAP fue un trabajo 'top secret,' Entrevista a la Dra. María Elena Solé Arrondo," *Cuban Studies* 44 (2016) where he interviews a psychologist who participated as a researcher and in the presumed rehabilitation of "anti-social" citizens in the UMAP camps.
20 Sierra Madero, "Lo de las UMAP," 358, 359.
21 Enrico Mario Santí, "Fresa y Chocolate: The Rhetoric of Cuban Reconciliation" *Institute for Cuban & Cuban-American Studeis Occasional Papers,* Paper 24, 16–17. Lawrence Chua, "I Scream You Scream: Lawrence Chua Talks with Tomás Gutiérrez Alea," *Artforum* 33, 4 (1994), 62.
22 Chua, "I Scream You Scream," 63. See also Gemma Casadevall, "Con o sin el embargo, la película se estrenará en Estados Unidos," *El Mundo* (February 22, 1994)
23 Chua, "I Scream You Scream," 63.
24 Chua, "I Scream You Scream."
25 See Quiroga and Cruz Malavé, which I will discuss in more detail further ahead.
26 See Henken and especially *Conducta Impropia.*
27 Aristotle, *Nicomachean Ethics,* (Oxford: Oxford University Press, 2002), 221.
28 Cicerón, *Lelio: Sobre la amistad; Sobre la vejez, sobre la amistad* (Madrid: Alianza Editorial, 2009), 120.
29 Jacques Derrida, *Politics of Friendship*, translated by George Collins (London and New York: Verso, 2005), 13.
30 Derrida, *Politics of Friendship*, 9.
31 Derrida, *Politics of Friendship*, chapter ten, passim.
32 Deleuze and Guattari, *What is Philosophy?*, 87.
33 Roach, *Friendship as a Way of Life,* 60. [needs full reference]
34 Deleuze and Guattari, *What is Philosophy?*, 107.
35 Tom Roach, *Friendship as a Way of Life: Foucault, AIDS, and the Politics of Shared Estrangement* (Albany: State University of New York Press, 2012), 60.
36 Deleuze and Guattari, *What is Philosophy?*, 71.
37 Deleuze and Guattari, *What is Philosophy?*, 108.
38 Barbara Cassin, Emily Apter, Jacques Lezra, and Michael Wood (eds.), *Dictionary of Untranslatables: A Philosophical Lexicon* (Princeton: Princeton University Press, 2014), 1196.
39 Deleuze and Guattari, *What is Philosophy?*, 4.
40 De Ferrari's study of friendship in the Post-Soviet Cuban novel illustrates another sense in which classical formulations of friendship have served totalitarian ends. She observes that the rhetoric of the Cuban state has "coopted values commonly associated with male friendships" and in so doing retained the loyalty of its citizens even after failing to comply with its social contract. In the novels she looks at, artistic integrity, revolutionary compliance, and friendship are simultaneously unsustainable. The three cannot coexist not only because of "the high demands placed on individuals by the socialist government, but also the fact that all three social formations feed off a common fund of virtues: loyalty, honor and courage [. . .] the very definitions of manliness." "Embargoed Masculinities," 84.

41 Senel Paz, *El lobo, el bosque y el hombre nuevo* (Ciudad de México: Ediciones Era, 2007), 19. While the focus of this chapter is on the film adaptation, I will also cite relevant passages from Paz's text. Any dialogue that is not footnoted is taken from the film.
42 Reynaldo Gonzaléz's article, "La cultura cubana con sabor a fresa y chocolate: Un artículo salido del closet," *La Gaceta de Cuba* (marzo-abril 2007) is one example of the more celebratory readings of the film.
43 While there were no explicit policies against a particular aesthetic, Eloy E. Merino explains in his essay, "Los usos del almuerzo lezamiano en *El lobo, el bosque y el hombre nuevo* de Senel Paz," *Chasqui* 33, 1 (May 2004), "la visión barroca ante la vida, de exceso, [fue] reputada tradicionalmente de femenina, contra una austeridad, de tirante contención masculina, que la Revolución auspicia en sus abanderados," 43. More significantly, the UMAPs and the laws designed to persecute gays reflect a desire for standardization and utilitarianism, which is antithetical to a Baroque aesthetic.
44 Santí, "Fresa y Chocolat," passim.
45 Emilio Bejel, *Gay Cuban Nation* (Chicago: The University of Chicago Press, 2001), 160.
46 Bejel, *Gay Cuban Nation*, 165.
47 Bejel, *Gay Cuban Nation*, 160, 165–169.
48 Quiroga, *Tropics of Desire*, 132.
49 Quiroga, *Tropics of Desire*, 133.
50 José Quiroga, "Cuba: la desaparición de la homosexualidad," in *Una ventana a Cuba y los estudios cubanos*, edited by Amalia Cabezas, Ivette N. Hernández-Torres, Sara Johnson, and Rodrigo Lazo (San Juán: Ediciones Callejon, 2010), 193.
51 In regard to the political and cultural status of gays in the 90s, Quiroga writes: "En este nuevo capítulo en la historia de la homosexualidad con la revolución cubana, el hombre homosexual va adquirir un significado diametralmente opuesto al de la 'escoria' con el que había sido identificado. Primero, va a representar la alegoría de una restitución, para finalmente convertirse en una identidad avalada por el estado, despojado de su carga opositora y rebelde." "Cuba: la desaparición de la homosexualidad," 195.
52 Quiroga, *Tropics of Desire*, 131, 132.
53 Cruz-Malavé, "Lecciones en cub*anía*," 143, 144.
54 Cruz-Malavé, "Lecciones en cub*anía*," 133.
55 Cruz-Malavé, "Lecciones en cub*anía*," 144.
56 Esposito, *Immunitas*, 8.
57 Esposito, *Immunitas*.
58 Cruz-Malavé, "Lecciones en cub*anía*," 145.
59 Santí, "Fresa y Chocolate," passim.
60 Esposito, *Immunitas*, 8.
61 Esposito, *Immunitas*, 6.
62 Henken, *Cuba*, 210.

63 Various accounts in *Conducta Impropia* recount the extensive policing, paranoia, and distrust that these committees generated within the Cuban community.
64 Bejel, "*Fresa y chocolate* o la salida de la guarida," passim.
65 See Michel Foucault's "The Meaning and Evolution of the Word Parrhesia," in *Discourse and Truth: The Problematization of Parrhesia*, edited by Joseph Pearson (Digital Archive: Foucault.info, 1999). Drawing from Foucault, my use of this word is meant to invoke the event of truth telling, in plain speech, and the political dangers it entails.
66 Esposito, *Immunitas,* 9.
67 Esposito, *Immunitas,* 17, 18.
68 "Lespri Endepandan: Discovering Haitian Sculpture," exhibition catalog, Frost Art Museum, Miami Florida, 2004.
69 Lois Parkinson Zamora uses these same adjectives to describe the Baroque in her book, *The Inordinate Eye: The New World Baroque and Latin American Fiction* (Chicago: University of Chicago Press, 2006).
70 Roach, *Friendship as a Way of Life,* 5.
71 Derrida, *Of Hospitality*, 25.
72 Derrida, *Of Hospitality*, 51.
73 Derrida, *Of Hospitality.*
74 Cicerón, *Lelio,* 123.
75 Paz, *El lobo,* 11.
76 Paz, *El lobo,* 12.
77 Paz, *El lobo,* 13.
78 Paz, *El lobo,* 18.
79 Plutarch, *Obras morales y de costumbres: (Moralia)/ Plutarco. 1, 1* (Madrid: Gredos, 2007), 73.
80 Plutarch, *Obras morales* , 125.
81 Plutarch, *Obras morales* , 73.
82 Judith Butler, *Precarious Life: The Powers of Mourning and Violence* (London: Verso, 2006), 44.
83 In *Precarious Life*, Butler writes, "When we recognize another, or when we ask for recognition for ourselves, we are not asking for an Other to see us as we are, as we already are, as we have always been, as we were constituted prior to the encounter itself. Instead, in the asking, in the petition, we have already become something new, since we are constituted by virtue of the address, a need and desire for the Other that takes place [. . .] To ask for recognition, or to offer it, is precisely not to ask for recognition for what one already is. It is to solicit a becoming, to instigate a transformation, to petition the future always in relation to the Other" (44).
84 Butler, *Precarious Life.*
85 This phrasing is taken from Leela Gandhi, *Affective Communities: Anticolonial Thought, Fin-De-Siécle Radicalism, and the Politics of Friendship* (Durham: Duke University Press, 2006) , 30.
86 Paz, *El lobo*, 12.
87 Derrida, *Politics of Friendship*, 9.

88 Derrida, *Politics of Friendship*, 18.
89 Cassin, *Dictionary of Untranslatables,* 1196.
90 Cassin, *Dictionary of Untranslatables.*
91 Roach, *Friendship as a Way of Life*, 45, 47. See also Luis F. Avilés, "En los límites de la Amistad: silencio, risa, honestidad," 80grados.net, May 8, 2015, https://www.80grados.net/en-los-limites-de-la-amistad-silencio-risa-honestidad/, for an analysis on the ethics of discomfort, truth telling, and the capacity of transformation in friendship.
92 Roach, *Friendship as a way of life*, 9.
93 Roach, *Friendship as a way of life*, 14, 15.
94 Roach, *Friendship as a way of life* , 5.
95 Roach, *Friendship as a way of life* , 7, 8.
96 Roach, *Friendship as a way of life* , 94, 95.
97 Roach, *Friendship as a way of life.*
98 Michel Foucault, *Technologies of the Self: A Seminar with Michel Foucault*, edited by Luther H. Martin, Huck Gutman, and Patrick H. Hutton (Amherst: University of Massachusetts Press, 1988), 25.
99 Foucault, *Technologies of the Self.*
100 Roach, *Friendship as a Way of Life*, chapter 2, passim.
101 Gandhi, *Affective Communities,* 30.
102 Gandhi, *Affective Communities*, 17, 25.
103 Aristotle, *Nicomachean Ethics*, 225.
104 Esposito, *Communitas*, Introduction, passim.
105 See Bejel, *Gay Cuban Nation.*
106 Hernández Salván, *Mínima Cuba,* 48, 49. See also Suquet Martínez's "De testimonios y de reos."
107 Hernández Salván, *Mínima Cuba,* 48, 49. See also Suquet Martínez's "De testimonios y de reos."
108 Ignaas Devisch, *Jean-Luc Nancy and the Question of Community* (London: Bloomsbury Academic, 2012), 203.
109 See Quiroga, "Cuba: la desaparición de la homosexualidad" and Cruz-Malavé, "Lecciones de cub*anía*."
110 Deleuze and Guattari, *What is Philosophy?*, 108.
111 Portela, *Cien botellas en una pared*, 7.
112 Portela, *Cien botellas en una pared*, 6, 5.
113 Portela, *Cien botellas en una pared*, 35.
114 Portela, *Cien botellas en una pared*, 1.
115 "Beyond Essence," 189.
116 Christian, "Beyond Essence," 192.
117 Portela, *Cien botellas en una pared*, 124, 6.
118 Portela, *Cien botellas en una pared*, 124, asterisks footnote, 5.
119 See chapter 3, the description of the character Fabián, title of *El pájaro*'s first chapter.
120 See chapter 4, section "The Latin American Cannibal and the Civilized Cuban."
121 Rama, *The Lettered City*, 18.

122 Rama, *The Lettered City*, 22
123 Javier Sanjinés C., "Subalternity within the 'Mestizaje Ideal': Negotiating the 'Lettered Project' with the Visual Arts," *Nepantla: Views from South*, 1, 2 (2000), 323.
124 Rama, *The Lettered City*, 190.
125 Luisa Campuzano translated and cited by Jonathan Dettman in "Literature as Reproductive Labor in Post-Soviet Cuba," *Chasquí* 47, 2 (2018), 101. Complicating this generational distinction are Leonardo Padura's detective novels, which are written in a Post-Soviet context and offer a more critical view of revolutionary discourse. His novels however continue to be more masculinist, traditionally constructed and market bound.
126 *Cien botellas*, xii. We can also look at the close ties between writers such as Nicolás Guillén and Alejo Carpentier and Cuban government to appreciate the relationship between letrados and political power.
127 In her book, *Community and Culture in Post-Soviet Cuba*, De Ferrari traces the historical relationship between Cuban intellectuals and the government. It seemed that immediately following the revolution, "the political vanguard and the artistic avant-garde had a common cause." However, "by the end of the 1960s politicians had grown more suspicious of local intellectuals." What followed were decades of censorship and self-censorship with events such as Heberto Padilla's 1971 auto-de-fé. Guevara's 1964 essay "El socialism y el hombre en Cuba," together with Castro's 1961 "Palabras a los intelectuales," although vague, created a culture where the intellectual needed to be understood as serving the interests of the revolution, otherwise they were betraying their revolutionary obligation. De Ferrari describes how the Cuban intellectual was in a paradoxical situation. On the one hand, unlike capitalist states, they were given material and cultural support from the government in exchange for using their voices for the social good; on the other hand, that perceived social good was already prescribed by the state, 10, 11. De Ferrari's account suggests that those that would have been published may not have wielded power per se as in Rama's *ciudad letrada*, but did need to produce along the lines dictated by the state.
128 De Ferrari, *Community and Culture in Post-Soviet Cuba*, 13, 14.
129 Portela, *Cien botellas*, 167.
130 Portela, *Cien botellas*, 176.
131 In French and in political theory (such as Hobbes) the sovereign is associated with, or conceived as, artifice. Claire E. Rasmussen, "The Beast and the Sovereign, Biopolitics and Derrida's Menagerie," *Environment and Planning D: Society and Space* 31 (2013), 1125.
132 Derrida, *The Beast and the Sovereign*.
133 See note 114.
134 Portela, *Cien botellas*, 5 (foot note).
135 Portela, *Cien botellas*, 169.
136 Portela, *Cien botellas*, 169 (foot note).
137 In "El socialism y el hombre en Cuba," Guevera writes, "El hombre comienza a liberar su pensamiento de . . . la necesidad de satisfacer sus necesidades animales me-

diate el trabajo. Empieza a verse retratado en su obra y comprender su magnitud humana."

138 Nickolas Pappas, "Plato's Aesthetics," *The Stanford Encyclopedia of Philosophy* , edited by Edward N. Zalta (Fall 2020 Edition) Last updated June 22, 2020, https://plato.stanford.edu/archives/fall2020/entries/plato-aesthetics/.

139 Pappas, "Plato's Aesthetics."

140 See section "Tocar la Tecla," note 79.

141 Portela, *Cien botellas*, 173.

142 Portela, *Cien botellas*, 174.

143 Portela, *Cien botellas.*

144 See chapter 3, where I discuss W.J.T. Mitchell's, "Illusion: Looking at Animals Looking," note 44.

145 Portela, *Cien botellas*, 34.

146 Portela, *Cien botellas*, 171–172.

147 Portela, *Cien botellas*, 172.

148 Portela, *Cien botellas.*

149 Portela, *Cien botellas*. 172.

150 Portela, *Cien botellas*. 171.

151 Portela, *Cien botellas*. 95.

152 Portela, *Cien botellas*. 87.

153 See chapter 4, note 37.

154 See chapter 4, section "Talking Pigs."

155 See chapter 2, section "Thinking Ecologically."

156 Portela, *Cien botellas*, 11, 4.

157 See note 136.

158 Portela, *Cien botellas*, 16–17.

159 Portela, *Cien botellas*, 21.

160 Portela, *Cien botellas*, 116.

161 See note 114.

162 *The Lettered City*, 21.

163 See note 43.

164 I am indebted to José Chavarry's reading of the liquid in Zeta and the opposition that Portela creates between Zeta's and Linda's writing style.

165 Portela, *Cien botellas*, 121.

166 Portela, *Cien botellas*, 235.

167 See section "Non-Dialectical Mingling, Betrayal, and Discomfort," from this chapter and note 98.

168 In my analysis of Portela's first novel, *El pajaro: pincel y tinta china*, in chapter 3, I underscored a similar tendency with descriptions of the sonogram. See section "Making Bodies Trans-lucid."

169 See note 83.

170 See note 67.

171 See note 66.

172 Ramas, *The Lettered City*, 1–5.

173 Portela, *Cien botellas*, 24.
174 Portela, *Cien botellas*.
175 Portela, *Cien botellas*, 43.
176 Portela, *Cien botellas*, 39, 44.
177 Portela, *Cien botellas*, 44, 43.
178 Portela, *Cien botellas*, 45.
179 Portela, *Cien botellas*, 44.
180 Portela, *Cien botellas*, 7, (footnote 16).
181 Portela, *Cien botellas*, 254.
182 Portela, *Cien botellas*.
183 Portela, *Cien botellas*, 256.
184 See section, "Philosophies of Friendship."
185 See note 101.
186 Christian, "Beyond Essence," 196.
187 See note 8.
188 Portela, *Cien botellas*, 196.
189 Portela, *Cien botellas*, 197.
190 Portela, *Cien botellas*, 197–198.
191 Portela, *Cien botellas*, 137, 156.
192 Portela, *Cien botellas*, 137, 158.
193 Portela, *Cien botellas*, 218.
194 See note 31.
195 Portela, *Cien botellas,* 138.
196 Portela, *Cien botellas*, 95.
197 Portela, *Cien botellas*, 217.
198 Portela, *Cien botellas*, 215.
199 Portela, *Cien botellas*, 123, 227.
200 Portela, *Cien botellas*, 148.
201 Portela, *Cien botellas*, 163.
202 See note 160.
203 Esposito, *Communitas*, 10.
204 Portela, *Cien botellas*, 95.
205 Nancy, *The Inoperative Community,* 21.
206 Nancy, *The Inoperative Community,* passim.
207 Esposito, *Communitas,* 95.
208 Smith, "Lu mujer negra, lesbiana y punk," 83.
209 Dettman citing Negrón-Muntaner, "Literature as Reproductive Labor in Post-Soviet Cuba," 109.
210 Dettman citing Negrón-Muntaner.
211 Portela, *Cien botellas*, 74.

Coda

1 Ponte, *La fiesta vigilada*, 203.
2 Whitfield, *Cuban Currency,* 143.

3 See Eduardo Lalo's photography and essay book, *donde* (San Juan: Editorial Tal Cual, 2005).

4 See La Vaughn Belle's series *Storm (How to Imagine the Tropical as Monumental)* 2016, http://www.lavaughnbelle.com/home-1#/storm-how-to-imagine-the-tropicalia-as-monumental/

5 See Tony Capellan's installations *Mar Caribe* and *Mar Invadido,* Perez Art Museum, "Watch Tony Capellán discuss his works in 'Poetics of Relation,'" YouTube video, 4:28, May 29, 2015, https://www.youtube.com/watch?v=zT5WnhJqx9A

6 See for example, Marc Perry, "What's Wrong With Literary Studies?" *Chronicle of Higher Education,* November 27, 2016, https://www.chronicle.com/article/whats-wrong-with-literary-studies/; Jennifer Schuessler, "What is Literary Criticism For?" The New York Times, February 3, 2023; https://www.nytimes.com/2023/02/03/arts/john-guillory-literary-criticism.html; Tyler Harper, "What the Last of Us, Snowpiercer and 'climate fiction' get wrong," BBC Culture, April 18, 2023, https://www.bbc.com/culture/article/20230418-what-snowpiercer-and-climate-fiction-get-wrong; Merve Emre, "Has Academia Ruined Literary Criticism?," *New Yorker*, January 16, 2023.

7 See Caroline Levine, "In Praise of Happy Endings: Precarity, Sustainability, and the Novel," *Novel* 55, 3 (November 2022).

8 Stacy Alaimo, *Bodily Natures: Science, Environment, and the Material Self* (Bloomington: Indiana University Press, 2010), 2.

BIBLIOGRAPHY

Abbate, Carolyn. "Music—Drastic or Gnostic?" *Critical Inquiry* 30 (2004): 505–36.

Abraham, Nicolas, and Mária Török. *The Shell and the Kernel: Renewals of Psychoanalysis, Volume 1.* Edited and translated by Nicholas T. Rand. Chicago: University of Chicago Press, 1994.

Aguirre, Ángel M. "Elementos Afronegroides en dos poemas de Luis de Góngora y Argote y en cinco villancicos de Sor Juana Inés de la Cruz." *Atti del Convegno di Roma* 1, 15–16 (March, 1995): 296–298.

Alaimo, Stacy. *Bodily Natures: Science, Environment, and the Material Self.* Bloomington: Indiana University Press, 2010.

Aldarondo, Cecilia, Lale Namerrow Pastor, directors. *Landfall.* Blackscrackle Films, Independent Television Service, POV (Firm), Field of Vision and Good Docs (Firm), 2020.

Almendros, Néstor, and Orlando Jiménez-Leal. *Conducta impropia.* Barcelona: Eagles Editorial, 2008.

Aloi, Giovanni. "On a Wing and a Prayer: Butterflies in Contemporary Art." Lecture at the Natural History Museum in London, April 2014.

Anderson, Thomas F. *Carnival and National Identity in the Poetry of Afrocubanismo.* Gainesville: University Press of Florida, 2011.

———. *Everything in Its Place: The Life and Works of Virgilio Piñera.* Lewisburg: Bucknell University Press, 2006.

Andrade, Oswald de. "Cannibalist Manifesto." Translated by Leslie Bary. *Literary Review* 19, 38 (July–December, 1991): 35–47.

Araújo, Nara. "Erizar y divertir: La poética de Ena Lucía Portela." *Cuban Studies* 32 (2001): 55–73.

Aristotle. *On the Soul, Book II.* Translated by J.A. Smith, http://classics.mit.edu/Aristotle/soul.2.ii.html.

———. *Nicomachean Ethics.* Oxford: Oxford University Press, 2002.

———. *Poetics.* Chicago: Dover Thrift Editions, 1997.

Arnedo-Gómez, Miguel. *Uniting Blacks in a Raceless Nation: Blackness, Afro-Cuban Culture and Mestizaje in the Prose and Poetry of Nicolás Guillén.* Lewisburg: Bucknell University Press, 2016.

———. *Writing Rumba: The Afrocubanista Movement in Poetry.* Charlottesville: University of Virginia Press, 2006.

Asad, Talal. “Reflections on Violence, Law, and Humanitarianism.” *Critical Inquiry* (Features). http://criticalinquiry.uchicago.edu/reflections_on_violence_law_and_humanitarianism/#_ftn13.

Atterton, Peter, and Matthew Calarco (eds.) Animal Philosophy: Essential Readings in Continental Thought. London: Continuum, 2004.

Avilés, Luis F. “En los límites de la amistad: silencio, risa, honestidad.” *80grados.net*, May 8, 2015. https://www.80grados.net/en-los-limites-de-la-amistad-silencio-risa-honestidad/

Baker, Steve. *The Postmodern Animal.* London: Reaktion Books, 2000.

Balibar, Étienne. *Masses, Classes, Ideas: Studies on Politics and Philosophy After Marx.* Translated by James Swenson. London: Routledge, 1994.

———. “Racism as universalism.” *New Political Science* 8, 1 (1989): 9–22.

Barad, Karen. “Transmaterialities: Tran*/Matter/Realities and Queer Political Imaginings.” *GLQ: A Journal of Lesbian and Gay Studies* 21, 2–3 (2015): 387–422.

———. “Posthumanist Performativity: Toward an Understanding of How Matter Comes to Matter.” *Signs: Journal of Women in Culture and Society* 28, 3 (2003): 801–831.

Barbas-Rhoden, Laura. *Ecological Imaginations in Latin American Fiction.* Gainesville: University Press of Florida, 2011.

Barthes, Roland. *The Pleasure of the Text.* Translated by Richard Miller. New York: Hill and Wang, 1975.

———. “Sarduy: La face baroque,” *La quinzaine littéraire* 28 (1967).

Bassnett, Susan and Harish Trivedi. “Of colonies, cannibals and vernacular.” Introduction to *Post-Colonial Translation.* London and New York: Routledge, 1999.

Bataille, Georges. *Accursed Share Vol. 1, 2 & 3.* Translated by Robert Hurley. New York: Zone Books, 1993.

Bateson, Gregory. *Steps to an Ecology of Mind: Collected Essays in Anthropology, Psychiatry, Evolution, and Epistemology.* London: Jason Aronson, 1972.

Bauman, Zygmunt. *Wasted Lives: Modernity and its Outcasts.* Boston: Polity Press, 2004.

Bazterrica, Agustina. *Cadáver exquisito.* Buenos Aires: Alfaguara, 2017.

Bejel, Emilio. *Gay Cuban Nation.* Chicago: The University of Chicago Press, 2001.

———. “*Fresa y chocolate* o la salida de la guardia: Hacia una teoría del sujeto homosexual en Cuba.” *Casa de las Américas* 35, 196 (1994): 10–22.

Benítez-Rojo, Antonio. *The Repeating Island: The Caribbean and the Postmodern Perspective.* Durham: Duke University Press, 1996.

Bennett, Jane. *Vibrant Matter: A Political Ecology of Things.* Durham: Duke University Press, 2009.

Berger, John. *Why Look at Animals.* London: Penguin, 2009.

Blanchot, Maurice. *The Unavowable Community.* Barrytown: Station Hill Press, 1988.

Blanco de la Cruz, Caridad. “Roberto Fabelo.” *Art Nexus* 60, 5 (2006): 130–131.

Birkenmaier, Anke. “El linchamiento, el teléfono móvil y la gran ciudad: dos ficciones negras de Ena Lucía Portela.” *Mitologías hoy* 10 (Winter 2014): 63–71.

Bolognese, Chiara. “El pájaro: Pincel y tinta china de Ena Lucía Portela: Escritura y cuerpo en escena.” *Mitologías hoy* 10 (Winter 2014): 49–62.

Borchmeyer, Florian, and Matthias Hentschler, directors. *Habana - Arte nuevo de hacer ruinas.* Cinema Guild, 2007.

Bowie, Andrew. *Music, Philosophy, and Modernity.* Cambridge: Cambridge University Press, 2007.

Braidotti, Rosi. *Metamorphoses: Towards a Materialist Theory of Becoming.* Malden: Blackwell Publishers, 2002.

Breton, André. "First Manifesto of Surrealism." In *Art in Theory 1900–1990: An Anthology of Changing Ideas*, edited by Charles Harrison and Paul Woods. Malden: Blackwell Publishers, 1992.

Brathwaite, Kamau. "The African Presence in Literature." *Daedalus* 103, 2 (Spring 1974): 73–109.

Brizuela, Natalia. "Sense of Place: Paz Encina's Radical Poetics." *Film Quarterly* 70, 4 (2017): 49–64.

Brennan, Teresa. *The Transmission of Affect.* Ithaca: Cornell University Press, 2004.

Broglio, Ron. "'Living Flesh': Animal–Human Surfaces." *Journal of Visual Culture* 7, 1 (2008): 103–121.

Bruno, Giuliana. *Surface: Matters of Aesthetics, Materiality, and Media.* Chicago: University of Chicago Press, 2014.

Burke, Nancy. "Precarity in the Time of COVID-19: Aging Housing and Aging Population in Cuba." *Global Perspective* 2, 1 (2021): 1–10.

Bustamante, Michael J. and Jennifer L. Lambe (eds.) *The Revolution from Within: Cuba, 1959–1980.* Durham: Duke University Press, 2019.

Butler, Judith. *Precarious Life: The Powers of Mourning and Violence.* London: Verso, 2006.

Bry, Theodor de. *Collected travels in the East Indies and West Indies* (1594), https://smarthistory.org/engravings-theodore-de-bry/.

Carpentier, Alejo. "The Baroque and the Marvelous Real." In *Magical Realism,* edited by Lois Parkinson Zamora and Wendy B. Faris. Durham: Duke University Press, 1995.

Casas, Bartolomé de las. *Brevísima relación de la destrucción de las Indias.* Edited by André Saint-Lu. Madrid: Ediciones Cátedra, 2003.

Casadevall, Gemma. "Con o sin el embargo, la película se estrenará en Estados Unidos." *El Mundo*, February 22, 1994.

Casamayor-Cisneros, Odette. "Incertidumbre resplandeciente. Breve incursión en la narrativa escrita durante la década del 90 en la Isla de Cuba." *Caravelle* 78 (June 2002): 179–196.

Cassin, Barbara, Emily Apter, Jacques Lezra, and Michael Wood, (eds.) *Dictionary of Untranslatables: A Philosophical Lexicon.* Princeton: Princeton University Press, 2014.

Castro, Fidel. "Palabras a los intelectuales." In *Política cultural de la Revolución Cubana.* La Habana: Editorial de Ciencias Sociales, 1977.

Chomsky, Aviva, Barry Carr, and Pamela Maria Smorkaloff, (eds.) *The Cuba Reader: History, Culture, Politics.* Durham: Duke University Press, 2003.

Christian, Karen. "Beyond Essence: Performing Gender and Sexuality in Ena Lucía Portela's *Cien botellas en una pared.*" *International Journal of Cuban Studies* 5, 2 (Summer 2013): 184–201.

Chua, Lawrence. "I Scream You Scream: Lawrence Chua Talks with Tomás Gutiérrez Alea." *Artforum* 33, 4 (1994): 62–64.

Cixous, Hélène. "O,C,O,B,R,A,B,A,R,O,O: A Text-Twsiter." *Literature and Arts of the Americas* 8, 13 (1974): 26–31.

Colas, Santiago. "Toward an Ethics of Close Reading in the age of neo-liberalism." *CR: The New Centennial Review* 7, 3 (2007): 171–211.

Colón, Cristóbal. *La carta de Colón: Anunciando el descubrimiento.* Barcelona: Linkgua Ediciones, 2007.

Cruz-Malavé, Arnaldo. "Lecciones de cub*anía*: Identidad nacional y errancia sexual en Martí Senel Paz y Lezama Lima." *Cuban Studies* 29 (1999): 129–154.

Dash, zj. Michael. *The Other America: Caribbean Literature in a New World Context.* Charlottesville: University Press of Virginia, 1998.

Dayan, Joan. "Vodoun, or the Voice of the Gods." In *Sacred Possessions: Vocou, Santería, Obeah, and the Caribbean*, edited by Margarite Fernández Olmos and Lizabeth Paravisini-Gebert. New Brunswick: Rutgers University Press, 2000.

De Ferrari, Guillermina. *Community and Culture in Post-Soviet Cuba.* New York: Routledge, 2014.

———. "Embargoed Masculinities: Loyalty, Friendship and the Role of the Intellectual in Post-Soviet Cuban Novel." *Latin American Literary* Review 35, 69 (January–June 2007): 82–103.

Deleuze, Gilles, and Francis Bacon. *Francis Bacon: The Logic of Sensation.* Translated and with an introduction by Daniel W. Smith. Afterword by Tom Conley. Minneapolis: University of Minnesota Press, 2003.

Deleuze, Gilles, and Félix Guattari. *What Is Philosophy?* Translated by Hugh Tomlinson and Graham Burchell. New York: Columbia University Press, 1994.

———. *Kafka: Toward a Minor Literature*. Minneapolis: University of Minnesota Press, 1987.

DeLoughrey, Elizabeth M., Renée K. Gosson, and George B. Handley, (eds.) *Caribbean Literature and the Environment: Between Nature and Culture.* Charlottesville: University of Virginia Press, 2005.

Derrida, Jacques. *The Beast and the Sovereign,* Volume I. Chicago: The University of Chicago Press, 2009.

———. *Politics of Friendship.* Translated by George Collins. London and New York: Verso, 2005.

———. "'Eating Well,' or the calculation of the subject: An interview with Jacques Derrida." *Who comes after the subject.* Edited by Eduardo Cadava, Peter Connor, and Jean-Luc Nancy. New York: Routledge, 1991.

Derrida, Jacques, and Anne Dufourmantelle. *Of Hospitality.* Stanford: Stanford University Press, 2000.

Dettman, Jonathan. "Literature as Reproductive Labor in Post-Soviet Cuba" *Chasquí* 47, 2 (2018): 100–112.

Devisch, Ignaas. *Jean-Luc Nancy and the Question of Community.* London: Bloomsbury Academic, 2012.

Dolar, Mladen. *A Voice and Nothing More.* Edited by Slavoj Žižek. Cambridge: The MIT Press, 2006.

Donovan, Thom. "A grave in exchange for the commons: Fred Moten and the resistance of the object." *Jacket2,* April 2011, http://jacket2.org/article/grave-exchange-commons.

Duany, Jorge. "Neither Golden Exile nor Dirty Worm: Ethnic Identity in Recent Cuban-American Novels." *Cuban Studies* 23 (1993): 167–183.

Duchesne Winter, Juan. *Caribe, Caribana: Cosmografías literarias.* San Juán: Ediciones Callejón, 2015.

———. *Comunismo literario y teorías deseantes: Inscripciones latinoamericanas.* La Paz: Plural Editores, 2009.

Duno-Gottberg, Luis. *Solventando las diferencias: La ideología del mestizaje en Cuba.* Madrid: Iberoamericana—Vervuert, 2003.

Echevarría, Ahmel. *Caballo con arzones.* La Habana: Editorial Letras Cubanas, 2017.

———. *Búfalos camino al matadero.* Santiago: Editorial Oriente, 2013.

Echeverría, Esteban. *El matadero.* New York: Las Americas Publishing Company, 1959.

Emre, Merve. "Has Academia Ruined Literary Criticism?" *New Yorker,* January 16, 2023.

Esposito, Roberto. *Immunitas: The Protection and Negation of Life.* Translated by Zakiya Hanafi. Malden: Polity, 2011.

———. *Communitas: The Origin and Destiny of Community.* Translated by Timothy Campbell. Stanford: Stanford University Press, 2010.

Evans, Brad, and Henry A. Giroux. *Disposable Futures: The Seduction of Violence in the Age of Spectacle.* San Francisco: City Lights Books, 2015.

Fabelo's Anatomy, Museum of Latin American Art Long Beach exhibition catalogue, 2014, 16.

Fantham, Elaine. *Ovid's Metamorphoses.* Oxford and New York: Oxford University Press, 2004.

Fernández, Raul A. *From Afro-Cuban Rhythms to Latin Jazz.* Berkeley: University of California Press, 2006.

Fernández Retamar, Roberto. *Calibán: Apuntes sobre la cultura en nuestra América.* Ciudad de México: Editorial Diógenes, 1972.

Ferreira da Silva, Denise. "Hacking the Subject: Black Feminism and Refusal beyond the Limits of Critique." *philoSOPHIA* 8, 1 (Winter 2018): 19–41.

French, Jennifer, and Gisela Heffes, (eds.) *The Latin American Ecocultural Reader.* Evanston: Northwestern University Press, 2021.

Foucault, Michel. "*The Meaning and Evolution of the Word Parrhesia.*" In *Discourse and Truth: The Problematization of Parrhesia,* edited by Joseph Pearson. Digital Archive: Foucault.info, 1999.

———. *Technologies of the Self: A Seminar with Michel Foucault.* Edited by Luther H. Martin, Huck Gutman, and Patrick H. Hutton. Amherst: University of Massachusetts Press, 1988.

Frost, Samantha. "The Implications of The New Materialisms for Feminist Epistemology." In *Feminist Epistemology and Philosophy of Science: Power in Knowledge,* edited by H.E. Grasswick, 69–83. London and New York: Springer Netherlands, 2011.

Fuentes, Elvis. "The Art of Growing Skin." Brochure essay for the exhibition of Roberto Diago's work at the Halsey Museum of Contemporary Art, Charleston, South Carolina, 2018.

Fusco, Coco. "Artists in Cuba Spearhead First Major Protests in Decades," *NACLA* (December 14, 2020), https://nacla.org/news/2020/12/14/artists-cuba-spearhead-first-major-protest-decades.

———. "The Artist as Hostage: Luis Manuel Otero Alcántara." *e-flux* (May 21, 2021), https://www.e-flux.com/announcements/398535/coco-fusco-in-e-flux-journal-the-artist-as-hostage/.

Galán, Natalio. *Cuba y sus sones.* Prologue by Guillermo Cabrera Infante. Madrid: Artegraf, 1997.

Galinsky, G. Karl. *Ovid's Metamorphoses: An Introduction to the Basic Aspects.* Berkeley and Los Angeles: University of California Press, 1975.

Gandhi, Leela. *Affective Communities: Anticolonial Thought, Fin-De-Siècle Radicalism, and the Politics of Friendship.* Durham: Duke University Press, 2006.

Gikandi, Simon. "E. K. Brathwaite and the Poetics of the Voice: The Allegory of History in *Rights of Passage.*" In *The Critical Response to Kamau Brathwaite,* edited by Emily Allen Williams. Westport: Praeger, 2004.

Giorgi, Gabriel. *Formas comunes: Animalidad, cultura, biopolítica.* Buenos Aires: Eterna Cadencia Editora, 2014.

Glissant, Édouard. *Caribbean Discourse: Selected Essays.* Translated by J. Michael Dash. Charlottesville: University Press of Virginia, 1989.

Goebel, James. "Uncanny Meat." *French Journal of English Studies* 55 (2016): 169–190.

Golán, María. "El grotesco popular en la obra de Nicolás Guillén: Motivos de son." In *Nicolás Guillén: Hispanidad, vanguardia y compromiso social,* edited by Matías Barchino, and María Rubio Martín. Cuenca: Ediciones de la Universidad de Castilla-La Mancha, 2004.

González Echevarría, Roberto (ed.) "Introducción." *De donde son los cantantes de Severo Sarduy.* Madrid: Cátedra, 1993.

———. "Guillén as Baroque: Meaning in Motivos de son." *Callaloo* 31 (Spring, 1987): 302–317.

———. *La ruta de Severo Sarduy.* Hanover, New Hampshire: Ediciones del Norte, 1987.

———. "Rehearsal for Cobra." *Review 74: Focus on Cobra,* Winter (1974): 38–44.

Gonzaléz, Reynaldo. "La cultura cubana con sabor a fresa y chocolate: Un artículo salido del closet." *La Gaceta de Cuba* (marzo-abril 2007): 43–47.

Guerra, Lillian. "What to Know about the Ongoing Protests in Cuba." By Nicci Brown. *University of Florida News* (November 23, 2021): https://news.ufl.edu/2021/11/from-florida-episode-11/?fbclid=IwAR1Gi1F37Xs4Q0uFq3qJ1mWnFZ0m58MTNaG-R9K30XMm0GpgwS6b7nqn34c.

Guerra, Lucía. *Ciudad, género e imaginarios urbanos en la narrativa latinoamericana.* Santiago: Editorial Cuartopropio, 2014.

Guevara, Ernesto Che. "El socialismo y el hombre en Cuba (1965)," https://www.marxists.org/espanol/guevara/65-socyh.htm#n*.

Guillén, Nicolás. *Obra poética 1920–1958 tomo I.* La Habana: Instituto Cubano del Libro, 1972.

Guillory, John. *Professing Criticism: Essays on the Organization of Literary Study.* Chicago: University of Chicago Press, 2022.

Guridy, Andre. *Forging Diaspora: Afro-Cubans and African Americans in a World of Empire and Jim Crow.* Chapel Hill: University of North Carolina, 2010.

Guzmán, Patricio, director. *Nostalgia for the Light.* New Wave Films UK, 2010.

Hallward, Peter. *Absolutely Postcolonial: Writing Between the Singular and the Specific.* Manchester: Manchester University Press, 2001.

Haraway, Donna J. *Simians, Cyborgs, and Women: The Reinvention of Nature.* New York: Routledge, 1991.

Harper, Douglas. Online Etymology Dictionary, August 29, 2023, https://www.etymonline.com/search?q=kaleidoscope.

Hayward, Eva, and Jami Weinstein. "Introduction: Tranimalities in the Age of Trans* Life." *TSQ: Transgender Studies Quarterly* 2, 2 (2015): 195–208.

Hearn, Maxwell. The Metropolitan Museum of Art History, Heilbrunn Timeline of Art History, Chinese Painting, https://www.metmuseum.org/toah/hd/chin/hd_chin.htm.

Henken, Ted. *Cuba: A Global Studies Handbook.* Santa Barbara: ABC-CLIO, 2008.

Hernández-Reguant, Ariana, Susannah Rodríguez Drissi, and Carlos Juárez. "Anti-Government Protests in Cuba." *Think Tech Hawaii,* July 16, 2021, https://thinktechhawaii.com/anti-government-protests-in-cuba-global-connections/.

Hernández Salván, Marta. *Mínima Cuba: Heretical Poetics and Power in Post-Soviet Cuba.* Albany: SUNY Press, 2015.

Hoyos, Héctor. *Things with a History: Transcultural Materialism and the Literatures of Extraction in Contemporary Latin America.* New York: Columbia University Press, 2019.

Jesús, Pedro de. *Imagen y libertad vigilada: Ejercicios de retórica sobre Severo Sarduy.* La Habana: Editorial Letras Cubanas, 2014.

Jackson, Richard. *Black Literature and Humanism in Latin America.* Athens: The University of Georgia Press, 1988.

James, Ian. *The Fragmentary Demand: An Introduction to the Philosophy of Jean-Luc Nancy.* Stanford: Stanford University Press, 2006.

Jankélévitch, Vladimir. *Music and the Ineffable.* Translated by Carolyn Abbate. Princeton: Princeton University Press, 1983.

Jay, Martin. "The Disenchantment of the Eye in Surrealism and the Crisis of the Ocularcentrism." In *Visualizing Theory, Selected Essays from V.A.R. 1990–1994.* Edited by Lucien Taylor. New York: Routledge, 1994.

Johnson, Adriana. "Precolumbian Writing Systems." Lecture at the University of California, Irvine, Summer, 2018.

Kafka, Franz. *The metamorphosis.* New York: Modern Library, 2013.

Kanzepolsky, Adriana. "¿Yo no soy el tema de mi libro? *La fiesta vigilada* de Antonio José Ponte." *Abehache* 1–2 (2011): 59–69.

Kaup, Monika. "Becoming-baroque: Folding European forms into the new world baroque with Alejo Carpentier." *CR: The New Centennial Review* 5, 2 (2005): 107–149.

Khlebnikov, Velimir. *The King of Time: Selected Writings of the Russian Futurism.* Translated by Paul Schmidt. Cambridge: Harvard University Press, 1990.

Kilgour, Maggie. *From Communion to Cannibalism: An Anatomy of Metaphors of Incorporation.* Princeton: Princeton University Press, 1990.

Kormondy, Edward J. "A Brief Introduction to the History of Ecology." *The American Biology Teacher* 74, 7 (2012): 441–43.

Kulez, Ali. "Eating (by) Oneself: The Wasteful Pleasure of Self-Cannibalism in Virgilio Piñera's 'La carne.'" *Revista de Estudios Hispánicos* 53, 3 (octubre 2019): 879–898.

Kupfer, Monica E. "Roberto Fabelo." *Art Nexus* 82, 128 (September/November 2011): 146–147.

Kutzinski, Vera. *Sugar's Secrets: Race and the Erotics of Cuban Nationalism.* Charlottesville: University Press of Virginia, 1993.

"Lespri Endepandan: Discovering Haitian Sculpture." Exhibition catalog, Frost Art Museum, Miami, Florida, 2004.

Levine, Caroline. "In Praise of Happy Endings: Precarity, Sustainability, and the Novel." *Novel* 55, 3 (November 2022): 388–405.

Levine, Suzanne Jill. "Discourse as Bricolage." *Review 74: Focus on Cobra* (Winter 1974): 32–37.

López-Cabrales, María del Mar. "La Habana, una ciudad que nunca duerme. Género y escritura durante y después del periodo especial." *Studies in Latin American Popular Culture* 27 (2007): 179–196.

Loss, Jacqueline. "Notes on Cuba, Taste, and Mobility." *The Global South* 13, 1 (Spring 2019): 33–58.

Luis, William. *Las vanguardias literarias en el Caribe, Cuba, Puerto Rico y República Dominicana.* Madrid: Iberoamericana—Vervuert, 2010.

Lyotard, Jean-François. *The Inhuman: Reflections on time.* Translated by Geoffrey Bennington and Rachel Bowlby. Stanford: Stanford University Press, 1991.

Lyotard, Jean-François, Adam Krims, and Henry James Klumpenhouwer. *Music/Ideology: Resisting the Aesthetic: Essays.* Amsterdam: G + B Arts International, 1998.

Mackie, Elliott. "Ernesto Oroza's Technological Disobedience project celebrates Cuban ingenuity." *Assemblepapers* (2017), https://assemblepapers.com.au/2017/04/28/technological-disobedience-ernesto-oroza/.

Maeseneer, Rita de. *Devorando a lo cubano: Una aproximación gastrocrítica a textos relacionados con el siglo XIX y el Período Especial.* Madrid: Iberoamericana—Vervuert, 2012.

Maguire, Emily. "Temporal Palimpsests: Critical Irrealism in Generation Zero's *Cuba in Splinters.*" *Revista de Estudios Hispánicos* 2 (June 2017): 325–348.

———. *Racial Experiments in Cuban Literature and Ethnography.* Gainesville: University Press of Florida, 2011.

Márquez, Enrique. "Cobra: De aquel oscuro objeto del deseo." *Revista Iberoamericana* 154 (enero-marzo 1991): 301–307.

Martí, José. "Nuestra América." *La Revista Ilustrada de Nueva York,* United States, January 10, 1891, and in *El Partido Liberal,* México, January 30, 1891, *Aportes:* 133–139.

———. *Poesías completas.* Prólogo y Notas de Luis Alberto Ruiz. Bueno Aires: Ediciones Antonio Zamora, 1975.

Martín Sevillano, Ana Belén. "Violencia de género en la narrativa cubana contemporánea: Deseo femenino y masculinidad hegemónica." *Hispanic Review* 82 (Spring 2014): 175–197.

Martínez, Juan A. *Cuban Art and National Identity: The Vanguardia Painters, 1927–1950.* Gainesville: University Press of Florida, 1994.

Marx, Karl. *Capital: A Critique of Political Economy,* vol. 1. Translated by Ben Fowkes. London: Penguin Books, 1990.

Mbembe, Achille. "Necropolitics." *Public Culture* 15, 1 (2003): 11–40.

Merino, Eloy E. "Los usos del almuerzo lezamiano en *El lobo, el bosque y el hombre nuevo* de Senel Paz." *Chasqui* 33, 1 (May 2004): 42–55.

Mignolo, Walter. "On the Colonization of Amerindian Languages and Memories: Renaissance Theories of Writing and Discontinuity of the Classical Tradition." *Comparative Studies in Society and History* 34, 2 (April 1992): 301–330.

———. *The Darker Side of the Renaissance: Literacy, Territoriality, & Colonization.* Ann Arbor: The University of Michigan Press, 1995, 2003.

Miller, Daniel, (ed.) *Materiality.* Durham: Duke University Press, 2005.

Mitchell, W.J.T. "Illusion: Looking at Animals Looking." In *Picture Theory: Essays on verbal and Visual Representation.* Chicago: University of Chicago Press, 1994.

"Montaje de Sobrevivientes," *Museo Nacional de Bellas Artes,* 10 Edición de la Bienal de la Habana, Video, March 2009, http://www.youtube.com/watch?v=ZZVWmzY4sPY.

Morejón, Nancy. "Su obra: Introducción." 1972, http://www.cervantesvirtual.com/portales/nicolas_guillen/su_obra_introduccion/.

Moore, Robin D. *Nationalizing Blackness: Afrocubanismo and Artistic Revolution in Havana, 1920–1940.* Pittsburgh: University of Pittsburgh Press, 1997.

Moten, Fred. *In the Break: The Aesthetics of the Black Radical Tradition.* Minneapolis: University of Minnesota Press, 2003.

Nancy, Jean-Luc. *The Ground of the Image.* New York: Fordham University Press, 2005.

———. "Corpus." In *Thinking Bodies,* edited by Juliet Flower MacCannell and Laura Zakarin. Stanford: Stanford University Press, 1994.

———. *The Inoperative Community.* Edited and translated by Peter Connor, Lisa Garbus, Michael Holland, and Simona Sawhney. Minneapolis: University of Minnesota Press, 1991.

Negrón-Muntaner, Frances. "'Mariconerías' de estado: Mariela Castro, los homosexuales y la política cubana." *Nueva Sociedad* 218 (noviembre-diciembre 2008): 163–179.

Neruda, Pablo. *Canto general.* http://www.literatura.us/neruda/general.pdf. 1950.

Nixon, Rob. *Slow Violence and the Environmentalism of the Poor.* Cambridge: Harvard University Press, 2011.

Ochoa Gautier, Ana María. *Aurality: Listening and Knowledge in Nineteenth-Century Colombia*. Durham: Duke University Press, 2014.

Oliver, Kelly. "Derrida and Eating." In *Encyclopedia of Food and Agricultural Ethics*, edited by Paul B. Thompson and David M. Kaplan. Dordrecht: Springer Reference, 2014.

Ortega y Gasset, José. "La deshumanización del arte." *Obras Completas José Ortega y Gasset, Tomo III*, 368-376. Madrid: Revista de Occidente, 1994.

Ortiz, Fernando. *Cuban Counterpoint: Tobacco and Sugar*. Translated by Harriet de Onís. Durham: Duke University Press, 1995.

Ovid, *The Metamorphoses*. Translated into English prose by A. S. Kline. The Netherlands: Poetry in Translation, 2000.

Palés Matos, Luis. *Tutún de pasa y grifería*. San Juan: Editorial de la Universidad de Puerto Rico, 1993.

Palmié, Stephan. "The Cuban factors: Reproductive biology, historical ontology and the metapragmatics of race," *Anthropological Theory* 16, 1 (2016): 3–21.

Pappas, Nickolas. "Plato's Aesthetics." *The Stanford Encyclopedia of Philosophy*. Edited by Edward N. Zalta (Fall 2020 Edition).

Parkinson Zamora, Lois. *The Inordinate Eye: New World Baroque and Latin American Fiction*. Chicago: University of Chicago Press, 2006.

"Plato's Aesthetics" Stanford Encyclopedia of Philosophy Archive, https://plato.stanford.edu/archives/fall2020/entries/plato-aesthetics/.

Paravisini-Gebert, Lizabeth. "Caribbean Utopias and Dystopias: The Emergence of the Environmental Writer and Artist." In *The Natural World in Latin American Literatures: Ecocritical Essays on Twentieth Century Writings*, edited by Adrian Taylor Kane, Jefferson: MacFarland & Co., 2009.

PBS. "Traces of the Trade: A Story from the Deep North." http://www.tracesofthetrade.org/guides-and-materials/.

Paz, Senel. *El lobo, el bosque y el hombre nuevo*. Ciudad de México: Biblioteca Era, 2007.

Pérez, Rolando. *Severo Sarduy and the Neo-Baroque Image in the Visual Arts*. West Lafayette: Purdue University Press, 2012.

———. *Severo Sarduy and the Religion of the Text*. Lanham: University of America Press, 1988.

Piñera, Virgilio. *Cuentos frios*. Buenos Aires: Editorial Losada, 1956.

Phillips, Tara. "Residuos Cubanos: The Aesthetics and Politics of Virgilio Piñera's 'La carne' and 'La cena.'" In *Undisciplined Cuba*, edited by Christina García with Mrinalini Tankha and Yairamaren Maldonado, forthcoming.

———. "The Politics and Aesthetics of Virgilio Piñera's 'Carne.'" Presentation at the Latin American Studies Association conference in May of 2022.

Piedra, José. "From Monkey Tales to Cuban Songs." In *Sacred Possessions: Vodou, Santería, Obeah, and the Caribbean*, edited by Margarite Fernández Olmos and Lizabeth Paravisini-Gebert. New Brunswick: Rutgers University Press, 1997.

Plutarch. *Obras morales y de costumbres: (Moralia) / Plutarco. 1, 1*. Madrid: Gredos, 2007.

Ponte, Antonio José. *La fiesta vigilada*. Barcelona: Editorial Anagrama, 2007.

———. "Un arte de hacer ruinas." In *Un arte de hacer ruinas y otros cuentos*, edited by Esther Whitfield. Ciudad de México: Fondo de Cultura Económica, 2005.

———. *Un seguidor de Montaigne mira La Habana & Las comidas profundas.* Madrid: Editorial Verbum, 2001.

Portela, Ena Lucía. *Cien botellas en una pared.* Edited by Iraida H. López. Doral: Stockcero, 2009.

———. *El viejo, el asesino y yo y otros cuentos.* Edited by Iraida H. López. Doral: Stockcero, 2009.

———. *El pájaro: Pincel y tinta china.* Barcelona: Editorial Casiopea, 1998.

Povinelli, Elizabeth A. *Economies of Abandonment: Social Belonging and Endurance in Late Liberalism.* Durham: Duke University Press, 2011.

Puig, Manuel. *Kiss of the Spider Woman.* Translated by Thomas Colchie. London: Vintage Books, 1991.

Price, Rachel. *Planet/Cuba: Art, Culture, and the Future of the Island.* London and New York: Verso Books, 2016.

Quintero Herencia, Juan Carlos. "La escucha caribeña de un cuerpo." *Papel Máquina* 2, 4 (2010): 181–193.

———. *La hoja de mar (:) Efecto archipiélago I.* Leiden: Almanera, 2006.

Quiroga, José. "Cuba: La desaparición de la homosexualidad." In *Una ventana a Cuba y los estudios cubanos,* edited by Amalia Cabezas, Ivette N. Hernández-Torres, Sara Johnson, and Rodrigo Lazo. San Juan: Ediciones Callejón, 2010.

———. *Cuban Palimpsests. Vol. 19.* University of Minnesota Press, 2005.

———. *Tropics of Desire: Interventions From Queer Latino America.* New York: New York University Press, 2000.

———. "Spanish American Poetry from 1922 to 1975." In *The Cambridge History of Latin American Literature,* vol. 1, edited by Roberto González Echevarría and Enrique Pupo-Walker. Cambridge: Cambridge University Press, 1996.

Rama, Ángel. *The Lettered City.* Edited and translated by John Charles Chasteen. Durham: Duke University Press, 1996.

Ramos, Julio. *Los archivos de Guillén Landrián.* 2013. http://www.lafuga.cl/dossier/especial-nicolas-guillen-landrian/15/.

———. "Descarga acústica." *Papel Máquina* 2, 4. 2010: 49–77.

———. *Desencuentros de la modernidad en América Latina: literatura y política en el siglo XIX.* Ciudad de México: Fondo de Cultura Económica, 1989.

Rancière, Jacques. *The Politics of Aesthetics: The Distribution of the Sensible.* Edited and translated by Gabriel Rockhill. London: Bloomsbury, 2004.

Rasmussen, Claire E. "The Beast and the Sovereign, Biopolitics and Derrida's Menagerie." *Environment and Planning D: Society and Space* 31 (2013): 1125–1133.

Reckin, Anna. "Tidalectic Lectures: Kamau Brathwaite's Prose/Poetry as Sound-Space." *Anthurium: A Caribbean Studies Journal* 1, 1 (2003): 1–16.

Ríos, Julián (ed.) *Severo Sarduy,* Espiral/Figuras. Madrid: Editorial Fundamentos, 1976.

Roach, Tom. *Friendship as a Way of Life: Foucault, AIDS, and the Politics of Shared Estrangement.* Albany: State University of New York Press, 2012.

Rodó, José Enrique. *Ariel*, translated by Margaret Sayers Peden, foreword by James W. Symington and prologue by Carlos Fuentes. Austin: University of Texas Press, 1988.

Rodríguez Monegal, Emir. "Metamorphoses of the text." *Review 74: Focus on Cobra* (Winter 1974): 16–22.

Rojas, Rafael. "Cuba la historia en rebanadas." *El Cultural* (Suplemento de La Razón) 338 (Sábado 12.02.22): 6–7, https://www.razon.com.mx/220211/cultural-338. Accessed February 10, 2022.

———. "Dilemas de la nueva historia." In *Una ventana a Cuba y los estudios cubanos*, edited by Amalia Cabezas, Ivette N. Hernández-Torres, Sara Johnson, and Rodrigo Lazo. San Juan: Ediciones Callejón, 2010.

———. *Tumbas sin sosiego. Revolución, disidencia y exilio del intelectual cubano.* Barcelona: Anagrama, 2006.

Ruffinelli, Jorge. *Poesía y descolonización: Viaje por la poesía de Nicolás Guillén.* Xalapa: Universidad Veracruzana, 1985.

Salemi, Joseph S. "Kalos Kai Agathos." *The Pennsylvania Review*, May 2009.

Santí, Enrico Mario. "Fresa y Chocolate: The Rhetoric of Cuban Reconcilliation." *Institute for Cuban & Cuban-American Studies Occasional Papers.* Paper 24, https://scholarship.miami.edu/esploro/outputs/journalArticle/Fresa-y-Chocolate-The-Rhetoric-of-Cuban-Reconcilliation/991031447769002976.

Sarduy, Mercedes. *Severo Sarduy: Cartas a mi hermana en La Habana.* Coral Gables: Severo Sarduy Cultural Foundation, 2013.

Sarduy, Severo. *Ensayos generales sobre el barroco.* Buenos Aires: Fondo de Cultura Económica USA, 1987.

———. *La simulación.* Caracas: Monte Ávila Editores, 1982.

———. *Cobra.* Buenos Aires: Editorial Sudamericana, 1972.

———. *Gestos.* Barcelona: Editorial Seix Barral, 1963.

———. "Pintura y revolución." *Revolución* (January 31, 1953).

Sarmiento, Domingo. *Facundo. Civilización y barbarie.* Buenos Aires: Editorial Universitaria de Buenos Aires, 1965.

Schwab, Gabriele. "Haunting from the Future: Psychic Life in the Wake of Nuclear Necropolitics." *The Undecidable Unconscious: A Journal of Deconstruction and Psychoanalysis* 1, (2014): 85–101.

———. *Imaginary Ethnographies: Literature, Culture, and Subjectivity.* New York: Columbia University Press, 2012.

Seed, Patricia. "Failing to Marvel': Atahualpa's Encounter with the Word." *Latin American Research Review* 26, 1 (1991): 7–32.

Sierra Madero, Abel. *El cuerpo nunca olvida: Trabajo forzado, hombre nuevo y memoria en Cuba (1959–1980).* Santiago de Querétaro: Rialta Ediciones, 2022.

———. "Lo de las UMAP fue un trabajo 'top secret': Entrevista a la Dra. María Elena Solé Arrondo." *Cuban Studies* 44 (2016): 357–366.

Silva, María Guadalupe. "Antonio José Ponte: El espacio como texto." *Iberoamericana* 14, 53 (2014): 69–83.

Simal, Mónica. "*La noria* de Ahmel Echevarría Peré o la máquina contra el olvido." *Revista LETRAL* 18 (2017): 56–75.

Smith, Anna Lucinda. "La mujer negra, lesbiana y punk en Cuba: La representación de La Gofia en *Cien Botellas en una pared* de Ena Lucía Portela." *Ogigia-Revista electrónica de estudios hispánicos* 29 (2021): 79–96.

Soler Serrano, Joaquín. "Severo Sarduy, a fondo." *A Fondo* de RTVE, Ministerio de Cultura, Expte. no. 63. 158, 1976.

Sollers, Philippe. "La Boca Obra." *Review 74: Focus on Cobra,* Winter (1974): 13–15.

Sommer, Doris. "Ethical Asymmetries: Learning to Love a Loss." In *The Ethics of Latin American Literary Criticism: Reading Otherwise*, edited by E. Graff Zivin. New York: Palgrave Macmillan, 2007.

Spangler, Ryan Anthony. "Ninguna patria tengo yo: Cuba's Poetic and Political Redemption in José Martí." *Journal of Critical Southern Studies* 3 (Winter 2015): 72–95.

Stokes, Adrian. *Smooth and Rough.* London: Faber & Faber, 1951.

Straet, Jan van der. "Allegory of America" ca. 1587–89, https://www.metmuseum.org/art/collection/search/343845.

Suquet Martínez, Mirta. "De testimonios y de reos: Biopolítica y revolución, el seropositivo cubano." PhD dissertation, Universidad de Santiago de Compostela, 2015,

Tallet, José Zacarías. *La rumba.* Buenos Aires: Biblioteca Virtual Universal, 2003.

Thompson, Robert Farris. *Flash of the Spirit: African & African American Art & Philosophy.* New York: Random House, 1983.

Tillis, Antonio D. "Language as Vernacular Cultural Performance in Black Communities in Cuba and the USA." *Estudos Anglo Americanos* 39 (2013): 142–161.

Timmer, Nanne. "Sujeto y comunidad: Voz, isla y muerte en la narrativa cubana del siglo XXI." *Mitologías hoy* 12 (Winter 2015): 71–82.

Tous, Adriana, *La poesía de Nicolás Guillén.* Madrid: Ediciones Cultura Hispánica, 1971.

United Nations Chronicle, "The Legacy of Slavery in the Caribbean and the Journey Towards Justice," last modified March 24, 2022, https://www.un.org/en/un-chronicle/legacy-slavery-caribbean-and-journey-towards-justice.

Unruh, Vicky. *Latin American Vanguards: The Art of Contentious Encounters.* Los Angeles: University of California Press, 1994.

Vidler, Anthony. "The Smooth and the Rough: Surfaces Psychological and Architectural from Adrian Stokes to Rem Koolhaas," School of Criticism and Theory, Cornell, July 12, 2017.

Viera, Katia. "Ahmel Echevarría: Dialogo desde su obra," *Recial* 8, 12 (2017): 292–297.

Viveiros de Castro, Eduardo. *Cannibal Metaphysics: For a Post-Structural Anthropology.* Edited and translated by Peter Skafish. Minneapolis: Univocal Publishing, 2014.

Von Heyking, John, and Richard Avramenko, Eds. *Friendship and Politics: Essays in Political thought.* Notre Dame: University of Notre Dame Press, 2008.

Whitfield, Esther Katheryn. *Cuban Currency: The Dollar and "Special Period" Fiction,* volume 21. Minneapolis: University of Minnesota Press, 2008.

Wiedorn, Michael. *Think Like an Archipelago: Paradox in the Work of Édouard Glissant.* Albany: State University of New York Press, 2018.

Wolfe, Cary. *Animal Rites: American Culture, the Discourse of Species, and Posthumanist Theory.* Foreword by W.J.T. Mitchell. Chicago: University of Chicago Press, 2003.

INDEX

Page numbers in *italics* refer to illustrations.

Christina M. García is assistant professor at the Department of Hispanic Studies and affiliate faculty in the African American Studies, Women and Gender Studies, and Latin American and Caribbean Studies programs at the College of Charleston. Her work has appeared in edited volumes and the journals *Cuban Studies, Revista de Estudios Hispánicos,* and *Chasquí.*

www.ingramcontent.com/pod-product-compliance
Lightning Source LLC
LaVergne TN
LVHW052350100826
845147LV00013B/803
* 9 7 8 1 6 8 3 4 0 4 4 1 5 *